Lawrence B. Krause and Walter S. Salant are senior fellows in the Brookings Economic Studies program. Mr. Krause is the author of many articles and books on international economic affairs, including *Sequel to Bretton Woods: A Proposal to Reform the World Monetary System* (Brookings, 1971) and *European Economic Integration and the United States* (Brookings, 1968). Mr. Salant, who has also written extensively in the field of international economics, is co-author of *Import Liberalization and Employment* (Brookings, 1961) and *The United States Balance of Payments in 1968* (Brookings, 1963).

European Monetary Unification

and Its Meaning
for the United States

LAWRENCE B. KRAUSE
and
WALTER S. SALANT
Editors

ONFERENCE ON the # European
Monetary Unification
and Its Meaning
for the United States

Papers by
ARTHUR I. BLOOMFIELD

JOSEPH S. NYE

HARRY G. JOHNSON

LAWRENCE B. KRAUSE

W. MAX CORDEN

WALTER S. SALANT

RICHARD N. COOPER

PHILIP H. TREZISE

THE BROOKINGS INSTITUTION
Washington, D.C.

Library of Congress Cataloging in Publication Data:
Conference on the Implications of European Monetary Integration for the United States, Brookings Institution, 1972.
European monetary unification and its meaning for the United States.

1. Monetary policy—European Economic Community countries—Congresses. 2. Foreign exchange problem—European Economic Community countries—Congresses. 3. Monetary unions—Congresses. I. Krause, Lawrence B., ed. II. Salant, Walter S., 1911– ed. III. Title.
HG930.5.C67   1972   332.4'94   73-1084
ISBN 0-8157-5032-3

9 8 7 6 5 4 3 2 1

THE BROOKINGS INSTITUTION is an independent organization devoted to nonpartisan research, education, and publication in economics, government, foreign policy, and the social sciences generally. Its principal purposes are to aid in the development of sound public policies and to promote public understanding of issues of national importance.

The Institution was founded on December 8, 1927, to merge the activities of the Institute for Government Research, founded in 1916, the Institute of Economics, founded in 1922, and the Robert Brookings Graduate School of Economics and Government, founded in 1924.

The Board of Trustees is responsible for the general administration of the Institution, while the immediate direction of the policies, program, and staff is vested in the President, assisted by an advisory committee of the officers and staff. The by-laws of the Institution state, "It is the function of the Trustees to make possible the conduct of scientific research, and publication, under the most favorable conditions, and to safeguard the independence of the research staff in the pursuit of their studies and in the publication of the results of such studies. It is not a part of their function to determine, control, or influence the conduct of particular investigations or the conclusions reached."

The President bears final responsibility for the decision to publish a manuscript as a Brookings book or staff paper. In reaching his judgment on the competence, accuracy, and objectivity of each study, the President is advised by the director of the appropriate research program and weighs the views of a panel of expert outside readers who report to him in confidence on the quality of the work. Publication of a work signifies that it is deemed to be a competent treatment worthy of public consideration; such publication does not imply endorsement of conclusions or recommendations contained in the study.

The Institution maintains its position of neutrality on issues of public policy in order to safeguard the intellectual freedom of the staff. Hence interpretations or conclusions in Brookings publications should be understood to be solely those of the author or authors and should not be attributed to the Institution, to its trustees, officers, or other staff members, or to the organizations that support its research.

Foreword

THE REOPENING of official foreign exchange markets on March 19, 1973, after a crisis that had forced their closing for two weeks marked the beginning of a period of floating rates among the world's major currencies. Even among these currencies, however, all exchange rates were not set entirely free; six of the nine members of the European Community agreed to continue to support each other's currencies so as to maintain a special relationship among themselves, and the other three members promised to assume a similar obligation as soon as they were able to do so. Thus the fledgling movement toward European monetary union survived another crisis—the third since it was first conceived at the Hague Conference in 1969.

Monetary union has long been recognized as the logical culmination of a customs union. As national economies of member countries become more interdependent, trade flows among members become increasingly responsive to small shifts in relative costs. Similarly, capital flows become increasingly sensitive to changes in relative interest rates and other influences on the movement of capital. One result is that changes in both current and capital accounts can cause frequent balance-of-payments difficulties among member countries. Since such difficulties may threaten the very existence of the customs union, it is regarded as preferable to prevent such disequilibria rather than to adjust to them. Prevention requires that member countries coordinate and harmonize important economic policies and, if efforts to do so are successful, exchange rates of the member countries are likely to remain fairly stable and parities, in time, to become rigid.

Monetary union, with its fixed exchange rate parities, would be the natural consequence of such an evolutionary process.

Yet the inevitability of monetary union in those circumstances would not in itself make the European Community's effort to attain it important. That effort is important because it reflects a political decision made by the heads of state of member countries in 1969 to accelerate the unification process with a view to attaining economic and monetary union by the end of the 1970s. Accelerating the process involves internal adjustments and external tensions that many observers considered too costly at the time. But the March 1973 decision of the members of the Community to continue to support each other's currencies suggests that their governments were prepared to run some risks to attain monetary union.

It is one thing, however, to seek monetary union when the alternative is thought to be a world of more or less fixed exchange rates. It is quite another to do so when the alternative is a system of floating rates. Without monetary union, floating rates among member countries might well lead to unnecessary adjustments involving substantial real costs. Some form of joint floating would seem to be essential for the European Community; thus the effort to accelerate the unification process has assumed greater significance than ever before and its success may now be a requirement for the very existence of the Community; the longer the floating-rate system lasts, the more urgent unification becomes.

None of the problems and difficulties of achieving monetary union in Europe has been changed because exchange rates are floating; only the costs of failure have increased. The papers in this book are therefore perhaps more relevant and important today than when they were first presented in September 1972 at the Conference on the Implications of European Monetary Integration for the United States, organized by the Brookings Institution with the cooperation of the U.S. Department of State. The papers analyze in some detail the economic and political problems involved in monetary union, the economic changes that union would bring, and their consequences for the United States.

In the first paper Arthur I. Bloomfield traces the evolution, since the Treaty of Rome, of efforts to foster monetary integration in the countries of the European Community. He also reviews more recent attempts to achieve eventual monetary union. After examining some of the economic, political, and intellectual forces affecting the movement toward monetary unification, he draws conclusions from this experience and assesses future prospects for European union. In a brief addendum he relates these to the March 1973 crisis.

Next, Joseph S. Nye, Jr., cites opinion surveys and the statements of political leaders to illustrate Europe's commitment, or lack of it, to unification. He then uses the insights obtained from the institutional, policy-making, and attitudinal aspects of political integration theory to assess the European monetary union as a serious step toward regional organization. He outlines the political consequences of such a union for the member states and European Community institutions.

Harry G. Johnson examines, in the third paper, some of the technical problems involved in narrowing the bands of exchange rate variation among European currencies. He analyzes the benefits expected from narrowing the bands, both in the operation of exchange markets and in furthering economic integration among member countries. He also assesses what costs might be involved, considers the technical problems of narrowing the bands under alternative international monetary arrangements, and draws attention to some interests of the United States.

The consequences of European monetary union for private capital markets are examined by Lawrence B. Krause. He points out that the freeing of capital movements, as well as promising certain economic benefits, is a necessary condition for the success of monetary union. The benefits are examined from the point of view of borrowers, investors, and financial institutions. Krause considers the difficulties of the transition period and the dilemma arising from pressures for greater capital controls. He examines implications for the United States of a successful union and also the consequences of failure.

In the fifth paper W. Max Corden investigates the difficulty of reaching and maintaining balance-of-payments equilibrium in a monetary union. He explores the different meanings of union and draws an important distinction between what he terms a pseudo monetary union and a complete union. He considers a model of developed countries characterized by a wage standard and analyzes the problem of internal and external balance in such a setting. Corden then examines alternative solutions to the adjustment problem. Finally, he considers the interests of the United States in both a pseudo union and a complete union.

Walter S. Salant explores the complex implications of European monetary union for international reserves. He points out the distinction between internal and external reserves that necessarily arises from monetary union.

evaluates the need for total reserves of member countries by examining the forces affecting the size and duration of imbalances, and then considers the substitutes for external reserves in settlement of imbalances within the Community. Salant later investigates the effects of monetary union on the need for reserves by nonmember countries, and in particular on their demand for dollars. Finally, he suggests how all this may affect U.S. policy.

The effects of European monetary union on the integration of the world economy are considered by Richard N. Cooper in the seventh essay. He examines the consequences of achievement of a single currency within Europe for world trade flows and capital movements, and for the role of the dollar as a world currency. He also reviews the economic difficulties likely to be encountered during the European transition to a single currency and their impact on the United States. Cooper notes the lack of agreement within Europe on the political basis for monetary union and relates it to the disagreement between France (with some European support) and the United States on conceptions of a proper world economic order.

Finally, Philip H. Trezise considers in his essay the policy of the United States toward Europe as it is affected by monetary union. Noting that the United States has consistently supported European efforts to integrate since the end of the Second World War, he analyzes the political importance of monetary union and possible conflicts of interest with the United States. Trezise foresees complications in U.S.–European relations as a result of the unification process, and he concludes with some observations concerning U.S. policy toward Europe and the appropriate attitude to adopt in relation to European monetary union.

Included in this volume are numerous comments on the papers, which considerably broadened the scope of conference debate. They were prepared for the September 1972 conference by Bela Balassa, C. Fred Bergsten, Edward M. Bernstein, Robert R. Bowie, Harold van Buren Cleveland, Benjamin J. Cohen, William Diebold, Jr., William J. Fellner, Edward R. Fried, Theodore Geiger, Gottfried Haberler, James C. Ingram, Peter B. Kenen, Charles P. Kindleberger, Fritz Machlup, Edward L. Morse, and J. Carter Murphy. Highlights of the lively conference debates have been reported by the editors, Lawrence B. Krause and Walter S. Salant. The book concludes with Harry G. Johnson's summary of the entire conference and a partial glossary by Walter S. Salant.

The editors were assisted in the preparation of the papers for publication by Ann O'Connor and Evelyn P. Fisher, who checked the accuracy of data and sources. Barbara P. Haskins edited the manuscript, and Florence Robinson prepared the index.

As explained in the first preface, the conference was partially financed by the Department of State.

The views expressed in this book are those of the authors and the conference participants and should not be attributed to the trustees, officers, or other staff members of the Brookings Institution or to the State Department.

KERMIT GORDON
President

August 1973
Washington, D.C.

Prefaces

Preface by the Under Secretary for Economic Affairs,
U.S. Department of State

IN 1971 the European Community decided to begin working toward the goal of complete monetary union by the end of the decade. If that effort succeeds, it will have major political as well as economic significance. Its many implications for the United States assumed even greater importance when the International Monetary Fund Committee of Twenty began its examination of how to reshape the world monetary system.

In 1971 and 1972 the U.S. Department of State held a number of meetings—some including outside consultants—to explore the meaning of European monetary unification for the United States. As a result, the Department and the Brookings Institution arranged a conference that brought together academic economists, government officials, international civil servants, and business representatives, embracing a variety of national and disciplinary points of view, to examine these implications. The eight papers presented at the conference and the prepared and informal commentary on them by various participants form the contents of this volume.

Convocations of private experts are a regular part of the Department's External Research Program, whose aim is to provide independent views on major foreign policy issues. The conference on which this book is based was unusual, however, in that it was one of the few instances in which the Department entered into a joint funding arrangement with a private institution, under which the private institution—Brookings—was to organize the conference and publish its results. Publication by Brookings will permit these papers and the discussion that followed their presentation to reach a wide audience. Of course, neither the papers nor the proceedings necessarily reflect the views of the U.S. Government or the U.S. Department of State.

The Department is pleased with the success of this form of joint venture and looks forward to the prospect of future explorations of difficult foreign policy issues in circumstances equally conducive to a free-ranging examination of the issues.

WILLIAM J. CASEY

Preface by the Conference Chairman

THE AGREEMENT which the European Community reached in 1971 to begin moving immediately toward the goal of monetary union marks a new phase in European economic integration. In a sense, all the prior progress of the Community can be viewed as laying the groundwork for this step—a step which, if it is to succeed, would be the first serious attempt to unify the economies of a number of disparate countries.

The economic and political implications of this decision for the United States are enormous. They would be so even if the Community's decision had been taken in a period of financial stability. The decision is of even greater significance because it coincides with the most thorough reexamination of the world's monetary system in nearly three decades and with a marked increase in the size and the economic importance of the Common Market owing to the admission of the United Kingdom and other countries as members.

Now that the major portions of the Bretton Woods system are being called into question, the task of replacing those parts or of developing an entirely new system must be faced. The reform of the international monetary system has many complex aspects. Not the least of them is the subject of this conference. What, for example, will be the impact upon the pace and substance of international monetary reform of the EC decision to move toward monetary union? Certainly, reform of the international system cannot wait upon European union. On the other hand, how far can we go toward global reform without a greater measure of agreement among the Europeans than now appears to exist on the details of the monetary unification they have in mind?

The entry of the United Kingdom into the Community compounds the problem and increases its impact on American interests.

Against this background, not long after the publication of the Werner Report in 1971, the Department asked Arthur I. Bloomfield to meet with a small number of department officials and give them his preliminary views on the subject. Mr. Bloomfield, who is a consultant to the Department's Bureau of Intelligence and Research, made a most provocative presentation, outlining a number of alternatives with differing implications for American interests. After this meeting, the Department decided that, in order to go into these aspects more thoroughly, it ought to have a preliminary, informal meeting with other experts, to be followed by a more comprehensive conference based on prepared papers and including a wider group of participants. That meeting, held in February 1972, confirmed the Department's judgment that such a conference ought to be held. Accordingly, the Department collaborated with the Brookings Institution in organizing the conference to consider these matters further.

LEONARD WEISS
U.S. Department of State

Contents

Figure

European
Monetary Unification
and Its Meaning
for the United States

ARTHUR I. BLOOMFIELD

The Historical Setting

THIS PAPER TRACES the evolution, since the Treaty of Rome, of efforts to foster monetary integration in the countries of the European Community (EC) and recent efforts to achieve eventual monetary union.[1] It examines the changing fortunes of these efforts in the light of some of the economic and political forces that influenced them. Certain conclusions are drawn from this experience and future prospects briefly assessed.

The Treaty of Rome laid down rather detailed provisions and timetables for the creation of a customs union and the removal of barriers to factor movements among member countries. Looking beyond to "an ever closer union among the European peoples" and "the unity of their economies" (Preamble), it also established guidelines for common agricultural and transport policies and for concerted action in other sectors. Its provisions on monetary and general economic policies, however, were particularly sketchy and members' commitments ambiguous. There was no reference to common macroeconomic policies or to eventual monetary union.

For example, the treaty (establishing the European Economic Community [EEC]) specifies that member countries "shall consider their policy relating to economic trends as a matter of common interest" and "shall

---

The author is indebted to Irving B. Kravis for helpful discussions.

1. *Treaty Establishing the European Economic Community and Connected Documents* (English translation: Publishing Services of the European Communities, 1962). The treaty was signed in Rome, March 25, 1957, by the representatives of Belgium, France, Germany, Italy, Luxembourg, and the Netherlands. The six participating states had all ratified the treaty by January 1, 1958. (Hereinafter referred to as the Treaty of Rome.)

1

consult with each other and the [EEC] Commission on measures to be taken in response to current circumstances" (Article 103).

Each must pursue the policy necessary to ensure equilibrium in its overall balance of payments and to maintain confidence in its currency, while ensuring a high level of employment and price level stability (Article 104). To facilitate the achievement of these objectives, members "shall co-ordinate their economic policies" through collaboration between their administrative departments and central banks. A monetary committee with consultative status shall be established to promote the coordination of monetary policies "to the full extent necessary for the functioning of the Common Market" (Article 105). In similar vein, Article 6 states that the members "shall co-ordinate their respective economic policies to the extent that is necessary to attain the objectives of this Treaty."[2] Each member is further enjoined to "treat its policy with regard to exchange rates as a matter of common interest." Remedies are provided in the event of changes in exchange rates incompatible with treaty objectives (Article 107).

Article 108 establishes procedures to be followed when a member's actual or prospective balance-of-payments difficulties threaten to jeopardize the functioning of the Common Market. The Commission shall recommend measures to be taken. If these prove insufficient, it shall after consultation with the EEC Monetary Committee recommend to the Council of Ministers the granting of mutual assistance in the form, for example, of limited credits by and with the consent of other members. If such assistance is not granted, or if it and other actions are inadequate, the Commission shall then authorize the member in difficulties to take its own safeguard measures, but these in turn shall be subject to amendment or suspension by the Council.

The cautious wording of these various provisions reflects the fact that they touch upon particularly sensitive areas of national sovereignty. Members are not prohibited in the treaty from altering their exchange rates. The consultations and recommendations provided for do not carry any obligation to adopt policies running counter to perceived national interests.

---

2. Similarly, Article 3 (g) states that the activities of the Community shall include, among others, "the application of procedures which shall make it possible to co-ordinate the economic policies of Member States and to remedy disequilibria in their balances of payments." Article 2 refers to "progressively approximating the economic policies of Member States."

The coordination of monetary and economic policies—and even the progressive abolition of restrictions on intra-Community capital movements called for in Article 67—are required only to the extent necessary for the functioning of the Common Market or the attainment of treaty objectives. The grant of credits to other members in balance-of-payments difficulties is in no way obligatory.

Despite all this, the intent of these various provisions seems clear. It was hoped that consultations, coordination of policies, and mutual aid would mitigate or prevent payments difficulties that might require the imposition of fresh trade and payments controls (to the detriment of progress toward the Common Market), or that might lead to changes in exchange rate parities that could otherwise have been avoided.

Early Efforts, 1960–68

Procedures for consultation and policy coordination were organized after the signing of the Treaty of Rome. In addition to the creation of the Monetary Committee already provided for, the Council of Ministers on March 9, 1960, authorized the establishment of a Committee on Short-term Economic Policy to ensure consultation on business-cycle policies. At the same time, the Council requested member governments to keep the EEC Commission informed of planned measures likely to affect economic trends in other member countries. An exception was made when secrecy was necessary to ensure the success of the measures contemplated.[3] At an early stage, moreover, the ministers of finance of the Six began regular meetings to discuss matters of mutual concern.

The first years of the Community saw developments especially favorable for progress toward economic integration. The devaluation of the French franc at the end of 1958 and the associated French stabilization measures removed the most likely reason for activating the safeguard clauses. At the same time, the members (along with eight other Western European countries) made their currencies externally convertible for current transactions and for some capital transactions. Indeed, Germany removed exchange controls altogether. Agreement was reached in May 1960 on a directive

3. *Journal Officiel des Communautés Européennes*, No. 31, 1960, pp. 764–65. (Hereinafter referred to as *Journal Officiel*.)

to free certain categories of capital transfers within the Community and to impose less restrictive rules on others. A second directive amended and supplemented the first in December 1962. (In practice, both directives were also applied to non-Community countries.) All of the members experienced balance-of-payments surpluses and reserve accumulations. The trend of economic activity within the Community was satisfactory.

Under such circumstances, further steps did not seem urgent. Even the 5 percent currency appreciations of the German mark and Dutch guilder in early March 1961, apparently decided upon without prior consultation, did not seem to cause any great anxiety within the Community despite their backwash on the exchange markets.[4] The rate changes were modest in size and "due less to imbalances in relations with the other Member States than to imbalances in relations with non-member countries."[5]

Commission Memorandum, October 1962

Nevertheless, in an important October 1962 memorandum, the Commission submitted to the Council, along with other recommendations, a set of proposals for increasing consultations and coordination of monetary and economic policies within the Community, with a view to the eventual establishment of a monetary and economic union.[6] In the monetary sphere proper, the Commission recommended the creation of a committee of governors of member central banks, and joint meetings of the governors and ministers of finance. Their function was to review monetary problems and to hold prior consultations on important monetary decisions relating to credit policies, alterations of rates of exchange between the member currencies, and recourse by member countries to the facilities of the International Monetary Fund (IMF). Together with the ministers of finance, the committee would work out common policies in monetary relations with outside countries and common positions on the international monetary system and its possible reform.

4. ". . . the final decisions on these changes were not preceded by perfect coordination within the Community." European Economic Community, *Fourth Report on the Activities of the Monetary Committee* (Brussels: March 23, 1962), p. 9.

5. *Ibid.*

6. European Economic Community Commission, *Memorandum of the Commission on the Action Programme of the Community for the Second Stage* (Brussels: October 24, 1962), esp. Chap. 8.

The memorandum stated that coordination of monetary policies was needed not only to support the progressive merger of short- and long-term economic policies generally, but also because "from the end of the transition period on, if not even sooner, economic union will involve fixed rates of exchange between Member States with very narrow limits on the variations allowed." Major parity changes were also to be avoided because they would imperil the common agricultural policy, although the possibility of such changes was not ruled out during the transitional period. The memorandum emphasized three imperatives: agreement on the extent of each member's obligations under the mutual-assistance provisions of the treaty; a "confrontation" of national budgets; and further liberalization of capital movements within the Community. Particular attention was also given to the need for a medium-term economic policy program for the Community.

Council Decisions, 1963–64

A number of developments in 1963 and 1964, including growing inflationary pressures in the Community, diverging price-cost trends in some member countries, and the intense Italian balance-of-payments crisis, finally led to action on some of the Commission's proposals in the form of a series of Council decisions and recommendations in April–May 1964.[7] The Committee of Governors of the Central Banks of the Member States of EEC was set up. Its function was to review credit policies and, if timing and circumstances permitted, to deliberate on important monetary measures before they were authorized. Member governments were also requested to confer with each other before making any changes in exchange parities. The mandate of the Monetary Committee was officially broadened to include discussions and, where possible, prior consultation on important international monetary questions.

Other directives established a Budgetary Policy Committee and a Medium-term Economic Policy Committee in keeping with the Commission's October 1962 memorandum.

Finally, the Council addressed its first formal recommendation on economic policy to member states: a request for the adoption of a concerted

7. *Journal Officiel,*.No. 64, 1964, pp. 1029–33; No. 77, 1964, pp. 1205–08; and No. 78, 1964, p. 1226.

anti-inflationary program, the proposed elements of which were outlined in some detail. This comprehensive package of measures and recommendations was accepted. The Commission wrote: "This round of decisions marks a decisive stage on the road to economic union; it represents, so to speak, the birth certificate of the Community's economic policy which, having been foreshadowed in the Treaty, can now become a reality."[8]

Years of Indifference, 1964–68

In the four years following the Council's decisions, however, no significant action was taken to promote monetary integration. Existing machinery and procedures for consultation on monetary and general economic policies seemed to the members to be adequate. Such procedures may have encouraged better policy coordination than before, but growing divergences in economic trends were evident in individual member countries, especially after 1966. The procedures also probably facilitated the adoption of common positions on some, though not all, international monetary deliberations (the discussion in regard to the Special Drawing Rights [SDR] scheme was a notable exception). Such positions were taken in the face of the various sterling crises, notably in November 1967 when the pound was devalued.

The Commission and Council continued to make periodic recommendations to the Community as a group or as individual members; the members were of course free to reject them and sometimes did. No effort was made to reach an understanding on the extent of the obligations that each member would be prepared to accept under the treaty's mutual-aid provisions. Agreement could not be reached on a third and broader directive on the liberalization of intra-Community capital movements proposed by the Commission in 1964. The Segré Report called attention to the many obstacles in the way of eventual establishment of a European capital

8. European Economic Community Commission, *Seventh General Report on the Activities of the Community* (Brussels: June 1964), p. 14. In its communication, "Initiative 1964," addressed to the EEC Council of Ministers on October 1, 1964, the Commission again emphasized the need for pushing on to a monetary and economic union. See European Economic Community, *Bulletin of the EEC*, November 1964, pp. 5–11, esp. p. 10.

market.[9] In February 1967, however, the Council adopted the first Medium-term Economic Policy Program.[10]

The failure to make any appreciable advance in monetary integration during this period seems primarily to reflect the continuing payments surpluses and mounting reserves of the individual member countries. The mutual-aid provisions of the treaty, for example, never had to be invoked, even during the heavy speculative attack on the Italian lira in the spring of 1964 when Italy had turned mainly to the United States for support. Nor had recourse ever been necessary to the safeguard provisions covering serious balance-of-payments difficulties. Indeed, despite diverging economic trends, the complacent attitude gained ground that exchange rate adjustments by members were becoming more and more unlikely because of the general progress being made by the Community and especially because of the fixing of common agricultural support prices in terms of a unit of account which, it was believed, would make such adjustments increasingly difficult.[11]

During this period, however, the Commission continued to stress the need to move on toward monetary solidarity. It argued that, with the growing integration of the Community on other fronts, especially because of the rapid removal of trade barriers, economic developments and policies in one member country tended to have greater impact on the economies of the others. As a result, coordinated policy decisions became correspondingly more urgent.[12] In a memorandum submitted to the Conference of Finance Ministers in February 1968, the Commission suggested that the following be studied: First, the possibility of getting member govern-

9. European Economic Community Commission, *The Development of a European Capital Market,* Report by a Group of Experts, Claudio Segré, chairman (Brussels: November 1966). It might be noted, however, that the growth of the Eurobond market was making possible a greater degree of linkage among the national capital markets in the Community.

10. For a discussion of the underlying principles of the Medium-term Economic Policy Program, see G. R. Denton, "Planning and Integration: Medium-term Policy as an Instrument of Integration," in G. R. Denton (ed.), *Economic Integration in Europe* (London: Weidenfeld and Nicholson, 1969), pp. 330–56.

11. See European Economic Community Commission, *Seventh Report on the Activities of the Monetary Committee* (Brussels: February 12, 1965), p. 12.

12. European Communities Commission, *First General Report on the Activities of the Communities, 1967* (Brussels-Luxembourg: February 1968), p. 124. See also *Seventh Report on the Activities of the Monetary Committee,* pp. 12–13, and European Economic Community Commission, *Ninth Report on the Activities of the Monetary Committee* (Brussels: March 1, 1967), p. 8, for similar ideas.

ments to commit themselves to change their exchange rate parities only by common agreement, a step far beyond the commitment of May 1964 to hold prior consultations on parity changes; and second, the feasibility of eliminating margins of exchange rate fluctuations between member currencies around the established parities. These and other suggestions met with no response.

Crises of 1968 and 1969

Members' indifference to closer monetary cooperation in the four years following May 1964 was severely jolted by the series of international monetary crises in 1968 and 1969 affecting the French franc and German mark. The French payments crisis in May–June 1968 was sparked by serious civil strife and student strikes. France imposed safeguard measures with the Commission's authorization. It instituted exchange controls over resident capital outflows, quotas on certain imports, and export subsidies, all of which applied to other member countries as well as to outsiders.

The speculative crisis that developed later in the year, associated with pervasive expectations of an appreciation of the mark and a devaluation of the franc, led to an emergency meeting in Bonn in November 1968 at which Germany and France were unable to agree on steps to be taken.[13] In the end, both countries acted unilaterally to maintain their existing parities. France introduced more severe exchange controls, along with extremely restrictive financial and economic policies at home; while Germany imposed a 4 percent tax on exports and a 4 percent tax rebate on imports (involving a revaluation of the mark in commodity trade).

Further upheavals, associated with large-scale speculative movements of short-term funds across the exchanges, occurred in 1969. The franc, subject to heavy intermittent pressure accompanied by French reserve losses, was finally devalued on August 8, 1969, by 11.1 percent. Germany, flooded with massive speculative inflows of funds in late April and early May, and again in the early fall, unpegged the mark on September 29,

13. The EC Commission expressed this bluntly: "... the machinery for prior community consultation established in 1964 did not function satisfactorily during the monetary crisis in November." It also admitted that the Community was "very poorly prepared" to deal with the 1968 crises. European Communities Commission, *Second General Report on the Activities of the Communities, 1968* (Brussels-Luxembourg: February 1969), pp. 17 and 126, respectively.

1969, and allowed it to float upward until October 24, when it was officially appreciated by 9.3 percent. These exchange rate actions were in each instance, according to the Monetary Committee, the subject of prior consultations, but the evidence the committee submitted to support this contention is somewhat conflicting.[14] The common agricultural policy, far from serving as a deterrent to parity changes as had been believed in some quarters, had to be propped up. Or, more correctly, it was suspended by a complex system of border taxes and subsidies on trade in agricultural goods which France and Germany were authorized to take following their respective exchange rate actions.[15]

Already the events of 1968 had led to renewed impetus within the Community for greater harmonization of economic policies, intensification of monetary cooperation, and improved consultation procedures. This theme was stressed, shortly after the November 1968 crisis, in a December 5, 1968, memorandum of the Commission, at a Council session on December 12, and in an interim report on January 15, 1969, of the Monetary Committee.

More important than all of these, however, was the appearance of the Commission's memorandum of February 12, 1969, on the coordination of economic policies and on monetary cooperation within the Community— the so-called Barre Report.[16] That report emphasized the need for joint determination of more realistic and compatible medium-term objectives for each country, and for more effective "concertation" of economic policies, than had been the case in the two earlier medium-term programs. It also called for more effective coordination of short-term economic policies within the framework of the medium-term guidelines to ensure that the various economies did not depart too far from those guidelines. This re-

14. The committee stated that the date on which the "prior" consultations on the French move took place was August 10, 1969, which was two days after the franc devaluation took place. Discussions on the floating of the mark were held on September 29, the day on which the float occurred. See European Economic Community Commission, *Twelfth Report on the Activities of the Monetary Committee* (Brussels: June 30, 1970), p. 13.

15. European Communities Commission, *Third General Report on the Activities of the Communities, 1969* (Brussels-Luxembourg: February 1970), pp. 151–55.

16. European Communities Commission, *Memorandum of the Commission to the Council on the Coordination of Economic Policies and Monetary Cooperation within the Community* (hereinafter referred to as the Barre Report). Published as a supplement to European Communities Commission, *Bulletin of the European Communities* (hereafter referred to as *Bulletin*), Vol. 2, No. 3, 1969.

quired more effective procedures for prior consultation and their extension to short-term economic policy measures generally. Finally, the report drew up a concrete proposal for a system of short-term monetary support and medium-term financial assistance among members of the Community to supplement the existing international monetary cooperation mechanisms.

Many of these recommendations were repeated on March 20, 1969, in a section of the Commission's memorandum on the Community's work program for the next three years.[17] The Commission also recommended that margins of fluctuation around parities of the exchange rates of member currencies against each other be eliminated.

The Council expressed agreement with many of the Barre Report's proposals and, in keeping with one of them, issued a directive on July 17, 1969, to apply procedures for prior consultation to short-term economic policy measures in general, not merely to exchange rate adjustments and to decisions and positions on international monetary matters which were already covered in the May 1964 Council decisions.[18] More specifically, unless circumstances prevented, prior consultations were to be held if any member country intended to change its short-term economic policy in ways that would have an "important" impact on the economies of other members or on its own internal and external equilibrium. Also, prior consultations were to take place if such steps might lead to a marked divergence between economic developments in one member country and the medium-term targets that had been jointly agreed.

Further impetus to the forging of closer monetary and economic links within the Community was given by the parity changes in the last half of 1969 and by their consequences for the common agricultural market.

Meantime, other forces, both internal and external to the Community, were working in the same direction. By December 31, 1969, the transitional period envisaged in the Treaty of Rome was to be over. The Community had already completed the customs union and, however unsatisfactorily, the common agricultural market, which had engaged so much of its attention during its first decade. A new thrust forward seemed necessary to maintain the momentum already achieved and even to avoid retrogression. To many, the logical course was a drive to full economic and monetary union. In certain member countries this view was reinforced by belief in the desirability of eventual political union. France was eager

17. Supplement to *Bulletin*, Vol. 2, No. 4, 1969.
18. *Twelfth Report on the Activities of the Monetary Committee*, p. 15.

for a more rigid fixing of exchange rates within the Community to preserve the common agricultural policy of which it was the main beneficiary. In most of the member countries, especially France, there was growing resentment at the privileged position and dominance of the dollar in international finance and a desire, through closer monetary integration, to counterbalance the weight of the dollar and to have a Community "monetary individuality" of its own. There was growing recognition of the need for a common external monetary policy and for a united front if the Community's influence in international monetary affairs was to be enhanced. The limitations of consultations and attempted coordination of national economic and monetary policies had already been dramatically illustrated. The growing interdependence of the member economies through trade and factor movements was becoming increasingly apparent. A new Community thrust forward thus seemed to be imperative.

New Initiatives, 1969–71

A summit conference of the Community heads of state was convened at The Hague on December 1 and 2, 1969.[19] The final communiqué requested among other things that during 1970 the Council draw up a plan, based on the Barre Report of February 12, 1969, to establish by stages an economic and monetary union in the Community. By a decision of March 6, 1970, the Council set up a committee, headed by Pierre Werner of Luxembourg, to draw up such a plan. Other committee members were the chairmen of the Committee of Governors of the central banks, the Monetary Committee, the Medium- and Short-term Economic Policy Committees, and the Budgetary Policy Committee, as well as a Commission representative.

In the meantime, the Council had agreed to a system of short-term monetary support among member central banks along lines suggested in the Barre Report. Under the scheme, which went into force on February 9, 1970, the central banks agreed to make available the equivalent of a total of $2 billion for mutual balance-of-payments support for a period of up to three months, with possible extension of the credits for a further three months. Of this total, $1 billion could be drawn almost automatically by

19. "Integral Text of the Final Communiqué of the Heads of State of Government on 1 and 2 December 1969 at The Hague," Werner Report, Annex 1 (see note 21).

members in payments difficulties up to the limits of their individual quotas, which also set the limits of their individual financing liabilities under the scheme.

In the meantime also, a long debate was developing as to the timing and priority of the various steps toward economic and monetary union. Belgium and Luxembourg, for example, had submitted their own plan for a union early in 1970 in which priority was to be given to monetary integration. They envisaged a reduction in the margins of exchange rate fluctuations among the member currencies and the establishment of a European Reserve Fund and a European unit of account. Such timing, it was believed, would put pressure on members to proceed more quickly to the required coordination of economic policies. The approach was largely supported by France, but opposed by Germany and the Netherlands, which considered a greater convergence of policies necessary before formal moves to monetary union. An intermediate position, ultimately to prevail, was taken by the Commission in a memorandum of March 4, 1970, on a scheme for the phased establishment of an economic and monetary union.[20] That memorandum anticipated many of the later recommendations of the Werner Committee and was, in fact, more precise as to timetable and agenda for each of the contemplated stages. It generally followed the principle of parallel moves on both the "monetary" and "economic" integration fronts.

The Werner Report

The Werner Report of October 8, 1970, the basis for all subsequent Community discussions and decisions in this field, laid down a program for the establishment by stages of an economic and monetary union by 1980.[21] In its final form, the envisaged union was to have the following main features: (1) a single Community currency or, what would in principle amount to much the same thing, the rigid fixing of the exchange rates of the member currencies inter se, with complete elimination of margins of fluctuations and the "total and irreversible" interconvertibility of such cur-

20. Published as a supplement to *Bulletin*, Vol. 3, No. 3, 1970.

21. *Report to the Council and the Commission on the Realisation by Stages of Economic and Monetary Union in the Community.* Supplement to *Bulletin* 11-1970 of the European Communities, the Werner Group, under the chairmanship of Pierre Werner (Luxembourg: Office for Official Publications of the European Communities, October 8, 1970). (Hereinafter referred to as the Werner Report.)

rencies; (2) complete liberalization of all capital movements within the area; (3) a common central banking system, organized along the lines of the Federal Reserve System, involving common management of internal and external monetary policy and pooling of external monetary reserves; and (4) centralized responsibility in a Community "center of decision for economic policy" politically responsible to a European Parliament.

The final goal was to be approached in a series of stages, of which only the first was spelled out in any detail, through the progressive coordination, convergence, and unification of mutually supporting policies on a wide front. These were to be effected through existing and new Community organs to which growing responsibilities and decision-making powers would be gradually transferred.

The proposed program for the first stage (1971–73) called mainly for a series of measures to reinforce procedures for consultations and policy coordination, to further liberalize intra-Community capital movements and to move toward a European capital market, to standardize various instruments of economic policy, and, from the beginning, to narrow margins of exchange rate fluctuations among member currencies around parities. The hope was expressed that before the end of the first stage there also could be established a European Fund for Monetary Cooperation which would serve as a forerunner of the eventual unified central banking system. An intergovernmental conference was to be called during this stage to draw up the modifications to the Treaty of Rome necessary for eventual establishment of the full union (mainly the transfer of the principal decision-making powers in economic policy to the Community level). The mechanics and effects of narrowing exchange margins were discussed in a report prepared by a committee of experts for the Committee of Governors of the central banks.[22]

Although France had signed the Hague communiqué in December 1969, the supranational aspects of the Werner Report were unacceptable to it. Indeed, French influence is apparent in the content of a report and draft resolutions on the Werner plan submitted by the Commission to the Council on October 30, 1970.[23] In that report the Commission stated that it was impossible to prejudge how powers would be divided between the

22. Werner Report, Annex 1.
23. "Commission Memorandum and Proposals to the Council on the Establishment by Stages of Economic and Monetary Union," *Bulletin*, Vol. 3, No. 11, 1970, pp. 15–25

Community institutions and the member states; the draft resolution omitted all reference to the "center of decision" and the intergovernmental conference to plan modifications in the Treaty of Rome; and attention was focused on the first stage only.

Council Modifications, February 1971

The broad substance of the Werner Report proposals, as amended by the Commission, was adopted by the Council in a resolution and series of decisions on February 9, 1971, and agreement was reached on an ensemble of actions to be taken during the first three-year stage beginning January 1, 1971.[24] Intra-Community exchange rate margins were to be experimentally narrowed from the outset; the member central banks subsequently agreed that from June 15, 1971, an initial reduction would be made from 0.75 percent on either side of parity to 0.60 percent. Machinery was set up for medium-term (2–5 years) financial assistance among members up to the equivalent of $2 billion to supplement the short-term, monetary-support arrangements already in force. The Council requested a report by June 30, 1972, on the organization and functions of a European Fund for Monetary Cooperation with a view to its establishment during the first stage. Procedures were authorized for strengthening central-bank cooperation and coordination of economic policies within the Community. It was decided that the Council would meet three times a year to establish guidelines on short-term economic policy for the Community and individual members to follow. Measures were to be taken further to liberalize capital movements within the Community, to foster a European capital market, and to implement other first-stage proposals of the Werner Report. At the same time the Council adopted the Third Medium-term Economic Policy Program for 1971–75.

While affirming their political determination to establish an economic and monetary union over the next ten years, the members were able to reach agreement only on the contents of the first stage. France welcomed the measures for monetary cooperation planned for the first stage, but it was unwilling to commit itself further at that time. Germany, on the other hand, was unwilling to commit itself indefinitely to these measures, and the financial burdens or constraints they implied, unless continued advance

24. For the text of the Council resolution and decisions, see *Bulletin*, Vol. 4, No. 4, 1971, pp. 19–29.

toward centralized economic and monetary policies was assured. In the end, a compromise was reached. The members committed themselves only to the first stage and laid down a procedure for possible transition to the second. At German insistence, a "precautionary clause" was introduced in the resolution to the effect that, unless agreement were reached to move on to the second stage (allowing for a two-year grace period) by January 1, 1976, at the latest, the monetary-cooperation measures to be initiated during the first stage would be terminated by that date.

Crises of 1971

As it happened, implementation of the first concrete step toward monetary union—the narrowing of exchange margins scheduled for June 15, 1971—was postponed as a result of the currency upheavals in early May and the failure of the members to agree on a concerted external monetary policy to meet the situation. On May 5, as a result of massive, speculatively induced inflows of short-term funds, Germany, the Netherlands, and Belgium temporarily closed their foreign exchange markets.

In keeping with established consultative procedures, a series of meetings was held within the Community to decide upon appropriate joint action. The Commission proposed that members affirm their determination to maintain exchange parities and take concerted action to curb the inflows of funds through regulation of the Eurodollar market. France, eager to avoid disruption of the common agricultural market, supported this position. Germany, on the other hand, finding the suggested antispeculative measures too interventionist to suit its tastes, proposed that the member currencies float jointly against the dollar, while remaining fixed against each other within narrow margins (the so-called European solution). Agreement could be reached on neither proposal.

On May 10, when the exchange markets reopened, the mark and the guilder were floated and the Belgian authorities ceased intervention in the "free" sector of their two-tier exchange market reserved for capital movements. Under these circumstances, the central-bank governors had no choice but to suspend their previous decision to narrow the fluctuation margins of their currencies against each other from June 15, 1971. Indeed, the whole project for economic and monetary union became temporarily paralyzed. In a resolution of May 9, the Council noted the need in certain circumstances for members temporarily to widen the fluctuation margins of their currencies around existing parities—technically, this is what Germany and the Netherlands argued that they were doing—and called for action to discourage excessive capital inflows.[25] To offset the effects of the floats upon the common agricultural policy, the Council on May 12 once again had to authorize taxes and subsidies on intra-Community trade in agricultural products.[26]

In summing up the reasons for the failure of the Community to agree upon a common approach in the May crisis, Raymond Barre commented:

This situation . . . derives from the dissimilarity of the situations, and consequently of the interests, of the various countries within the Community, from disagreement among member countries on economic doctrine, and from differing viewpoints on the methods to be used to solve international monetary problems.

So long as the Member States do not arrive at some measure of political consensus on certain major problems, we shall always have to live . . . with qualified commitments and, in difficult situations, with decisions designed mainly to safeguard what each country considers to be its own vital interests.[27]

The member countries as a group were again unable—and for similar reasons—to agree upon a common external monetary policy in the face of the new challenge posed on August 15, 1971, by the suspension of the convertibility of the dollar into gold and other reserve assets. Germany again proposed a joint float of the member currencies, but this was rejected by France. In the end, Italy and BLEU (Belgium-Luxembourg Economic Union) joined Germany and the Netherlands in allowing their currencies to rise against the dollar. France introduced a two-tier foreign exchange market and new controls on capital inflows, while maintaining its existing parity and intervention limits for current-account transactions. The Netherlands and Belgium-Luxembourg, however, were able to agree on a joint floating of their currencies; from August 23, they limited the

25. *Bulletin*, Vol. 4, No. 6, 1971, pp. 26–27. Later, on June 25, 1971, the Commission placed before the Council a proposed directive for the regulation of short-term capital flows and for the neutralization of their undesirable effects on internal liquidity. The Council, while expressing agreement with the principles involved, postponed formal adoption (*Bulletin*, Vol. 4, No. 8, 1971, p. 43). This directive was to be adopted in March 1972.

26. *Bulletin*, Vol. 4, No. 6, 1971, pp. 27–30.

27. From a statement before the European Parliament on May 18, 1971. See *Bulletin*, Vol. 4, No. 6, 1971, p. 22.

maximum fluctuation of the guilder-franc spot exchange rate to 3 percent by standing ready to support each other's currency when necessary.[28]

Despite their inability as a group to agree upon a common policy, the members were able to adopt and maintain a common position, in keeping with conclusions reached by the Council on September 13, in the various negotiations of the Group of Ten countries that led up to the Washington agreement in mid-December. The Council had emphasized the need for a stabilization of the exchange rates of the leading countries on the basis of the par value system, for a differential realignment of relative parities, including that of the dollar, and for measures of control over capital movements (including a possible limited widening of the band of exchange rate variation against the dollar permissible under the IMF rules).[29] During these months the attention of the member countries was directed much more to the wider issue of international monetary stabilization than to the problem of monetary relations among themselves. But the issue of future monetary union was kept alive in some of the discussions and communications within the Community. Indeed, many held the view that the upheavals since May 1971 strengthened the case for integration.

The opportunity to proceed was provided by the Smithsonian Agreement in Washington by the Group of Ten on December 18, 1971.[30] The exchange rates of the leading currencies (except the Canadian dollar) were restabilized on the basis of new par values or "central rates" involving a substantial appreciation against the dollar of Community currencies and those of the prospective members (Britain, Ireland, Denmark, and—at that time—Norway), and a considerable realignment of some of these currencies against others. At the same time, "pending agreement on longer-term monetary reforms," provision was made for a widening of the margins of exchange rate fluctuations to 2¼ percent on either side of the new

28. Belgium retained its two-tier foreign exchange market, and the joint float applied only to the commercial franc rate.

29. *Bulletin*, Vol. 4, No. 9/10, 1971, pp. 41–43. For discussion of terms, see pp. 310–14.

30. The Group of Ten comprises the countries that participate in the General Arrangements to Borrow of the International Monetary Fund (IMF), viz., Belgium, Canada, France, Germany, Italy, Japan, the Netherlands, Sweden, the United Kingdom, and the United States. Provisions of the Smithsonian Agreement are given in "Central Rates and Wider Margins—A Temporary Decision," IMF Executive Board Decision No. 3463 (71/126), December 18, 1971. See *International Financial News Survey*, Vol. 23 (December 22–30, 1971), p. 419.

central rates. All of the member countries (and the prospective members) were among those to avail themselves of this provision.

Agreement on the new structure of exchange rates, and the emergence of a more "realistic" pattern of rates within the Community and against the dollar, cleared the way for a reactivation of the plan for monetary union stalled since May 1971. Indeed, a new sense of urgency seemed to be lent to the enterprise, not only because of the dismal experience of the preceding six months, but also because of the continued inconvertibility of the dollar into reserve assets. The new exchange rate margins against the dollar, moreover, would have made possible, in principle at least, swings of up to 9 percent between any two Community currencies, compared with those of up to 3 percent before May 1971. Swings of that magnitude could, according to Community officials, have seriously affected the competitive trade position among members, disrupted the common agricultural policy, and severely impeded the convergence of economic policies required in a move to economic and monetary union.

Renewed Drive in 1972

On January 12, 1972, the Commission proposed a resumption of the first phase of the plan for economic and monetary union. In a memorandum on the organization of Community monetary and financial relations during that phase, it made a number of recommendations differing from or supplementing those on which agreement had been reached a year earlier in connection with the original plan.[31] It recommended that the band of exchange fluctuations between the highest and lowest member currencies be fixed initially at 2.0 percent. The Commission believed that the original proposed band of 1.2 percent would no longer be realistic in view of the new wider band against the dollar. Further, it recommended that member central banks intervene in member currencies to maintain the 2.0 percent band, intervening in dollars in principle only when the limits of the 4.5 percent dollar band were reached. The original agreement had called for initial intervention in dollars alone. Finally, the Commission called for implementation of its proposed directive of June 23, 1971, regarding the regulation of capital movements and neutralization of their undesirable internal effects.

31. *Bulletin*, Vol. 5, No. 1, 1971, pp. 25–34.

The decision to proceed with plans for the first stage was taken by the Council at a meeting early in March and embodied in a resolution of March 21, 1972, which supplemented and amended the decisions of a year earlier.[32] Virtually all of the Commission's recommendations were adopted, along with others on a wider front that the Commission had submitted in the interim. The member central banks also reached certain understandings. They were instructed to reduce the band between the highest and lowest Community currencies initially to 2¼ percent, beginning July 1, 1972, at the latest. The choice of this figure, instead of the 2 percent recommended by the Commission, meant that the swings between any two member currencies, on the basis of any given parities, could not exceed 4½ percent, or exactly the same amount that any one member currency could swing against the dollar. The Community band could, in turn, move within the wider band against the dollar (hence the phrase, "the snake in the tunnel").[33] According to the expressed intention, the Community band would itself be subject to progressive narrowing over time.

It was clear, although not explicitly stated, that member countries reserved the right to alter their parities or central rates, subject to the established prior consultative procedures. Any such alterations could, in principle, be accommodated within the framework of the scheme, which was concerned only with maximum deviations from parities of member currencies against each other. The French and Belgian "free" exchange rates were not covered by the scheme.

The member central banks were asked to intervene in member currencies only when the limits of the Community band were reached. It was understood that this would be effected by sales of the strongest currency, or currencies, and purchases of the weakest currency, by the central banks concerned. The latter would intervene in dollars only when the limits of the dollar band (the "Smithsonian limits") were reached. Intervention within the limits would require a concerted decision.

The evident purpose of these provisions was to reduce the importance of the dollar as an intervention currency for Community central banks and perhaps also to limit the possibility of any one member currency becoming

32. *Bulletin*, Vol. 5, No. 4, 1972, pp. 41–44.
33. While an individual member currency could in principle move over time within the full range of the tunnel, its actual range of fluctuation at any time was constrained by the position of the snake within the tunnel. As a result, a member could be forced to intervene in the exchange market before either of the limits of its potential variation against the dollar was reached.

a major intervention medium in intra-Community exchange transactions. Of more interest, the requirement to intervene in dollars only at the dollar limits obviated the problem, on which some concern had been expressed in an appendix to the Werner Report, of otherwise having to reach agreement among the members as to the appropriate position and movements of the Community band within the dollar band. Members with weak currencies might have wanted to move the Community band down at times when members with strong currencies might have wanted it up. By permitting the undulations of the snake within the tunnel to be determined by market forces, the problem of how to reconcile possible conflicting interests of this kind was avoided.

It was also agreed that inter-central bank liabilities resulting from intervention in member currencies would be settled at the end of the month following the month of intervention. This time limit was no doubt intended to remove fears on the part of certain members, notably Germany, that in supporting the weaker currencies they would assume an obligation to extend credit indefinitely to the weaker member countries. Furthermore, when a country settled its liabilities in its own reserves—it could also avail itself within limits of the short- and medium-term credit facilities established in 1970 and 1971—it would have to use its reserves, such as gold, dollars, and SDRs, in proportion to the composition of these assets in its total reserves. This rule was mainly designed to prevent members from settling exclusively in dollars, as they would otherwise have done.

The Council also called for a report by June 30, 1972, on the proposed European Monetary Cooperation Fund, whose initial function would presumably be to facilitate the coordination of the exchange market interventions and the reserve policies of the member central banks. Also at the March meeting, the Council approved the directive proposed by the Commission on June 23, 1971, regarding the control of capital movements and neutralization of their adverse internal effects. That directive had merely recommended that each member equip its monetary authority with specific instruments for use in case of need, their exact application being left to the member's judgment. At the time that the directive was adopted, nearly all of the countries had virtually all of these instruments already at their disposal. It was not made clear in the directive whether, or to what extent, these instruments when used to control capital movements would apply to member as contrasted with nonmember countries.

On the nonmonetary front, the Council established a coordination group. This was one more piece of administrative machinery designed to reinforce existing procedures for consultation and coordination of short-term economic and financial policies within the framework of the policy guidelines laid down by the Council.

These decisions and understandings, and the discussions that preceded them, indicated a somewhat greater degree of flexibility in the positions of the various member countries, notably France and Germany. To be sure, only the first stage of the envisaged unification process was again involved, and the question of the eventual distribution of powers between Community institutions and national authorities was left open as before. But both France and Germany made certain concessions to each other, perhaps because of the chastening experiences of 1971. The French, for example, seem to have taken a less hostile line to joint supervision of economic policies (for example, in agreeing to the coordination group), while Germany yielded to the French view on the regulation of capital movements (although on March 1, 1972, it had already introduced a strong measure of capital-movements control in the form of a 40 percent cash-deposit requirement on borrowings abroad).

Crisis of Mid-1972

The narrowing of intra-Community exchange margins got under way on April 24, 1972. In the immediately preceding months, the spread between the highest and lowest Community currencies, in terms of their deviations from the central rates, had generally exceeded the specified band of 2¼ percent. With the Council's March resolution, however, intra-Community exchange rates promptly moved within that range before the July 1 deadline. In anticipation of their accession to the Community, Great Britain, Ireland, and Denmark joined the scheme on May 1 and Norway on May 23.

The new Community band was soon put to its first major test. By mid-June the pound was under heavy speculative selling pressure and moved to the floor of the band. To prevent the band being breached, a number of the member central banks had to buy large quantities of sterling, while the Bank of England in turn had to sell some member currencies obtained under bilateral swaps. With most of the participating currencies in the upper half of the dollar band, these support operations became necessary well before the pound had fallen to the dollar floor. Faced with a heavy loss of reserves, the British authorities decided on June 23 to float the pound. They therefore no longer had to keep the pound within the Community band or the dollar band and they relieved other participants of their obligation to support the pound against their own currencies. Under the pressure of market forces, the pound quickly floated out of both the "snake" and the "tunnel." (Ireland followed suit.)

Shortly thereafter, Denmark removed the krone from the Community band because it feared unsupportable reserve losses, but continued to maintain the dollar band. Italy, whose currency was being heavily supported, wanted to drop out of the scheme, and indeed to float like the pound. But it was induced by its Community partners to remain within the snake only by an alteration of the settlement rules for three months whereby Italy was permitted to pay its partners entirely in dollars for liabilities incurred under the support operations.[34] In 1972, Italy, unlike Britain, held a high proportion (50 percent) of its reserves in the form of nondollar assets, and it was reluctant to give up these assets in that proportion to settle with its partners.

Thus, by September 1972, three of the partners had dropped out of the scheme, at least temporarily, while a fourth remained only because of a suspension in the settlement rules. The Six and Norway continued to keep their currencies within the Community band.

In the wake of the speculative attack on the dollar that followed the sterling crisis, the Community considered the possibility of a joint float of member currencies against the dollar. This was rejected, among other reasons because of the differing payments positions of the various countries. Instead, direct controls over capital inflows (outflows in the case of Italy) were tightened, even by Germany. Since these controls applied equally to all countries, there was a further setback to liberalization of capital movements within the Community, one of the essential ingredients in a move to monetary unification.

Conclusion

Over the period as a whole—from 1957 to 1972—Community efforts at monetary integration have been unimpressive. There has been little success in meaningful coordination of domestic monetary and economic

34. These arrangements were extended until December 1972.

policies. This failure has in part been responsible for the differential rates of inflation and diverging economic trends in many of the member countries, especially after 1966, and in the series of balance-of-payments crises experienced in the later years of the period. To the extent that members' economies have moved in step during the period, it has been because of the pressure of market forces or their growing interdependence through trade and integration on certain other fronts. At times of crisis members have generally been unable to agree on common external monetary policies and have gone their separate ways. (Somewhat more success has been achieved, however, in reaching agreement on common positions in various international monetary negotiations.) When agreement was finally reached in February 1971 to move to eventual monetary and economic union, a joint commitment could be obtained only with regard to the first and most innocuous stage of the envisaged unification process.

The first planned attempt to narrow intra-Community margins of exchange rate fluctuations never got off the ground. The second, when launched, almost immediately ran into difficulties, with three of the participants dropping out of the experiment and a fourth remaining in only because of special inducements. The liberalization of intra-Community capital movements made no headway after 1962; in 1971–72, on the contrary, movements were more restricted. No visible progress has been made in developing a Community capital market. Only after considerable prodding from the Commission was a system of short- and medium-term financial support finally set up in the early 1970s. And only in September 1972 was agreement reached on the details of an embryonic European Monetary Cooperation Fund.

The reason for this unimpressive performance does not lie in any lack of machinery and procedures for consultation and cooperation within the Community. On the contrary, there have been ample administrative facilities for promoting the coordination of monetary and economic policies and the harmonization of policy instruments and targets. These facilities have undoubtedly served a useful role in fostering exchange of views and proposed strategies among high officials of the member countries, in making each member more aware of the repercussions of its actions on the economies of the others. Perhaps it has been easier for members to mutually adopt national targets and policies, and to conform more in attitudes generally, than would otherwise have been the case. Admittedly, however, the terms "coordination" and "harmonization" are by no means operationally clear, and there has not always been agreement among the members as to what they were meant to imply in particular circumstances.

Under fair-weather conditions, such as those prevailing up to the fall of 1963 and in the four years following the spring of 1964, there has been no strong pressure for coordination of policies or for other steps toward monetary integration. Policy recommendations emanating from Community institutions have generally been adopted by members, at least so long as they do not clash with their national interests. At times of crisis, however, such as those that occurred during 1968–72, individual members have chosen to be guided by their own economic and political interests when these conflicted with those of other members or of the Community as a whole.

Periods of crisis have invariably been followed by the introduction of new or strengthened consultative procedures, by solemn affirmation of pledges to coordinate policies more closely and, as in spring 1971 and spring 1972, by expressed resolve to move forward to full economic and monetary union. As late as 1971, the Commission lamented the fact that progress "has been much more rapid in creating interdependence between the member countries than in aligning their behavior, objectives, and policies."[35] And the European Parliament, in a resolution of February 9, 1972, expressed the hope that from then on "the Community's economic policy shall not be determined so much by the particular requirements of the Member States as by the needs of the Community as a whole."[36]

The lack of effective coordination of domestic monetary and economic policies stems mainly from differences among members in their priorities and tradeoffs among the various economic policy goals. In relation to France, Germany, for example, places more importance upon restraining inflation than upon reducing unemployment. Preferences for different policy instruments and mixes tend to differ from country to country and also their relative effectiveness. So do the economic characteristics of the individual countries. As a result efforts to reach agreement on coordinated or joint policies have been impeded if they ran counter to the preferred mix of objectives and policies of individual countries. Members have held

35. European Communities Commission, *Fourth General Report on the Activities of the Communities, 1970* (Brussels-Luxembourg: February 1971), p. 85.
36. *Bulletin,* Vol. 5, No. 4, 1972, p. 25.

firmly to their autonomy in decision making on domestic monetary and economic policies, relying on their right to alter exchange rates or to impose safeguard measures if need be in case of balance-of-payments problems. Even perfect coordination, whatever that means, will be no guarantee that such problems will not still emerge.[37]

With regard to external monetary policy, it has also been difficult to reach agreement on a common stance in the face of external challenges. This difficulty has reflected not only the differing payments positions of individual members, but also differing economic philosophies. Germany, for example, was sympathetic to a joint float of Community currencies during the crises of 1971, whereas France, in part because of its desire to minimize disruptions to the common agricultural policy, favored the maintenance of fixed exchange rates. Likewise, at least until the fall of 1972, Germany was opposed to direct controls over capital movements, a position not shared by France. Differing political considerations have also added to the problems.

Doubtless, more can be done in the future than in the past, by way of consultations, to promote greater convergence of economic trends, policies, and objectives in the various member countries. But at some point successful progress to eventual monetary and economic union will require a move from attempted coordination to a unification of policies, at least in key areas such as money creation, determination of exchange rates, and pooling of reserves. This in turn will necessitate the transfer of relevant decision-making powers from national authorities to Community institutions. It remains to be seen whether individual member countries will, in the end, be prepared to accept the political implications of such a transfer: Will they accept the loss of economic autonomy involved, the subordination of their national economic interests to the majority or average interests of the group with which their own may not coincide, and the dis-

37. As one writer has put it: "Cost movements in different national economies may diverge over time for a variety of reasons, including differential strengths and tactics of labor unions, different rates of adoption of new technology, and the like; and demand for foreign products may grow at differential rates.... For all these reasons, and others, a country's balance-of-payments position may gradually slip out of equilibrium under a regime of fixed exchange rates, even when monetary and fiscal policies have been 'harmonized' in some conventional sense of the term...." See Richard N. Cooper, *Sterling, European Monetary Unification, and the International Monetary System* (British-North American Committee, 1972), p. 20.

ciplines or burdens that might be required or imposed—at least in the absence of sufficiently large fiscal transfers to distressed regions—by adherence to unified exchange rates?[33] As indicated earlier, however, the crucial issue of transfer of powers has been postponed during the first three-year stage of the envisaged unification process.

In the meantime, what are the prospects for the narrowed (and prospectively narrowing) intra-Community exchange rate band—the most visible symbol of the Community's move to monetary union? The defections in June 1972 have admittedly been a psychological setback. But so long as the remaining participants, the original Six, do not get too far out of line in their balance-of-payments trends, there is in principle no reason why the scheme in truncated form cannot continue in the foreseeable future. From the very inception of the idea of a narrower and narrowing Community band, the possibility of occasional adjustments of individual parities before achievement of full monetary union has always been recognized. These could be accommodated within the framework of the scheme, which commits the participants only to certain maximum percentage deviations of their currencies relative to those of the others around parities, whatever the latter might be. Admittedly, the possibility of members dropping out of the scheme, at least temporarily as in the case of Britain and Denmark, was never explicitly considered. But it is conceivable that these two countries may return to the scheme before too long. In the case of Britain, this would undoubtedly involve repegging the pound at a lower level. In the case of the lira, too, there may also be a devaluation in the reasonably near future, but this would not be inconsistent with the band scheme. (For developments since September 1972, see pp. 28–30.)

Looking somewhat farther ahead, however, a greater degree of flexibility than the frequent adjustments of the peg will probably be necessary if the band scheme is to survive at all; differential price-cost trends are likely to prevail among the participants for some time to come. For one thing, formal changes in the settlement rules for liabilities incurred through market intervention by individual members in the currencies of others may be needed to take account of differences in the reserve composition

38. For detailed analyses of the costs and of the larger problems of monetary union, see J. Marcus Fleming, "On Exchange Rate Unification," *Economic Journal*, Vol. 81 (September 1971), pp. 467–88, and W. M. Corden, *Monetary Integration*, Essays in International Finance 93 (Princeton University, International Finance Section, 1972).

of the various members.[39] Of more importance, formal provision may have to be made during the transitional period for temporary currency floats or withdrawals from the scheme by individual members whose currencies are subject to strong upward or downward pressures. Or provision might be made for a system of "crawling pegs" (graduated changes in parities) for individual member currencies against others (and thus against the dollar) to compensate for emerging differences in price-cost trends within the group.[40] The latter system is consistent with the narrowed (or narrowing) Community band which, to repeat, is concerned only with deviations from parities. It would also be more consistent with the aims of the common agricultural policy than large, infrequent changes in the pegs.[41]

Of course, the band scheme could be suspended altogether until there is a greater convergence in economic developments and policies in the member countries. Each currency could be allowed to take full advantage of the wider band against the dollar. Germany, while not supporting such an alternative, has consistently argued that the band scheme and other moves toward monetary union will have a solid base only when substantial progress has been made toward such convergence. In discussing initial moves to monetary union, another view has stressed not so much the band scheme and its possible modifications as the need for the early commencement of operations of the European Monetary Cooperation Fund and establishment of a European unit of account.

39. In late July 1972 France had apparently suggested a higher bookkeeping price for gold in settlement of official transactions between Community central banks, but this suggestion was opposed by Germany and Britain. See *The Economist*, Vol. 244 (August 26, 1972), p. 34.

40. This possibility was suggested by Governor Carli of the Bank of Italy. See Guido Carli, "The Monetary Aspects of British Entry into the Common Market," in *Problems of British Entry into the EEC*, Reports to the Action Committee for the United States of Europe, European Series No. 11 (London: Chatham House and Political and Economic Planning [PEP], 1969), p. 47. This suggestion was also endorsed by Rinaldo Ossola in the event that greater progress toward unified economic policies within the Community was not achieved. See *Successo* (Milan— International edition), March 1972, p. 94. A transitional system of crawling pegs within the Community pending the establishment of full monetary union was also supported and analyzed in some detail by Bela Balassa, "Monetary Integration in the European Common Market" (paper presented at the Conference on Europe and the Evolution of the International Monetary System, Graduate Institute of International Studies, Geneva, Switzerland, 1972; processed).

41. Stephen Marris, *The Bürgenstock Communiqué: A Critical Examination of the Case for Limited Flexibility of Exchange Rates*, Essays in International Finance 80 (Princeton University, International Finance Section, 1970), pp. 29–30.

With regard to external monetary policy, the Community will face no major problems in the longer run if full monetary union is achieved. The Community as a group can adjust to external disequilibria, if it decides to do so, by a joint adjustment of parities or agreement to crawl or float. Indeed, one of the hoped-for benefits of monetary union, from the view-point of the United States, is that it will facilitate desirable movements of exchange rates between the United States and Europe, but until monetary union is achieved the picture will be different. Unless the payments posi-tions of the individual members happen to be broadly in line with each other, agreement on a common external monetary policy in the face of major external disequilibria for the group as a whole might be extremely difficult if not impossible. With payments positions—and national interests —differing, each member may choose to go its own way through exchange rate policies or exchange control actions suited to its own national needs.

Looking still farther ahead, the prospects of achieving eventual eco-nomic and monetary union in an enlarged European Community are going to depend fundamentally upon the willingness of the individual countries to accept the inevitable costs, referred to earlier, in the hope of the presumed greater politico-economic benefits. This is essentially a matter of political determination. And whether or not that determination will be forthcoming in the face of the many economic and political ob-stacles to union only the future will tell.

Addendum

THIS NOTE briefly summarizes developments affecting the plan for Euro-pean monetary union that have occurred since September 1972.

On January 22, 1973, Italy established a two-tier foreign exchange market, following continued speculative pressure against the lira. The "commercial" (as opposed to the "financial") lira was to be officially supported around its Smithsonian central rate and was also to be main-tained within the Community exchange rate band of 2¼ percent. On the following day the Swiss franc, which was most immediately affected by the Italian action, was floated and promptly moved sharply above its former ceiling. This in turn precipitated heavy speculative movements of funds into other European countries, especially Germany, in anticipation of further exchange appreciations. In the first nine days of February, the

German Bundesbank alone had to make dollar purchases of almost $6 billion to maintain the ceiling of the mark. On February 12 and 13, European and Japanese exchange markets were closed down. On the evening of February 12, the United States announced a 10 percent devaluation of the dollar.

When the exchange markets were reopened, the Japanese yen and the Italian commercial lira were floated (the financial lira had been floating since January 22). Germany, France, the Netherlands, Belgium, Luxembourg, and Denmark kept their central rates or par values unaltered in terms of gold and SDRs, thus allowing the market relations between their currencies and the dollar to reflect the full extent of the dollar devaluation. The snake-in-the-tunnel scheme remained in force for these countries, but Italy, with its currency now floating, dropped out of the arrangement. The British and Irish pounds continued to remain on a floating basis. (Denmark had returned to the scheme following the referendum of October 2, 1972, whereby it had voted in favor of joining the European Community, whereas Norway had removed itself from the scheme following its own referendum of September 25, 1972, which opposed entry into the Community.)

A renewal of large-scale speculative movements of funds into European centers occurred within a few weeks of the devaluation of the dollar. By February 23, the dollar had fallen to its new floor against the mark, guilder, and French and Belgian francs. Speculative pressures reached a peak on March 1, when European central banks had to purchase dollars to the extent of over $3.6 billion to maintain their exchange rate ceilings. The official exchange markets of the leading countries were closed on March 2 and did not reopen until March 19. With official exchange dealings suspended, the snake floated above the tunnel in trading by commercial banks. During this period a number of emergency meetings were held by Community members, and collectively by them, the Group of Ten countries, and Switzerland, in an effort to resolve the crisis that had prompted the closing of exchange markets.

Announcement was made on March 12, 1973, that, when the markets were reopened on March 19, the Community band of 2¼ percent would be maintained between the mark, Danish crown, guilder, and French and Belgian francs (the financial francs of France and Belgium were to be exempt from the scheme as before), but that the central banks concerned, while intervening in each other's currency to maintain the band, would not intervene any longer to maintain the 4½ percent range of fluctuation of these currencies against the dollar. In short, these currencies were to float jointly against the dollar and other outside currencies. Simultaneously, Germany announced its intention to revalue the mark by 3 percent prior to the reopening of the exchange markets. The currencies of the United Kingdom, Ireland, and Italy were to continue to float independently, but all three expressed their intention to associate themselves as soon as possible with the Community decision regarding exchange rates. Sweden and Norway, not members of the Community, subsequently decided to keep their currencies within the band on an informal basis.

For about two months after the reopening of the exchange markets, the snake remained within the limits of the old tunnel, although it was no longer bound by that range as a result of the March 12 decision. With the renewal of strong pressures against the dollar in mid-May, however, the snake floated above the upper limit of that tunnel.

In the crises of February and March 1973, the various European countries tightened their controls against speculative movements of short-term funds. These additional controls were applied to Community and non-Community countries alike, thereby involving a further setback to the projected liberalization of intra-Community capital movements.

The European Monetary Cooperation Fund formally came into existence on April 6, 1973. Initially, it will supervise the concerted intervention in Community currencies on the exchange markets, administer short-term financing among the member central banks, and multilateralize positions and intra-Community settlements resulting from central-bank market interventions in Community currencies. The Fund will also facilitate the progressive narrowing of the Community exchange rate margins, the progressive pooling of member reserves, and the achievement of other goals for which it had originally been established.

A. I. Bloomfield
June 10, 1973

Comments by Benjamin J. Cohen

ARTHUR BLOOMFIELD has done yeoman's work in providing a historical review of the monetary aspects of the European Community. This could not have been an easy task. The Community's efforts to foster monetary integration have been like a slowly incoming tide: uneven, episodic, uncertain, now leaping forward, now slipping back. It is only when we look back over the experience of the Common Market as a whole that we can see that progress has indeed been made. Bloomfield has successfully assimilated this whole experience and made it intelligible for us. His survey is comprehensive and lucid.

Of course, one might quibble. For example, one might ask why Bloomfield is so averse to naming names when he discusses historical events. His impersonal historical analysis is perhaps a bit too categorical. He notes that in the five years from 1964 through 1968, no significant action was taken to promote the process of monetary integration, that it was only in 1969 that progress was made again. Yet in attempting to explain the reasons for this prolonged hiatus, Bloomfield chooses merely to cite "prevailing circumstances." Can anyone doubt that one of the most fundamental of these "prevailing circumstances" was a man named Charles de Gaulle? It sems to me that we can ignore the historical role of the personalist government of France in the mid-1960s only at our own peril. The general was directly responsible for France's stubborn resistance to any hint of supranationalism in those years, in the monetary sphere no less than in any other. Likewise, his resignation in 1969 was the single most influential factor opening the floodgates to renewed movement toward monetary integration in the years since.

Such quibbling aside, I believe that two issues raised by the paper deserve greater discussion than they have received. One concerns specification of the objective of monetary integration that has been declared by the European Community. The other concerns specification of the forces that have propelled the Europeans toward that declared objective.

First as to objective: Bloomfield's paper talks about monetary integration as if we all know perfectly well what it means. But what in fact *does* it mean? A common currency, or merely separate national currencies linked together? Full unification of private financial markets, or merely fixed rates of exchange? Supranational centralization of all monetary and economic policies, or merely periodic harmonization of the short-term activities of central banks? At one time or another over the years, the Europeans themselves have seemed to suggest that any or all of these things are what monetary integration means. Such ambiguity is embedded in the debates between the so-called monetarists and economists, to which Bloomfield refers. Unfortunately, Bloomfield does nothing to clarify the ambiguity of the Europeans in this regard; his remarks on the economist–

monetarist debate are all too brief and cursory. As a result, his discussion is less enlightening than it might be. The distinctions among alternative interpretations are by no means unimportant. In practice, each would have significantly different implications for capital movements, for the adjustment process, for international liquidity, and for relations in general between Europe and the United States. In practice also, each would have significantly different economic and political feasibility. It is precisely these matters of effect and feasibility that are our main concern.

For such purposes, I think, like some of the contributors here, that it is necessary to distinguish among at least three different meanings of monetary integration.

First is the form of monetary integration that involves fixing of currency exchange rates, perhaps supplemented by some kind of mutual balance-of-payments support or joint reserve fund. For convenience, this may be called *currency integration.* W. Max Corden in his paper calls this form an "exchange rate union." It is the only form of monetary integration that the Community has come even close to achieving. It is the most feasible form, perhaps the *only* feasible form in the mid-seventies. It is also perhaps the least significant for the United States in either economic or political terms.

Second is the form of monetary integration that involves freeing capital movements and the unification of financial institutions and markets. For convenience, this may be called *financial integration.* Corden's term here is "capital market integration." It should be noted that to achieve this form of monetary integration, it is not absolutely necessary to achieve the first. Financial integration may be perfectly feasible even in the absence of currency integration (that is, fixed exchange rates), as, for instance, the postwar history of the sterling area demonstrated. Also, in the absence of currency integration, financial integration need not imply harmonization or unification of monetary policy either.

The third form of monetary integration does involve unification at the level of policy, and may or may not go beyond monetary policy to include other general economic policies as well. This might be called *pure monetary integration.* Corden says that this is "literally monetary integration." It is presumably what the Europeans mean when they say that their ultimate objective is an economic and monetary union. It probably has the most far-reaching implications for the United States, and for the international monetary system in general, of any of the three forms. It is also undoubtedly the least feasible in present circumstances, certainly in political terms.

The other issue which deserves greater discussion concerns the forces motivating monetary integration in Europe. Are these forces internal to the Community itself, reflecting the divergence of economic trends between the members? Or are they primarily external, generated by a resentment of the dollar and a desire for greater bargaining strength in international monetary negotiations? At times, Bloomfield seems to suggest the former, at times the latter, without regard to any differences between the two. Yet differences there are, and surely they are important. Both the form of monetary integration, and its implications for the United States, will depend greatly on which forces are most determining in the decision-making process. It will make a real difference whether the Europeans are pursuing their present course out of need, or out of spite. This matter too should be among our main concerns.

Comments by Gottfried Haberler

ARTHUR BLOOMFIELD gave an excellent description of the movement toward monetary integration. I share his general skepticism, and so, I believe, do many economists. Is the right approach to start with monetary integration instead of waiting until harmonization of economic policies has reached a certain point? This widespread skepticism is well illustrated by the fact that two economists as far apart as Nicholas Kaldor and Ludwig Erhard, each in his own language, used the same phrase: Kaldor said that it is putting the cart before the horse and Erhard, quite independently, said that it is putting the bridle on the tail of the horse, which means the same thing in German.[42]

I think I share their view. Now you may say this issue has nothing to do with our discussion. After all, the Europeans are moving toward monetary integration. We take this as a fact. But we should keep in mind that it is questionable if this is the right approach because it casts doubt on whether

42. Kaldor discussed the problem at the Ninth Colloquium of the List Society. See Nicholas Kaldor, "Reform of Bretton Woods," in Bertram Schefold (ed.), *Floating-Realignment-Integration*, 9th Colloquium of the List Society: Proceedings and Papers (Basel, Switzerland: Kyklos Verlag, 1972), pp. 12–26. Erhard's remark was made on another occasion as reported in the press.

it will be possible to move very far ahead with monetary integration before basic policies are much more unified than they were in September 1972.

If I may take up one or two points: Bloomfield says that narrowing of the margin—the famous snake in the tunnel—is a technical matter and that market forces are allowed to determine the location and movement of the snake inside the tunnel. I doubt whether that is really the case. It requires some more or less arbitrary decisions to fix the location of the snake and those decisions in turn require prior agreement among the parties involved and provide opportunities for disagreement. However, Harry Johnson's paper in this volume deals with this aspect of monetary unification.

Another question relates to capital controls. It would be a good idea here to distinguish between monetary integration of countries with controls, whose currencies are not entirely convertible, and monetary integration of countries with entirely convertible currencies. The European countries are somewhere in between; there are numerous capital controls, especially those which were introduced in 1971 by France, and in 1972 by the Germans and Swiss. Germany—and this is very important—has imposed capital controls that apply not only to transactions with the outside, but also to transactions between members of the group.

That is, as Bloomfield pointed out, a step backward in integration. The alternative would be to have unified capital controls against the outside and no capital controls inside. This is the theoretical possibility, but I would suggest that it is extremely difficult to do.

Again, apart from these capital controls on balance-of-payments grounds, there is the question of a unified capital market. This is one of the objectives of monetary integration. The idea is that permanently fixed exchange rates will help to unify the capital markets of the participating countries. Here again, I believe some skepticism is in order. It is an extremely complicated area. The members of the Common Market are working on the problem, talking all the time about unifying these types of controls—largely administrative in nature. This is one of those subjects that can be discussed for decades without making much progress. But I would like to recall that two massive studies have been made: one by the Organisation for Economic Co-operation and Development (OECD) and another one, the so-called Segré report, made for EEC.[43] These reports

43. Organisation for Economic Co-operation and Development, Committee for Invisible Transactions, *Capital Market Survey* (Paris: OECD, 1967–68), Vols. 1–4; European Economic Community Commission, *The Development of a Capital Market* (Brussels: November 1966).

describe in great detail the innumerable regulations in all the participating countries which restrict capital flows and prevent unified interest
structures.

I would suggest that monetary unification in the sense in which it is used
in Corden's paper, which freezes exchange rates and fixes them once and
for all, is not enough to bring about the unified capital market. I missed
in Lawrence Krause's paper a discussion of these issues and any reference
to the two detailed studies I mentioned.

Monetary integration between countries with exchange control (inconvertible currencies) means preferential abolition of the controls among
themselves with or without unification of the controls against the outside.
Intricate problems arise in both cases corresponding to those posed by
customs unions and free trade areas. Various techniques have been proposed, for example, formation of a payments union analogous to the
European Payments Union of the 1950s. The Pearson Report has recommended that approach for less developed countries.[44] To my mind, this is
bad advice because such an approach to remove controls on a regional
preferential basis is at the most a second-best solution. In this case the best
solution—to get rid of all controls by currency depreciation or floating—is
technically easier than the second-best solution.[45]

In Europe exchange controls, mainly capital controls, have *not* been
unified and are being applied also on intra-Community transactions. This
means disintegration and must cause distortions in capital flows as well as
in commodity trade, for it must be assumed that there is a good deal of
evasion of the controls: current transactions masquerading as capital transactions, or the reverse situation. France has on several occasions proposed
that unified controls for the whole Community be set up against the
outside.

Monetary integration of countries whose currencies are fully convertible
means freezing exchange rates once and for all. It is, in fact, a step back
toward the gold standard. Where macroeconomic policies are not sufficiently harmonized—which surely is still the case in Europe—monetary
integration is premature and must lead to friction and the imposition of
controls that are not in the interest of true integration. Some experts—

44. *Partners in Development*, Report of the Commission on International Development, Lester B. Pearson, Chairman (Praeger, 1969).

45. The problem is further discussed in Gottfried Haberler, "Reflections on the
Economics of International Monetary Integration," in *Verstehen und Gestalten der
Wirtschaft, Festgabe für Friedrich A. Lutz* (Tübingen, Germany: J. C. B. Mohr
[Paul Siebeck], 1972), pp. 269–78.

Kaldor, for instance—argue that monetary integration also requires regional policies in favor of the weaker members. It is not clear what useful purpose is served by the halfway house of the narrower band (the snake in the tunnel), which has its own special drawbacks.

We are told that such halfway measures should be regarded as symbolic acts and should not be judged in cold economic terms. One can only say that it is an expensive symbolism. The creation of the symbols produces friction and diverts attention and energies from more useful and integrative work. After macroeconomic policies have been sufficiently coordinated, exchange rates will automatically settle down in a stable pattern. Then is the time to link them rigidly.[46]

46. For general discussion of Arthur Bloomfield's paper, see pp. 70–77.

JOSEPH S. NYE

The Political Context

WITHIN A DECADE, the member states of the European Community intend to have established an economic and monetary union. As planned, this means that in regard to each other, the members plan to renounce a vital instrument of national sovereignty: the ability to devalue or revalue their respective currencies. When differences arise in national rates of productivity growth in relation to wages, intercountry adjustment will have to be achieved by politically difficult means such as severe unemployment in the countries experiencing greater inflation, flow of labor from weak to strong areas ("regional depopulation"), or large-scale fiscal transfer from stronger to weaker countries. Willingness to tolerate externally generated deflation, migration, or income redistribution implies a very high degree of political community. In addition, some sort of central institution will be needed not only to coordinate intercountry economic stabilization, but also to create some instrument of monetary control for the European Community (EC) as a whole. Otherwise, as one critic notes, "by establishing a monetary union they are not transferring it to the Community. They are simply throwing it away."[1]

The Political Paradox

Does this high degree of political integration exist in Europe? Apparently not. In May 1971, after experiencing a massive inflow of short-term capital, Germany rejected French, Italian, and EC Commission pleas for

1. Uwe Kitzinger, "Problems of a European Political Economy," in Steven J. Warnecke (ed.), *The European Community in the 1970's* (Praeger, 1972), p. 47.

37

jointly imposed exchange controls and proceeded to let market forces determine the value of the mark. The float meant the postponement of the first move to monetary union—the reduction of the margins in which the six currencies fluctuated against each other from 0.75 to 0.60 percent either side of parity scheduled to begin the following month.[2] This German exercise of sovereignty, however unpopular with its partners, conforms with their views on political integration as expressed in 1971. According to a 1971 British White Paper, there is no question of any erosion of essential national sovereignty.[3] Or as French President Georges Pompidou is reputed to have said:

There is no European nation. There are British and French and German and Italian nations. So I do not believe that a purely technical and administrative power can impose itself on the various states and the various nations.[4]

The French president was reflecting, not thwarting, the views of his electorate. Indeed, given his setback in the 1972 referendum in which he attempted to link his regime's popularity with British entry into Europe, he could be accused of *over*estimating the intensity of popular support for the concept of Europe.

Public opinion studies show that mass opinion determines elite behavior only when such opinion is clear and intense. Support for a "united Europe" has been consistently high in all countries (slightly more so in Germany and the Netherlands), rising from just over 50 percent in 1950 to fluctuations between 60 and 70 percent in the 1960s.[5] Nonetheless, public opinion has tended to provide only a permissive consensus rather than clear directives leaving a range of freedom of action for political leaders. A majority of Frenchmen supported political unification of Europe and voted as Gaullists at the same time.[6] When probed for intensity, public

2. Richard Norton-Taylor, "Currency Crisis Strains Solidarity," *European Community*, Vol. 146 (June 1971), pp. 12–14.

3. *The United Kingdom and the European Community*, Command Paper 4715 (London: Her Majesty's Stationery Office, 1971).

4. Quoted in Steven J. Warnecke, "The European Community After British Entry: Federation or Confederation?" in Warnecke (ed.), *The European Community in the 1970's*, p. 6.

5. Leon N. Lindberg and Stuart A. Scheingold, *Europe's Would-be Polity: Patterns of Change in the European Community* (Prentice-Hall, 1970), p. 39; Ronald Inglehart, "Public Opinion and Regional Integration," *International Organization*, Vol. 24 (Autumn 1970), pp. 773–76.

6. Jacques Réné Rabier, *L'Opinion Publique et l'Europe* (Brussels: Institute de Sociologie de l'Université Libre de Bruxelles, 1966), p. 23.

support often varied with the costs implied in the question asked. For instance, 66 percent of Frenchmen sampled in 1969 were in favor of a European Defence Community (EDC) and indicated they would vote for a non-French president of Europe, but only 35 percent said they were willing to accept a slight diminution of their buying power for several years if that were necessary to create a unified Europe.[7] Charges of obsolescence notwithstanding, the nation-state remains the primary guarantor of public welfare and the source of political legitimacy in Europe today.

Given this discrepancy between prevalent political attitudes and the political constraints on member states implicit in the notion of monetary union, how can the apparent paradox be explained? Prevailing arguments tend to be skeptical ones. For example, Fred Hirsch states that it "is not a serious issue. It belongs to the category of commitments that are endorsed by national authorities at the highest level, but are in fact ranked low in their priorities when it comes to the test."[8] In the view of another skeptic, "the Germans have managed to avoid more than a very limited commitment to monetary co-operation in the absence of an accompanying French commitment to economic co-operation."[9] In other words, one could interpret the monetary arrangements as a politician's gesture designed to satisfy a widespread but diffuse public taste for European symbolism.

One could also regard the plan as simply a Machiavellian French stratagem designed to constrain its partners to adopt the French view of international financial questions in particular, and foreign policy in general. Certainly the Nixon-Connally challenge of August 1971 helped to reinstate monetary union at the top of the European agenda from which it had been demoted by the monetary crisis of May 1971. In the view of a German bank official, "there is no other answer to the problem of the dollar standard and how to live with it."[10]

Undoubtedly there is merit in the prevailing skeptical explanations of European Monetary Union (EMU) as mere symbolic politics and diplomatic ploy. If that were *all* there were to EMU, however, the policy implications for the United States and international monetary reform would be quite different than they would be if EMU were really likely to lead to

7. *Paris-Match*, No. 1072 (November 22, 1969), pp. 18–19.

8. Fred Hirsch, "The Politics of World Money," *The Economist*, Vol. 244 (August 5, 1972), p. 55.

9. M. S. Mendelsohn, "European Monetary Union—Again," *Euromoney*, Vol. 3 (April 1972), p. 30.

10. Kurt Richebacher, Dresdner Bank official, quoted in "Prospects Weak for Money Union," *New York Times*, July 3, 1972.

higher degrees of European integration.[11] Others taking the latter position argue that EMU is a serious step toward European integration, the latest application of the "Monnet method" that has worked so well in the past. They point out that similar skepticism in the 1950s was unwarranted.

Assessing the sincerity of motives is a task better left to diplomats. The purpose here is to make a "best case" assumption that EMU is, in part at least, a serious strategy of integration, an effort to "pull the movement up by its own bootstraps." The insights of political integration theory are used to assess EMU as a calculated step in regional integration, and to outline the consequent political implications for the member states and Community institutions.

A Feasible Strategy

The implications of European monetary integration for domestic politics and European institutions will depend, of course, upon the degree and types of political integration that are achieved. How ought the prospects for European Monetary Union to be assessed? Political science theory provides no crystal-ball answer. There is, however, more than a decade of empirical research and middle-level (inductive) theorizing about integration processes that at least make it possible to identify the major variables and some of the relationships between them.[12] These variables and relationships are portrayed in Figure 1.

An essential aspect of the model and the following argument is a conceptual distinction among three types of political integration that are generally run together in popular discourse:

1. Institutional integration is the creation and development of common institutions. This dimension is measurable in terms of the respective jurisdictions and budgetary resources of the institutions involved.

2. Policy integration is the extent to which a set of countries act as a group (with or without institutional growth) in making policy decisions. This "political division of labor" is measurable by a locus-of-decision scale ranging from totally national to totally communal.[13]

11. See Richard N. Cooper's paper in this volume.

12. A useful collection of studies in this area is in Leon N. Lindberg and Stuart A. Scheingold (eds.), *Regional Integration: Theory and Research*, special issue of *International Organization*, Vol. 24 (Autumn 1970).

13. For details, see J. S. Nye, *Peace in Parts: Integration and Conflict in Regional Organization* (Little, Brown, 1971), Chap. 2.

3. Attitudinal integration is the extent to which people develop a sense of common identity and mutual obligation. This can be measured by survey research data.

The important point is that these three aspects of political integration do ✗ not all change at the same rate. It is possible to have greater progress in one than in the others. There are also good theoretical reasons (sketched below) for believing that the leads and lags among the three types are of great importance. Successful integration requires relatively high degrees of integration in each area to be stable in the long run. In this view, the European monetary union project represents an effort to make progress in the policy-type integration with expectations and hopes that institutional and attitudinal political integration will catch up before the decade is out.

Convergence of Actors' Goals

An interpretation of EMU as a serious step in European integration might start with the argument that Pompidou's statement would have been as true in 1957 as in 1971, yet the absence of a high degree of political integration did not prevent impressive achievements in European commercial and agricultural integration. A leading student of European integration wrote in 1967, "Converging economic goals, embedded in the bureaucratic, pluralistic and industrial life . . ." contributed more to the uniting of Europe than the symbols and goals of ". . . the politician, the scholar, the poet or the writer."[14] In other words, the necessary degree of political integration may evolve as the *result* of monetary integration rather than be a precondition for it. In the words of the Werner Report: "The economic and monetary union thus appears as a leaven for the development of political union which in the long run it will be unable to do without."[15]

On December 2, 1969, the heads of state or government of the six members of the European Community agreed to work out a plan for the creation of an economic and monetary union. At the same meeting,

14. Ernst B. Haas, "*The Uniting of Europe* and the Uniting of Latin America," *Journal of Common Market Studies*, Vol. 5 (June 1967), p. 322.

15. *Report to the Council and the Commission on the Realisation by Stages of Economic and Monetary Union in the Community.* Supplement to Bulletin 11-1970 of the European Communities, the Werner Group, under the chairmanship of Pierre Werner (Luxembourg: Office for Official Publications of the European Communities, October 8, 1970), p. 26. (Hereinafter referred to as the Werner Report.)

Figure 1. *Regional Integration Process over Time*

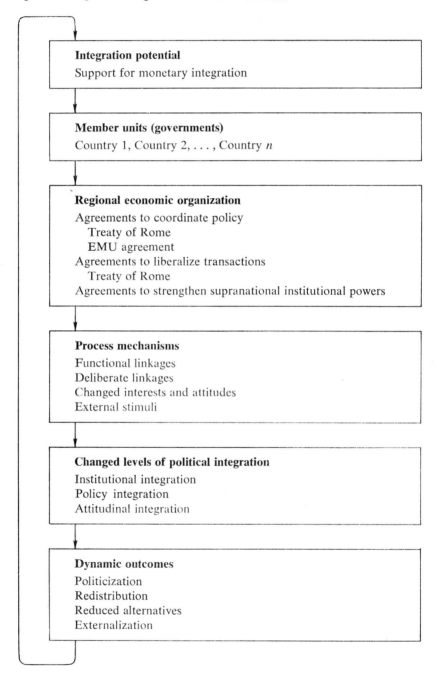

Integration potential
Support for monetary integration

Member units (governments)
Country 1, Country 2, . . . , Country *n*

Regional economic organization
Agreements to coordinate policy
    Treaty of Rome
    EMU agreement
Agreements to liberalize transactions
    Treaty of Rome
Agreements to strengthen supranational institutional powers

Process mechanisms
Functional linkages
Deliberate linkages
Changed interests and attitudes
External stimuli

Changed levels of political integration
Institutional integration
Policy integration
Attitudinal integration

Dynamic outcomes
Politicization
Redistribution
Reduced alternatives
Externalization

France agreed not to block negotiations over British entry if its five partners would agree on a new regime to finance the common agricultural
policy (CAP). Within a few weeks, a marathon session of the Council of
Ministers achieved agreement on financing the CAP, providing the Community with its own budgetary resources (to cover the entire budget by
1978), and increasing (marginally) the budgetary power of the European
Parliament. Thus the European Community completed its transitional
period on a note of optimism.

The December agreements were the first large "package deal" since the
debacle of 1965 when President de Gaulle had "untied" a proposed package of progress on agriculture, providing the Community with its own resources, and arranging for the direct election of the European Parliament.
The outcome of that crisis had been the 1966 Luxembourg Compromise
in which the six partners agreed to disagree on majority voting, leaving
intact the French notice that regardless of treaty provisions when vital
interests were at stake, unanimity would be the only acceptable procedure.

The 1965 crisis did not arrest all progress in the European Community
but progress was uneven. European bureaucrats (or Eurocrats) in Brussels
and French diplomats had convergent interests in further developing the
CAP. The basic deal between French agriculture and German industry (as
Walter Lippmann had caricatured the Community a decade earlier)
proved to be a successful one. But success in establishing the customs
union and common agricultural policy was not matched in other areas.
Elsewhere, as Uwe Kitzinger notes, Community progress lagged behind
plans, and agricultural policy absorbed 70 percent of the ministers' time
and 95 percent of the Community budget.[16] Similarly, according to esti-
mates by Lindberg and Scheingold in 1970, of some twenty-two governmental functions, Community activity predominated over national processes in only four: customs union, agricultural protection, commercial
relations with other polities, and balance-of-payments stability.[17]

Moreover, in 1969, even these achievements were threatened by the
devaluation of the French franc and revaluation of the German mark that
followed a period of diverging rates of inflation. In 1964, when the Community had fixed agricultural support prices in a common unit of account
equal to the dollar, it was frequently said that this would prevent divergent
change in exchange rate parities. This in turn would lead to coordination

16. Uwe Kitzinger, "Problems of a European Political Economy," p. 31.
17. Lindberg and Scheingold, *Europe's Would-be Polity*, p. 71.

of balance-of-payments policies. The alternative that countries accept a sharp rise in food costs or a fall in farmers' incomes was regarded as unacceptable. In fact it was not accepted, but the initial reaction did not lead to the predicted spillover into greater integration, but rather to a "spillback," as temporary border taxes and subsidies were implemented to protect French food prices and German farmers' incomes.

This monetary threat to the agricultural component of the basic political bargain underlying the Community was an important factor leading the member states (particularly France) to contemplate monetary integration. In May 1968, the EC Commission had wrestled unsuccessfully with the problem of reconciling changes in parity with the common agricultural unit of account.[18] In 1969 and again in 1971, the feared disruptions had occurred. While France and Germany had important differences of interest over the degree of economic coordination, supranationality of institutions, timing of limitations on exchange rate fluctuations, and international monetary questions, they shared a concern that monetary fluctuations not be allowed to undo the key agricultural policy.[19] The wider bands of fluctuation agreed to internationally at the December 1971 Smithsonian meeting accentuated this concern because of fear that cross rates within the 4.5 percent dollar bands would be too volatile for CAP border taxes to keep up with them.[20] In other words, initiatives on monetary integration were linked to very real and very powerful interests.

A second set of goals that converged in the monetary initiative were less tangible than agricultural interests, but no less real. These were the goals of promoting European integration, shared both by politicians concerned with foreign policy, and by a transnational network of "Europeanists," some inside and some outside the Brussels institutions. The European Community accorded legitimacy to West German foreign policy goals (and to the Sozialdemokratische Partei Deutschlands [SPD], a westward anchor for playing the game of Ostpolitik). To British foreign policy elites, it offered a new role after the end of empire. To French elites, it provided additional opportunities for leadership. Many of these foreign policy elites feared that unless the political integration process advanced, there was

18. "Parity Changes and Prices in Agriculture," *Common Market* (The Hague), Vol. 8 (November 1968), pp. 250–52.

19. For the difference between the Karl Schiller and Raymond Barre plans, see Dennis Swann, *The Economics of the Common Market*, 2nd ed. (Penguin, 1972), pp. 151–53.

20. "Oh No, Not Emu Again," *The Economist*, Vol. 242 (Feb. 12, 1972), p. 62.

danger of retrogression. Others felt that divisiveness on international monetary matters might be destructive. They shared Triffin's view that "the monetary, economic, and political unity of the European Economic Community would inevitably founder in the most redoubtable chaos, if the Community were to fail to reach agreement on a common policy to cope with this problem."[21]

Members of the Europeanist network saw monetary integration as a major opportunity for pursuing the strategy of *engrenage* which had earlier been so successful. In the words of Pierre Uri:

We have been able to devise many gradual steps towards economic integration. . . . In terms of political union, this is much more difficult, because when it comes to foreign policy it presupposes almost an overnight change in regard to what is the essential character of a national government. But then the answer should also be that there is already something political in the Common Market as it stands. . . . [E]conomic union and the steps towards monetary union are also political in a very wide sense of the word. . . . [W]e are already almost unconsciously following the real way towards political union.[22]

Integration Potential

Monetary policy seems to fit well into the Monnet-type strategy of integration. The Monnet, or neofunctionalist, method that has characterized the European Community was to avoid frontal clashes over sovereignty, and rather to let the natural linkages inherent in complex societies draw political actors gradually from integration in one sector to integration in another. The secret of successful *engrenage* is in finding initial sectors which are (a) politically symbolic but sufficiently noncontroversial so as to be susceptible to a technocratic style of decision making, and (b) not so technically autonomous that integration might fail to spill over into related sectors.

Monetary policy has the advantage of political symbolism without rousing intense natonalist feelings. In the words of Richard Cooper, money is "a somewhat arcane subject, thus offering the prospect that symbolic

21. Robert Triffin, "Monetary Aspects of the Accession of Britain to the Common Market," in *Problems of British Entry into the EEC* (London: Chatham House and Political and Economic Planning [PEP], 1969), p. 56.
22. Pierre Uri, "Steps Towards Monetary Union" in *European Monetary Cooperation*, Federal Trust Report, Special Series, 4 (London: Federal Trust for Education and Research, 1969), p. 81.

value could be achieved without provoking public controversy."[23] For instance, in 1968, 53 percent of a sample of French citizens were reported as willing to have French money replaced by European money. (In contrast, only 18 percent were reported as willing to see the French flag replaced by a European flag.)[24] In other words, money appeared as a field for technocrats, par excellence.

At the same time, money was a field rich in linkages to other sectors and with favorable implications for the growth of central institutions:

Fiscal policy. As Cooper points out, differences in fiscal policy will become increasingly important as the monetary instrument is removed from national governments.[25] Although the fiscal policy need not (and in Cooper's view *should* not) be uniform, there will be strong incentives for stronger states in a position to extend credit to fellow members to press for coordinated rates of economic growth and centralized decision making on budgetary policy and countercyclical measures. In fact, Germany has made this an explicit condition for participation in the second stage of monetary union.

Regional policy. Differences in economic activity that previously appeared as balance-of-payments problems will, under monetary union, appear as country and regional maladjustments. This will strengthen the demands for compensatory regional policies advocated thus far primarily by Britain and Italy. There is some speculation that the next summit package deal may involve a stronger commitment to regional policies in return for a fixed parity for the pound.[26]

Social policies. Among the programs designed to countervail regional maladjustments might be a Community-wide program of unemployment compensation, and various programs related to mobilization of labor.

Foreign policy. Once the European countries are committed to a monetary union, there will be strong incentives for them to take common positions on financial aspects of foreign policy issues. Efforts to hold a common position during negotiations over Special Drawing Rights (SDRs) in the 1960s were weakened by the divergence of German and

23. Richard N. Cooper, "Monetary Unification in Europe: When and How?" *The Morgan Guaranty Survey* (May 1972), p. 5.

24. Lindberg and Scheingold, *Europe's Would-be Polity*, p. 255.

25. Cooper, "Monetary Unification in Europe," p. 9.

26. "Why Do Today That Which Can Be Put Off Until Tomorrow?" *The Economist*, Vol. 244 (July 22, 1972), p. 31.

French views of the American presence in Europe. The French and the Commission regarded monetary union as strengthening the incentives for a common position.

The institutional implications of monetary union have also appealed to Europeanists:

Institutions for joint control of money supply. As Cooper argues, some single source of monetary expansion will be necessary. Different growth rates and national ratios of money supply to GNP ranging between 13 percent (Germany) and 42 percent (Italy) make it difficult to employ mechanical standards such as uniform rates of growth in money supplies.[27] Eventually, such an institution might evolve into a European reserve bank regulating both domestic credit and common external reserves.

Institutions for economic coordination. Institutions such as the Commission and the Medium-term Economic Policy Committee will increase in importance and "therefore the necessary powers will be transferred from the national plane to the Community plane."[28]

Community budget. An active regional policy and compensatory social policies imply a greatly enlarged Community budget. An enlarged budget leads to enlarged programs. As one Eurocrat put it, after 1978, ". . . we can begin to put into effect the proper industrial policies, regional policies, social fund policies and all the other things that we are at present writing memoranda about in this building."[29]

European Parliament. With the economic powers of administrative institutions expanded in the above manner, and with intercountry adjustment affecting such vital issues as unemployment, migration, and regional redistribution, the need under democratic theory for direct parliamentary control will become more apparent to those who now regard the European Parliament as a largely irrelevant body. In the words of the Werner Report, "The centre of economic decision will be politically responsible to a European Parliament."[30]

The initial arrangements for EMU were much more modest than the Europeanists envisaged. In the first stage there was to be policy integration but not institutional integration. The Council's February 1971 agreement

27. Cooper, "Monetary Unification in Europe," p. 8.
28. Werner Report, p. 26.
29. Quoted in *The Economist*, Vol. 235 (May 16, 1970; supplement), p. 16.
30. Werner Report, p. 26.

on implementation dropped the Werner Report's various references to supranational institutional powers. The provisions for narrowing exchange rate bands and extension of credits benefited France, which was concerned about the effects of monetary fluctuations upon the CAP, and which expected to borrow from Germany. At the same time, Germany (and the other four member countries) insured forward movement on policy integration, and a hint of progress on institutions, by the provision that the benefits of the first stage of monetary union would cease to be available if the Community did not enter a second stage within two years (i.e., by 1976) of the completion of the first stage. Subsequently, when a revised EMU was agreed upon and implemented a year later, Britain acceded with the understanding that there would be early progress on regional policy.[31]

In short, the goals of the European states as they embarked upon monetary union were convergent rather than identical. This presents the possibility of dispute and rupture as latent conflicts come to the surface. Supporters of supranational institutions, for example, will resist "automatic" schemes for market or policy integration that diminish institutional responsibilities. Similarly, disputes among states over leadership may burden progress. However, the monetary initiative is also linked to strong interests both in agricultural policy and foreign policies. This presents the possibility of greater policy integration, and thus a means of moving forward toward unification without waiting for the distant day of intense popular pressure for political federation.

Process Mechanisms

Given the ambivalence of public opinion in Europe and the existence of a permissive consensus, but not intense pressure for European unity, what is it that prevents political leaders from merely maintaining the existing level of integration? To simplify, the forces for change are: (1) functional linkage of issues, (2) deliberate linkage of issues, (3) the learning of new interests and attitudes, and (4) external stimuli (see Figure 1).[32]

31. "Yes, They Hatched A Snake," *The Economist*, Vol. 242 (March 11, 1972), p. 87.
32. This is a simplified version of discussion in J. S. Nye, *Peace in Parts*, Chap. 3. Legal commitments are treated as instances of deliberate linkages. The chapter also discusses the conditions that determine whether a process mechanism leads to positive or negative change.

1. Many sectors of complex societies are interdependent and there is a functional linkage of issues among them that makes it difficult to limit integration to a single sector. The imbalances created by these functional linkages of issues can press political actors to redefine their common tasks in either a more integrative or a more disintegrative fashion. In Walter Hallstein's view, "the material logic of the facts of integration urges us relentlessly on from one step to the next, from one field to another."[33]

As seen earlier, once the European states had agreed upon uniform agricultural support prices expressed in a common unit of account, agricultural policy was functionally linked to stability of exchange rate parities. Stable parities are in turn linked to differences in national rates of economic activity. The trouble with the Hallstein view of functional linkages, however, is that it does not allow for disintegrative responses. When the little wheels of societies are meshed, but the resistance of the larger wheels is too great, the little wheels are either disengaged or broken. Agricultural and monetary policies were disengaged both in 1969 and in 1971. Unless other conditions are favorable, it may be easier again to disengage agriculture from money rather than try to turn such large societal wheels as coordination of monetary and budgetary policies.

2. The functional linkage of issues may be reinforced or supplemented by deliberate linkage of issues. Deliberate linkage of issues creates "packages" in which progress on one issue is tied to progress on another. Initiatives for linkage may come from such sources as interest groups wishing to take advantage of new opportunities, national politicians concerned about an imbalance of benefits, external actors interested in promoting or retarding integration, and international bureaucrats who present proposals linking issues and who try to act as honest brokers during bargaining.

One of the important questions during the next phase of the transition period will be whether leadership will be forthcoming to assist in constructing positive linkages that serve to upgrade the common interest. According to the Treaty of Rome, and in practice before 1965, the Commission exercised this leadership role. Many observers are skeptical of the Commission's ability to fill such a role in the future, and point to the apparent anomaly that as European affairs have assumed prominence, states have tended to *withdraw* responsibility from the Commission. Even a commissioner has (anonymously) suggested "the common exercise of

33. Walter Hallstein, "The Dynamics of the European Community," *European Community*, No. 103 (June 1967), p. 11.

sovereignty" as a more realistic formula than supranationality.[34] On the other hand, Germany's deliberate linkage of progress on institutions with entry into the second phase of monetary union may help to restore the Commission's role.

Geographical enlargement is also sometimes cited as a possible source of new leadership for the construction of positive linkages. As more geographically peripheral areas are added to the Community, problems of regional distribution may be exacerbated, and there will be a stronger coalition of states interested in serious progress on such issues as a common transport policy, regional policy, and industrial policy. Britain and Italy have already linked progress on monetary union to progress on regional policy. On the other hand, British attitudes on institutional integration bear close resemblance to those of the French.

3. New ventures in joint policy integration provide opportunities for both the general publics and elites to learn new interests and develop new attitudes favorable or unfavorable to further integration. At the official level, transnational contacts are increased both among officials seconded to common institutions and among officials attending intergovernmental meetings. One estimate made for the mid-sixties is that some 12,000 national bureaucrats are involved in 1,200 meetings of various committees of the EEC system.[35] There is some evidence that these contacts tend to create enlarged perspectives.[36]

At the private level, the desire to reap promised benefits, and the practical problems of influencing central institutions, stimulates the formation of a variety of formal and informal transnational organizations to reflect common interests at the regional level. By the mid-sixties, there were some 350 regional interest groups with offices in Brussels.[37]

Thus far, such transnational groups have not been particularly powerful lobbies for further integration. Their common interests tend to be less

34. As reported in Warnecke, "The European Community After British Entry," p. 11; see also p. 23.

35. Stephen Holt, *The Common Market: The Conflict of Theory and Practice* (London: Hamish Hamilton, 1967), p. 60.

36. Lawrence Scheinman and Werner Feld, "The European Economic Community and National Civil Servants of the Member States," *International Organization*, Vol. 26 (Winter 1972), pp. 121–35.

37. Lindberg and Scheingold, *Europe's Would-be Polity*, p. 79. See also C. J. Friedrich, *Europe: An Emergent Nation?* (Harper and Row, 1969), passim.

intense than their special concerns and it is therefore still most profitable for the groups to lobby their respective governments. There seems no reason to believe that the situation will be different for the contacts made and groups formed in response to the initial phases of monetary integration. At a later stage, some common interests of public and private networks may be a positive force for further monetary integration.

4. External factors are often strong forces promoting integration. Certainly, the Soviet threat and American support were important stimuli in an earlier period. More recently the American decision to make the dollar inconvertible and to link discussions of trade and monetary affairs helped to relaunch the EMU scheme. It is sometimes quipped that "Europe has two fathers—Stalin and Connally."

To have an integrative rather than a disintegrative effect, however, the actions of the external actor must be perceived and evaluated in a way that leads to similar policies among the Community members. This was frequently not the case during the 1960s when French and German evaluations of the American presence in Europe reflected their different leaderships, historical experiences, and security situations.[38] Thus, although the Germans shared French dislike of an "inflationary" American deficit, they were unwilling to use a common financial policy as a means of weakening the American presence in Europe.[39]

European defense is currently based upon the American nuclear deterrent. Despite détente and a possible European security conference, the political leaders of Western Europe will need a credible defense position to neutralize what would otherwise be a powerful Soviet political influence in their affairs. Given the costs of maintaining a credible second-strike deterrent and the anxieties aroused by a nuclear Europe with a German component, it seems likely that during the EMU transition the members of the enlarged Community will remain heavily (and differentially) dependent on the United States. The United States will be tempted to link security issues (where it is relatively stronger) with monetary issues (where it is relatively weaker). Presumably this would tend to brake rather than accelerate European monetary integration.

38. This point is developed in Stanley Hoffmann, "Obstinate or Obsolete? The Fate of the Nation-State and the Case of Western Europe," *Daedalus*, Vol. 95 (Summer 1966), pp. 862–915.

39. See Stephen D. Cohen, *International Monetary Reform, 1964–69: The Political Dimension* (Praeger, 1970), Chap. 5.

Dynamic Outcomes

Over time, an integrative process is likely to encounter four conditions: politicization, redistribution, reduction of alternatives, and externalization. If there is a severe imbalance among the three types of political integration distinguished above (and shown in Figure 1), these conditions can lead to stagnation or disintegration. Here are some hypotheses:

Politicization. Controversy will grow as the arena covered by the participants broadens and as more and more groups find their interests affected by each succeeding phase of monetary policy integration. As the effects of monetary integration spread, its importance will increase and money will no longer appear as a merely technical matter. Politicization is not necessarily bad for an integration process. It is inevitable that public opinion become more heavily involved as policy integration makes incursions upon national sovereignty. But if attitudinal integration lags seriously behind policy integration, politicization will lead to stagnation or disintegration.

Redistribution. Higher levels of monetary policy integration are almost certain to have an effect on the distribution of welfare, status, and power, both among groups and among states. Some redistribution of an expanding Community output "may be both healthy and necessary if there are to be incentives for increased policy integration."[40] Monetary integration may disproportionately benefit strong currency economies like Germany, while costing them credit and fiscal transfers to partners. For redistribution to be tolerable (and thus productive), however, there must be strong enough institutions to plan and administer common compensatory policies. If institutional integration lags too seriously behind, it seems likely that the redistributive effects of monetary policy integration will be disruptive.

Reduction of alternatives. As policy integration increases, the independent alternatives open to national decision makers are reduced. As more issues become interrelated through functional or deliberate linkages, the costs of independent action become greater because there is the danger of disintegration. "Fewer alternatives" are not the same as "no alternatives," however, and some leaders may precipitate crises inadvertently or through deliberate brinksmanship (witness de Gaulle in 1965). The further

40. See the comparison of agricultural policy and transport policy in Lindberg and Scheingold, *Europe's Would-be Polity*, Chap. 5.

monetary policy integration progresses, the larger such crises are likely to become, due to greater interdependence and greater infringement of sovereignty.

Such crises can encourage greater integration if they help to overcome inertia by temporarily focusing popular attention on the alternatives to the status quo. But for the crises that accompany the reduction of alternatives to be productive, attitudinal integration must have progressed to the point where the opportunity costs of noncooperation are intolerable for a politically significant portion of the population.

Externalization. The further monetary policy integration proceeds, the more the member states will be forced to work out a collective external position toward third parties, and the more third parties are likely to react either in support or hostility. The closer the linkages (whether generated internally or externally) to other areas of foreign policy, the greater will be the politicization of monetary policy—with the implications in relation to attitudinal integration mentioned above. In addition, if institutional integration lags seriously, the capacity to arrive at and administer a common external policy is likely to be diminished. If, as Cooper points out, disagreements lead to immobility and inability to negotiate international monetary reform seriously, there will be more financial crises and more occasions when the United States will be tempted to play upon different foreign policy preferences among Community members.[41]

If these hypotheses about the future effects of increasing monetary policy integration are correct, what are the prospects that the success of the integration process will of itself generate the higher levels of attitudinal integration that seem to be necessary if the process is to succeed?

There are at least three major ways in which the process of monetary policy integration may stimulate greater attitudinal integration. First, the symbolism of success (including, some day, a common currency) may strengthen public attitudes toward the concept of Europe and toward the partner countries, but there is also some evidence to the contrary. Declines in public support have been associated with failures, as in the instances of EDC and de Gaulle's veto.[42] And in general terms the striking rise in Franco-German net amity (favorable responses minus unfavorable responses) from −20 in 1955 to +36 in 1965, coincided with and prob-

41. Cooper, "Monetary Unification in Europe," p. 10.
42. Inglehart, "Public Opinion and Regional Integration," p. 773.

ably to some extent was causally related to the success of the European Community.[43]

A second possible way in which the success of policy integration may create greater attitudinal integration is through generating benefits. Evidence from the 1960s, however, indicates that a majority of the public did not know whether they were directly benefited or hurt by European integration.[44] This would probably be true of the early stages of monetary union. At a later point, it does not seem that monetary union would provide clearly perceptible benefits to large segments of the public (financial interests and farmers notwithstanding), while it might be blamed for costs such as unemployment or budgetary burdens in certain areas.

Finally, successful monetary policy integration may stimulate the formation of transnational elite networks of public officials and private groups with a vested interest in the success of the process, and these elites may lobby to develop the requisite public support. As indicated earlier, however, the strength of these networks in the early stages of the project should not be overestimated.

Exogenous Variables

In short, while the process of increasing monetary policy integration will contribute something toward the development of requisite levels of attitudinal integration, it seems unlikely that the internal dynamics of the process will develop a sufficient level to prevent stagnation or spillback. If this is true, then the ultimate success of monetary integration will depend upon "dei ex machina," which by definition are difficult to predict.

What are some of the factors not related to the integration process that might cause large-scale changes in public opinion in Europe? One possibility is generational change. Studies by Ronald Inglehart indicate that both younger groups and more educated groups are stronger supporters of European integration than those older and less well educated.[45] Whether the attitudes of those now young will persist as they age is an open question.

43. Donald J. Puchala, "Integration and Disintegration in Franco-German Relations, 1954–1965," *International Organization*, Vol. 24 (Spring 1970), pp. 183–208.
44. Lindberg and Scheingold, *Europe's Would-be Polity*, pp. 42, 78.
45. Ronald Inglehart, "Cognitive Mobilization and European Identity," *Comparative Politics*, Vol. 3 (October 1970), pp. 45–70.

Another possibility is that dramatic external events, such as an unintended war or rise of a new type of regime in the USSR or United States might lead to a great intensity of public interest. Yet another possibility is that changing technology or environmental pollution will politicize new issues that involve a clear and current need for stronger regional institutions.

Whether such exogenous factors will bring about the integration of attitudes that seems necessary for the heavy infringement on national sovereignty implied by monetary union is beyond the scope of this paper to review. It is possible that a plan for monetary integration that was more flexible in the early stages and relied more on capital flows for payments adjustment might lessen the initial blow to national sovereignty, but favorable smiles from gods outside the machine would still be necessary.[46]

There are general reasons to believe that one day Europe may have a common currency.

The advantages of fixed exchange rates and the disturbances of fluctuating rates grow progressively with the degree of economic interpenetration. At the same time, the mutual credit facilities needed to make fixed exchange rates tolerable should be attainable more easily between countries that trust each other politically.[47]

The politics of the transitional period, that is, the next decade, have been the focus of discussion here. Given the unknowns in the equations, long-run predictions would not be very meaningful.

Comments by Edward L. Morse

JOSEPH NYE's discussion of the political context of monetary integration in Europe provides a succinct and virtually exhaustive account of hypotheses found in the current body of writings on political integration. That its conclusions on the likelihood of monetary integration in Europe are ambiguous and skeptical should not be surprising. The theoretical basis of this literature remains rudimentary and political conditions in Europe still appear to be indeterminate.

One might well quibble with incidental points in Nye's analysis. I wonder, for example, whether the notion of "spillback," as an alternative

46. See the papers presented by Lawrence B. Krause and W. Max Corden.
47. Fred Hirsch, *Money International* (Penguin, 1967; Doubleday, 1969), pp. 460 and 319, respectively.

and symmetrical outcome to "spillover" resulting from "functional" processes is useful if one does not specify the conditions under which the one or the other is likely to occur. I question also whether a Community Reserve Fund need evolve into anything that would add to the Community's institutional powers. Its operation is likely to be supervised closely by the finance ministries of the members and would quite purposively be maintained on a separate track from existing Community political bodies. Finally, I would challenge the asserted belief that in the monetary field, what the current political literature refers to as "attitudinal integration" need bear a close relationship to a stable level of policy coordination among the Community's members.

I find a few additional intellectual problems in Nye's approach. It seems to me that the current debate over monetary integration has been formulated on somewhat misleading premises about politics in Europe. This does not imply that the conclusions of integration theory as so fully and articulately stated by Nye are wrong. In fact, I agree with them on the whole. But they must be weighed against conclusions derived from an analysis of domestic politics in Europe—that is to say, in precisely those areas in which integration theory is lacking.

Let me clarify this by reviewing Nye's discussion of the EMU paradox. As he states it, members of the expanded European Community have committed themselves to the establishment of an economic and monetary union, yet none of them is willing to surrender the sovereignty necessary for the plan to be implemented. He explains this paradox, first, as a combination of political hypocrisy and French diplomatic tactics and, then, through the insights of political integration theory. What these explanations omit is an analysis of domestic political conditions in the societies of Western Europe, conditions that are largely responsible for the profound malaise in Europe today. What I would like to suggest is that these factors are preponderant and, if analyzed, provide a more powerful explanation of the EMU paradox.

The basic political condition in Europe from this point of view is that not since World War II have the European governments had so many occasions to reassert some influence over their own destinies as in the past two or three years (since 1969). Yet, wherever one looks for a response to the challenges before them, one finds passive acquiescence in the status quo, the submission of potentially significant foreign policy decisions to domestic pressures, or, worst of all, nostalgic efforts to patch up the outmoded system of the 1950s and 1960s. Political rhetoric would tell us that, since the December 1969 summit conference at The Hague, the commitment to a united Europe has been renewed and invigorated. It is the contrast between this rhetoric and actual political motivations that is at the heart of the EMU paradox. If this rhetoric, even in such issues as monetary union, is far removed from the intentions of European statesmen, how can we, as analysts, explain it?

In the case of monetary reform, I would argue, an illusion has been fostered by the decisions of March 1972 to renew the process of monetary integration by narrowing margins of exchange rate variations. This would be not only a first step toward European monetary unification, but also the major European contribution to the reorganization of the international monetary system. But the decision was taken more under pressure to act in such a way as to prove the existence of a European will to independence than from a desire actually to create a monetary union. That and subsequent decisions on the establishment of a European Fund did not carry with them any commitment to accept the consequences of monetary unification on other policy areas, either internal or external to the European Community.

The agreements, after all, still paper over essential Franco-German differences on the requisites of European monetary union. These differences are likely to come to the fore once again when the next crisis erupts. Agreement also was reached without any regard to the consequences of monetary unification on unemployment levels or inflation, both of which are likely to increase under a unified currency to a degree unacceptable to any of the major European governments. And, in spite of vague references to the European contribution to the reorganization of the international monetary system, there is no clear consensus or even outline of how a unified currency area in Europe would fit into a reorganized monetary system.

Some people would argue that the leaders of Western Europe have in fact been active in articulating medium-term goals for the evolution of the relationship of their societies to the rest of the world. The successful ratification of Chancellor Willy Brandt's Ostpolitik in May 1972, upon which hinged the implementation of the four-power Berlin accords and further steps toward détente, would certainly be illustrative. So would the active expansion of the EC to other states that has been hailed as the new prime to the European pump.

All of these policies and statements, however, smack of a superficial reechoing of past hopes and fears. They reflect an almost aimless action where activity, largely devoid of objectives, has assumed a value for its own sake. Brandt, for example, has been utterly unable to get any legislation passed in education, in tax reform, or in social welfare reform that reflects his own and the traditional goals of European socialism. To prove that he can be effective, he has made the most of ratifying the postwar status quo through his Eastern policy. Georges Pompidou's rhetoric strikes a balance between right-wing Gaullism and traditional French pro-European interests—no mean achievement, but one where compromise has overcome coherence in foreign policy. Restricted in their ability to implement or reform domestic programs, the European governments have been carrying out a new transcendental foreign policy. Unlike the transcendental politics of the past when the monarchs of Europe sought "power" and "glory," the new transcendentalism in European foreign policy is one of activity for its own sake, activity uninformed by either grand designs or short-term foreign policy goals.

What these actions reveal, it seems to me, is a profound fatalism and historical pessimism. This malaise in Europe is not simply a fear of change from the status quo, although that is certainly characteristic. Nor does it seem to me to be simply the result of an objective inability to achieve stated goals in all fields. Rather, the malaise in contemporary Western Europe stems from a condition inherent in modern industrialized societies, one that prevents or impedes the articulation of long-term visions and goals. And, with no consensus on political goals and objectives, the malaise and sense of aimlessness feeds upon itself in a vicious circle. The more ambiguous and static political rhetoric becomes, the more it reinforces a sense of fatalism that itself impedes, indeed makes silly, the further articulation of idealized views of what Western Europe ought to become.

Several overlapping factors may be distinguished. None of them alone would be sufficient to explain the current crisis of confidence in Europe. But taken together, they have presented a formidable obstacle to the constructive revitalization of Europeanism.

First, it has often been noted that the most persistent impediment to the coordination of policies in Europe has been the inevitable intrusion of electoral politics into foreign policy. In any one year the probability is high that one of the major European states is preparing for or in the process of an electoral campaign. Each time one of the countries faces an important election, it is obliged to suspend its own momentum in the organization of Europe. The enlargement of the Community to include states whose electoral processes have not yet become familiar to the original Six will exacerbate the condition.

Of the four major European countries, three have had or will soon have important elections. In two of them, Germany and France, the question of monetary union has become an issue of domestic politics. Some apparent success is needed to illustrate that the respective governments are capable of achieving their stated goals, in contrast to domestic sectors where they have been virtually ineffective. Actual implementation, however, need not be carried as far as rhetoric would imply. It is more important for electoral purposes to avoid failure than to achieve success. The distinction is important when policy agreements in Europe affirm basic consensus but postpone difficult decisions.

Second, a different kind of rigidity is shown in the twin problems of labor unrest and inflation that confront every major West European capital. Working classes have never been as rich as they are today, and never so afraid of any adverse change in their employment opportunities and relative wage levels. One result is that union officials have become unable to exercise effective control over their own members. Their loss of authority reflects a broader crisis of authority in European societies where governmental legitimacy is everywhere challenged. In the case of unions, even when they are able effectively to bargain with management or governments, negotiations have grown to look more like international conferences culminating in peace treaties than like traditional labor settlements.

Anticipated increases in personal income on the part of the rank and file, coupled with union tactics, have also become a major source of inflationary wage settlements. These problems have had a double and paradoxical effect on external policy. On the one hand, they have made it exigent that policy coordination be institutionalized in the EC countries. On the other hand, the activities that give rise to inflationary and other policy pressures reflect a growing introversion, which makes it harder to escape the national decision-making framework.

Third, the expansion of the EC itself has been bringing mixed benefits to the current state of European affairs. It has served as a symbolic example of the tenacity of the original European idea. However, the expansion brings with it almost insurmountable barriers to common solutions. Negotiation among six countries has been difficult enough. With more, it is hard to see how any dramatic steps in policy can be taken with the agreement of all parties.

This will be especially noticeable in two aspects of the Community's relationships with the outside world and, in particular, with the United States. On the one hand, if there are to be future trade negotiations among all the industrialized societies and if the Europeans are to negotiate as a block, as they did during the Kennedy Round, then it is doubtful that a position can be reached that will give the negotiators sufficient flexibility to strike any bargains. On the other hand, the intrusion of the outside world, and especially of the United States, will have an effect on potential tradeoffs on major issues within the Community that will enable it to forge common policies. Nye mentioned the basic tradeoff between France and Germany that enabled the Community to implement its customs union and to create a common agricultural policy. Now potential tradeoffs within the Community have to do with fundamental relationships with the United States. And the United States can carry out its own share of bargaining with some of the Community's members so that it, too, must figure in the European bargaining equations. The degree to which the United States will agree to serve as a "common enemy" inducing the expanded Community to accept a common set of goals will probably be much lower in the future than it was in 1971. If that is the case, it does not portend well for the articulation of a clear set of objectives for the new Common Market.

Fourth, inter-European political jealousy will continue to play its own role in impeding imaginative political efforts. With British entry, the opportunities presented to the member countries of the EC for manipulating one another is, of course, increased, and the old Franco-German game will in no way cease. Reluctance to replace the international dollar standard is an example of this. Neither the French nor the Germans want to see the mark begin to play the role in Europe that the dollar played in the fifties and sixties. And neither wishes to give up some of the central-bank functions that it would have to if a common currency actually were agreed upon.

Edward Heath and Georges Pompidou would each like to play the leading role in federation but neither can do this alone. Only Germany seems to have the capacity to do that and, unlike the other two countries, does not want the part because of the substantial constraints on German action in almost every field. Fearful that other parties may come to the fore as the focus of a new Europe, each of the major governments counterbalances the others so that none is able to play the essential centralizing role. And none of the states is yet willing to see an all-European body with this function if the rules by which that body operates are different from its own domestic rules.

A fifth factor responsible for the current fatalism in European politics has to do with a double uncertainty about the future. On the one hand, there is the attachment to a status quo with which everyone feels comfortable, whose rules are easy to understand, whose continuance seems to be relatively costless. But there is uncertainty as to whether it can be continued. On the other hand, there are uncertainties that have developed from the novelty of the contemporary situation. These uncertainties are the most formidable obstacles to innovative thinking in Europe today. It is clear that a major part of the current paralysis of political thought in Western Europe has to do with the trap that the Europeans feel themselves to be in between living with outmoded structures unable to handle problems that arise on a transnational basis and the fear that adapting or changing these structures to new conditions will involve costs in terms of budgets or autonomy that no one is willing to accept.

But the current uncertainty goes beyond that, for it pervades not only political circles but intellectual groups as well. It is an uncertainty that has to do with the knowledge available to handle the problems confronting the governments in the industrialized world today. These uncertainties pertain to the unprecedented web of interdependencies that involve the relationships among the European countries and between them and the United States. They are compounded by uncertainties about the governance of modern industrialized societies. These are paradoxically both stable and fragile structures. Their stability seems to hinge upon political traditions, political cultures if you will, that have emerged in the long process of nation-building in Western Europe. Their fragility stems from the incredibly rapid rate of change that these societies have undergone since World War II and the dislocating effects of change on various social strata, but particularly the working classes. The result has been that governance in modern industrialized societies has become based on daily decision making rather than long-term planning. Governments are concerned more with keeping the status quo and preserving the machinery of public policy than with steering a course for the future. The result is what French political scientist Pierre Hassner refers to as a state of agitated immobility rather than either revolution or integration.

My conclusions, then, are no less skeptical than are Nye's. The Europeans are anxiously waiting for initiatives from America, knowing full well that their actions will be inevitably reactive, the formulation of their objectives made in contrast or in complementarity to those of the United States. Or, given contemporary political constraints, they know that they will muddle along until another series of crises, as inevitable as the prolongation of their current malaise, stemming from domestic unrest or from relatively unstable international transactions, forces them to think together about their future.

Comments by Theodore Geiger

JOSEPH NYE has covered the internal sociopolitical aspects of the integration process so well and with such conceptual rigor that other economists will, I believe, share my admiration for his analysis. I shall direct my remarks largely to the external environment conditioning European integration.

The subject of the external environment of European integration is so enormously complex and heterogeneous that I can only paint certain trends and countertrends with a very broad brush. Those of you who are interested will find a fuller discussion of this and other related subjects in my recent book.[48]

Today, we are in a period between two worlds; the international political and economic system is in a transitional state. However, unlike Matthew Arnold's famous description of his period a hundred years ago as being "between two worlds, one dead and the other powerless to be born," ours is actively schizophrenic. While the postwar world is still very much alive in many of its most important aspects (notably the continuing competition between the two superpowers), the characteristics of a new world are gradually emerging within the postwar pattern of relationships. Some see only the old world and insist that nothing significant has changed. Others foresee what the new world might eventually be like and proclaim that it has already come. Many of us see both and are trying to make a coherent whole out of our double vision. Here is my contribution to that effort.

Since the late 1960s, there has been a pronounced trend toward multi-

48. Theodore Geiger, *The Fortunes of the West: The Future of the Atlantic Nations* (Indiana University Press, 1973).

polarity in world political and economic relationships that is gradually permeating the bilateral polarity persisting from the postwar period. New centers of political and economic power are evolving alongside the two existing superpowers, the Soviet Union and the United States. Three—China, Japan, and the enlarged European Community—are already increasingly important, although in different ways, in the international system. By the end of the century, others are likely to emerge from among such potential great powers as India and Indonesia in Asia, Brazil and Mexico in Latin America.

However, one major reason for the transitional character of the current situation is that each of the new great powers is developing its economic, military, and political capabilities at different rates. The European Community is the world's largest trading entity, with influence in world economic affairs second, if not equal, to that of the United States. But it lacks a world military capability and, hence, its influence in world political affairs is not commensurate with its size, wealth, and history. In contrast, China's economy is underdeveloped and its trade comparatively small but its sheer size and its military capabilities give it a rapidly growing importance in the international system, as evidenced by the current competition for its friendship and a share in its commerce. Japan, with the fourth largest (after the United States, the Soviet Union, and the European Community) and the fastest growing economy on the planet, has emerged in recent years as a world economic power center but lacks significant military capabilities and international political importance. In the course of the 1970s, it is likely that developments in Asia and in the international political and economic system as a whole will impel Japan to develop its own nuclear force, a change already presaged by the current doubling of its conventional defense expenditures.

These differential rates of development of economic, military, and political capabilities generate enormous tensions and strains not only among the existing and emerging great power centers but also within them. The latter effect is at present most pronounced in the European Community, which is confronted with a series of dilemmas in its internal evolution that also strongly affect its relationship with the United States.

For much of the postwar period, roughly defined as the two decades from the mid-1940s to the mid-1960s, each of the West European nations related to the United States on a bilateral basis. Hence, each saw itself confronted by an American economy many times larger than its own and on which it was substantially reliant for its economic well-being. This economic disparity and extreme economic dependence were paralleled by the disproportionate military and political capabilities of the United States and the consequent dependence of each European country on American military protection and political support.

By contrast, in the early seventies, most of the West European nations relate to the United States not only bilaterally but also collectively as members of the European Community. Thanks to European economic growth since World War II and to European integration, the economic capabilities of the United States and the European Community are more nearly equal and their dependence is mutual and not nearly so great. At the same time, however, Europe's defense dependence persists. Although they possess the requisite techno-economic capabilities, the West European nations, individually and collectively, are unwilling either to divert sufficient resources from nonmilitary domestic goals or to institute the integrated arrangements needed to develop independent defense forces.

Western Europe's unwillingness to allocate resources for developing its own military capabilities reflects another of the basic trends shaping the emerging new period of world politics and economics: the tendency in all of the developed nations—in Western Europe, North America, and the Pacific countries—for claims on resources by the politically and economically effective interest groups to proliferate in number and to grow in size. Moreover, these groups are becoming more impatient and less inclined to compromise. The national goals being sought and the means to achieve them naturally vary from country to country and from year to year. But, in greater or lesser degree in all of the developed nations, these trends are wholly or in part responsible for the increased politicizing of the process of resource allocation, for the now endemic tendency to inflation, and for the growing importance of the national governments both in resolving conflicting claims on resources and in implementing the resulting allocations to national goals.

In Western Europe, this strengthening of the central institutions of the nation-state has occurred concurrently with the process of European integration, which requires the governments involved to give up or to agree not to use unilaterally such major sovereign powers as control over their external trade and payments. These opposing trends underlie the European Community's present difficulty in moving beyond its customs union to monetary, and eventually full economic, union.

They are also important at the level of transatlantic relationships. European economic recovery, the six rounds of tariff reductions under the aegis of the General Agreement on Tariffs and Trade (GATT), and the great improvements in transportation and communication have brought to nations of North America and Western Europe an unprecedented degree of economic integration in the course of the 1960s, which is reflected in trade and capital flows. As within the European Community, many of the current economic issues among the United States, the European Community, and Japan are caused by the conflicting trends of the internal strengthening of the institutions of the nation-state and the external restraints imposed on their freedom of action by Atlantic economic integration.

In the postwar decades, the international economic difficulties confronting the United States and the West European countries largely related to their common interests in the reconstruction of the world economy, which had been shattered by two world wars and the intervening Great Depression. The means for doing so—U.S. economic aid, the reduction of barriers to the movement of goods and capital, and the adoption of rules for achieving a worldwide, nondiscriminatory system of trade and payments—were widely perceived, and hence could be officially justified, as producing benefits for all concerned. Now, however, the internal changes in the United States, the European Community, and Japan, the narrowing of the economic disparities among them, and the reduction of their barriers to trade and capital movements during the 1960s are making conceptions of the interests at stake more conflicting. Increasingly, a gain for one is seen as a loss for the other. Neither the United States, nor the European Community, nor Japan is willing to incur short-run losses in employment and income, sometimes not even to forgo potential gains, for the sake of possible longer term or indirect benefits for all concerned.

The basic problem is no longer seen as the overriding common interest in the reconstruction of the world economy. The system is now in being, and its current difficulties are perceived as involving only the not nearly so pressing common interest in the system's reasonably effective functioning. In these circumstances, disputes over trade, monetary arrangements, balance-of-payments adjustment, foreign investment, defense costs, and other problems become much harder to resolve. Nor can gains in one aspect of economic relations always be traded off for losses in another. National governments have increasing difficulty in making such bargains because the normal resistance of the particular groups adversely affected is more and more reinforced by the general expectation of continually improving conditions of life.

Moreover, not only do the particular problems involve conflicting conceptions of national interests but also implicit in them are competing designs of world economic order. In the postwar period, the West European countries willingly or perforce acquiesced in the U.S. goal of a worldwide multilateral nondiscriminatory system. Today, both the institutional development of the European Community and the revival of the historical European predilection for preferential arrangements and market-sharing incline Western Europe—and, in its own way, Japan—to policies that markedly foster the process of world economic bloc formation. The danger arises that relationships may deteriorate into a vicious spiral of mercantilist restrictions and retaliations that will sooner or later be costly to all participants.

As domestic developments and the changing nature of international relationships narrow the freedom of action of the national governments, their willingness and ability to make concessions to resolve the issues among them are correspondingly reduced. Reaching agreements on international economic problems becomes more difficult, slower, and more highly politicized, and the results are less satisfactory than during the postwar period. This difference does not mean that international economic problems are insolvable. It does mean, however, that in most cases prolonged negotiations will lead only to marginal adjustments among the participants, and to the smallest possible structural changes required to preserve the main elements of a functioning world economic system. Within this framework, the great powers and the smaller nations will live as best they can with persisting economic difficulties and recurrent crises.

The process of maneuvering to advance or protect national and bloc interests increasingly involves shifting alignments dictated by short-run expediency. Already the United States seeks to enlist the support of Japan to press the European Community into making economic concessions, and joins with the Community to exact similar concessions from Japan. At the same time, the Europeans concert their tactics with the Japanese to put pressure on the United States for monetary changes. And, for its part, Japan is being impelled into a much more complex maneuver of playing off the United States, China, and the Soviet Union against one another in order to achieve not only economic but also political gains. True, such temporary tactical alignments to advance particular national interests were practiced during the postwar period. But, they were then only incidental features of the larger cooperative effort to achieve the shared goal of a reconstructed world economic order. In contrast, they are now becoming central elements of international relationships because the conflicting interests involved more and more constitute the essence of the problems with which the nations are grappling.

In short, the emerging polycentric pattern of world relationships constitutes a more complex and ambiguous international system than that of the postwar bipolar confrontation. Its characteristics will increasingly be mutual nuclear deterrence, continuous maneuvering for political advantages, shifting economic alignments among the existing and prospective great powers, and efforts to preserve or increase their influence over middle-size and small nations in their own or other regions.

The danger of a world nuclear war among the great powers is probably less in this kind of balance-of-power configuration than it was in the bipolar pattern of the cold war. Hence, unless one of the nuclear nations makes a revolutionary assault on the international system, world politics will very likely consist of marginal adjustments in relative power positions that do not threaten to change fundamentally the political security or economic well-being of the major participants. This means that each of the major powers will be under pressure to develop and thereafter maintain military forces and diplomatic capabilities sufficient to assure that the inevitable shifts will be marginal and to inhibit the others from trying to bring about revolutionary changes. It means also that the most likely kinds of agreements on international economic problems will be those that both reflect and further reinforce the process of world economic bloc formation. These complexities and ambiguities of the emerging pattern of world politics and economics in the 1970s pose much more difficult problems for political and economic diplomacy, as well as for defense policy, than did the bipolar confrontation and the common interests of the postwar period.

On balance, the trends and countertrends characteristic of the emerging new period of world politics and economics over the longer term—the next decade or so—will increasingly foster the sense of European identity and impel the members of the Community to act more and more as a unit. In the current transitional phase, however, these external forces are not yet powerful or pervasive enough to produce this effect, particularly in the face of internal forces which, as Nye so cogently demonstrates, are not now working decisively for European unification. Thus, in the shorter term—the next two or three years, the time span on which national policy makers perforce concentrate their attention—the probability is much greater that the European Community will *not* achieve the essential merger of sovereignty requisite for a true monetary union than that it will.

However, the formation of a true monetary union—that is, an arrangement under which the powers to tax and to regulate money and credit are exercised by central supranational institutions—is not the only possible development in Western Europe. I believe it is useful to make a distinction between integration and unification. European economic integration can continue and intensify without necessarily leading to monetary or full economic union. Therefore, although the members of the European Community are unlikely in the shorter term to form a true monetary union, they are likely to push for closer coordination of their policies and increased mutual credit facilities so as to restrict fluctuations among their exchange rates—developments that by no means preclude the possibility and desirability of occasional devaluations and revaluations by individual countries. And they will more and more endeavor to make common cause when negotiating with the United States and Japan regarding reforms in the international monetary system.

Moreover, I believe it would be imprudent for U.S. policy makers, in devising their strategy for the likely shorter term developments, to omit the longer term possibilities from their conceptual framework. The desirability and feasibility of policy prescriptions, and the tactics for their carrying them out, depend not only on their consistency with the opportunities and limitations of the existing situation but also on their congruence with the more basic continuing trends that are shaping the future as well as the present. In evaluating the probabilities of the possible long-term developments and in analyzing their implications for policy, I would urge that four general considerations be kept in mind.

The most basic is the dynamism of Western societies: their capacity for rapid change and for generating unforeseeable novelties in their institutions and cultures. Western societies have been historically and are still today the most dynamic on the planet. Their continuing high propensity for change and innovation must qualify every socioeconomic projection, no matter how scientifically it is made.

The second consideration follows from the first: the nation-state is not an immutable and eternal form of macrosocial organization. It developed within Western societies over the past five hundred years and, in our own day, has spread to all parts of the planet. In the West, especially in its homeland in Western Europe, it is under new pressures and strains that are sooner or later bound to modify it further. Nor is it most likely to evolve into, or to be replaced by, another already familiar form of macrosocial organization. The outcome of the ongoing transformation is most probably going to be something new.

Third, despite the obvious differences in their societies and cultures and in their rates of sociocultural change, all of the countries of Western Europe are internally evolving in the same general direction: their institutions, values, and behavioral norms are undergoing similar or analogous modifications. This process of gradual convergence will make explicit economic and political unification decisions less and less difficult to accomplish. Owing to internal pressures and restraints, the initial stage in the unification of European nation-states will probably be some kind of confederal arrangement, in which essential sovereign powers are retained at the national level while the implementation of agreed-upon policies is delegated to central agencies. It is less likely to be a federal union, in which such powers are transferred to supranational authorities.

Finally, the harmonizing effects over time of the market process should not be underestimated. Policy makers naturally focus their attention on the decision-making process, that is, on what policy measures should and could be applied and on how to carry them out. But, however much it may be guided by deliberate policy choices, the "invisible hand" of market forces is operating to harmonize economic conditions within the Community and to build more and more institutional links at the level of the individual organizations comprising the members' economies. The integrating effects of market forces are not sufficient in themselves to bring about a monetary, or any other kind, of European union, but they work powerfully and ceaselessly toward it.

In sum, insofar as rational analysis can foresee the course of events, European monetary union seems unlikely in the shorter term. In the longer term, however, some form of European economic and political confederation would appear to be an increasingly probable outcome of basic internal and external trends.

Discussion of the Bloomfield and Nye Papers

THE GENERAL DISCUSSIONS based on the papers by Arthur Bloomfield and Joseph Nye were devoted almost entirely to whether the Community had made any progress in promoting monetary integration; identifying the policy objectives of that integration, the forces motivating the members to seek it, the similarities and differences of national interests among the members, and the effects of conflict among their political objectives; identifying the tactics and procedures followed in the effort to attain unification; and appraising them in the light of the objectives and motivations. This discussion of objectives, motivations, national interests, and tactics elicited additional and, in general, less pessimistic views concerning the progress made and likely to be made.

With regard to the meaning of monetary integration, Bloomfield agreed with Benjamin Cohen's comment that it was necessary to distinguish various meanings of "monetary integration." He noted that the Europeans themselves, at least up to the time of the Werner Report, were apparently uncertain as to exactly what they meant by it. Prior to the 1969 Hague communiqué, they had no intention of moving eventually to monetary union, although it had been vaguely hinted at before by the EC Commission. The Europeans merely wanted to draw their economies closer together to offset the possibility that one member's serious balance-of-payments trouble would require de-liberalization of trade or payments. After 1971, with the goal of monetary union clearly articulated, they meant by monetary integration, Bloomfield explained, simply accelerating the process of bringing the members' economies closer together on all fronts; even then, they did not distinguish harmonization of objectives, of policies, and of instruments from each other.

Peter Kenen suggested that it was necessary to distinguish not only among currency, financial, and monetary-policy integration, as Cohen had described them, but between monetary policy proper and credit policy. Kenen sensed that the Europeans make the latter distinction sharply, talking of unifying or harmonizing monetary policies but having important mental reservations about harmonizing controls over domestic credit markets. The latter include not only control of capital imports, but controls to support selective domestic credit policies. Harmonization or joint use of

such credit policies may make monetary unification even more difficult
than we now perceive it to be.

Harold van B. Cleveland noted the contradiction Bloomfield had mentioned between the Community's failure to achieve substantive progress in
monetary unification and its repeated efforts to begin the process over
again. He observed that this has been the pattern of the Common Market
since the beginning. It indicates both the deep conflict in national interests
and members' unwillingness to give up hope that such conflict can be
resolved. Using technical matters to precipitate the process of unification,
in other fields as well as the monetary field, was Jean Monnet's idea. It no
doubt reflected his belief that doing this would foster a Community spirit
so that, eventually, the European idea would take a political form. Although it has not exactly worked that way, Cleveland noted, we can expect,
and must assume, that this symbolic acting-out of the European idea will
survive one substantive or technical failure after another. Leonard Weiss,
carrying this point farther, noted that it is premature to regard the setbacks
that have occurred so far in monetary unification as auguring failure. The
Werner Report envisaged monetary unification as a ten-year, step-by-step
process. That the steps have been small is not a fair criticism. Although it
may be fairly argued that the steps taken have been wrong ones, Weiss
questioned that their smallness has adverse implications for success.

Discussion showed that the issues of conflicting policy objectives, the
small-step tactic, and possibly wrong choices in steps to be taken were
interrelated. The metaphors of putting the cart of monetary unification
before the horse of economic integration and policy coordination and its
German equivalent, putting the bridle on the tail of the horse, were frequently invoked. Edward M. Bernstein noted that a reason for putting the
bridle on the horse's tail may be that it is easier, if a person fears that it is a
biting horse; he puts it on the front if he thinks it a kicking horse. J. Carter
Murphy noted that it has been recognized since the beginning that the
process of European integration meant taking at least one step backward
for every two steps forward. This showed the importance of "feeling out"
the horse. For many Europeans, Murphy said, the nature of the difficulties
is probably only dimly understood, and it is essential to take some steps,
even if they later prove to be wrong, to reveal clearly the precise nature of
the commitments and responsibilities of political integration and of ultimate monetary integration.

Kenen suggested that there are three impediments to the harmonization of national policies—outright conflicts of interest such as those which emerge in debates about the composition of the balance of payments, differences in attitude toward tradeoff between domestic objectives, and different degrees of national reliance on various policy instruments. Although debate tends to focus on the difference in preferences concerning domestic objectives, the first and the third of the impediments may be more important.

Lawrence Krause noted that a model of the political process in which nationalism and regionalism are the only alternatives may be too simplified. One needs to include other possibilities, because integrating influences, such as market forces, that lead away from nationalism often do not lead to regionalism. As to the convergence of national economic or political goals mentioned by Nye as making monetary union possible, goals may converge at a particular moment in time—for example, the German, British, and French desires to have larger roles and opportunities for leadership. Members may utilize integration as a means of realizing them, but the goals themselves are a denial of political unification. In the longer run, those converging national goals might prevent regional integration.

These and other points made in the course of the discussion of national goals and objectives made clear that a distinction should be drawn between avowed or explicitly expressed policy goals and those motivating forces which might be implicit and of which policy makers might not even be aware. Noting Cohen's distinction between internal and external motivation, Krause said he thought that the idea of monetary union came to the fore at the 1969 Hague conference primarily because of motivations internal to the Community. The background was that the French franc and the German mark had deviated from their equilibrium values in opposite directions and needed to be realigned. A 20 percent change in their relationship brought several industries that had been competitive in export markets suddenly face to face with severe import competition. This identified the need either for more prompt changes in exchange rates or for better policy coordination to prevent disequilibrium from developing. If coordination can be achieved, it is the preferable alternative.

There was also political motivation, Krause observed; the French did not want Germany to take political leadership at that moment. The later renewed effort at monetary integration was externally generated; it resulted from overvaluation of the dollar. From the point of view of the United States, monetary integration stimulated by internal factors is likely to be highly desirable (or at least not recognizably undesirable), but one that is externally motivated may hurt the United States. For example, if monetary integration can be achieved only with maladjustment and external exchange crises, Europeanists who recognize that fact may be less eager for an international system that adjusts well with the United States. Better adjustment with the outside world then is a threat to European integration.

William Diebold, who also attached importance to the distinction between internal and external forces, thought that although external forces were certainly important in the first phase of European integration, internal forces—the need to overcome internal quarrels and to break down economic barriers—are also very important. However, by late 1972 and in the foreseeable future, internal forces do not appear of much significance to the Europeans. The ratio of internal benefits to internal costs has decreased. Europe's desire to make its weight felt in the world, especially in the matter of world monetary reform, may have become more important.

Henry C. Wallich thought that one motivation for integration was to make the monetary reserves of one group of countries available to others by pooling reserves, since one was a powerful earner of reserves and others had shortages. When the growth of the United States deficit enabled all of the members to earn reserves, this motivation lost its force; it is quite weak now in late 1972. He observed that the general problem might be analyzed along lines analogous to that used in analyzing control of a market by an oligopolistic industry seeking to maximize profits of the industry. One can think of the EC as such an industry with no natural leader, that is, with no single member having a market share so large that it is willing to make sacrifices to control conditions in the market as a whole, as the United States has done with the world as a whole. Indeed, accession of new members further diminishes ability to achieve a common goal. Perhaps new groupings or coalitions will emerge, and one group may develop enough power or cohesion to become a center of action. Probably not agriculture, but perhaps manufacturing industry or even labor might develop a transnational common interest that would enable it to pull the whole Community together. While the analogy led him to no firm prognosis, he thought this line of analysis might prove fruitful.

Upon being invited to comment, Frédéric Boyer de la Giroday (an official of the European Commission and an observer at the September 1972 conference) said that in his view the prime reason for the apparent incoherence in European economic and monetary integration is that this integration is being forced on the Europeans by the development of modern technology in a geographical setting of contiguous nation-states, but in the face of political establishments that are organized nationally.

To illustrate how technology is increasing the cost and inconvenience for everyday transactions of having separate monetary and economic regimes, he cited the growth in air travel and the resulting greater frequency with which national boundaries are being crossed. The removal of formal barriers to movement of goods and persons, however, would not alone substantially reduce the difficulties of international transport if currency relationships were still constantly changing. When the value of one or another currency is uncertain, even deciding what currency to use to tip a porter is a problem.

De la Giroday felt that, on the one hand, monetary integration is a necessary partner of the economic integration that modern technology is forcing on European countries. On the other hand, national establishments that have held the reins for centuries—ten, in the case of France—obviously are not going to surrender their powers quickly. Thus, there is a continuous tug-of-war between these economic and political forces. This is what gives rise to the incoherent picture described in the discussion. Given the difficulties, the process is bound to be long and to involve inconsistencies, but there is no solution other than to keep trying until the forces of resistance are eroded.

W. Max Corden believed the main issue underlying the discussion of objectives to be one of motives. He listed seven: (1) Economies of scale in the use of money by avoiding the use of different moneys whose exchange rates alter. That is a sound reason, he said, but that benefit must be weighed against its cost. (2) Avoidance of speculative capital movements and crises resulting from expectations of changes in exchange rates. Crises cannot entirely be avoided by fixing exchange rates, but it is a natural instinct of practical men to believe so and it was prominent in European thinking. (3) Antidollar and anti-American attitudes. (4) Desire to avoid the inconvenience to the common agricultural policy of changes in exchange rates, as the CAP was then constructed. (5) The idea of pooling of reserves; this in practice really means extension of credits by probable surplus countries to probable deficit countries. (6) What may be called "megaphonism": the desire of the two greatest imperial nations to continue to "make a big noise" in the world when they are no longer really big noises but have not yet adjusted themselves to their new situation. (7) The familiar motive of Europeanism, subdivided into idealism of the Monnet type (which had been very important once but was less so in 1972), and self-interest of groups and institutions established in the first instance to promote Europeanism, but that then managed to sustain themselves and exert pressures to maintain their status.

Cleveland thought this a useful enumeration of specific motives but felt that it omitted what he thought had been the overriding motive from the beginning, which Theodore Geiger had previously stressed: political identity or world power. He agreed with Geiger that the very impotence of states tends to reenforce this motive; the natural way to overcome the impotence is to expand. The contradiction is that this same impotence, especially in external matters, inhibits movement toward union. That, as Edward L. Morse had said, is probably the reason for the play-acting or symbolic character of so many of the actions taken. Europe not only suffers from a malaise, a frustration, a turning from reality; there is an element of "waiting for Godot." To make the European ideal real, some miracle must occur, and there is a feeling that until it does activity is required to keep the ideal and the hope alive. He thought the discussion had shown that it is wrong to analyze monetary union primarily as a function of economic phenomena; it is much more a social-symbolic phenomenon.

Weiss, noting that one could argue that some of the most vital steps taken in Europe since establishment of the Common Market were being taken in 1972–73, asked whether the discussants generally accepted the characterization of Europe as being in a state of malaise or rigidity. Robert Bowie thought comparison of the position in the fall of 1972 with the earlier stages of unification misleading. Earlier, the Europeanists were essentially a small elitist group able to act at a very high level without worrying much about the political process. Now, in fall 1972, by contrast, any movement forward had to be part of the political process. General talk about motives is misleading. There are all sorts of groups with different motives. Ways must be found to mobilize these motives and adjust the conflicts among them. That is a much more tedious and slower process. If one compares the working of that political process in Europe today with its working in the United States, Bowie said, the Europeans do not look bad. The decision of Britain to enter, or of the Community to admit Britain, the continued concern about how to move forward despite conflicting pressures and the absence of any critical pressure to do so from an external threat—all these indicate considerable consensus about moving ahead. To depict these efforts as fake or phony rhetoric is not quite valid. They may be messy, confused, or formless, but so are efforts in the United States to deal with its own problems, domestic and foreign. Americans are doing much worse with much smaller problems. In thinking about European integration, we should correct our perspective and then ask whether the steps being taken, inadequate as they may be, are tackling the problem. Bowie thought they were, and did not feel as pessimistic as the other discussants. Europe is attempting to do something politically on a scale that has seldom been attempted.

Diebold reinforced this interpretation by recalling that everybody who had looked at the problem of European integration expected that a decision to admit Britain to the Community would be followed by several years of great uncertainty; "all the equations would have to be rebalanced." That is part of what is going on in 1972–73. In addition, the Community is having to deal with the problem of the international monetary system and the change in American foreign policy. These two factors, plus those listed by Morse, make a period of very considerable confusion and uncertainty inevitable. Although Diebold did not fully share Bowie's calm confidence, he regarded such confusion as not very alarming.

These views of the conflicts of interest and motivations led to some discussion of the point made by Geiger, in his formal comments on Nye's paper, that in the early stages of formation of the Community, the Western European countries and the United States were involved in a game in which all participants benefited, but that an increasing number of issues involve zero-sum games, in which one party's gain is another's loss.

Fritz Machlup questioned that present issues could be so interpreted, at least without specifying who interpreted gains and losses. If Europe were to surrender part of its output to the United States, economists would interpret that as a loss for Europe and a gain for the United States, but mercantilists would interpret it as a gain for Europe and a loss for the United States. Some changes in trade that mercantilists would regard as involving offsetting gains and losses, moreover, would be interpreted by economists as net gains for the combined parties, and so not a zero-sum game.

Geiger explained that he did not mean that the relationship had now become wholly a zero-sum game, but merely that, whereas in the postwar period common interests had outweighed conflicting interests, today in the early seventies conflicting interests have become relatively more important. By "interests" in this context he meant perceptions of national interests by key politicians and opinion leaders in the major groups and the mass media of communications. It is such perceptions of the issues that take on increasingly the character of a zero-sum game, regardless of whether in the long run or in some larger context both sides may gain. Machlup thought this response left open the question of whose perception of national interests was intended, and asked whether the discussants' purpose was to analyze the economists' meaning of gain and loss or that of "the misguided vocal majority."

Diebold agreed with Geiger's view that more issues are now seen as conflicting, but he also agreed with the view, implied in Machlup's question, that some issues perceived by mercantilists as zero-sum games are really not; for example, controls over international trade result in net losses. Diebold thought that both sorts of issues arise, and the important thing is to find out whether the issues that participants perceive as involving conflicts of interest really do involve such conflicts. The serious underlying issue of concern is that, despite apparent conflicts of interest in how the monetary system should be reshaped, all have a stake in a system that works. It is also important to recognize that there are conflicts of interest among groups within a country, because this implies that there are natural common ties between groups in different countries. Constructive economic diplomacy should build on these natural transnational coalitions of interest.

HARRY G. JOHNSON

Narrowing the Exchange Rate Bands

THIS PAPER is concerned with what appears to be a fairly narrow technical problem, alternative methods of narrowing the bands of exchange rate variation among the European currencies. The technical problem is seen in the perspective of broader economic and political issues. Treatment of these issues is brief, however, since they are dealt with more fully in other papers.

The technical problem of alternative methods for narrowing exchange rate bands is related to the first stage in establishing a common European currency. The aim underlying the ultimate objective is to harmonize economic policies among the European countries. This aim rests on a questionable assumption: that disturbances causing balance-of-payments disequilibria in Europe and hence the need to resort to exchange rate changes, trade and payments restrictions, or both, are primarily caused by the pursuit of independent national policy objectives and by a lack of coordination in the use of national policy instruments (including changes in exchange rates). The assumption is questionable as seen by the actual experience of exchange rate crises, especially the events of May 1968 in France.

This paper owes a great deal to the pioneering work of Richard N. Cooper, especially to his paper, *Sterling, European Monetary Unification, and the International Monetary System* (British–North American Committee, 1972), notably pp. 18–26; and to his article, "Eurodollars, Reserve Dollars, and Asymmetries in the International Monetary System," *Journal of International Economics*, Vol. 2 (September 1972), pp. 325–44.

Even if the assumption is accepted, there are still two alternative positions on monetary unification in European discussion. One is the "economist" position: that it is futile to seek monetary unification until the required degree of economic policy harmonization has been achieved. The other, the "monetarist" position, is that monetary unification is the only way to force member governments to accept the required degree of policy harmonization.

In addition, there are conflicting objectives among the European countries with respect to the underlying political purpose of achieving monetary unification, or at least taking steps toward achieving it. Specifically, the other members of the European Community (EC) accept the objective of a full community with a common currency, but disagree about the strategic sequence of monetary unification and policy harmonization; France, however, seems determined to preserve its monetary autonomy but accepts the objective of monetary unification as a means of bringing concerted European pressure to bear on the United States, with respect to both U.S. national economic policy and the shape of future reform of the international monetary system.

Finally, monetary unification is only one possible form of monetary cooperation among a regional grouping of states. For example, Robert Triffin, basing himself on the experience of the European Payments Union, has for many years been advocating plans for reserve pooling and reciprocal credit lines, for other regions (Latin America, Asia) as well as Europe.[1]

These reasons and the past history of exchange rate changes among the European countries justify skepticism about the likelihood of progress in European monetary unification.[2] One can argue that the Europeans have become accustomed to making gestures toward integration as a fair-weather system while retaining autonomy of domestic economic policy because of their ability to change their exchange rates as a last resort, and that it is only their common chagrin over the franc devaluation and mark revaluation of 1969 and their dislike of the American-induced world in-

1. The Triffin proposals have not carried much weight in the European discussions of recent years because Europe has been suffering from a plethora rather than a shortage of international reserves. Indeed, under present circumstances of world inflation the economics of reserves achievable by pooling might exacerbate the inflation. The probable effects of European monetary unification on the international reserves situation are discussed in the paper by Walter S. Salant in this volume.

2. See the paper by W. Max Corden.

flation of recent years that have led them to adopt the objective of a common currency. Three possible outcomes are conceivable. European monetary union may turn out to be a futile gesture and nothing more. In this case, there is little point in detailed study of the alternatives involved in the first step of narrowing the bands of exchange rate variation among European currencies. Alternatively, the first step may be successful enough to lead on fairly speedily toward establishment of a genuine European currency. In this case, United States policy makers might be better advised to study the implications of such a single currency for the international monetary system and for proposals to reform it. However, since it is conceivable European countries may succeed in narrowing the bands but get no further, it is worth devoting some attention to alternative methods of narrowing the bands, and their implications.

Economic Background

Under the traditional gold standard, countries fixed the values of their national currencies at a par value in terms of gold, and guaranteed the convertibility of domestic currency into gold at this par value by buying and selling gold in exchange for domestic money at the central bank. The exchange rate of a currency in the foreign exchange market could vary around the par value within the "gold export" and "gold import" points. That is to say, if the currency depreciated enough in the market it became cheaper for domestic traders to buy gold from the domestic market or central bank and ship it to a foreign country for conversion into foreign currency at that country's central bank, than for them to buy the foreign currency in the market at the prevailing foreign exchange rate. Conversely, if the domestic currency's value in the foreign exchange market appreciated sufficiently, it paid traders to convert foreign currency into gold, to import the gold, and then convert it into domestic currency at the central bank, rather than convert the foreign currency directly into domestic currency through the foreign exchange market. The costs of transacting indirectly via gold shipments rather than directly through the foreign exchange market included insurance, freight, abrasion, and loss of interest on the capital invested in the gold while it is in transit. Hence the "band" (in modern terminology) of market exchange rate fluctuations around the par value was set by the real cost of shipping gold. Moreover, the positions of currencies were symmetrical, since each was pegged onto a nonnational-currency numéraire, gold.[3]

Under the international monetary system as it has developed since sometime in the interwar period, and especially later since the establishment of the International Monetary Fund (IMF), the bands no longer correspond to or are determined by economic factors. In the first place, transfers of gold are no longer made by private purchase from and international shipment and sale to central banks. Instead, the transactions were (until August 15, 1971) conducted directly between central banks, predominantly by exchanges of dollars for gold, and vice versa, with the Federal Reserve System. Moreover, the practice of "earmarking," whereby gold is not shipped internationally but is merely moved a few yards down the corridors of the vault of the Federal Reserve Bank of New York by men in steel boots armed with wooden pegs for insertion in gold mountains to prevent landslides, is virtually costless.

Second, the permitted bands of exchange rate variation for national currencies are fixed by international agreement through the International Monetary Fund.[4] Confinement of exchange rate movements within the bands is implemented by exchange market intervention by the national

3. This brief account ignores a complication which is in important respects parallel to the situation in 1972, namely, that central banks frequently set a higher selling price than buying price for gold, thereby adding a "seigniorage," or tax element to the band of market exchange rate variation around the par value. When gold coins still circulated among the public, the price difference had to exceed the real costs of melting coin into bullion and minting bullion into coin to yield seigniorage, but when gold coins were removed from circulation, the differential was retained and became almost entirely seigniorage. In fact, as will appear from subsequent argument, the "bands" of current times consist virtually entirely of seigniorage for the central bank; and the existence of this seigniorage gives a profit incentive to the private foreign exchange market to undertake part of the exchange rate stabilization operations that would otherwise fall on the central bank.

4. The bands were 2 percent, the sum of margins fixed by the IMF Articles of Agreement at a maximum of 1 percent above and below parity, although the European countries had implemented a somewhat smaller band, and the Fund, by a decision in 1959, in effect interpreted "parity" as meaning parity with the dollar. (See Glossary, note 3.) In the Smithsonian Agreement of December 18, 1971, however, the permitted margin of variation was fixed at 2¼ percent above and below parity with the dollar, which permitted nondollar currencies to vary within margins of 4½ percent above and below their parities with each other. The subject of this paper is the March 1972 decision of the European countries to permit their currencies to vary within only half of this range around their parities between pairs of their own currencies.

central banks. The implications of the techniques employed to do this are discussed later. It is useful to review here, however, what economic benefits result from the provision of a wider range of variation of exchange rates around parities than is occasioned by the economic costs of maintaining fixed exchange rates (more accurately, fixed parities) in an international monetary system that purports to be a fixed exchange rate system.

One incidental effect of exchange rate bands, noticed long ago by theorists of the traditional gold standard, is that within the bands the system is one, not of fixed exchange rates, but of floating exchange rates. To this extent it brings into play the same automatic mechanisms of adjustment as a floating exchange rate system would. Under the traditional gold standard, this effect is a necessary and unavoidable by-product of the economic costs of gold shipments, so that there is no point in arguing about its desirability. Under the IMF system, the arbitrary (that is, not cost-related) choice of the width of the band necessarily entails an arbitrary choice of how far a floating rate system is desirable. The only argument for having a restricted band at all, instead of a fully freely floating rate system and for choosing one band rather than another, rests on either the proposition that the market process of price determination can be trusted only within certain limits or the proposition that unless limits are set to the possible range of price variation the market process will function badly and all sorts of disasters may occur. (Neither proposition is held to be applicable generally in economics, with the major exception of agricultural and primary product prices.)

The provision of a limited degree of automatic exchange rate flexibility under the guise of maintaining a fixed exchange rate system, however, is not the prime consideration, at least as central bankers see the matter. From their point of view, the existence of a band of variation that does not reflect real economic costs of transacting in one direction or the other has three advantages. Assuming that domestic economic policy can normally avoid the need for a change in the par value itself and can keep the exchange rate within the band around the par value, these three advantages are:

First, by confining its exchange market interventions to sales of its own currency for foreign exchange at the upper limit of its value in terms of foreign currencies, and purchases of its own currency with foreign currency at the lower limit of its value in terms of foreign currencies, the central bank automatically makes a profit on its interventions in the foreign exchange market.

NARROWING THE EXCHANGE RATE BANDS

Second, the existence of this profit attracts into the foreign exchange market "stabilizing speculators" because they, too, can make a profit by buying the currency when it is low in foreign exchange value and by selling it when it is high in foreign exchange value. Hence, the volume of stabilizing transactions the central bank needs to conduct itself is reduced, and so is the amount of foreign exchange reserves it needs to hold.[5]

Third, when speculation against or in favor of a currency is unjustified by the objective ability of the country to maintain its currency's present par value, the central bank is enabled to penalize the speculators at a profit to itself by intervening in the market. Of course, if the allegedly destabilizing speculation is based on a justified view that national economic policies make the existing exchange rate untenable, while central bank intervention is based on irrational loyalty to the government's declaration that this rate is tenable, the central bank stands to make losses instead of profits.

These considerations, as well as the general theoretical case for floating exchange rates, suggest that the wider the bands permitted by the conventions and rules of the international monetary system the better for the individual nation-member of that system. Narrowing of the bands on either an individual or a group basis involves a loss of autonomy of national economic policy that has to be justified on some other grounds. (This is not to say that wide bands can take care of all problems. Circumstances may arise in which parity changes are necessary, and wide bands may even encourage nations to pursue policies that lead to such circumstances.)

The foregoing argument has not specified precisely how national central banks intervene in the foreign exchange market to keep variations in the foreign exchange values of their currencies within the band, other than the vague statement that they do it by buying and selling "foreign exchange." In fact, the international monetary system after World War II (the International Monetary Fund system), operated until August 15, 1971, on the basis of the United States pegging the dollar rigidly to gold at $35 an ounce, standing ready to buy or sell gold in exchange for dollars at that price, with other countries using the dollar as their intervention currency.

This system involves an asymmetry in the relations between the U.S.

5. There is an interesting theoretical problem here, not relevant to the purposes of this paper: What width of band will maximize the profits of an individual central bank, or of central banks collectively, given that the wider the band, the larger the seigniorage profit per unit of intervention but the smaller the amount of intervention required?

dollar and all the other national currencies on the one hand, and the relations between other individual national currencies on the other. Assuming a margin of 1 percent each way about the gold (and dollar) parity for other countries and a fixed par value for the dollar, the exchange rate between the dollar and any other currency could move only 1 percent each way from parity, whereas the exchange rate between any other two currencies could move 2 percent each way from parity (one going 1 percent up, the other 1 percent down). This asymmetry has been generally assumed—by those who have thought about it at all—to constitute a disadvantage for the United States. How important the handicap is empirically is doubtful, at least for a world trading system still dominated by the United States and in which balance-of-payments adjustments have to be made primarily against the United States. However, from the point of view of the objective of European economic integration, it has meant that European countries have twice the degree of exchange rate variability against each other's currencies as they have against the U.S. dollar. Assuming maintenance of given par values, this implies more automatic integration of each country with the United States than with other EC member countries. It is partly for this reason that the Europeans decided to narrow the range of variation of exchange rates among their currencies as the first step toward monetary unification: to produce the same degree of monetary integration among the European countries as there is between them and the United States.

It may be noted that an alternative means to achieve the same end would be to establish some sort of new international reserve money, the obvious candidate being a modified form of Special Drawing Rights (SDRs). All countries would specify their par values in relation to the SDR and each, including the United States, would have a permitted band of variation of market exchange rates. Such a proposal lies outside the scope of this paper. But it may be observed that, unless there were privately tradable, or perhaps only officially tradable, liabilities expressed in terms of the new international reserve asset, it would be difficult to establish the latter as an international numéraire in terms of which countries could conduct exchange market interventions. In other words, markets deal in tangible assets and liabilities, not in terms of numéraire. The development of an exchange rate system that dealt in tangible assets and liabilities within price limits set by a prescribed band of variation around a par value in terms of a numéraire would be a very difficult undertaking.

The Problem

If what the EC member countries want to do is merely to narrow the variation of exchange rates among themselves, it would be simple enough to do so by narrowing the permitted range of variation around their parities with each other. To do so, however, with the dollar remaining as intervention currency and the fundamental reserve asset of the international system, would still leave the range of variation of exchange rates between member currencies at double the range of variation of each against the dollar, with the implications for the relative degrees of intra-Community and Community-U.S. monetary integration already mentioned. The technical problem, therefore, is to narrow the range of exchange rate variation among the EC currencies in relation to one another, without narrowing their range of variation collectively against the dollar. This involves imposing two constraints on the movement of any individual member currency: it must stay within the permitted margin of variation in relation to the U.S. dollar; and it must stay within the permitted "spread" of Community rates in relation to each other.

Since this set of constraints is not easy to appreciate, assume that the permissible margin is 2¼ percent above and below parity with the dollar, and that the limit of variation of the EC currencies is also 2¼ percent, above and below their parities with each other. Both constraints could be fulfilled at the limit if, say, one member country's extreme currency rate was at parity with the dollar and the one at the other extreme was at a 2¼ percent premium over (or discount under) the dollar; or if there were any intermediate position, such as one extreme exchange rate at a 1⅛ percent premium and the other at a 1⅛ percent discount in relation to the dollar. But, assuming for simplicity that the average Community exchange rate (in some sense) lies halfway between the extremes, these cases would imply that the average variation of the Community currencies versus the U.S. dollar would still be only half of the variations of the European currencies against each other. To take full advantage of the permitted range of variation against the dollar, the member currencies would have to maintain their parity exchange ratios against one another, while departing from parity with the dollar by the same percentage (i.e., all rise above or fall below parity with the dollar by the same percentage).

The problem is: Which country is to set the pace in determining where the average Community rate on the dollar is to lie? Or, alternatively, how will a collective decision on this issue be reached? Do the member countries in surplus have to forgo full use of the limited degree of appreciation against the dollar permitted them by the band against the dollar in order to let the deficit members make full use of the limited degree of depreciation against the dollar permitted them by that band? Or, on the contrary, are the deficit countries constrained to forgo some part of their permitted exchange rate freedom for the sake of the surplus countries?[6] Or, is this issue to be negotiated centrally?

To raise a related but different point, suppose that one country's currency is at the lower limit of the band against the dollar (maximum permitted depreciation), can that country prevent others from reducing the values of their currencies to the same limit, to its own competitive disadvantage?

It should be noted that these issues would not arise in a complete monetary union, because then all European currency movements would be perfectly synchronized. These problems result from narrowing but not completely eliminating the variation of the market exchange rates of the member countries vis-à-vis one another, as compared with the variation permitted by the band allowed each in relation to the dollar. In other words, they arise from substituting a constraint on individual countries' exchange rate variations based on the discretionary behavior of the other member countries, for a constraint based on a fixed rule of permissible percentage variation about the parity with the dollar.

The constraint of a fixed band of permitted variation about parity with the dollar is an important one, at least so long as the dollar remains the de facto standard of the international monetary system and is not replaced by a new genuinely symmetrical international reserve asset. Yet it is frequently overlooked in discussions of methods of narrowing the band of permitted exchange rate variation among the European currencies. As will be discussed in the next section, the most obvious way of accomplishing the result is to select an existing European currency, or to establish a new Community currency, which will fluctuate against the dollar within the dollar band, and have the other (or all) member currencies fix a parity in terms of that currency and fluctuate against it within the permitted

6. On these issues, see Pascal Salin, "A Note on the Problem of Symmetry in the Process of Adjustment and the Reform of the International Monetary System" (University of Paris-Dauphine, 1971; processed).

Community band of fluctuations. For example, if there were a supranational European currency, and each national currency could fluctuate against it within a 1⅛ percent margin on each side, the exchange rates of member countries would be confined within a range of variation of 2¼ percent against the supranational currency and a 4½ percent range of variation in relation to each other. But such a system would in principle allow the market values of individual member currencies (other than the chosen currency) to get outside the permitted band of fluctuation against the dollar. This would involve a substantive change in the constraints now imposed by the international monetary system. Take, for instance, the pound sterling as the chosen currency; if its value hit the lower limit of the dollar band—2¼ percent below parity—all the other member currencies could go to 2¼ + 1⅛ = 3⅜ percent below dollar parity. From the European point of view, of course, this would mean more monetary integration within the Community than between the Community and the United States, and hence would probably be considered desirable. But it would involve a substantive change of the rules of the international monetary game.[7,8] If, on the other hand, the constraint prevails, countries will not have the freedom to utilize the permitted European range of exchange rate variation as the market value of the chosen currency approaches one of the permitted limits of the band against the dollar.

Alternative Techniques

The objective of the European Community is to narrow the band of variation of exchange rates among the members' currencies without narrowing the range of variation between them and the dollar.

7. An implicit assumption of the "Europa" plan developed by Magnifico and Williamson is that such a change in the rules of exchange rate variation will raise no objections; this implicit assumption was admitted by Williamson at the September 1972 conference. See Giovanni Magnifico and John Williamson, *European Monetary Integration*, Federal Trust Report (London: Federal Trust for Education and Research, 1972). Their plan is referred to in the next section of my paper.

8. It is easily seen that the international monetary system could be completely changed if each country could peg its currency onto another currency, with a permitted margin of variation of its exchange rate around parity with that currency, instead of establishing a par value in relation to all other currencies together, with a permitted range of variation around that par value.

Using "Paper Gold" as a Reserve Asset

If some sort of "paper gold" standard were to be established, say through one or other of the schemes for consolidating existing reserve assets into a sort of "super-SDR," in relation to which the dollar played a role symmetrical with the roles of other currencies—that is, fluctuated within a band around its par value in terms of paper gold—the problem could in one sense be easily resolved. Under such a system, the Community countries would have the same band against each other as against the dollar. If they wished to go further they could fix a narrower band around their par values than the permitted band, leaving the dollar to fluctuate within the full permitted band.

However, there are two snags to this. First, the United States authorities would have the same freedom to employ a narrower band than the full permitted range, and might well do so (after all, the present asymmetrical system originated in the American insistence on maintaining a fixed value of the dollar in terms of gold). Second, even if the United States used the full internationally permissible band, the European countries, while having a narrower band among themselves than either the full internationally permissible band or the band against the dollar, would also have less than the full internationally permissible band against the dollar.

To illustrate the second point, let $2B$ be the full internationally permissible range of variation around par value, and $2b$ be the (narrower) Community band around par value. Then $B+b$ and not $2B$ would be the maximum range of variation of any European currency against the dollar (e.g., the dollar could be B above par value, and the Community currency b below par value, or vice versa). If the Europeans wished to narrow the band among their exchange rates to $2b$ while retaining the full range of variation of $2B$ against the dollar, they would face the same problems as they face under the present dollar standard: they would have to arrange for their exchange rates to be able to move up and down within the full internationally permitted band, while not varying from each other by more than the Community-permitted band.

The establishment of such a paper-gold standard would require one or other of two substantial changes in the international monetary system.

The first would be to devise techniques for operating an international monetary system in which the numéraire currency (SDRs) was not privately tradable and traded but constituted only a nonmarketed means of settlement among central banks and between them and the International Monetary Fund. Under the traditional gold standard, gold was privately marketable and the bands were determined by the economic costs of moving gold between central banks. Under the two-tier gold-market system prevailing from March 1968 to August 1971, gold served as a numéraire of this type, but on the basis of an asymmetry between the dollar and other currencies (the dollar having no band against gold), and de facto with increasingly restricted freedom for other countries to use gold as a settlement medium. This system culminated in the crisis of August 1971 which deprived gold of the latter role entirely. A system based on a freely usable reserve-settlement asset which was not privately marketed and in relation to which all currencies could vary within a permitted band would be a difficult one to set up.

The second alternative would be to develop paper gold as a privately usable and used form of money. Institutionally, this would require the development of securities denominated and paying interest in terms of paper gold. These could be created by deliberate efforts by central banks and their governments (for example, through the issue of national government debts denominated in paper gold and the acceptance of tax payments in paper gold), but it would have to be a major cooperative effort. From the point of view of international monetary organization, it would confront the controllers of the supply of paper gold with the same problem as national central banks now face: offsetting the destabilizing effects of shifts between private and central bank holdings of base money ("high-powered money").

Displacing the Dollar as Intervention Currency

For the above reasons, it seems more reasonable to discuss the alternative methods of narrowing the bands among the currencies of the EC members in the context of the existing dollar standard, in which the dollar is used as the intervention currency by other countries in order to keep their exchange rates within the permitted range of variation around parity.

As Richard Cooper points out, it makes a crucial difference whether the effort to narrow the bands among the member currencies retains the dollar as the intervention currency or not.

If the dollar were not to be retained, the European countries could simply peg exchange rates among their own currencies, each country undertaking to buy and sell any of the other currencies at mutually agreed intervention prices, and settling any resulting payments imbalances in some stipulated international reserve asset other than the dollar.

What sounds simple in theory, however, would not be so simple in practice, for four reasons. First, to "make a market" in member currencies among member central banks without reference to the private market in exchanges of their currencies for dollars, and vice versa, would involve forgoing the convenience of using an intervention currency. It would put the member central banks in the position of being (at least normally) the only speculators in their own and other members' currencies and it would oblige them to maintain reserves of internationally acceptable assets (acceptable, that is, to each other on the one hand and to the United States on the other) adequate for the purpose.

Second, the problem mentioned in the previous section—of whether the surplus or the deficit member countries set the pace for the determination of the central average of the value of Community currencies in terms of other currencies—would still remain, though in a somewhat altered form. Specifically, when some member country's currency hit the limit of the band of permissible variation in relation to the dollar, it would be necessary to have either a standard rule or an individual ad hoc determination governing the question of whether the other EC member countries should cooperate with that country's need for currency adjustment by narrowing the band among member currencies or not. A member country in surplus might or might not be assisted by appreciation of other members' currencies that put their countries into deficit, and vice versa.

Third, payments imbalances would have to be settled in some international reserve asset other than dollars; that is, other than something with an immediately realizable and ascertainable market value. In other words, settlements would have to be made in a nonmarketable asset of fictitiously specified monetary value. This is not impossible, given that central banks are deliberately nonprofit-making institutions, and that they can take paper losses (or gains) without necessarily being influenced thereby. They typically earn more seigniorage on the domestic money supply than they are allowed to retain as profits or as inflated staff and building expenses, the surplus being returnable to the state. But central banks are still subject to legislative scrutiny, and a system of artificial valuation of transactions in reserve assets might well run into domestic political criticism, even though in the long run it was a zero-sum game for each participant.

Fourth, some member or members of the group would be obliged to exchange either holdings of dollars, or holdings of some other international reserve asset (say SDRs) for its own or other Community currencies when one or more of their currencies hit the limits of the band; and this would aggravate the problem of intra-Community dealings in reserve assets at arbitrary and fictitious prices.

Retaining the Dollar as Intervention Currency

If, on the contrary, the dollar were to be retained as intervention currency, there would be three alternatives of varying degrees of difficulty, each involving some sort of coordination of policy in the use of the dollar for purposes of intervention.

1. The simplest, most workable, and most "natural" method would be to develop an existing national European currency into the Community currency, to peg other national currencies onto that currency with the posited narrower Community range of permissible variation around it, and to put the management of the exchange value of that currency in relation to the U.S. dollar in Community hands. This procedure, as Cooper cogently argues, would not necessarily entail any "unwarranted" benefits to the country that managed the currency in question, in the form of seigniorage profits on the issue of the currency and command over the real resources of other countries in exchange for issues of that currency. But it would, if the narrowing of the range of European exchange rate variation were combined (as may be assumed) with no widening of the band of variation of individual member currencies against the dollar, raise the previously mentioned problem of whether, as the exchange value of the chosen member's currency approached one or other limit of the band against the dollar, the other European countries had to narrow (one way) their range around it, or whether the managers of that currency had to avoid using the full range of permissible variation against the dollar in order to allow the other members the full range of variation permitted by the Community against that currency.

If this alternative were adopted, the obvious candidate for a national currency to stand for the Community against the dollar would be the pound sterling. In fact, the main motivation of the City of London in favoring entry into the European Community has been to extend the domain of the pound sterling, though for commercial rather than monetary purposes. Unfortunately for this alternative, the world role of sterling is regarded with deep suspicion in Europe, and by France in particular, on the grounds that it enables the British to obtain unwarranted advantages in the form of seigniorage and the capacity to finance balance-of-payments deficits. As mentioned, advantages of this kind are by no means necessary; but the fact that they are thought to be institutionally inevitable, combined with Britain's action in June 1972 of floating the pound for purely domestic policy reasons, probably means that the use of the pound as the European currency is ruled out.

The only other obvious candidate for that role is the German mark, which has the advantage that Germany is both a structural capital exporter and the least inflation-prone country in Europe. Here, again, there are deep political reasons for distrusting the Germans as managers of European money. Apart from the mark, the Dutch guilder or some other currency might be elevated to the position of the Community's currency; but the amount of effort involved rapidly appears at least as great as that of constructing a new genuinely European currency.

2. The proposal to construct a new European currency—the "Europa" —has been explored in most detail by Magnifico and Williamson.[9] The basic idea is simple: a new currency to be managed by the equivalent of a new European central bank, onto which the individual members of the Community would peg the values of their currencies within the permitted range of variation of intra-Community exchange rates. But the authors of this proposal implicitly assume that in order to give themselves the full range of permitted intra-Community variation of relative currency values, the member countries will be permitted to let their currency values go beyond the permitted range of variation in relation to the dollar, to the extent of the full European band. Magnifico and Williamson also contemplate with unjustified equanimity the use of such devices as the imposition on commercial banks of required cash reserve ratios in terms of Europas, devices which would establish the Europa as a mandatory commercially useful currency at the expense of reducing the efficiency of the European commercial banking system. This already is suffering from the superior competitive power of American branch banks though, if the reserve requirements applied to all banks, all would suffer from the implicit tax and there would be no relative loss of efficiency on the part of European banks.

9. Magnifico and Williamson, *European Monetary Integration*.

The main reservation about the Magnifico-Williamson proposal, however, is that the weight of historical evidence strongly suggests that it is difficult, if not impossible, to establish by artificial governmental devices a commercially acceptable and conventionally used money. Almost without exception, moneys have acquired their legal status after, not before, they have acquired commercial acceptability—Knapp's little-known *The State Theory of Money* to the contrary.[10] One can force the public and the banking system to pay implicit taxes by enacting legislation requiring the holding of bank reserves in Europas rather than real money (a parallel is the imposition on banks of required liquid assets ratios in the form of Treasury bills). One can also bribe the public to use the new money by issuing assets denominated in it on specially favorable terms, or by enabling taxes to be paid in terms of it, again on favorable terms. Two assumptions, both extremely doubtful, are made without question by Magnifico and Williamson. One is that such devices implement an "infant industry argument" for protection of the infant monetary asset. The other is that very quickly the public and the commercial world will come to accept the new asset in an unsubsidized (or not induced through taxation) form as the asset superior to mere national currency assets—that these authors would like to see established as a means to their objectives of European unity and independence.

3. Given the unacceptability in Europe of the elevation of a single national currency into a commonly used European money, and the difficulties of establishing a new and neutral European money, the third alternative is to seek similar results by the coordination, without a central institution, of national economic policies; specifically, coordination of policies for foreign exchange market intervention. This was the recommendation of the celebrated Werner Report. The trouble with this recommendation, as with many other proposed "solutions" to European Community problems, is that it seeks to solve a problem on the basis of a vague agreement that there is a problem that should be solved, but no agreement on the principles on which the solution should be tackled. The hope is that these principles will somehow emerge from the process of negotiations among countries that have a vaguely defined moral commitment to arrive at some sort of solution. The difficulty of arriving at any such solution is exemplified by the conflict of interest between deficit and surplus countries over

10. Georg F. Knapp, *The State Theory of Money* (London: Macmillan for the Royal Economic Society, 1924).

whether the average of Community exchange rates should be set near the top or near the bottom of the permissible range of variation against the U.S. dollar.

In the event, instead of the Werner Committee's recommendation of close coordination of intervention policies in the market for U.S. dollars, the Community countries agreed that each would intervene in the market only in each other's currencies so long as its exchange rate was within the permitted range of variation against the dollar, and that they would intervene in dollars when their exchange rates hit the limit of permissible variation against the dollar. This system, which ran into trouble almost immediately, has the advantage that countries deal only in marketable assets: each other's currencies within the Community band and inside the dollar band, dollars at the limits of the dollar band. But it has the disadvantage from the viewpoint of an individual national central bank that it is no longer free, as it had become accustomed to being, to use dollar reserves to intervene to control the foreign exchange value of its currency within the permissible dollar band itself. Because the agreed system involves such a sacrifice of national discretionary power over the exchange rate, the agreed system is unlikely to be able to withstand in the longer run the pressures that make countries and their central banks desire to exercise the maximum discretionary control over their exchange rates with the dollar.

Impact on U.S. Policy

The United States has a variety of interests in the international monetary system and in international economic relations generally. These interests are not always compatible, and they reflect the somewhat inconsistent historical phases of the U.S. stake in the world economy and its relations with Europe in particular. In the late 1940s and during the 1950s, the United States viewed European economic integration as its top priority. The cold war had indicated the need to establish a strong European military ally, and Americans also still believed that the main trouble with Europe was that its peoples were not as cosmopolitan as its emigrant sons and daughters in the United States. Then, toward the end of the 1950s and in the early 1960s, the United States became more concerned with the commercial role of the dollar and the economic advantages resulting from its use as an international reserve currency. Europe's reaction at that time, as exemplified by Gaullism, still exerts a strong influence on European thinking. Even more recently, the United States, troubled about its waning position as the economically strongest and most technologically advanced country in the world, has become concerned about the need to reform the international monetary and trading system. It seeks greater exchange rate flexibility and what it considers "fair competition" between the United States and the other advanced industrial countries.

The prospect of narrower bands of exchange rate variation among the major currencies looks very different according to the perspective from which it is viewed. A particular viewpoint may be perfectly reasonable in itself but anachronistic and obsolete in terms of current U.S. interests. Thus, taking the viewpoint of the early 1950s, any move that looks plausibly like a step toward further European integration should be encouraged, whatever the immediate cost to the United States; it is worth attempting even if the capacity of the Europeans to effect it is in doubt. On this basis, the narrowing of the bands of exchange rate variation among the main European currencies is a worthwhile objective in terms of broad U.S. foreign economic policy objectives, whatever its costs in cash terms to the United States.

Alternatively, there is the view that the United States could gain greatly through the international monetary role of the dollar: in seigniorage profits and ability to employ Americans at high salaries in prestigious activities. Any European initiatives tending to reduce the international role of the dollar would be regarded as adverse to U.S. national interests. If an individual adopted this point of view, he could be either a pessimist or an optimist, either credulous or Machiavellian. Either he could assume that the Europeans will be successful in establishing some form of common European currency that will sooner or later rival the dollar, in which case any move toward that objective should be resisted by all available means. Or he could assume, with a great deal of historical justification, that any efforts the Europeans may make in this direction are not only doomed but will actually extend the hegemony of the dollar. Whether Europe establishes exchange rate flexibility against the dollar, or resorts to exchange controls of various kinds, it may be argued, the result will be to make the dollar a still more attractive and usable private international currency than anything the Europeans can devise. Moreover, if, in the process of establishing more internal exchange rate rigidity, the Community restricts or eliminates individual national exchange rate flexibility against the dollar without establishing a comparable degree of collective exchange rate flexibility against it, the dollar will have more opportunities to dominate than it had for most of the postwar period. Only if the Community can establish a better record in maintaining stability of prices can it hope to provide a better money than the U.S. dollar has done. Recent evidence indicates that Europe as a whole is doing considerably less well than the United States in the matter of price stability.

The third viewpoint on which to base U.S. policy relates to international monetary reform. The United States has only recently realized that the International Monetary Fund system, as practiced up to August 1971, offers a wonderful opportunity for other countries to pursue mercantilist policies of growth through exports; for attraction of foreign capital investments by a combination of exchange rate undervaluation and high tariffs; and for comfortable domestic policy making on the strength of a balance-of-payments surplus—all at the expense of U.S. unemployment (particularly of youth, blacks, and women), slow growth, and loss of technological leadership in the United States. The interests of the United States demand an international monetary system that will on the one hand demand and enforce prompt adjustment of exchange rates to balance-of-payments disequilibria, and on the other hand force other countries to review their institutional machinery and policy thinking to solve their own problems rather than relying on the benevolent self-disregard of the United States. There has been a great deal of criticism in recent years of the United States for its "benign neglect" of its balance of payments. One could with equal justice say that the United States, despite domestic vested interests, has "benignly ignored" the failure of other countries to live up to their obligation to adopt intelligent policies of economic management.

From this third point of view, the United States faces a real dilemma. One of the main problems of the present international monetary system is that individual European countries have been extremely reluctant to undertake exchange rate changes because the main impact of such changes would fall on their trade with one another, rather than their trade with the United States. This was tolerable, for the United States, as long as most payments imbalances were imbalances between individual European countries and the world in general, incurred by deviations between their domestic policies and the average trend of other countries' policies. But when the United States moved from being a (statistically) stable-price country to one that is a source of inflationary pressure for the rest of the world, it then became a problem for the United States itself. Under the impact of these conditions, it would be in the interest of the United States to have an international monetary system under which other countries had to appreciate when U.S. inflation made their currencies undervalued.

The narrowing of the bands of exchange rate variation among European currencies would be of substantial advantage to the United States if such a move presaged a conscious management of the exchange rates of the European currencies on average against the U.S. dollar, *and* if this management were directed toward preserving balance-of-payments equilibrium between the United States and Europe rather than snatching mercantilistic export surpluses for Europe against U.S. industry's competitive power. In such a case, it would be the mechanism for institutionalizing the fact that the Community constitutes a bloc with common interests vis-à-vis the United States, and should act accordingly. If, instead, the process of establishing a Community currency meant a freezing of exchange rates of member currencies against the dollar, and a deliberate abandonment of the degrees of freedom of exchange rate variation permitted by the present system in exchange for an artificial rigidity of exchange rates—especially if supported by exchange controls and a two-tier system of different exchange rates for current- and capital-account transactions—the United States would find itself confronted by an international monetary system of an interventionist and *dirigiste* kind quite different from what its own long-run interests in a liberal international economy require.

Comments by Edward M. Bernstein

IN ITS ANNUAL REPORT for 1972, the National Bank of Belgium, commenting on the wider margins of the Smithsonian Agreement and their effect on integration in the European Community, said that it should be possible for operations between residents of different countries within the Community to be concluded as easily and smoothly as transactions between residents of the same country. The central bank of Belgium meant by this not merely that exchange transfers between countries in the Community should be free of all restrictions, but that exchange rates between their currencies should vary very little from their parities. What the Federal Reserve System sought in par clearings of checks throughout the

United States, the EC countries seem to be seeking in limiting exchange rate fluctuations among their currencies.

I shall discuss only two aspects of this problem, both of which are analyzed in Harry Johnson's paper. The first is how the interest of the United States may be affected by narrower margins among the Community's currencies. The second is the technical problem of how the Community can maintain narrower margins among its currencies within the framework of wider margins with respect to the U.S. dollar. The problems are, of course, interrelated.

The United States is in favor of wider margins of exchange rate fluctuation above and below the parities among currencies. The Smithsonian Agreement and the action of the International Monetary Fund have temporarily established margins of 2¼ percent above and below the par value as the permitted range of fluctuation in exchange rates. As this margin relates to a designated currency—the dollar—the possible range of fluctuations for the currencies of members making use of the wider margins is 4½ percent of their parities with the dollar but 9 percent of their parities with each other.

All but about twenty members of the International Monetary Fund with established par values (prior to the floating of sterling in June 1972) availed themselves of the wider margins. They include the applicant members of the enlarged European Community. After the Smithsonian Agreement, the European Community agreed that the exchange rates between any two of their currencies should not exceed 2¼ percent above or below their parities with each other. The new arrangement came into operation on April 24, 1972, and the United Kingdom joined the scheme at the beginning of May. At the 1972 annual meeting of the governors of the International Monetary Fund, Treasury Secretary George Shultz said that the United States prefers a margin of 4½ percent above and below parity for the dollar in terms of other currencies—the range now available between two currencies, each of which has a limit of 2¼ percent above and below its dollar parity. At the same time, Secretary Shultz recognized "that countries in the process of forming a monetary union—with the higher degree of political and economic integration that that implies—may want to maintain narrower bands among themselves, and should be allowed to do so."[11] In short, the United States does not object to a narrower band for

11. U.S. Treasury, "News," Release S-56 (Sept. 26, 1972; processed), pp. 9–10.

exchange rate fluctuations among the currencies of the European Community.

On the face of it, if wider margins are in fact desirable for facilitating balance-of-payments adjustments, it would seem that a narrowing of the range of exchange rate fluctuations among the currencies of the largest trading area in the world would to some extent impede balance-of-payments adjustments. While the primary interest of the United States is to maintain a balanced payments position for itself with the world as a whole, it is also interested in seeing a well-balanced pattern of payments among all the large trading countries. Otherwise, the imbalance of payments in some countries—persistent surpluses or deficits—will require them to adopt corrective measures, such as deflation, that may adversely affect either the United States' balance of payments or its domestic economy.

I recognize that some European countries, and many less developed countries, are skeptical of the benefits of wider margins. I also recognize that even with the limited deviations permitted from their parities, the exchange rates for the Community currencies can vary more with respect to each other than before the Smithsonian Agreement, when the margin set by the International Monetary Fund was 1 percent and the de facto margin relative to the dollar for these currencies was ¾ percent. Thus, there is considerably more range for exchange rate variations among the Community currencies than there was prior to December 1971, even though there is less range for such variations than would be permitted by the Smithsonian Agreement and much less than the United States is now proposing for the dollar in a reformed international monetary system.

The first interest of the United States is how the action of the European Economic Community on exchange rates among their currencies will affect its balance-of-payments adjustment. If the Community had a single currency and were, in fact, a completely integrated economic area, the question would not arise. The exchange rate for the European currency would be determined by the overall balance of payments of the Community with the rest of the world, of which the United States would be by far the largest part. If the United States needed to adjust its balance of payments, and that adjustment could be facilitated by exchange rate changes within the wider range, it would still be able to do so. But the Community is not completely integrated, and each country in the Community has a balance-of-payments position of its own. How then would the exchange rates for the Community currencies array themselves with respect to each other and with respect to the dollar, assuming significant differences in the balance of payments among the members of the Community?

One assumption is that somehow the total or weighted average balance of payments of the members of the Community would determine their individual or average rates of exchange with the dollar. If this were true, it might in some respects even be helpful to the United States. In fact, each member of the Community must be concerned about its own balance of payments, regardless of the reserve credit help they may extend to each other. Thus, if one country in the Community has an overall payments deficit and other countries have an overall payments surplus exceeding this deficit, it does not follow that the average exchange rates of their currencies with the dollar will be the same as if there were a single European currency whose exchange rate is determined by the overall balance-of-payments surplus of the Community with the rest of the world.

The deficit country in the Community may have a serious balance-of-payments problem which requires all the help it can get from flexible exchange rates. For this reason, it may want the price of its currency to be at the bottom of the permitted range with the dollar. On the other hand, the surplus of other members of the Community would require their currencies to be above their parities with the dollar. As this combination of exchange rates is not permitted in Community currencies, the question is whether the deficit country should be permitted to pull down the currencies of the surplus countries or the surplus countries be permitted to pull up the currency of the deficit country. As the problems of deficit countries usually seem more urgent than the problems of the surplus countries, the deficit country rather than the surplus countries may be the determinant of the general level of the dollar exchange rates of the Community currencies.

A practical example of this was the way the dollar exchange rates for the Community currencies behaved during the speculation against sterling. On June 14, 1972, the French commercial franc was the strongest currency in the group, 2¼ percent above the dollar parity, and sterling was the weakest, just above its dollar parity. In the following week, sterling fell to about 1¼ percent below its dollar parity, and in response to the EC exchange rate arrangements, the strong European currencies began to decline against the dollar—the Belgian franc by 1.3 percent, the French commercial franc by 1.0 percent, and the D-mark by 0.9 percent. This method of keeping the margins among the Community currencies was clearly prejudicial to the United States. The general weakness of the U.S. balance of payments should have been accompanied by an exchange rate for the strongest Community currencies at or close to the upper limit of the range. Instead, the dollar prices of these currencies began to decline toward their dollar parities. No wonder billions of dollars flowed from the United States to Europe in a very short period. Fortunately, with the floating of sterling, this anomalous behavior came to an end, and the dollar prices of the strong European currencies rose to the upper limit of the range. One would hope that this is not typical of the way the Community will maintain the narrower range among its currencies if a similar situation should arise in the future.

There is another problem that touches the interest of the United States and that is the method of balance-of-payments settlements. When the dollar is used as the intervention currency, the dollars put into the exchange market by the deficit countries and the dollars taken out of the exchange market by the surplus countries become in the first instance the means of international settlements. When the dollar was convertible, countries that acquired dollars could convert them into other reserve assets to meet their asset preference. That has not been possible since the dollar ceased to be convertible into gold and other reserve assets. Dollars are still used for intervention and countries that acquire them hold them as reserves— ignoring for the moment the conversion of some official dollar holdings by a few countries into German D-marks, Swiss francs, and probably Japanese yen through the exchange market. The countries in the Community were not willing to agree on settlement in inconvertible dollars among themselves. They provided, therefore, that within the Community balance-of-payments settlements would be made pro rata in all of the different reserve assets held by the deficit countries. At a time when the dollar was not convertible into other reserve assets, this method of settlement within the Community was almost certain to lead to difficulties.

The fact is that countries do not regard their different reserve assets as equally attractive at the present time (September 1972), and in the hierarchy of their preference gold is very high and the dollar is very low. Thus, a country in the Community having a balance in its overall payments, but with a deficit in the Community and a surplus in the rest of the world, would be taking in dollars in settlement of its surplus, but paying out gold, SDRs, and dollars in settlement of its deficit. If the structure of its balance of payments involved a permanent deficit with the Community and a permanent surplus with the rest of the world, the composition of the reserves of this EC member could change in the opposite direction of its asset preference. This in itself would seem an untenable payments position if the preference for gold over dollars were very great. If continued, it would ultimately lead to measures designed to limit the deficit of the country with the rest of the Community, although the same measures would tend to augment its surplus with the rest of the world. At best, it would involve exaggerated payments problems for countries outside the Community, particularly the United States. At worst it would result in a division of the balance of payments of each member of the Community into two distinct parts: one settled in dollars and one settled in other reserve assets as well as dollars. Fortunately, this method of settlement within the Community had to be suspended because Italy had a large deficit that it was not willing to settle by transfers of gold.

I come now to the technical difficulty of maintaining a narrower range of exchange rate fluctuations among the EC currencies than with the dollar. A great deal has been made of the asymmetry existing between the dollar and other currencies which, with the same margins, permits wider fluctuations in the exchange rates among other currencies in terms of each other than in their exchange rates with the dollar. This is the situation at present. It did not exist under the gold standard, and it does not have to exist under the Bretton Woods system. As Johnson pointed out, under the classical gold standard, exchange rates were kept within defined limits from mint parities through gold and exchange arbitrage by banks and bullion dealers. When the United States modified the gold standard in 1934 by confining its sales of gold to foreign central banks, this did not alter the gold points, except to the extent that its charge of ¼ percent for buying and selling gold had the effect of widening them. What the action of the United States did do was to compel central-bank intervention in the exchange market to keep exchange rates within the new gold points. The United States did not take an active part in this intervention, except as agent for other central banks, not because it regarded the dollar as unique, but because it felt no need to intervene and because other central banks were performing this function.

The Bretton Woods system did not set up the dollar as an intervention currency and it did not establish a wider range of exchange rate fluctuations for other currencies in terms of each other than for the dollar. The economists at Bretton Woods were well aware of the interrelationship of the gold points, the transactions charge of the International Monetary Fund, and the margins above and below par values which were to be the limits of exchange rates. They even considered the contribution that wider fluctuations around par values could make to balance-of-payments adjustment. These questions were discussed in the U.S. Treasury document, *Questions and Answers on the International Monetary Fund*, prepared for the Bretton Woods conference and recently published by the IMF in the third volume of its history or chronicle.[12]

The Articles of Agreement of the International Monetary Fund state in Article IV, section 3: "The maximum and the minimum rates for exchange transactions between the currencies of members taking place within their territories shall not differ from parity (i) in the case of spot exchange transactions, by more than one percent. . . ." On the face of it, this means that the exchange rate for the lira, for example, cannot differ by more than 1 percent from either its dollar or sterling parities. The rule that the dollar parity was the test of the margin evolved in a practical way. As the European currencies were inconvertible in the early years of the Fund's operations, the question arose as to who had the responsibility for supporting an inconvertible currency—an interesting question in our present environment. (The first case which brought the question to the attention of the International Monetary Fund was the decline in sterling to more than 1 percent below its parity with the lira in the Milan and Rome exchange markets. The view of the British was that the IMF Articles of Agreement obligated Italy to prevent a decline in sterling in its markets below the 1 percent limit from parity, even if that meant acquiring and holding inconvertible sterling.) The Fund adopted the view that no country could be compelled to acquire inconvertible currencies in order to maintain exchange rates within the prescribed limits from parity. It was this special situation that led to the rule that the test of exchange stability would be applied by the Fund with respect to a designated currency, which was usually the dollar.

I see no technical difficulty in applying the same effective rule regarding the range of exchange rate fluctuations to all currencies, including the dollar, subject to the right of any country (or group of countries) to opt for a narrower band for its currency with respect to another currency (the

---

12. International Monetary Fund, *The International Monetary Fund, 1945–65: Twenty Years of International Monetary Cooperation*, Documents, Vol. 3 (The Fund, 1969), pp. 136–82.

dollar) or for their own currencies with respect to each other—the European case. In fact, the economics of the problem would dictate this, if countries always followed their financial interests and if all reserve assets were equally attractive. About twenty years ago I expounded the doctrine at the IMF that the currency that countries should draw from the Fund was the currency with the highest premium in the exchange market rather than the currency with which they usually intervened in the exchange market—that is, the dollar. If the D-mark, for example, were 1 percent above the dollar parity, a country drawing D-marks from the IMF could make 1 percent profit by supporting its currency with D-marks rather than with dollars. And if its exchange market was accustomed to the use of dollars for intervention, it would still be better off drawing D-marks from the IMF and selling them for dollars to be used in supporting its own currency. I can recall only one case in which a member of the IMF followed this principle—when Japan drew sterling, then at a premium relative to the dollar, and repaid the drawing almost immediately in dollars.

If all currencies were convertible into reserve assets and all countries used reserve assets in settling their balance of payments, this principle would definitely be established. Moreover, that is the way that members of the European Community could keep their currencies with the narrower band they establish for themselves. Suppose, for example, that the D-mark were at the limit of 2¼ percent above its parity with the lira. If the dollar were at par with the lira, it would be more costly for Italy to intervene to support the lira against the D-mark with dollars. Either it would sell reserves for the D-mark at par, using the D-marks to support the lira, or it would convert dollars into reserves which it could then sell for D-marks, both transactions at par. Of course, if the dollar were at par with the D-mark, or at a premium relative to the D-mark, it would be more economical for Italy to intervene with dollars to support the exchange rate for the lira in terms of the D-mark. It should be noted, however, that if there were a charge for buying and selling reserves for currencies, which I believe is essential with wider margins, these charges would have to be taken into account.

To put it simply, I see no reason for having a common European currency, to be used for intervention in the exchange market, in order to enable the members of the Community to maintain exchange rates for their currencies in terms of each other within any band they prefer. The supposed difficulty comes from their practice of using the dollar as an intervention currency, reinforced by the fact that their preference for dollars as reserves is now relatively low. Once all major currencies, including the dollar, are convertible into reserve assets on the same terms, I see no problem for the European Community in using any currency for intervention to maintain the spread of exchange rates among their currencies within an agreed band. They could use dollars, sterling, or D-marks for intervention, as all of these currencies have wide enough exchange markets in Europe to be used for this purpose. With all currencies convertible, the choice of the intervention currency would depend on which has the highest premium in the exchange market. There is no need to create a Europa for this purpose, particularly if it is to be used both as reserves of the monetary authorities and as a transactions currency held by the public. I can think of other reasons for creating a Europa as a central-bank reserve asset— say, as an instrument for compelling a common policy on monetary expansion—but not solely or primarily for the purpose of enabling the European Community to maintain exchange rates for their currencies within a narrower band.

Comments by William J. Fellner

I SHARE Harry Johnson's skepticism about the prospects of European economic integration. I think the policies that will be domestically acceptable in Germany, Italy, Britain, and other EC countries will in the predictable future remain sufficiently different to deprive the integration effort of any real promise. Among the many reasons for this, I will mention briefly only two—or rather two aspects of one.

Within specific ranges of labor-market tightness there may well exist fairly stable long-run tradeoffs between inflation and unemployment. At first, wage earners and their representatives might behave as if, given somewhat greater labor-market tightness, they were insisting on a steeper *real*-wage trend, and thus a monetary-fiscal policy attempting to avoid recession would at first have to accommodate some acceleration of inflation; yet at unchanging productivity trends the trend of real wages would not in fact become steeper. At some stage unions might give up this effort, so that a policy attempting to stabilize an increased rate of inflation will lead not to a serious recession but to fairly stable rates of increase in money wages and prices. In this regard, the available alternatives and the policy preferences are apt to be different in the different countries under consideration.

To turn to another aspect of the same problem, while I am convinced that a commitment to maintain very high degrees of tightness in major labor categories leads to increasingly sharp bidding for scarce labor and makes the inflationary process explosive (and the tradeoffs unstable), so that inflation would then have to be "beaten down" by shifting to the stop phase of pronounced stop-and-go alternations, I am also persuaded that these stop phases appear more objectionable in some countries than in others. They are felt to be more or less undesirable depending partly on institutional arrangements determining how much it hurts to be temporarily unemployed, and partly on other factors such as the number of foreign workers, the size of the agricultural sector, and so forth.

These and several other differences among countries bearing on exchange rates will remain. If monetary integration should nevertheless succeed in Europe—an assumption that even the skeptics like myself should perhaps accept in order to continue the discussion—then, as Johnson says, some potential consequences would be favorable for the United States, other potential consequences unfavorable.

Among the potential favorable outcomes is the greater willingness of a monetarily integrated economic unit to make the central dollar rates, around which the band is defined, reasonably adjustable. This would be a significant advantage also from the American point of view. One of the potential unfavorable effects is the increased scope for coordinating restrictive practices. It sems to me, however, that as long as the restrictive practices in question aim at reducing dollar inflows, intrabloc coordination would continue to be difficult, even in the event of monetary integration. In the contrary situation, restrictive practices creating obstacles not to dollar inflows but to commodity imports from the United States would be much easier to coordinate, and one can only hope that the danger of American retaliation would be obvious enough to discourage such measures.

The interim objective, as yet unrealized, appears to be to narrow the band for the currencies of the European bloc in relation to each other by keeping them at no more than a "snake's width" from one another, while utilizing the larger "tunnel" for movements of the block currencies relative to the dollar. The tunnel—the permissible width of the band in relation to the dollar as agreed upon at the Smithsonian Institution—is 2¼ percent in each direction from the central rates. Hence, the greatest "permissible" swing of any other currency within the band relative to the dollar is 4½ percent. If fluctuations of the European-bloc currencies were not to be subjected to any limitation beyond that implied in the Smithsonian Agreement, the greatest "permissible" swing between two European-bloc currencies vis-à-vis each other would be 9 percent, since any two of them could change places in relation to the dollar. For currency A relative to B, there is a 9 percent difference between the conditions prevailing when A is 2¼ percent above its parity with the dollar while B is 2¼ percent below and the conditions prevailing when A is 2¼ percent below while B is 2¼ percent above. Reducing the maximum swing between any two European-bloc currencies from 9 percent to 4½ percent (2¼ percent up and 2¼ percent down relative to each other) would merely make these currencies as flexible in relation to one another as they are supposed to be in relation to the dollar according to the Smithsonian Agreement.

A genuine snake-in-the-tunnel program—genuine in the sense that it would result from greater and prompter harmonization of policies within the bloc than between the European-bloc countries and the United States —would require finding viable means for reducing the flexibility of the European-bloc currencies in relation to each other *below* the flexibility these currencies have relative to the dollar (say, to 1⅛ percent up and down for the bloc currencies in relation to one another). This should presumably be done without reducing the flexibility of the bloc currencies vis-à-vis the dollar.

I will not comment in detail on Johnson's interesting discussion of the difficulties of finding viable means of implementing the snake-in-the-tunnel program. I will merely observe that, given any available technique for narrowing the band in intrabloc relations, one would indeed have to stretch one's imagination to describe sequences of events in which any of the currencies keeping at a not inconsiderable distance—rather than at zero distance—from its parity with another would typically make full or even nearly full use of the Smithsonian band in relation to the dollar. (It would be even harder to imagine sequences of events in which several bloc-currencies would develop such a record.)

For example, if bloc-currency A, when hitting the upper limit of the dollar band, is at some distance above B and the two do not change places in relation to each other when moving down in the dollar band, *neither* can make full use of the 4½ percent band in relation to the dollar. The two bloc currencies could change places during the downward movement in the dollar band, in which case *A* could make full use of the dollar band but the movement of *B* would then be all the more limited. To be sure, next time *B* could be in the situation in which *A* was initially, and vice versa, but it remains true that whenever conditions *happen* to develop in such a way that one of the two currencies can make full use of the dollar band, the other's movements are distinctly limited.

Discussion

THE GENERAL DISCUSSION of Harry Johnson's paper concentrated on alternative methods of keeping the exchange rates between members' currencies within the Community's band of permitted deviations from their parities (the "snake"); the possible incompatibility of doing so with maintenance or restoration of balance in the international payments of the members; the resulting conflicts of interest as to where the band should be within the wider band permitted under the Smithsonian Agreement (the "tunnel"); and, in view of these conflicts, what would determine the location of the snake in the tunnel.

Johnson had pointed out that when one member of the Community is in surplus and another in deficit, a question arises as to the relation between the European currencies as a whole and those of nonmembers, notably the dollar. Leonard Weiss thought that although Johnson had treated this question as a technical one, it really is a policy issue. There is no escape from the dilemma created by the constraints of the snake and the conflict between the interests of surplus and deficit members, except for one of them to cease being a member of the monetary union. Johnson agreed that a government's decision to enter a union involved a policy commitment to limit its authority, but the degree to which a member intended to "bind its hands" depended on the degree to which it thought it gave up freedom to change its exchange rate. Johnson thought that EC members were counting on the possibility, for at least some time ahead, of changing the par values of their currencies. In discussing the issue, he had assumed that divergences among the members would not reach the point where such changes would be necessary; he had intended to emphasize that conflict would arise even before that point was reached.

Richard Cooper said that there had been a well-defined technical problem, and that the Community had faced it. The problem was how to narrow exchange rate variations among the European currencies without narrowing their variations with the dollar by at least twice as much. That is a real problem as long as the dollar is used as an intervention currency. Three kinds of solution are conceivable. One is to abandon the market as a clearing mechanism and have central banks make the market by posting buying and selling prices for all currencies. This would eliminate any special role for the dollar and also whatever efficiency is to be gained from using the market as a clearing mechanism. Second, a single European currency could be used as the intervention currency for all European monetary authorities except one. The currency utilized might be an existing one or a new one, such as the Europa proposed by John Williamson and Giovanni Magnifico, although it would be difficult to have such a new one adopted by the market. If the pound sterling were used under this alternative, European central banks would not intervene in dollars but only in pounds, and the Bank of England would intervene in dollars. This would permit setting separately the width of the band between any pair of European currencies and that of the band between any one of them and the dollar. The pound is the natural choice for the intervention currency on economic if not political grounds, since the City of London has the necessary financial capacity and the volume of outstanding Treasury bills denominated in sterling is large. Such a choice, however, would give the pound less flexibility in relation to other European currencies than they would have in relation to each other; this may be regarded as a disadvantage for Britain. The third possibility, one variant of which was adopted, is some form of coordinated intervention. The Werner Report proposed coordinated intervention in dollars in a way that gave rise to the snake-in-the-tunnel metaphor. As William J. Fellner had noted, it required the European authorities to decide where in the tunnel the snake should be. Cooper's view, however, in contrast to those of Edward M. Bernstein and Fellner, is that the system actually adopted did not involve this problem. Market forces would determine the position of the snake in the tunnel, since each European central bank, while intervening in any other European currency whenever its currency threatened to be more than 2¼ percent from parity with that other currency, would not intervene in dollars until a member currency reached the outer limits permitted in relation to the dollar. It is true that policy actions affect market forces, but Cooper was not referring to that influence; the intervention system did not require decisions as to the location of the snake in the tunnel. What this system requires is some kind of nonmarket exchange of assets—either loans or sales of currencies —between the European central banks. What they have given up is the right to intervene within the 2¼ percent band.

Cooper expected that the great flexibility allowed by this band would not survive long before the central banks would want to intervene within the snake, as well as at its limits. That would create the problem of conflicting intervention and would require coordination, which may best be resolved by going back to the second solution (designating a single European currency) or, alternatively, a single intervening agency.[13]

C. Fred Bergsten noted that the presumption Cooper had mentioned against official intervention within the limits of the snake would tend to promote payments adjustment, whereas the limitation of possible fluctuations imposed by the snake would tend to retard it. He invited the discussants to strike a balance between these opposing influences on the adjustment process, asking whether less intervention within narrower margins might not result in a net improvement in the process, or at least not affect it adversely. His invitation elicited no response.

Fellner, taking up Cooper's point that under the intervention methods adopted, the location of the snake in the tunnel will be determined by market forces and will not require a Community decision, said that official intervention in the foreign exchange markets is only a temporary method of maintaining these limits. A more enduring maintenance of the limits would require harmonization of policies, and the location of the snake in the tunnel would ultimately be determined by the decision as to how policies were to be harmonized.[14] John Williamson addressed the question of where in the tunnel the snake should be when two European currencies

13. This outline of the possibilities by Cooper seemed to indicate that the means of limiting the fluctuations between pairs of Community currencies and the determination of their average value in relation to the dollar are interrelated, since the average value of the Community currencies in relation to the dollar depends in part on the method chosen to limit fluctuations in their relation to each other.—Editors' note.

14. This point is compatible with Cooper's view that the location of the snake in the tunnel would be determined by market forces. Indeed, Cooper had recognized that market forces are influenced by policy actions, although he said he was not talking about that influence when asserting that no decision about the location of the snake in the tunnel is required. Fellner's point implies that these forces, in turn, would be influenced by a decision, and that the need to make one could not be escaped. Even though the decision might not be addressed explicitly to the question of where the snake should be in the tunnel, it would imply an answer to that question. —Editors' note.

were pulling it in opposite directions. He said that in principle one would want its position to reflect some weighted average of the values of the member currencies. He thought such a result would be more easily attained if the proposed Europa were the intervention currency. Movement in the reserves of the proposed Community central bank that had issued it would show whether the currency should be rising above or falling below parity with the dollar. Since its movement would carry with it all the individual European currencies, there would still be conflicts of interest among the member countries, but they would be less troublesome than if one of the national currencies were the medium for intervention. For example, if the pound had been the intervention currency, its decline in June 1972 toward the bottom of the band with the dollar would have pulled down the other European currencies. That would have caused a conflict of interest with the other European countries more acute and difficult to manage than if there had been a common intervention medium managed in the collective interest of the members.

Charles Kindleberger thought that, from the point of view of the development of the world economy, it makes little difference whether exchange rates between a non-key currency and other currencies are fixed; for example, whether the European currencies have fixed rates among themselves or whether the Canadian dollar is fixed in relation to the U.S. dollar. What is important is that the rates between the key currencies be fixed. Discussion about the snake in the tunnel was significant, Kindleberger considered, because it brought out the importance of cross rates. Proposals to make the SDR or a new currency the numéraire disregard cross rates, he thought, and for that reason are nonsensical. He endorsed Cooper's view, expressed in a September 1972 article, that there is no way of getting rid of asymmetry.[15] Benjamin Cohen agreed that the SDR is irrelevant as a numéraire, but thought that the European Community's movement toward monetary integration might drive the members to promote use of SDRs as an intervention currency, which would require reforming the world monetary system in such a way that SDRs could be held privately. Bergsten, however, thought that to use SDRs in the private market as well as officially would be a disastrous replication of the history of gold.

15. Richard N. Cooper, "Eurodollars, Reserve Dollars, and Asymmetries in the International Monetary System," *Journal of International Economics*, Vol. 2 (September 1972), pp. 325–44.

Harold van B. Cleveland considered that the only practical alternative to the Community's decision to maintain the member currencies within the snake by intervening in each other's currencies was to intervene in dollars. The Community's reason for rejecting that alternative was essentially political: to reduce the role of the dollar and increase the members' control of their own affairs. The effect, however, was to make the relation between the member currencies as a group and the dollar more responsive to market forces.

In further discussion of the Magnifico-Williamson proposal to create a new European currency—the Europa—to which the existing European national currencies would be pegged, Williamson took up Johnson's observation that devices to establish the Europa as commercially useful, such as requiring commercial banks to hold minimum cash reserve ratios in assets denominated in Europas, would reduce the efficiency of the European commercial banking system, and that the authors of the proposal viewed the resulting loss of microefficiency with undue equanimity. Williamson's response was that, owing to the importance of economies of scale in financial markets, assets like the one they had proposed could be made widely attractive only after they were very widely held. The device they proposed to promote wide holding was an infant-industry type of protection that would become unnecessary after a time. Although it might be retained for purposes of monetary control, it would not be needed for protection. This implied that in the long run there would be no loss of microefficiency.

In response to questions by Bernstein and Johnson as to how the proposal was intended to operate, Williamson explained that under it there would be no direct intervention in the exchange rate between a European national currency and the dollar. The Community central bank that would be created along with the Europa would intervene between the Europa and the dollar, and the monetary authorities of the members would intervene in the rates between their national currencies and the Europa. If the deutsche mark were at the top of the snake, for example, Germany would acquire additional Europas. If Germany disliked taking in more Europas, it would be as free to act as it does at present when it does not want any more dollars. If the Europa were also at the top of its band with the dollar, the European central bank would acquire additional dollars and sell Europas on balance in the market. The position of the Europa in relation to the dollar thus would provide an automatic device for weighing the interests of the members against each other. If the Community bank disliked taking in more dollars, it could allow the Europa to rise against the dollar. The proposal envisaged adjustment of the parity between the Europa and the dollar, as well as a band of permissible fluctuations around the parity.

Johnson said that he had thought the proposal implied a major reform of the international system according to which either the Europa could move anywhere in relation to the dollar, in which case there would be a floating rate between them, or it would have a parity with the dollar and a defined band around that parity. The European member currencies, in turn, would have a band around the Europa, in which case any one of them could deviate from the dollar by more than the Europa was able to do. If that were not a correct understanding of the proposal, moving the Europa up and down would involve squeezing the national currencies at the top or bottom, respectively. Williamson responded that the proposal could work on either alternative, but that the first—a floating rate between the Europa and the dollar—was not the solution he and Magnifico preferred. Their preference was for the second alternative, which would indeed make the effective band between a European national currency and the dollar wider than that between the Europa and the dollar. Whether the band between a member currency and the dollar would be wider than it is now in September 1972 would depend on the size of the bands chosen. It would be wider if the margins between the Europa and the dollar were plus and minus 2¼ percent (or a total band of 4½ percent around their parity), since the intra-Community band would be a net addition to that, and would provide additional flexibility.

LAWRENCE B. KRAUSE

Implications for Private Capital Markets

WHAT DIFFERENCE will it make to private capital markets in the future if the European Community achieves its goal of becoming a complete economic and monetary union rather than remaining a more limited common market? That is the primary question addressed in this paper. But, to speculate about the future of private capital markets probably takes as much courage as it does to speculate in these markets. The inventiveness of private financiers has been demonstrated so vividly over the last twenty years that it borders on the foolhardy to try to anticipate the future. Nevertheless, an attempt needs to be made to analyze possibilities because of the importance of private capital movements to the economies and policies of the member countries of the European Community (EC), and because monetary union could have considerable impact on these monetary flows.

The Werner Report set down in 1970 the overall implications of monetary union for capital movements in explicit terms.[1] The report calls for the "total liberation" of movements of capital, along with the "total and

The views are those of the author and should not be attributed to other staff members, officers, or trustees of the Brookings Institution.

1. *Report to the Council and the Commission on the Realisation by Stages of Economic and Monetary Union in the Community*. Supplement to *Bulletin* 11-1970 of the European Communities, the Werner Group, under the chairmanship of Pierre Werner (Luxembourg: Office for Official Publications of the European Communities, October 8, 1970). (Hereinafter referred to as the Werner Report.)

irreversible" convertibility of currencies, the elimination of margins of fluctuation in rates of exchange, and the "irrevocable" fixing of parity ratios. The report also states that goods and services, people, and capital should all circulate freely among the member countries and without competitive distortions, indicating the nonseparability of capital flows from other economic links among members. At one point, it even chides the Community for its previous lack of progress in liberalizing capital movements. It is important to note that no distinction is drawn between long-term and short-term capital; all types are to circulate freely within the Community. Thus there is in the Werner Report none of the ambiguity about the desirability of private capital movements found, for instance, in the Articles of Agreement formulated at Bretton Woods.

One should not take the mistaken view that the Werner group was unaware of the problems that private capital movements may cause for governments; indeed, the report points to the enormous growth in speculation as an argument for monetary union. Rather, the report envisions a situation in which "policy harmonization and coordination" will eliminate speculative capital movements and avoid such problems.

The Werner group anticipates a staged transition toward complete liberation of capital movements, similar to the transition for other aspects of economic and monetary union. In the early stages, EC member governments are to set up explicit targets, or quotas, for new bond flotations in domestic capital markets for residents of other member countries, these targets being increased over time. Similarly, in each country, quotas for medium- and long-term credits are to be established on a nondiscriminatory basis for residents of other member countries, and its stock exchange opened to listings of equities from the others. Also during the transition, the member countries are to coordinate their policies in relation to financial markets, which presumably will cover short-term capital. Thus, the Community will arrive at a true common capital market by the progressive interpenetration of national markets.

The Werner Report makes no overt reference to the treatment of private capital movements to or from nonmember countries. The general provisions imply, however, that whatever treatment is to be accorded foreign capital would be applied uniformly throughout the Community. Of course, explicit targets or quotas for one class of borrowers implies less favorable treatment for other classes of borrowers. The European Community in other contexts, however, has so liberally defined Community residency that a subsidiary of an American firm incorporated in a member country qualifies as a resident for favored treatment.

Need for Free Movement of Capital

The free movement of private capital within the Community not only advances economic welfare; it is also an essential ingredient—possibly the most essential ingredient—in an effective economic and monetary union. Obviously, the greatest threat to monetary union is regional imbalance within the Community, recognizing that each region corresponds to a former sovereign state. In the face of imbalance, political pressures to alleviate distress may impel member countries to exercise sovereignty in ways inconsistent with monetary unity. For monetary union to succeed, therefore, regional imbalance must either be prevented or adjusted to without independent policy measures being taken by the member countries. Private capital movements are of great importance because they can perform this valuable adjustment function, replacing the need for policy action.

Not all imbalances can be assimilated through private capital movements. If regional disparities develop within the Community in the rate of growth of wage costs per unit of output and in the rate of general inflation, economic and monetary union will not be realized, because changes in exchange rate parities will be unavoidable. The strategy must be to prevent differential inflation rates among regions, not to correct for them. Thus a single monetary policy operated by a unitary monetary authority (in fact, if not in appearance) is a necessity. It is a necessity, however, that will severely constrain the access of member governments to capital markets to finance budget deficits: a constraint which implies that the overall fiscal domain should correspond to the single monetary union. It would still be possible to maintain concurrently lesser fiscal domains similar to states in the United States. Indeed, historical precedent dictates that some fiscal autonomy be maintained at the national level in the Community. But even the operation of such a mechanism constitutes only the necessary, not the sufficient, condition for regional balance.

Disturbances can occur, for instance, because of trend differentials in the productivity growth of industries in which particular regions specialize. Productivity differentials will be reflected in real-income differentials among regions. Productivity differentials are, in fact, inevitable in dynamic economies and could lead to permanently depressed member countries if no adjustment mechanism were operating. Possible adjustment mechanisms can be constructed from three general elements: governmental transfers from advanced to backward regions, labor migration from low to high productivity regions, and private capital movements from low to high yield areas. Obviously, an adjustment mechanism can be constructed with all three elements. To make the case for the necessity of the liberation of capital movements requires only an examination of how the adjustment mechanism would have to operate in their absence.

In his seminal study of the subject, Robert Mundell identified optimal currency areas with unified labor markets.[2] His concept of labor mobility used for adjustment purposes, however, is not compatible with the political, sociological, and cultural reality of the European Community today, nor is it likely to be in the foreseeable future. While some labor migration does occur, ample evidence demonstrates that few Europeans are prepared to move away from their native countries, even in response to large economic incentives, nor do they appear to be acceptable as permanent immigrants elsewhere in other than small concentrations. Depopulation just does not seem to be a politically viable answer for the depressed-region problem, particularly if the region constitutes all of a former sovereign state.

A solution based solely on governmental transfers seems only slightly more realistic. The required transfer payments appear to be quite large and would have to continue indefinitely. From a political point of view, such a solution is hard to implement, even between regions with strong cultural ties. It would be next to impossible where, as among EC member countries, such cultural identity does not exist. To be sure, some governmental transfers are possible, as in the case of the common agricultural policy (CAP). But a system that always increases taxes in advanced regions because of productivity gains (and thereby seemingly rewards laggard regions) would in time face serious opposition. The situation hardly changes if there is some labor mobility, for then the advanced regions will consider they are doubly taxed: once because of the transfer payments and again, because of the higher social overhead required to serve the new immigrants.

2. Robert A. Mundell, "A Theory of Optimum Currency Areas," *American Economic Review*, Vol. 51 (September 1961), pp. 657–65.

Private capital movements add an essential ingredient to these other two elements in the adjustment process, as James Ingram points out.[3] Particularly when combined with entrepreneurship, they can be an automatic and almost invisible adjustor among regions. Capital that is free to move will seek higher rates of return and thus spread productivity gains from advanced to backward regions. But if capital is to move in an equilibrating direction, some governmental transfers are also required to overcome barriers that may exist as a result of deficiencies in the public sectors of backward regions. Furthermore, without some labor mobility, skill shortages and surpluses in regional labor markets will not be corrected. Such cross-patterns of migration are seen between the South and other areas of the United States.

Thus, the opportunity for the free movement of private capital among regions in a monetary union should be highly favorable. In a properly working monetary system, private capital movements are not just to be tolerated, they are to be sought. It should be recognized that such movements serve an important economic and social function besides enriching their owners, but that they should be subject to regulation against possible abuses of market power.

The favorable climate for private capital markets to operate freely within a monetary union can be anticipated through analogy with capital markets in the United States. Monetary union will have implications for borrowers, for investors, for financial institutions or intermediaries, and therefore for capital markets as a whole.

Implications for Borrowers

The achievement of monetary unification could make a substantial difference for business firms and governments, and even for individuals when they enter capital markets as borrowers. By far the most important impact would come from the abolition of legal and administrative discrimination by EC member countries against nonnational borrowers. These discriminatory practices help to perpetuate separation of capital markets and are most effective against long-term debt and equity borrowings, the

3. James C. Ingram, "Comment: The Currency Area Problem," in Robert A. Mundell and Alexander K. Swoboda (eds.), *Monetary Problems of the International Economy* (University of Chicago Press, 1969), pp. 95–100.

part of the market that is usually considered the most productive from a social point of view. Such discrimination was recognized as undesirable even in 1957 by the Treaty of Rome establishing the European Economic Community.[4] Yet pressures caused by regional and external imbalance inhibited efforts to liberate private capital from progressing much beyond what had been achieved by the early 1960s. The abrogation of the obligation to free capital markets was permitted under Article 73 of the Treaty of Rome. Further restrictions have actually been imposed since 1967. When economic and monetary union relieves member countries of concern over regional imbalance, it should be possible to end these barriers to the free movement of capital.

Another but perhaps less important aspect of monetary unification that will have some impact on borrowers concerns exchange rate risk. Borrowers will no longer have to worry that the currency in which they borrow and have to repay will rise in value relative to their own domestic currencies. This anxiety relates to both the small fluctuations within the permissible band of fluctuation and larger parity changes among currencies. Although it is possible that such exchange rate risks weigh heavily on some borrowers, it is hard to believe that the overall consequences are very great and therefore constrain borrowing very much. Long-term borrowings are presumably even less affected than short-term borrowings, because any loss can be amortized more gradually and because long-term interest rates more clearly reflect price expectations, which in turn can compensate borrowers and lenders in advance for expected exchange rate fluctuations. In other words, the borrower who takes the risk of borrowing a strong currency, like the German D-mark or the Swiss franc, is compensated by a lower long-term interest rate than is available in the markets of countries with weak currencies. For short-term borrowers, a sudden and large parity change could make a substantial difference in the overall cost of borrowing; however, in this case, forward markets operate quite effectively.[5] Borrowers can hedge their risks by buying the currency in the forward market to be delivered at the time repayment is due. Of course, forward cover does involve an expense; hence, monetary union will reduce the cost of borrowing by eliminating the need for it.

Exchange rate risk also has another consequence for borrowings in

---

4. Treaty of Rome, Part 2, Title 3, Chapter 4, Articles 67–73.

5. Forward markets disintegrate during periods of currency crises, but weak currencies are not borrowed at such times except for pure speculation.

European Monetary Unification

Table 1. *New Security Issues in Domestic Markets, Seven European*
Countries and the United States, 1965–69
Millions of U.S. dollars

Country of issue and type of security	1965	1966	1967	1968	1969
Belgium					
Shares	250	330	325	460	476
Bonds	920	840	1,265	1,590	1,350
Debt certificates	50	75	190	135	210
Denmark					
Shares	143	139	123	119	142
Bonds	1,013	833	923	1,235	1,570
France					
Shares	930	690	640	735	1,525
Bonds	1,445	1,770	1,675	1,150	1,405
Germany					
Shares	990	678	477	786	711
Bonds	2,893	1,212	3,666	4,795	3,774
Debt certificates	727	691	624	605	916
Italy					
Shares	755	825	655	810	1,240
Bonds	3,175	4,555	3,890	4,950	5,360
Netherlands					
Shares	84	38	39	65	70
Bonds	422	427	391	396	498
Debt certificates	1,448	1,475	1,765	2,039	1,972
United Kingdom					
Shares	246	448	215	898	494
Bonds	4,530	2,027	2,774	−139	1,399
Total, seven European countries					
Shares	3,398	3,148	2,474	3,873	4,658
Bonds	14,398	11,664	14,584	13,977	15,356
Debt certificates	2,225	2,241	2,579	2,779	3,098
All securities	20,021	17,053	19,637	20,629	23,112
United States					
Shares	2,272	2,513	2,844	4,583	8,396
Bonds	16,380	16,627	37,049	37,424	24,210

Source: Organisation for Economic Co-operation and Development, *Financial Statistics*, No. 4 (December 1971), p. 514.

capital markets. Business firms usually accumulate assets denominated in other currencies as a normal part of their business. Trade credits are the most common form, but longer term investments, such as real and financial assets of local sales agents, are also frequently owned. Some firms feel at times that they should borrow foreign currencies (even though they may not actually need the funds) in order to have a liability in foreign currencies equal to the value of the assets they hold in those currencies, especially if they are short-term assets. The purpose is to avoid loss from devaluation of weak currencies. Possible losses may not be large, but they constitute capital losses and must appear that way on the income statements and balance sheets. This causes many firms to worry about their foreign exposure. The added cost of borrowing an appreciating currency (as discussed above) is hidden in an overall cost figure, but a capital loss from owning a depreciating asset frequently attracts an inordinate amount of attention, and firms may thus feel they have to borrow for insurance purposes. By ending the exchange rate risk, monetary union might well end the need for this kind of borrowing as well and thus reduce the costs of doing business within the Community.

In order to provide some insight into the possible dimensions of existing capital markets, some figures are presented in Tables 1 and 2. In Table 1, the total value of new issues in the domestic markets of the member countries of the expanded EC is shown covering five years in the 1960s.[6] Also shown are the comparable flotations in the United States. In Table 2 international bond issues outside the United States (including Eurobonds) are given for the years 1967–71. The conventional wisdom that suggests that European capital markets are not well developed in comparison with those of the United States does not seem to be supported, at least as far as domestic new issues are concerned (Table 1). Such issues are a higher proportion of gross capital formation or GNP in Europe than in the United States though less in absolute size. Indeed, during 1966–67, the years of the monetary crunch in the United States, even the absolute level of new issues was the same in Europe as in the United States.

The figures in Table 1 refer to domestic issues floated in individual member countries. An example is a bond flotation of a German company

6. The figures are for the seven major countries of the expanded EC. Inclusion of the two missing countries, Luxembourg and Ireland, presumably would not change the thrust of the argument.

Table 2. *International Bond Issues outside the United States, by Currency of Denomination, 1967–71*

Millions of U.S. dollars

Currency of denomination	1967	1968	1969	1970	1971
Eurobonds[a]					
U.S. dollar	1,780	2,554	1,723	1,775	2,221
German mark	171	914	1,338	688	786
Dutch guilder	...	...	17	391	298
Other[b]	51	105	78	112	337
Foreign bonds[c]					
German mark	10	674	531	89	308
Swiss franc	153	238	196	193	669
Italian lira	24	72	24	...	32
British pound	102	19	...	12	138
Other[d]	114	132	76	84	391
Total international bonds	2,405	4,708	3,983	3,344	5,180

Source: Morgan Guaranty Trust Company of New York, *World Financial Markets* (June 23, 1972), p. 14.

a. Eurobonds are issued and underwritten by an international syndicate and sold principally in countries other than the country of the currency in which the issues are denominated.

b. Includes European unit-of-account, European Currency Unit, and pound/deutsche mark option.

c. Foreign bonds are those underwritten by a syndicate composed of members from one country, sold principally in that country, and denominated in the currency of that country.

d. Includes pound/dollar option issues.

denominated in D-marks and sold through German underwriters to German nationals, at least in the first instance. In addition, the European market absorbs foreign and international bond issues or Eurobonds (Table 2). These new flotations differ in that, in at least some respects, a foreigner is involved.[7] This represents at present the international dimension of the European market. A comparison of Tables 1 and 2 for the same years indicates that the international portion generally represents less than 20 percent of total flotations. With the advent of monetary union, the distinction between the domestic market and the international market will disappear for member countries, but not for nonmember countries, as national currencies lose significance. For residents of individual member countries, unification will lead to a fivefold expansion of the market,

7. For a description and analysis of the Eurobond market, see Morris Mendelson, "The Eurobond and Capital Market Integration," *Journal of Finance*, Vol. 27 (March 1972), pp. 110–26. For purposes of strict comparability between Tables 1 and 2, an attempt would have to be made to eliminate Swiss participation. However, the Swiss often act as intermediaries for other Europeans and other foreigners, so no adjustments were attempted.

similar in size to the market in the United States. While this expansion will be of some value, even now the size of the individual national markets plus the present option of the Eurobond market appear to be adequate for all borrowers. A company whose demands are too great for a domestic market will probably have a good enough reputation and ties to a strong mercantile bank to float a Eurobond successfully. It is hard to believe that the market is now closed to prospective borrowers who would be accommodated only with monetary union. Nevertheless, some significant qualitative changes might occur, as noted in the discussion on capital markets below.

The conclusion reached above is reinforced when one takes into account the other Euromarkets besides Eurobonds. The short-term Eurocurrency markets have grown at a tremendous pace; by December 1970, deposits were $57 billion and by mid-1972 they had reached over $71 billion. While it is dangerous for firms to use such short-term money for long-term investments, some are no doubt doing so temporarily, until long-term financing becomes available. Furthermore, another very important development in 1970–72 has been the evolution of a medium-term Eurocredit market. It is now possible for borrowers to obtain bank credits in Eurocurrencies of from three to ten years.[8] This market was reported to have reached the $10 billion level in annual flotations in 1971 and is thus already a challenge to the Eurobond market. Thus, between domestic markets, Eurocurrency, Eurocredit, and Eurobond markets, sufficient finance would seem to be available already for all worthwhile European projects and those in many other places in the world as well.

Implications for Investors

Individuals or business firms seeking new investments through capital markets will also be affected by monetary union. Investors, like borrowers, will react to the end of discrimination among member countries, to the elimination of exchange rate risks, and also to the commitment to total and irreversible convertibility of currencies. Of the three, the end to discrimination appears to be the most important. With the diminishing im-

8. For a description of the Eurocredit market, see William Low, "Explosive Growth of Medium-Term Market," *Financial Times*, March 13, 1972, p. 18.

portance of national designations and with the ending of discriminatory taxes and regulations, individual investors will be able to satisfy more easily their desired portfolio positions.[9]

The second effect of monetary union on investors, the suppression of exchange rate risk, will certainly reduce the cost of investing in other member countries for those who are risk averse and should, therefore, stimulate cross flows of investment within the Community. On the other hand, risk-seeking investors will have to search for investments outside the Community—or more strictly, those denominated in nonmember-country currencies. Similarly, the adoption of unitary monetary policy for the whole of the Community will reduce the dispersion of interest rates available at any point of time on securities originating in member countries. This trend toward convergence of interest rates has, in fact, been going on for some time. Thus, investors who try to outwit the market in anticipating interest rate changes will have to look outside the Community to find the diversity of situations they require. With respect to convertibility, the effect is unidirectional. Investors have not been much concerned about inconvertibility of European currencies for quite a few years, but a guarantee of convertibility is obviously an advantage.

Implications for Institutions and Intermediaries

Financial institutions in Europe have been changing very rapidly with the development of Euromarkets and the appearance of new entrants, especially American banks. There is evidence, however, that even more change will take place with the advent of monetary unification. Some indication of this is seen in Table 3, in which the spread between commercial bank deposit and lending rates for the EC and the United States are shown. The spread can be interpreted as a rough measure of gross profit margins in the domestic banking business. These figures may not represent exactly comparable situations among countries nor in the same country over time.

9. Frequently in the past, individual investors were confined to domestic government issues and a few others, while many interesting nongovernment issues were being retailed essentially through private placement. As to be discussed subsequently, this relates more to the quality of capital markets than to their quantitative dimensions.

(For instance, the definition of a prime borrower or compensating balance requirements may change.) Nonetheless, they are suggestive.[10]

The eight countries named in Table 3 are classified in three groups: the high-gross-margin countries of Denmark and Italy; the low-gross-margin countries of the United Kingdom, the United States, the Netherlands, and Belgium; and the two median-gross-margin countries of France and Germany. The difference in gross profit margins does not relate to efficiency in banking, since banks in all of these countries participate in the Eurodollar market at much lower spreads. They reflect instead different conditions of competition prevailing in the domestic banking business. Commercial banking in some countries is still highly cartelized; and government regulation inhibits the undermining of the cartel. A comparison of the spreads in the same country over time shows that margins do respond to changes in general monetary conditions; the spread between deposit and lending rates generally diminishes when tight money prevails and

Table 3. *Spread between Commercial Bank Deposit Rates and Lending Rates to Prime Borrowers, Seven European Countries, Eurodollar Markets, and the United States, End of Year, 1967–71*[a]

Percent[b]

Country or Eurodollar market	1967	1968	1969	1970	1971
Belgium	1.50	−0.13	0.75	1.50	1.87
France	1.85	1.85	1.35	3.15	1.90
Germany	2.00	1.62	0.37	1.50	2.25
Italy	4.00	1.00	0.75	4.25	3.50
Netherlands	0.87	0.75	−0.50	1.50	1.50
Denmark	3.75	3.75	4.50	4.00	4.00
United Kingdom	0.62	−0.13	−0.13	1.00	1.00
Eurodollars	0.88	0.88	0.87	0.88	0.88
United States	0.50	0.75	2.50	1.12	1.00

Source: Morgan Guaranty Trust Company of New York, *World Financial Markets* (February 23, 1972), p. 20.

a. At or near end of December of each year.
b. Negative signs indicate loss of money on loans.

10. In the United States, for instance, the increase in the spread to 2.5 percent in 1969 resulted from the Regulation Q ceiling on CDs. Banks during that period of tight money were unable to attract money at home at the low CD rate and were forced to borrow Eurodollars at extremely high rates. Thus, actual profit spreads narrowed rather than increased in that year.

expands during periods of ease. The important point, however, is that there is no time trend toward a reduction of spreads, which would indicate that domestic banking is not becoming more competitive (recognizing that some countries may have already reached a minimum average level).

With the achievement of monetary integration, the compartmentalization of national capital markets would be ended. The banking business would become more competitive, particularly in the high-gross-margin countries. One would guess that the banks now operating in the City of London are going to be the first to cross the traditional boundary lines, since they have prospered in a very aggressive environment, but most banks in the Community will have to change in order to survive. The spread in the Eurodollar market indicates what might become typical throughout the Community, since this aspect of banking is already competitive. What this means is that, on average, depositors might receive higher rates and borrowers pay lower rates. There might be greater variance in the rates over time, and possibly fewer banks to serve the market.

The remarkable consistency of the spread on Eurodollars, shown in Table 3, requires some comment. Eurodollar lending and deposit rates have been quite variable over time, rising from 7.13 percent in 1967 to 11.00 percent in 1969 and falling to 6.63 percent in 1971 (lending rates at the end of December in each case).[11] There have been many fluctuations in between, yet the spread has not deviated from 0.88 percent. This fact presumably could be explained either by the existence of an administered price mechanism working extremely well or by a high degree of competition. Conditions in the industry strongly suggest that competition is the answer. First of all, the low absolute level of spreads relative to domestic banking implies competition. Entry into the industry is fairly easy for financial institutions with experience elsewhere. The product being offered is identical in all respects; the information system is near perfect for buyers and sellers; aggressive bidding is known to take place. While some indivisibilities may be present because of the size of transactions, a mechanism exists for sharing risks through temporary subcontracting. Furthermore, the absence of government regulation permits entry in the first place and also forces bank managers to pay close attention to business, because "Big Brother," the central bank, is not watching out for them. Thus, the Eurodollar market has become very efficient. It is a good

11. Morgan Guaranty Trust Company of New York, *World Financial Markets* (February 23, 1972), p. 20. See Table 3 for the Eurodollar spread.

indicator of what might occur in European domestic banking following
monetary integration.

Although the above refers to commercial banking, the same argument
may hold true for other aspects of European capital markets. In his 1967
study, Sidney Rolfe noted the compartmentalization of the long-term
domestic capital markets in Europe into noncompetitive sectors.[12] He contrasted the market for domestic issues in Europe with those in the United
States and also with the market for international issues in the process of
development in Europe. He indicated the inefficiencies of the European
domestic market in relation to the other two. Both tradition and government regulation have tended to inhibit competition among institutions in
the same country and to severely restrict intra-Community competition.
This aspect of European capital markets provided the basic rationale for
an explanation of the U.S. balance-of-payments performance in certain
years, as seen by Walter S. Salant and others of the "intermediation
school."[13] Monetary unification, however, will encourage competition and
break up the compartmentalization of the long-term market so that the
same benefits will accrue to it as to commercial banking.

Implications for Market Operations

The full significance of monetary union can best be understood by
looking at the capital market as a whole rather than at the individual
elements within it. It may well be that qualitative changes of considerable
importance may occur. If they do, they will affect the average size of transactions, the instruments and methods of finance being employed, and the
specialization and sophistication of the institutions involved.

One advantage of a unified market will be its ability to absorb much
larger issues than the individual national markets. Financing needs can
thus be met through a single transaction. Europe's capacity to save is
already adequate for such a market. While firms at present can usually

12. Sidney E. Rolfe, *Capital Markets in Atlantic Economic Relationships*
(Boulogne-sur-Seine, France: Atlantic Institute, 1967).

13. Walter S. Salant, "Financial Intermediation as an Explanation of Enduring
'Deficits' in the Balance of Payments," in Fritz Machlup, Walter S. Salant, and Lorie
Tarshis (eds.), *International Mobility and Movement of Capital*, A Conference of
the Universities–National Bureau Committee for Economic Research (Columbia
University Press for the National Bureau of Economic Research, 1972), pp. 607–59.

obtain the financing they need, they frequently have to tap several markets over a long period of time, sometimes at high interest rates and always at the expense of much management talent. Better capital markets permit nonfinancial firms to concentrate their management talent on nonfinancial matters.

With monetary integration, extensive development might well occur in the equity markets of the Community. The Werner Report calls for the opening of the stock exchanges in one member country to the listing of issues of firms in other member countries, but this change alone would not make much difference. Rolfe recognizes that equity markets in Europe have suffered from fragmentation into national units, from the expense to firms of equity financing as measured by low price–earnings ratios, and from inadequate institutional support in secondary markets.[14] The approximate size of European equity markets is seen in Table 4, which also indicates the low price–earnings ratios generally prevailing. A more compelling problem is the lack of reliable information concerning the profits and net-assets positions of European firms. European investors without inside connections have to rely on a firm's reputation or that of the underwriting institution because published income statements and balance sheets of firms are so unrevealing; some firms do not make any current information available to the general public. More aggressive institutions in the market are now eliminating some of these deficiencies, but much remains to be done.

Monetary unification will require governments to remove their legal discriminations and taxes. It will accelerate changes already in process and initiate new ones. The opening of markets will increase competition among financial intermediaries. Community-wide laws, requiring firms to provide reliable information, will no doubt be promulgated for the protection of investors, although to tap the large market successfully many firms will circulate the information without legislation. Unification will spur the development of unit trusts (mutual funds) specializing in Community securities. This would permit an increase of equity financing by many small firms as well as large ones. If equity financing were available, the general public could then share the risks of investing in enterprising and novel ventures, rather than leaving such investing to family businesses. Of

14. Sidney E. Rolfe, *Capital Markets in Atlantic Economic Relationships.*

Table 4. *Capitalization, Price–Earnings Ratios and Yields, Seven European and United States Equity Markets, 1971*[a]

Country or area	Market capitalization (billions of dollars)	Price–cash earnings ratio	Price– earnings ratio	Yield (percent)
All Europe	286	7.1	16.5	3.4
Britain	130	10.4	18.2	3.1
Germany	44	5.3	13.7	3.4
France	31	4.5	13.1	4.0
Switzerland	16	n.a.	11.7	2.2
Holland	13	4.0	9.7	5.1
Italy	12	9.6	n.a.	3.0
Belgium and Luxembourg	8	5.5	16.2	6.3
United States	1,030	n.a.	18.2	3.1

Sources: *The Economist*, Vol. 243 (May 20, 1972), p. 89, except U.S. data. Market capitalization for the United States, Board of Governors of the Federal Reserve System, *Federal Reserve Bulletin*, Vol. 58 (June 1972), Table 5, p. A73.10; the net worth of U.S. holdings is represented by the total holdings of corporate shares minus liabilities. U.S. price–earnings and yield figures, *Economic Indicators* (April 1972), p. 34.
n.a. Not available.
a. U.S. capitalization data are for December 31, 1971. Other U.S. data are for 1971. The dates for the other data were not given in the source cited, but were current when *The Economist* article was prepared.

course, all of this could take place now under the terms of the Treaty of Rome. However, the fact that insufficient progress has been made so far may indicate that to bring such changes about will take something like monetary unification.

It is even possible that markets will evolve for financial instruments not now in existence. For instance, a market could develop for short-term financial paper in Europe similar to the one in the United States. With deep enough markets, some firms might find it cheaper to raise short-term money through direct sales to investors by using only a financial specialist but no banking intermediary. Also, a Community-wide secondary market might be organized for real estate mortgages, particularly on commercial property appealing to institutions, such as life insurance companies or pension funds with long-term liabilities. Alternatively, the mortgage markets could be joined by cross-national solicitations of funds by savings and loan banks or other mortgage lending institutions. With the end of legal discriminations and the erosion of national prejudices, many of these new devices are possible.

Implications for the European Community

No doubt monetary unification will lead to more efficient capital markets and greater economic welfare. Part of the gain will be due to economies of scale, but part will be because financial resources are withheld from low-productivity uses or because favored borrowers are forced to pay the full cost of finance. The dynamic sectors of the economy will benefit a great deal, while some traditional sectors may be hurt. Economic change generally causes pain to some, and the evolution of private capital markets is no exception.

Monetary unification should also spur other aspects of integration within the Community, for financial, real, and institutional (political) development must evolve simultaneously. As Community-wide financing on reasonable terms becomes available on an increasing scale, business firms are likely to become more aggressive in invading the domain of other member countries through direct investment. The local control of finance has been one of the reasons that there has been little intra-European investment to date (September 1972). With monetary unification, political institutions in the Community will be challenged to keep pace with financial developments. Governments will have to find the means to countervail huge financial institutions that consort to abuse their market power. Differences in laws and administration dealing with business profit taxes, depreciation rules, accounting standards, and the like, will also be subject to more abuse with greater financial mobility within the Community unless steps are taken to reduce them.

The operation of Community monetary policy cannot follow the pattern, simply on a larger scale, of existing national policies. The effectiveness of national monetary policy rests in part on imperfections in capital markets, and monetary unification will substantially reduce these imperfections. Thus, with monetary unification, economic conditions are likely to be much less responsive to changes in monetary policy. This is not to suggest that monetary policy will be unimportant (the reverse is closer to the truth), but it does mean that it will be very hard for the authorities to obtain quick results by, say, restricting a particular class of borrowers. The evolution of sophisticated private capital markets means that new channels of borrowing will develop if the authorities press very hard on particular arteries. Monetary authorities will have to concentrate on the prevention of disequilibria rather than on their cure; they will have to take into account long lags between action and response. In general, authorities will be less successful at fine-tuning the economy than the national authorities have been in the past.

Implications for the United States

The United States will probably not be affected to any substantial degree by private capital market developments resulting from European monetary union. It is assumed that wholly owned American subsidiaries incorporated in the EC will be accorded Community status in all laws and regulations dealing with the capital market. Although American subsidiaries will also be helped, the improvement in the European capital market will make European firms more formidable competitors everywhere. Some American firms will thus feel the pinch of greater competition. But in general, assuming the maintenance of equilibrium exchange rates, the economic welfare of the United States is advanced by prosperity in other countries.

The United States does have particular interest in the Eurodollar and Eurobond markets. If economic and monetary union is achieved, much of the raison d'être for the Euromarkets will disappear, but not all. European borrowers and investors will find the large domestic market more attractive to them for their European business. But when European borrowers need funds for external investments or want external assets, the Euromarkets will still have appeal, the degree depending on what the United States does with its capital controls. Even though European controls are ended, there will be a Euromarket if U.S. controls are maintained. If the United States and Europe both end controls, then the Euromarkets will probably become little more than convenience banking. American financial institutions that now specialize in the Euromarkets would shift over into the domestic European business, assuming again that there is no discrimination against them. European markets might even attract other American institutions, particularly those that have specialized in organizing small equity underwritings.

If the European capital market develops the breadth and depth of the U.S. market, many ties will develop between the two. Private financial market connections will be just one of the many factors drawing the two areas together. Europeans will be investing in the United States, even if not to the same extent as Americans invest in Europe. Sophisticated financiers speak the same language in all countries; no doubt Europe and the United States would benefit from such a close dialogue.

Transition Problems and Possible Solutions

The European capital market is now fragmented for most purposes into national units. As discussed above, economic welfare and political unification will be advanced by the evolution of an integrated private capital market resulting from economic and monetary union. The transition from fragmentation to complete unification, however, raises some difficult problems. Some of the problems arise from conditions prevailing at the time the transition is begun and others arise from difficulties encountered when harmonizing and coordinating conflicting regional situations.

To effect economic and monetary union requires the harmonization of fiscal policies and the coordination of monetary policy relating to both targets and instruments. Even assuming that, at the time of implementation, the exchange rates of member countries are in equilibrium with each other, the actual act of harmonizing and coordinating is going to upset these relations. Investors in the member countries have different long-run price expectations because of different histories of price performance. These price expectations will be reflected in different long-run interest rates, which will cause capital flows among the members for some period of time and which will subsequently end as expectations harmonize. Thus, whatever pattern of exchange rates provides equilibrium at the outset will probably need revision during the transition. Also, monetary institutions and the monetary instruments of the authorities differ among member countries. These differences have implications for the time structure of interest rates, the competitiveness of debt relative to equity financing, and other characteristics of finance. As these instruments are harmonized, an adjustment will occur in capital markets that will require some other adjustments between members. Moreover, as in the past, the further integration of labor markets will require some adjustments. Finally, as differences in control relating to the inflow and outflow of capital from member to nonmember countries are harmonized, some adjustments will be required among the members as well as with nonmember countries. Hence, the act of harmonizing and coordinating will probably require exchange rate adjustments.

Is it reasonable to assume, however, that an equilibrium pattern of exchange rates exists at the starting point? The floating of the British pound in June 1972 indicates that this assumption is likely to be incorrect. Big disequilibria often hide smaller ones. The U.S. dollar was seriously out of balance with the currencies of other industrial countries, as was recognized by the December 1971 Smithsonian Agreement. Lesser disequilibria are appearing only as the U.S. payments position is corrected. Big exchange rate adjustments often reveal the need for smaller ones in their wake. This need was recognized in some degree on December 18, 1971, but perfect foresight did not crown that agreement. Because it is impossible to foresee the future, some flexibility must be maintained in exchange rates. The exchange rate adjustments necessary because of incomplete adjustment may not be additive to the requirements noted above, but it would be the height of coincidence if they were exactly offsetting.

The achievement of the required adjustments will not be easy, particularly because of the priorities established in the Werner Report. The Werner group agreed to make exchange rate parities rigid at the earliest stage of unification rather than as the final step, which is a logical alternative. Furthermore, monetary policy—an alternative method of adjustment among member countries during the transition—must be coordinated in order to serve the needs of the EC as a whole. What this describes is the classic dilemma of policy makers with too few instruments for the number of targets.

The dilemma is compounded by the position taken by the French government after the Werner Report was tabled.[15] The French were particularly strong supporters of the idea of monetary union at the time of the 1969 Hague conference. Clearly, rigid exchange rates remove one of the problems that have plagued the common agricultural policy, a policy of particular interest to the French. Also, Georges Pompidou recognized the advantage to French diplomacy of seizing the political initiative at the right moment. But as the political implications of monetary union were enunciated by the Werner group, the French reverted to the Gaullist position of opposing strong Community institutions that would challenge national sovereignty. Thus, the French want a currency with no head!

15. Hans Tietmeyer, "European Economic and Currency Union—A Political Challenge," *Europa Archiv*, Vol. 26 (June 25, 1971), pp. 409–20.

Some indication of French thinking on this point is seen in the writings of Edmond Giscard d'Estaing.[16] While his reasoning is addressed to world problems, the rationale also fits intra-Community problems. Giscard d'Estaing has regarded fixed exchange rates as an economic necessity and an article of faith. Freedom of action is recognized as leading to optimal results only if every member country has the same advantages to begin with. Unequal starting positions in terms of economic or political bargaining power require governmental intervention to compensate the weak. In the EC context, this would mean massive intra-Community fiscal transfers and transitional controls on private capital movements—a well-established French position. Freedom of capital movements would be permitted presumably only when equality was achieved. National institutions will thus have to retain their authority relative to Community institutions to maintain control.

The Alternative of Controls

This conclusion raises the issue of whether it is possible to design and administer a system of controls on private capital movements to serve the needs of internal balance during a transition period and also to proceed toward the ultimate goal of monetary union. This historical record raises serious questions in this regard, as indicated by the recent research of Alec Cairncross.[17] Of course, it makes a great difference whether the controls are intended to deal with capital inflows or outflows; whether the controls are meant to deal only with the form of financing or investment behavior; whether particular classes of flows or all flows are to be restricted; and, more specifically, whether short- and long-term flows are to be controlled or only one or the other. Some of these objectives can be achieved by controls, while many others clearly cannot.

The type of controls envisaged might include complete prohibitions (which will not be considered further because of their inconsistency with freedom of all commerce), controls on long-term portfolio capital or direct

16. Edmond Giscard d'Estaing, "Liberalization of World Trade and Monetary Circulation," in Wolfgang Schmitz (ed.), *Convertibility, Multilateralism and Freedom. Essays in Honor of Reinhard Kamitz* (Springer-Verlag, 1972), pp. 367–74.
17. Alec Cairncross, *Control of Long-Term International Capital Movements* (Brookings Institution, 1973).

investments, controls on short-term capital movements, and division of exchange markets into separate current and capital compartments. There is some evidence that limitations on outflows of portfolio capital through measures like the U.S. interest equalization tax or the British stamp duties of the 1920s are somewhat effective in limiting that particular flow, but little evidence that total outflows can be much affected. Similarly, controls on direct investment outflows, as practiced by the United States through its Office of Direct Investment and by the British controls on direct investments in nonsterling areas, appear only to have changed the form of the finance of such investment, not its amount. Conversely, the Japanese have been successful in limiting direct investment inflows. It is unlikely, however, that the Community will want to restrict long-term capital flows within its boundaries, because of their expected economic benefit.

There is less compunction about interfering with short-term capital flows within the Community, however, and even exponents of free capital movements like Hermann Abs agree to these controls, if they are required for the proper exercise of monetary policy.[18] Devices such as the German and Swiss prohibition against their banks' paying interest on deposits by foreigners, Italian restrictions on banks that force them to balance foreign asset and liability positions, secondary reserve requirements to be posted by firms on foreign borrowing, and the myriad controls imposed by the French and the British governments are all available—but to what purpose? Leads and lags still provide tremendous scope for uncontrolled capital movements. In extreme cases, paper currency can be carried across borders, as the Italians and Swiss have discovered. Many knowledgeable central bankers recognize that these controls have only a small effect on the aggregate of flows, although individual financial institutions can be severely restrained. With sufficient profit incentive, any business firm or individual can, like a bank, transfer funds from one country to another.

The split exchange market that has been utilized by the Belgians and the French also offers little help with the problem of controlling capital movements. The Belgian experience seems to indicate that the market for current and capital transactions can be separated successfully only as long as the exchange rates in the two markets do not diverge appreciably—that is, when the separation is little needed—but breaks down when they begin

---

18. Hermann J. Abs, "Some Thoughts on International Money and Capital Movements," in Schmitz (ed.), *Convertibility, Multilateralism and Freedom*, pp. 199–207.

to diverge a great deal.[19] Furthermore, the complexity of the apparatus to keep the several markets of the Community currencies separate appears to work against the general use of this device. Donald Hodgman suggests that three separate markets would be required for each currency to separate intra-Community and external capital movements as well as current transactions.[20] Clearly, the number of cross rates requiring arbitrage would create a nightmare for central banks.

The magnitude of the task involved in controlling capital movements within the Community for the purpose of maintaining internal balance over time would be enormous. The controls would have to be flexible enough to cause flows to reverse direction in response to changed conditions. Regardless of the methods used, controls almost certainly would fail to push overall flows in the desired direction. Rather, ineffective controls would be likely to lead to demands for and exercise of even greater interference in private transactions, creating further incentive to avoid them. It may well be that attempts to make a transition to monetary union through the use of controls would cause an unstable situation. As governments sought to ease an imbalance through controls, even greater imbalances might result. While governments learn from experience, so do private markets, and the anticipation of controls might itself cause instability.

Is it possible for the European Community to reach a position of eventual liberation of capital movements even though controls are utilized and intensified during the transition period? In all likelihood the answer is, No. Even maintaining the government bureaucratic and reporting system on a standby basis for emergencies may be sufficiently discouraging so that the full benefits of monetary union will not be realized. This does not mean that monetary unification is not possible; it means only that it does not appear to be achievable with the priorities set down in the Werner Report. In order to make the adjustments to regional imbalances that develop during the transition period, some flexibility of exchange rates will have to be maintained until the very end of the transition. This is the same con-

19. See Armin Gutowski, "Flexible Exchange Rates vs. Controls," in Fritz Machlup, Armin Gutowski, Friedrich A. Lutz, and others, *International Monetary Problems* (American Enterprise Institute for Public Policy Research, 1972), pp. 67–84.

20. Donald R. Hodgman, "European Monetary Integration: Problems and Prospects," *Kredit und Kapital* (Berlin), Vol. 5, No. 3 (1972), pp. 249–65.

clusion reached by Bela Balassa through a different route.[21] Since large parity changes would obviously be very disruptive to the Community, particularly if steps are taken—as they should be—to liberalize private capital movements, the best method of maintaining equilibrium would be through small and gradual parity changes.

Exchange Rate Flexibility during Transition

A regime of gradual exchange rate parity adjustments within the EC points to three areas of interest: the operations of the CAP, the need for a band within which spot exchange rates may fluctuate, and the possibility of developing a key currency within the Community. With respect to all three subjects, a regimen of gradual parity adjustments is of importance and subject to misunderstanding.

It is sometimes suggested that the CAP could not be maintained with flexible exchange rates or even frequent parity changes. The evidence for this position comes from the difficulties the CAP has experienced with every parity change in the past. But previous changes have all been of great magnitude. A regime of gradual parity changes would not introduce the same kind of problem. Even with fixed parities under the present system, farmers are not fully insulated from fluctuations in market prices. With gradual parity changes farmers would face only a moderate additional source of uncertainty, and the CAP would be saved more significant disruptions. Each year some corrections are possible in crop prices and in the overall unit of account to keep inequities from accumulating. Of course, a more basic reform of the CAP, which moved toward income supports and away from price supports, would be even better, because it would improve resource allocation, but a CAP under a regime of gradual parity changes would be no worse in this respect than it is at present.

If gradual parity changes were accepted, the Community would be bound not to narrow the band of permitted spot exchange rates drastically. The larger the permitted parity change, the larger must be the band in

21. Bela Balassa, "Monetary Integration in the European Common Market" (paper presented at the Conference on Europe and the Evolution of the International Monetary System, Graduate Institute of International Studies, Geneva, Switzerland, 1972; processed).

order to contain speculative capital flows.[22] The Community might still maintain a narrower band than permitted under the rules of the International Monetary Fund—the so-called snake within a tunnel. However, it would be wise if the snake were larger than half the size of the tunnel. If the snake is fairly wide, it guarantees that the direction of any parity change by any member country is indicated by its spot exchange rate.

With the prospects of frequent and small parity changes among member-country currencies, business firms may well begin to focus on a particular currency for use within the Community. As firms have growing involvement with other member countries and become even more dependent on this business, they will find that, for long-run planning purposes, they need to fix on a particular currency and gear their operations to it. This currency will become the "key" currency for the entire Community, and that role will fall to the most predictable currency in the group. While the Italian lira has had fewer parity changes than the others, the German D-mark is more likely to predominate because of its strong performance for many years. Baron Ansiaux has suggested that the British pound could serve this function for the Community because of London's large financial market, but firms may be hesitant to take a position in sterling, as would be required, because of Britain's problem with inflation over recent years.[23]

Harmonization and Coordination

Up to now it has been assumed that the member countries have no difficulty in overcoming regional imbalance in the process of moving toward economic and monetary union. The amount of imbalance was assumed to be small and could be handled by the automatic adjustment mechanism or supplemented by small parity changes which should become less frequent over time. But the major problems of different rates of general inflation among the member countries and different attitudes toward inflation may not disappear merely with a declaration of the intent to form a monetary union. Member countries will be forced to make hard choices.

22. The relation between the two is discussed in Lawrence B. Krause, *Sequel to Bretton Woods: A Proposal to Reform the World Monetary System* (Brookings Institution, 1971), Chap. 4.
23. Baron H. Ansiaux, "Achievement of Economic and Monetary Union by the Member Countries of the European Economic Community," in Schmitz (ed.), *Convertibility, Multilateralism and Freedom*, pp. 287–98.

Fritz Machlup summarizes the difficulty.[24] He suggests that each member country must be prepared to (a) oppose the imposition of trade restrictions and exchange controls, (b) accept unemployment without a policy response unless it is in regional surplus, (c) accept economic stagnation unless it is in regional surplus, (d) accept the market-determined rate of interest, and (e) accept the importation of inflation when in the position of regional surplus. If member countries are not prepared to accept all of these restraints, monetary union will not be achieved at all or only with great difficulty.

If the Community does not accept the necessity of gradual parity changes, the difficulties of harmonizing national rates of inflation will build up pressures that in time will force major parity realignments. The problems involved are similar to those encountered by the entire international monetary system in recent years. Essentially, the EC will live under the old Bretton Woods rules, while the rest of the world moves forward to a reformed system. If the EC is willing to accept gradual parity adjustments, major explosions can be avoided, but another danger may appear. After years of transition, the Community may find that there is no tendency to converge, that parity changes are not diminishing over time. This will be a sign that member countries have not made a basic commitment to unity.

The EC Commission apparently feels that there is little prospect for convergence without the pressure of fixed exchange rates, which accounts for their insistence that rates be made rigid early. Fixing the rates might work, but it is clearly a very high-risk strategy.

Impact on U.S. Policy

The U.S. interest in the developments of private capital markets following the successful European monetary union is of second-order importance. However, failure to achieve it may be of greater importance. The United States can still prosper if Europe remains at the stage of a common market. U.S. prosperity will probably be enhanced if Europe achieves economic and monetary union. On the other hand, the United States and Europe will both suffer if Europe attempts monetary union and fails. This is one of those cases where it is not better to try and fail; indeed, it would be much better not to try at all if the risks of failure are high.

24. Fritz Machlup, "Nationalism, Provincialism, Fixed Exchange Rates and Monetary Union," in *ibid.*, pp. 265–73.

An abortive attempt at monetary union will have particularly heavy impacts on private capital markets. As pressures build up within the Community because of the premature fixing of exchange rates, further tightening of capital controls will look very attractive, particularly on capital from nonmember countries. In time, the Community will assume the characteristics of a closed and inward-looking monetary bloc, rather than an open and natural optimal currency area. Such a closed bloc will cause economic and even diplomatic difficulties for the United States. As the Community members find controls less effective than they had hoped, they may well turn to the United States to restrict capital flows from its side. Such an appeal would be dressed up in a package described as "monetary cooperation" and would present a diplomatic challenge.

Nevertheless, the plea for the United States to institute controls is to be resisted. European controls may hurt economic interests outside the Community, but their major negative effects fall on Community residents. U.S. controls, on the other hand, will hurt primarily United States residents without serving any American interest. The United States, as on August 15, 1971, must be prepared to change the dollar's exchange rate parity for adjustment needs and should not resort to controls on capital, or on current-account items for that matter. Indeed, the optimal strategy for the United States to follow, now that it has discovered how to change the parity for the dollar, is a program of liberalizing capital controls until they are finally ended. This should be an on-going policy perhaps varying in intensity, but never in direction.

Conclusion

Since the Second World War, American capital has been attracted to Europe for a number of different reasons. In the early postwar years, there was a simple shortage of capital caused by the war which American capital, both public and private, helped to overcome. By the time the European Economic Community was in the process of formation in the later 1950s, the capital shortage as such had disappeared, but a managerial and technological shortage became apparent, which American firms again helped to overcome with packaged capital transfers through direct investment. By the 1970s, a state of near equality was achieved between Europe and the United States. Selective investment opportunities existed on both sides of the Atlantic, which called for relatively limited flows of capital in both directions. Yet at times torrents of capital flowed, primarily because of inappropriate monetary institutions and disequilibrated exchange rates maintained only through the actions of governments. Now that international monetary reform is a real possibility, future disequilibria may be avoided. A new era of freedom for capital movements may well be in the offing. It would be unfortunate if the opportunity were lost because the Community, for doctrinal reasons, failed to recognize the reality of the situation.

Comments by Harold van Buren Cleveland

THE IMPLICATIONS of European monetary unification for international capital markets during the next two to three years depend mainly on whether Common Market members make more or less use of exchange controls. Longer term capital market integration in the sense of the Werner Plan (elimination of discrimination against foreign borrowers; removal of restrictions on entry into financial intermediation and of other official and private obstacles to international competition in financial services) is not likely to be attempted seriously as long as capital flows are or seem likely to be interrupted by exchange controls.

I assume that the European Community will attempt to maintain pegged and relatively fixed exchange rates. It will continue to restrict the snake to the tunnel and to work seriously, but not supranationally, at policy harmonization. The question I want to discuss is whether these assumptions are compatible with a gradual easing of existing European exchange controls in the economic environment of the next few years—during the seventies.

Lawrence Krause's paper, along with most American and much European opinion, is highly skeptical on this score. The argument is that the attempt to maintain stable pegged parities in the absence of effective supranational coordination of domestic policies, particularly monetary policies, will lead to serious payments imbalances within the Community, destabilizing speculation, and, therefore, exchange controls. In other words, the German view that "harmonizing" of policies must precede any attempt to fix rates is correct, and the French view that an attempt to fix rates will in time lead to the necessary harmonization is either quixotic or simply mistaken. The practical conclusion is that the essential condition of capital market integration in Europe is a more automatically flexible exchange rate regime, pending effective supranational policy harmonization.

I shall take the opposite view here, presenting what I hope is a plausible scenario under which the EC may be more successful than the above argument suggests in achieving substantial stability of parities, while also liberalizing exchange controls over the next two or three years. Britain and probably Italy have to be treated as exceptions, however.

Two critical assumptions underlie this scenario. First, the U.S. balance of payments on current account must improve greatly in this period as a result of the exchange rate realignments that have already occurred in 1972, a lower rate of price-cost inflation in the United States, a probable further appreciation of the yen, and substantial growth in U.S. exports to the USSR and China, financed in part by long-term dollar credits. Second, the EC member countries must make far more effort than they have in the past to finance each other's payments deficits and surpluses, through such means as liberal credit arrangements and the creation of paper reserve assets on the European level.

Exchange Rate Stability: When the Dollar Was King

During the period 1959–67, a remarkably high degree of exchange stability was maintained in Europe under the par-value system, along with considerable liberalization of capital movements. This gross fact has been played down in the extensive economic literature critical of the par-value system. The literature makes little or no distinction between the period before 1967, when the system in general could hardly be called "crisis-prone" (except with the wisdom of hindsight), and the subsequent period when the criticism clearly applies.

This curious oversight may be due to a failure to grasp adequately the nature and operations of a key-currency system. In the period 1959–67, the Western European countries except Britain normally had overall payment surpluses in an accounting sense, of which the counterparts were U.S. liquidity and official-settlements deficits. Yet, the imbalance did not lead to speculative pressure on the dollar or on European currencies, or to exchange controls, because the dollar's exchange rate was presumed to be immutable downward. This made dollar-denominated assets even more attractive relative to financial assets denominated in other currencies than they already were for many other reasons; there was no effective limit on the amount Europeans were willing to hold, counting official and private holdings together. Some European central banks would rather have held more gold and fewer dollars, but none believed in this period that their total international reserves were excessive.

Thus, there was little or no excess supply of dollars on the exchange markets in this period, although the dollar outflow may have resulted in somewhat more domestic money creation and price inflation in Europe than Europeans would have chosen for themselves if they had been in full control of the volume of high-powered money in their banking systems. But, of course, it all depended on the presumption that the exchange value of the key currency would never decline, either by reason of a U.S. devaluation or by virtue of a general appreciation of other currencies. This presumption derived essentially from the hegemonic postwar power position of the United States and was reinforced by the improving trend in the U.S. current balance between 1959 and 1964, based on declining relative prices. Also, Japan was still a minor factor in world industrial competition and the United States still had technological leadership in many industries.

In these circumstances, the substantial intercountry differences in the pace of inflation in Europe had relatively little effect on the stability of European exchange rates. The French franc was undervalued and the pound overvalued on the European plane, but the markets overlooked it. The strong external (that is, dollar) liquidity position of European central banks and of the private economy, along with the experience of exchange rate stability, the presumed immutability of the dollar, and the ideological commitment of governments and central bankers to fixed rates, all combined to inhibit destabilizing exchange speculation, except in the case of sterling.

These conditions have now changed drastically, of course. Yet, there are reasons for believing that the strengthening of the dollar that now (in September 1972) seems to be in the cards, along with the greater degree of "real" integration of the EC economies, may make it possible to maintain more or less fixed exchange parities within the EC for quite long periods.

"Openness" and Balance-of-Payments Adjustment

Recent developments in monetary theory suggest that the increased integration of the European economies and their increased "openness" to each other (the higher ratio of tradable to nontradable goods and services) tend to make monetary and fiscal policies a more effective means of maintaining payments equilibrium within the Community, and also a less costly one in terms of effects on employment or price inflation. The reason is that the marginal propensity to consume tradable goods is higher, so that a given change in aggregate income has a larger impact on the current-account balance.

Furthermore, greater openness also means that exchange rate changes have become a less effective tool of balance-of-payments adjustment because, with increasing integration, they affect the domestic price level more, and in a direction which tends to offset the competitive effect of the exchange rate change. Thus, a devaluation tends to raise domestic prices sharply both directly (competitively) and indirectly through the resulting impact on price expectations and wage decisions. The argument is that labor in open economies has learned that devaluation means more inflation; unions therefore force up wages in anticipation of a rise in living costs even before the rise has occurred (erosion of "money illusion"). This, in turn, forces the monetary authorities to "validate" the higher wage-price level in order to maintain employment.[25]

If the EC economies are, or will soon become, sufficiently open to each other to make these theoretical propositions practically important, the above considerations suggest that the problem of achieving sufficient policy harmonization to permit considerable exchange rate stability may have been exaggerated.

If relatively small changes in monetary policy, measured, for example, by changes in domestic credit expansion (DCE), are sufficient to restore current-account balance rather promptly, whereas rather large exchange rate changes are required to achieve the same result, and with considerably

---

25. It may be argued that any rise in the domestic price level resulting from a devaluation would tend to reduce the real value of the public's cash balances, which would tend to improve the country's balance of payments in two ways: (1) immediately, by pushing up interest rates and pulling in funds from abroad; and (2) with a certain lag, by causing people to spend less on goods and services, thus holding down aggregate demand and imports. However, it is doubtful that these "real balance effects" would be large, especially since the monetary authorities would be inclined to respond to an important rise in interest rates and a significant slowdown in spending by easing monetary policy.

Such real balance effects would in any event yield only a temporary improvement in the devaluing country's balance of payments, for they would not reverse the initial rise in the domestic price level, which must be assumed to be inflexible downward in the short run.

longer time lags, then policy harmonization within the EC looks much more attainable and exchange rate flexibility relatively less attractive— the more so because the structural (reallocation) effects of exchange rate changes on open economies can be politically troublesome.

The increased openness of the EC economies to each other has other implications supporting this conclusion. One is that openness tends to keep the business cycles of the European countries in phase. There is evidence that greater synchronization has, in fact, occurred. This has the direct (income) effect of keeping current payments among the members more in balance. Cyclical synchronization also means that the domestic and external ("European") objectives of stabilization policy are less likely to conflict, for at any time the members' monetary and fiscal policies are more likely to be pointing in the same direction, further easing the task of policy harmonization because less deliberate harmonization is required.

The U.S.-Canadian relationship provides a useful analogy. Canada has succeeded in stabilizing its currency relative to the U.S. dollar for long periods, whether the currency has been pegged or floating. This has been possible because Canadian monetary policy has normally been a carbon copy of Federal Reserve policy. Canada has accepted such leadership because of the openness of the Canadian economy to its southern neighbor and the resulting synchronization of the business cycles in the two countries. In these circumstances, stability of the exchange rate has mattered more to the Canadian authorities than monetary autonomy.

In principle, increased openness should help to keep price levels in European countries in line, via the direct competitive effects on market prices and via effects on price expectations and wage settlements. Moreover, if the member countries' monetary policies tend to be, on average, accommodating to the existing level of price expectations, in order to avoid prolonged business slowdowns, this, in itself, would also keep monetary policies in step. Similar monetary policies, of course, support and reinforce the tendency for inflation rates to stay in line and diminish the need for deliberate policy harmonization. However, experience in the last few years has not shown a strong tendency for a convergence of European inflation rates, perhaps because they have been affected by such "accidents" as the French general strike in 1968 and Germany's gross errors in fiscal and monetary management in 1966.

Here again, the U.S.-Canadian relationship may be relevant. The U.S. and Canadian wholesale price levels have stayed quite close together for long periods. The main divergence occurred after 1961–62, when the floating Canadian dollar was forced down from about 102 U.S. cents and then repegged at 92½ U.S. cents, a level generally considered to be substantially undervalued. During the 1960s, the Canadian wholesale price level rose more rapidly than that of the United States, with the result that by the end of the decade the normal relationship was approximately restored.

Some Qualifications

I would largely exclude Britain from these generalizations. The British economy is, and will probably remain for some years, much less open to the other main EC economies than the latter are among themselves. Moreover, its lower potential growth rate, its higher level of inflationary expectations (which is also likely to persist for several years), the greater militancy of its trade unions, and the political weakness of its monetary authorities—all these factors suggest that sterling will have a strong tendency to become periodically overvalued vis-à-vis the continental currencies.

Thus Britain is likely to be, within the EC, what it has long been in the wider monetary system: the country least able to maintain a stable parity and freedom of capital movements. Exceptions will have to be made periodically for Britain, and perhaps for Italy too, to keep them nominally in the system.

A further important qualification to the general thesis is that the exchange stability I foresee as possible within the Community is relative only. Major shocks, such as the 1968 events in France, Germany's policy errors in 1966 that produced the sharp 1966–67 recession, and labor unrest and political confusion in Italy, will no doubt recur, bringing in their wake exchange speculation and controls, and forcing parity changes from time to time. But such episodes are exogenous; they do not invalidate the main line of the argument.

Effects of a Stronger Dollar

Let me return now to the dollar and the effects of its assumed strengthening on the issue of exchange stability and controls within the European Community. The major cause of exchange controls in Europe over the last few years has not been disequilibria among European currencies but lack of confidence in the exchange rate of the key currency.

The dollar's weakness was troublesome, for two main reasons. In the first place, the supply of dollars for exchange speculation is highly elastic. Recent experience has demonstrated that the opportunity for speculative profit with a number of currencies can pull dollars at the rate of several billion a day out of the United States and the Eurodollar banking system into the exchange markets. The reasons for this remarkable supply elasticity are essentially the sheer size of the U.S. monetary system and its overseas extensions, in conjunction with the size and sophistication of U.S. multinational firms and rapid, cheap communications. The intense competition and low spreads in the Eurodollar market, which Krause's paper notes, is also an important contributing factor.

Second, the dollar's use as vehicle and intervention currency makes its presence felt, so to speak, in every exchange rate crisis. Thus, if the dollar is considered weak, an attack on any important currency in either an upward or a downward direction may develop into a general crisis involving the dollar and a number of other currencies. And the elastic supply of dollars assures that the crisis when it comes will be a big one.

All this was made clear in 1971 and again in the 1972 sterling crisis. The run on the pound in June 1972 turned into a run not simply *through* the dollar as vehicle and intervention currency but also *out of* the dollar into the stronger European currencies. If the dollar had played a purely intermediary role—that is, if there had been *no* net speculative sales of dollars for other currencies—the whole crisis would have been on a much smaller scale. The supply of pounds available for exchange speculation was much smaller than the potential supply of dollars. A sharp rise in short-term British interest rates and a temporary decline in continental money rates, in combination with Britain's existing "outward" exchange controls, would have kept the speculative movement within tolerable bounds. Germany would probably not have felt impelled to impose new controls for domestic monetary reasons. But with the dollar actively involved, the potential size of speculative inflows forced the Germans to act.

If the dollar grows strong enough so that speculation against it is not easily triggered, European exchange crises will become relatively isolated affairs, as they once were, with movements of funds on a considerably smaller scale than is at present regarded as normal. Movements of this nature can probably be financed by "recycling" or out of reserves, suitably enlarged; all but temporary controls could be avoided.

This analysis further suggests that as the dollar strengthens, European proposals for controls on the Eurodollar market may cease. The principal rationale for such controls is that the Eurodollar market provides such a large source of funds for speculation against the dollar in favor of European currencies. If this speculation is not so easily precipitated, the objections to the Eurodollar may weaken and its contribution to European welfare, as well as to the profits of European banks, may become significant again.

The additional reserves needed to defend European parities will be supplied in part by dollars. Despite many present indications to the contrary, I assume that if the dollar is seen to strengthen, European central banks will be more willing to accept dollars from each other and to increase their holdings, particularly if the United States makes some gesture in the direction of fractional convertibility, at least into Special Drawing Rights. The Federal Reserve, I assume, will normally make this liquidity available by following a generally expansive policy and offsetting the effect on U.S. bank reserves of any substantial outflows.

Dollars apart, the Europeans will surely have to make much more generous provision for the creation of international credit and reserve funds than they have done so far, if my scenario is to remain plausible. The present terms of settlement among the EC central banks of balances arising in their support operations in member currencies are obviously too onerous. The European Monetary Cooperation Fund, formally instituted in April 1973, provides the vehicle, but not yet the money. Of course, generous provision of liquidity through such a fund is likely to contribute to the inflationary bias of domestic policies in Europe. But this might, paradoxically, contribute to exchange stability in Europe, if its effect were to prolong the period in which the dollar is relatively strong vis-à-vis European currencies.

One concluding comment: The European Community is bound, I believe, to continue its efforts for European monetary unification and, as a means to that end as well as for more immediate reasons, to try to keep fixed parities with relatively narrow bands among their currencies. This effort may well break down repeatedly over the next few years, as it has twice already since spring 1972. Also, I have previously noted that Britain and probably Italy will be able to participate only partially. Traumatic events and gross policy errors will undoubtedly force parity adjustments from time to time.

Sooner or later, however, the combination of deliberate policy coordination and increased "real" integration will make it possible for something close to a European exchange rate union to emerge. I would not expect such an arrangement to amount to a full-fledged unitary monetary system with a single currency within the next ten or fifteen years, if ever. I doubt that it would involve much formal supranationalism. The national currencies and central banks will live on indefinitely. The possibility of parity changes among the members' currencies will remain, although it may become increasingly remote.

My sense of the historical inevitability of such a development reflects in part a feeling that the diffusion of industrial power in the world is strongly conducive to bloc formation. More precisely, I judge that a tolerable international monetary order—tolerable for the United States as well as for Europe—depends critically upon the emergence of a European monetary bloc unified enough to be able to tolerate a rather flexible joint exchange rate vis-à-vis the dollar.

In the shorter run, we shall have to make do with a revived but still rather wobbly and crisis-prone dollar standard, and pegged parities. It will work tolerably well, or badly, depending chiefly on the quality of U.S. domestic demand management. But in the longer run, the forces that brought the dollar down in 1971 will prevent the survival of a dollar-centered, key-currency system.

In the longer run, however, since I do not believe in the possibility of a multinational monetary system involving a high degree of automatic exchange rate flexibility for currencies generally, such as that which is implicitly advocated in Krause's paper, the only alternative to international monetary anarchy seems to be a two- (or three-) bloc system with substantial exchange rate flexibility between the blocs.

Comments by Charles P. Kindleberger

LAWRENCE KRAUSE kept to his assigned task of discussing private capital markets for most of his paper but finally broke down and addressed the question he found more interesting: whether the European Community should fix the structure of exchange rates at the beginning of the process of monetary integration or at the end. He argues that it is a mistake to start with a fixed structure and adapt national Phillips curves to it. It is better to maintain exchange rate flexibility until the last and freeze the structure as the final step.

He may be right, but I do not see how anyone knows. I recall Harold Stein saying at the end of the 1960s that, if the coal industry in the United States had been told it would be called upon to export 40 million tons of coal to Europe within a couple of years, it would have thrown up its hands and quit—the industry had to be led along. On the other hand, Roosevelt's goal of 50,000 airplanes a year, announced in 1941 when production was only a minuscule fraction of that amount, was exactly the stimulus the industry needed to gear up for a heroic effort. I cannot see that economists have any particular expertise in choosing between incremental steps and a heroic effort in monetary integration.

With this introduction, let me make a few small points about Krause's paper and then raise one aspect of the problem which he does not touch. First, my comments:

1. Krause postulates that the removal of government restrictions will improve the adjustment mechanism. I agree that this is possible, and even that it is likely. But one must recognize other possibilities. There are at least two. First, the removal of government restrictions may change nothing because the restrictions are redundant. Along with government discrimination there is also private discrimination. When the Belgians and the Dutch removed the barrier on freedom of worker movement in fashioning Benelux, workers stayed exactly where they were. Capital is likely to be more mobile than labor, but I do not regard it as proven that the only barriers to capital mobility have been governmental.

The other possibility which is likely to be realized from time to time is that capital will move the wrong way, from areas where it is scarce to areas where it is plentiful, harming rather than assisting adjustment. This may be for lack of complementary factors, or due to loss of confidence in political leadership, as in the Italian capital flight of 1963. The European Social Fund and the European Investment Bank were incorporated in the Rome Treaty against the possibility that capital would move from peripheral areas to the center. It still may do so, if not continuously, at least from time to time.

2. A small technical point: Krause discusses capital movements before and after monetary integration in relation to the need to hedge and the cost of hedging. In my judgment he does not go far enough. If all capitalists hedge exchange risk, there can be no capital movement (apart from changes in the current account), because for capital movements to take place, there must be an exchange risk. In hedging, the question is: Who

buys the counterpart of the forward exchange that the hedger is selling? If he is an arbitrageur, the capital movement is offset. If he is a speculator, the exchange risk is borne by the speculator in the forward market, rather than the initial capitalist, but the risk is still taken. It can happen that the decline of the forward exchange goes so far as to encourage new imports, which produces the current-account change previously ruled out by assumption. It is nonetheless an error, I believe, to assume a forward market with infinitely elastic demand or supply and not to take into account the counterpart of the hedging sale.

3. In his description of European capital markets, Krause presents some data on Eurodollar bonds and discusses Eurodollar short-term lending. He says these are alternatives to the European capital market, not a part of it. The root question is whether European monetary integration is to be achieved through direct connections between European capital and money markets, or whether it is to be accomplished through third markets: the Eurobond and Eurodollar markets in capital, south European workers in labor, and American-based international corporations in corporate enterprise. The issue is more political than economic. It is perfectly feasible for the German and the French money and capital markets to be integrated through the Eurobond and Eurodollar markets, as well as directly; it is possibly more efficient. Krause's paper presents the spreads between prime lending and borrowing rates as a measure of monopoly and efficiency, and it indicates that the spreads in the Eurodollar market are a small fraction of those in national money markets. In these circumstances, with economics of scale difficult to overcome, one would think that European lenders and borrowers would continue to use Eurobond and Eurodollar markets for their efficiency and regardless of their national label. Some part of the borrowing in the Eurodollar market, of course, has been a short sale of dollars, and this depends more on the rates between the dollar and the European currencies than on what happens to European monetary integration. A large part, perhaps a major part, has consisted of dollar intermediation in European capital markets, based on liquidity preference and efficiency. I should not expect that to change abruptly because of the removal of government regulations on European capital movements.

4. Is there a contradiction implicit in Krause's suggestion that locally controlled finance has limited European direct investment in the Community? Surely it has not limited direct investment by American-based

corporations, which also use local finance. I should have thought that the reason for the difference in the volume of direct investment by European and U.S. firms must be sought in other variables.

5. Krause makes the point that some capital movements which now take place in the European Community are due to a misunderstanding by investors of interest rates based on local rates of inflation. If this is the case and, for example, Italy has higher interest rates than France because of a higher rate of inflation (which is acknowledged by the Italians but not by the French), monetary integration with the wider spread of knowledge may eliminate the movement. Admittedly, such a consequence of monetary integration is possible. I find it implicit theorizing, however, to assume that money illusion on long-term contracts applies to foreign lending and borrowing but not to domestic lending. The point has been made before by analysts such as Robert Mundell. Is there, however, any evidence? On a priori grounds, I should have thought it equally feasible to maintain that all those who loaned internationally were more sophisticated than those who loaned only within the nation, with the consequence that there was less likelihood of money and exchange illusion in international lending than in domestic lending. But how does one know?

Having made these comments on the paper, let me raise a question of my own: As monetary integration proceeds in Europe, will the emerging money and capital market have a geographic location, and if so, what factors will attract it where?

On the first point, it can be held that the increased efficiency of telecommunications today obviates the need for agglomeration of financial markets which can function effectively via telephone, telegram, telex, and the like, without an actual geographic site. I would agree that this is true for new issues of bonds. I doubt that it holds for the money market, or for the secondary market. The costs of communication over distance can be readily borne by the underwriters as they spread over the financial world to sell new issues. The short-term borrower and the post-issue buyer or seller of a few bonds at retail, after the wholesaling has been completed, probably cannot carry the cost of arbitrage between markets, except for closely connected ones like London and Johannesburg in South African gold-mining shares traded on the London exchange, or Amsterdam and New York in a few U.S. and Anglo-Dutch equities. Therefore, unless there is a technical breakthrough which cheapens the picture telephone over long distances, I should forecast—admittedly on the basis of insufficient knowledge—that the European capital market would find a single center in the next ten to fifteen years.

Where? I do not know. There are a number of theories as to how a single financial center emerges and produces the economies of scale, at least in providing a liquid and efficient secondary market. Such theories argue for one or another candidate. Which is the more appropriate theory is something economists and economic historians have yet to determine.

In frequent instances the government center becomes the financial center as well. Examples are London, Paris, and Berlin. That theory argues for Brussels. If many international corporations establish European headquarters at Brussels to be near the EC Commission and European top branches of international banks move there to be near the corporations, it could happen that Brussels would become the financial center of Europe, despite its fourth or fifth place in European financial ranking.

Another theory relies on hysteresis and history. This argues for London. London was the world financial center in the century preceding 1914 or 1929. Its financiers have the skill and the tradition to enable it to dominate the European capital market the way these financiers have come to dominate the Eurodollar market (but not the Eurobond market). I have reservations. While banks like BOLSA (Bank of London and South America) have produced leadership in the Eurodollar market, the place of London is due in my judgment to the role of top branches of United States banks. In long-term lending, the British are out of it. Skill is necessary, but not sufficient. One needs capital as well. It is not enough to be a broker. The broker must also take a position and make a market. British savings are insufficient in amount, and too highly canalized into insurance companies, at least in my view, for London to be able to take leadership.

A number of purely financial towns have managed to dominate capitals and industrial cities. New York, Montreal, Frankfurt, Milan, Amsterdam, and Zurich are among these. At least one leading Italian bank moved from Florence to Rome with the transfer of the capital in 1870 but shortly thereafter transferred to Milan with its financial economies of scale. An accident of sorts may push one financial center ahead of the others (as Boston was said to have fallen behind New York in 1816 when the Boston harbor froze over, or, more likely, with the digging of the Erie Canal in 1825) and, from then on, economies of scale take over and push that center into the lead. The accident may be the political pulling and hauling that will precede the choice of location for the Committee of Governors of the Community central banks which will ultimately become the European central bank.

I raise these questions not because I can answer them but to note how seldom economics can find answers to precise questions involving familiar processes.

In summary, the crucial question is whether European monetary integration means the disintegration of European connections with American financial institutions by means of the Eurobond and Eurodollar markets. Krause guesses that it will. I guess it will not.

Discussion

THE GENERAL DISCUSSION of Lawrence Krause's paper focused on the questions of whether integration of the Community's capital markets should precede the narrowing of the bands of members' exchange rate fluctuations, the relative roles of financial and other considerations in the integration of capital markets, some of the relations between capital flows and the process of payments adjustment, and the feasibility of freeing capital movements inside the Community while controlling those between the Community and the rest of the world.

Addressing the question of whether integration of capital markets should precede limitations of intra-Community exchange rate fluctuations, Henry Wallich noted that the combination of a free capital market and absolutely fixed exchange rates implied that independent national monetary policies were impossible. To believe that private capital movements could be free, therefore, implied a belief that policies could be integrated, since every country would then be forced to act in concert with others. If integration of capital markets and establishment of fixed exchange rates really would force countries to harmonize their policies, combining those two actions would be an easier way to obtain coordination than negotiating a voluntary agreement to coordinate. Wallich could not believe, however, that this was feasible; a credible system of policy harmonization and of quasi-political arrangements permitting stable fixed rates and free capital movements would have to be established before integration of capital markets.

Frederick Strauss was also pessimistic about the possibility of integrating European capital markets before certain other conditions were met, but he emphasized difficulties created by industrial conditions. Strauss thought Krause's paper and the formal comments on it were too exclusively confined to financial considerations. In the short term, he thought a common monetary policy could not be adopted when there are tremendous divergences of economic structure and problems, and therefore of the measures that the members must take to solve their various problems. These divergences would require several years, not months, to overcome, so that even trying to arrive at a common monetary or any other policy in the short run is unthinkable. More important, even in five years or more, it is necessary to have some kind of common European company law or common industrial policy to permit mergers across national lines, which are now extremely difficult. Such mergers are necessary to maintain the scale of production needed, and to supplant what is now being accomplished only by U.S. multinational companies. These shortcomings make it difficult to organize an integrated capital market. The Canadian-American situation, to which Harold van B. Cleveland had alluded, is one in which a high percentage of Canadian production is financed and owned by American parents and the capital markets are closely related; it is not at all comparable with the relations among the Community members. Strauss considered it very unrealistic to expect capital market integration in Europe to be comparable to that between the United States and Canada.

J. Marcus Fleming also found Cleveland's citation of the Canadian-American relation unconvincing as evidence that close trading relations permitted freedom of capital movements to be combined with relative fixity of exchange rates. Fleming agreed that, in general, a high proportion of tradable goods in relation to national income increases the effectiveness of monetary and fiscal actions in adjusting balances of payments, but he thought it also increases the effectiveness of given changes in exchange rates, and for the same reason, although he conceded that money illusion might be less in the case of exchange rate changes. Moreover, the need for exchange rate changes, as well as their effectiveness, increases with the degree of economic integration. The closeness of Canadian-United States relations may permit or make necessary comparatively small changes in their relative price levels, but it does not make it easier for Canada to maintain a fixed exchange rate with the United States dollar. History demonstrates the opposite to be true. The high mobility of capital between the two countries and the high elasticity of substitution between their goods means that a slight price misalignment creates great balance-of-payments trouble for Canada; for that very reason Canada has found it more expedient than any other country to move its exchange rate. In fact, Fleming thought Canada's experience in this respect has foreshadowed what is becoming recognized in the rest of the world: the more completely one country is economically integrated with another, the more domestic autonomy requires freedom to move the exchange rate between their currencies, even though the necessary movement may be small.

Krause adduced another reason why the effectiveness of domestic policy and of exchange rate movements would be affected in the same direction. If a decrease in money illusion is making changes in exchange rates less effective, it is also enabling people to recognize more clearly the implications of monetary changes for real income, which implies that they will also offer greater resistance to small changes in monetary and fiscal policies. Deficit countries will resist adjustment by either mechanism because reduction of real income is what the adjustment process is all about.

W. Max Corden noted that Krause, in arguing that private capital movements may ease the adjustment process, had ruled out the problem of wage inflation. If one country suffers a relative loss in productivity or a reduction in demand for its products and, as a result, develops a deficit in its balance of payments, capital will flow out of rather than into the country and this will increase its unemployment problem. Fleming agreed.

Richard Cooper believed that Cleveland's analytical propositions, which suggested that market forces would tend to harmonize policies without conscious effort, were encouraging, but their validity depended on what was meant by saying monetary and fiscal policies were more effective when economies were more open. If "openness" is measured by the marginal propensity to import, an increase reduces the influence of fiscal policy on domestic demand and increases its influence on the balance of payments. But it is not clear, Cooper said, that this measure of openness is correlated with the ratio of tradable to nontradable output, which is a very different measure. As to the influence of openness on the effectiveness of exchange rate changes, the monetary view of how devaluation works suggests that greater openness, measured by the ratio of tradable to total output, should increase the efficacy of rate changes because a given percentage devaluation reduces the real value of money balances by a greater percentage, up to the point at which the public ceases entirely to hold its own country's money in favor of foreign money. The effect of openness is complicated; one cannot infer from simple propositions that adjustment will work out well.

The discussion then turned to the relation between the freedom of capital to move within the Community and its freedom to move between the Community and outside countries. C. Fred Bergsten agreed with Krause's optimism about the possibility of achieving a unified European capital market, but thought private capital flows could promote payments adjustment within the Community even if freedom of capital movements were limited to intra-Community movements. A European might even argue, he commented, that such limited freedom could promote payments adjustment more than complete freedom, because there would be no risk that the Community would lose capital to outside countries. That fact, coupled with the French preference for adjusting the Community balance of payments through a coordinated set of capital controls, raised the serious possibility that the Werner Plan's objectives will be modified to favor freedom of capital movements within the Community, retaining controls over movements into and out of it. That combination would achieve at least one of the major objectives of the Werner Plan, said Bergsten. William Cates then asked whether it was possible to have free intra-European capital movements without either extending that freedom on a most-favored-nation basis or erecting a Community set of controls, and whether it is technically and politically feasible for the Community to set up a common barrier to capital flows.

Peter Kenen argued that, apart from their feasibility, such discriminatory controls involve an important practical problem: any controls that discriminate effectively against capital flows across the boundary of the Community may seriously interfere in the short run with those markets and arrangements that are most important for encouraging capital mobility within the Community. For example, the Eurocurrency markets increase the mobility of short-term funds both within the Community and between it and outside markets. On which side of the Community barrier would these markets be placed? The same problem arises with respect to intra-firm transfers of capital by multinational firms. Controls that discriminate against flows into and out of the Community would substantially impair the prospects for greater mobility within the Community in the short run. Whether such discriminatory controls were established or not would depend in part, according to J. Carter Murphy, on what type of reformed international monetary system emerges and on the relationships between the European currencies and the dollar. How the Eurocurrency markets would be treated under discriminatory Community controls also would depend on that relationship. If their relationship is flexible but the European currencies are tightly bound to each other, the Eurodollar would presumably cease gradually to play a role in linking the European markets. Whether such discriminatory controls would be good or bad is still another question; it might be analyzed in the way the influences of customs unions on trade are analyzed, that is, by comparing the investment-creating and investment-diverting effects. Murphy had no view as to where, after such an analysis, the balance would lie.

Krause, responding to this discussion, thought the Community might develop discriminatory controls over capital movements, but that this would require restrictions on far more than capital movements. Capital controls cannot be enforced on firms operating both inside and outside the Community unless their trade is also subjected to controls. The controls that would be required are technically so demanding and would involve so great a welfare loss to the member countries that he did not believe they would be imposed. Krause thought, however, that the motivation for such controls is not merely, as Cleveland said, a lack of confidence in the exchange value of the dollar. That is one element motivating the Europeans to keep capital out so that they would not have to take more dollars into their reserves; a second factor, which appears to be more important, is that capital inflows undermine their monetary policies, whether they bring in dollars, francs, lire, or gold. This consideration suggests that capital controls will be eased only after the difficult problem of harmonizing policies is solved.

W. MAX CORDEN

The Adjustment Problem

THE PROCESS OF arriving at monetary integration and monetary integration itself are likely to affect the ways in which member countries of the
European Community (EC) eliminate, finance, or dispose of balance-of-
payments deficits and surpluses. Indeed, will there still be balance-of- $\cancel{k}$
payments deficits and surpluses? The answers to these questions are quite
simple, and the crucial question to be emphasized in this paper is: How
will these ways of adjustment affect employment and inflation within
countries?[1]

What Is Meant by Monetary Integration?

A monetary union has two essential components: exchange rate union
and capital market integration. The first component is a geographic area

The first six sections of this paper draw extensively on W. M. Corden, *Monetary
Integration*, Essays in International Finance 93 (Princeton University, International
Finance Section, 1972), which goes more fully into some of the issues raised. (Some
passages from this earlier study are directly incorporated in the first three sections.)
See also J. Marcus Fleming, "On Exchange Rate Unification," *Economic Journal*,
Vol. 81 (September 1971), pp. 467–88, and Richard N. Cooper, *Sterling, European
Monetary Unification, and the International Monetary System* (British-North
American Committee, 1972). I have benefited greatly from valuable comments by
Fred Hirsch on an earlier draft.

1. It is assumed here that the proposals to move to monetary integration in
Europe can be taken seriously. Severe doubts about that assumption are expressed
below (pp. 176–79), but such doubts are the inevitable sequel to the preceding
sections.

159

within which exchange rates bear a permanently fixed relationship to each other though the rates may vary in unison relative to nonunion currencies. The second component, an integrated capital market, is an area permanently without exchange controls for capital transactions, including interest and dividend payments. The latter also probably involves the harmonization of relevant taxes and other measures affecting the capital market. The exchange rate union component is the major concern of this paper, though the existence of capital market integration is relevant to the discussion.

A distinction should be drawn, first of all, between what I call a pseudo exchange rate union and a complete exchange rate union.

A Pseudo Exchange Rate Union

A group of countries may solemnly agree to maintain fixed exchange rates relative to each other. They may allow fluctuations of these rates within a narrow margin, but essentially they undertake to maintain fixed exchange rate relationships. At the same time each country within the group may retain its own foreign exchange reserves and its own monetary and fiscal system, and operate its monetary and fiscal policies to ensure that it does not exhaust reserves, or maybe to avoid undue accumulation. At intervals these countries' representatives meet in solemn conclave to decide whether they should, in unison, devalue or appreciate relative to the outside world.

The general system and its obvious weaknesses are readily recognized and need hardly be described in detail. In the European context, for example, at any point in time France's interests may require the union to devalue its currencies and Germany's to appreciate its currency. France in this instance would be running a balance-of-payments deficit, and to maintain a fixed rate, would have to deflate, hence creating unnecessary unemployment. If, owing to Germany's need to appreciate relative to the outside world, France is also forced to appreciate, it would have to deflate even more, suffering even greater unemployment.

There is then no real assurance that the agreed exchange rate relationships within a union will be maintained permanently. Of course, such rates are likely to be more rigid than in the absence of any agreements. But, because of the lack of assurance, this system is only a pseudo exchange rate union.

A Complete Exchange Rate Union

For real assurance of fixed exchange rate relationships, the countries must agree to do more than that. Surplus countries within the union must provide finance for deficit countries. It is not sufficient to have arrangements for limited financing, with an upper limit and with a repayment requirement. Such arrangements merely delay exchange rate changes and so allow a pseudo union a somewhat longer life than would otherwise be the case. To provide complete assurance of fixed exchange rate relationships within the union there must be unlimited, automatic, and undisputed financing within the union. Such a system is, at least technically, a complete exchange rate union. Foreign exchange reserves are, in fact, pooled.

But these measures are not really adequate, either. Unless something else is done, they do not permit a complete union to work. If each country still has freedom to manage its own monetary policy, then France, for example, can be busily expanding credit, and hence running a balance-of-payments deficit that has to be financed by its partners. If the reserves of the union run down as a result, there will be a general devaluation, which will increase partner countries' surpluses needed to finance France's deficit. There must thus be a central control over monetary policy. No country can be allowed to engage in unlimited domestic credit creation.

Consideration of common policy issues might then lead to "integration through talk," so popular in Europe: finance ministers getting together regularly to tell each other, no doubt solemnly, what their internal economic policies ought to be. But such meetings do not assure that countries will not expand, or indeed contract, credit unduly. Neither will it ensure the survival of their foreign exchange pooling, and hence the fixity of their exchange rate system. For a complete exchange rate union a communal central bank has to be established which not only holds the common foreign exchange reserves but also has the sole right to create money in the union. This is literally monetary integration. It means, of course, that there has to be a strong political authority to control the central bank, a crucial implication that goes beyond the scope of this paper.

When there is a complete exchange rate union the various countries within the union, like the regions within a country, can no longer have "balance-of-payments problems." Their balances of payments are still separate and show national deficits and surpluses, but there is only a "problem" when foreign exchange reserves are running down, or perhaps accumulating; member countries no longer have their own reserves, and national balance-of-payments problems become transmuted into an internal-balance problem.

The Central Problem

The main focus here is on the effects of European monetary integration on the United States. But the internal effects of monetary integration will govern actual European policies and are bound to attract most attention. If these internal effects are severely adverse—as is quite likely to be the case—and if this becomes clear to policy makers in Europe, there may be no monetary integration, whether pseudo or complete, and hence no external effects. Therefore, to assess how the adjustment problems of European union will affect the United States, it is essential to turn to the central problem of monetary integration, the problem of internal balance.

The Internal-balance Problem and the Wage Standard

The main point is simple, well known, but not always understood by influential non-economists in Europe. Internal balance can be thought of as the combination of unemployment and inflation that a specific country prefers from an internal point of view, given the various combinations it can choose from at any particular point in time. To take the hypothetical case:

In a world of at least three countries where fiscal and monetary policies in each country are used to maintain internal balance, country *A* may need to depreciate and country *B* to appreciate relative to the outside world, if each is to maintain internal and external balance. However, if *A* and *B* form an exchange rate union, they can jointly depreciate, which would suit *A*, or jointly appreciate, which would suit *B*. But they cannot alter the exchange rate to suit both. If the exchange rate adjustment leaves country *A* with a deficit, *A* will have to deflate, hence creating unemployment. If the adjustment leaves country *B* with a surplus, *B* will either have to be content with accumulating reserves or allow its wages and prices to rise.

The major argument is that if countries do not permit themselves appropriate exchange rate adjustments, they impose on themselves losses essentially resulting from enforced departure from internal balance. The concern here is with countries that have already formed a customs union and therefore cannot impose import restrictions or similar devices to solve their individual balance-of-payments problems.

In a complete exchange rate union as distinct from a pseudo union, the essential story is the same, although told in a slightly different way. The internal-balance problem should be viewed in terms of regions in a country. Broadly speaking, one particular level of aggregate demand associated with the appropriate exchange rate for the country (union) as a whole can maintain full employment in one region, but it may lead to inflation in another. If inflation in most regions is to be avoided, excessive unemployment in some regions may have to be tolerated.

All this can be described in dynamic terms, though it adds nothing to the main thesis. Assume that, at the outset, France and Germany are in internal and external balance, with the appropriate exchange rate relationships. Then money wages increase more rapidly in France, productivity rises more slowly, or both conditions arise; relative costs get out of line. The maintenance of internal and external balance requires France to devalue the franc relative to Germany's mark. If this is not permitted either France must deflate or Germany must inflate: one or both must depart from internal balance.

This approach, which seems to be the only one appropriate to the problem in hand, assumes that countries are on a wage standard. At any point in time each country has a certain level of money wages (or, in dynamic terms, a certain rate of increase in money wages) that, together with levels and rates of increase in productivity, determine levels of monetary demand required for full employment. Appropriate monetary and fiscal policies are then implemented to validate the money wage level. The crucial assumption is that governments are committed to full employment and that money wages are not sufficiently flexible downwards (if indeed they can be reduced at all) to "validate" given monetary and fiscal policies, rather than the other way around.

If monetary and fiscal policies were governed wholly by the requirements of the external situation rather than by the requirements of the wage standard, undue unemployment would be quite likely. Hence, exchange rate alterations are needed to adjust the external situation if both internal and external balance are to be maintained. They are required because relative costs change between countries. And relative costs change because labor costs per unit of output—the ratio of productivity increases to increases in money-wage rates—rise at different rates, the differences in money wage increases not necessarily offsetting the differences in rates of productivity increase.

Coordination of Economic Policies

In European discussions it is sometimes suggested, especially by the Germans and Dutch, that what is required within the monetary union is coordination of economic policies or, more specifically, of budget policies. The implication is that a country expanding aggregate monetary demand more than its fellow union members and then having to devalue its currency in relation to theirs does so for budgetary reasons, perhaps because it is profligate, and not in order to maintain full employment with a given rate of increase in money wages. One could accept this view if one believed either (a) that money wages are sufficiently flexible to maintain full employment with any given level of monetary demand, or (b) that full employment is not a target of policy. The logical conclusion is that, if differences in budgetary profligacy can be avoided, the need for exchange rate alterations can also be avoided. There have been various proposals in this vein that suggest economic policy should be coordinated before exchange rate relationships are fixed; these proposals imply that such coordination would make fixed exchange rate relationships possible. It is obviously contrary to the wage-standard approach and hardly seems realistic.

Clearly, what is principally required is not coordination or harmonization of budgetary policies but rather, if it were possible, some kind of coordination or harmonization of wage-rate changes. Even daily meetings of ministers of finance may find this rather difficult!

Hence, the central problem of exchange rate union is that some countries may have more unemployment and some more inflation than they want. This applies both to the pseudo union where member countries have their own foreign exchange reserves but keep exchange rate relationships fixed at least for a certain period and to the complete union where the countries have common reserves and a central source of credit creation.

Real-wage Flexibility

There is one crucial assumption in the wage-standard approach: while
money wages are not flexible downwards, real wages are. This assumption
is perhaps disputable, but in the short and medium run it seems to be
justified in the European case. A devaluation can reduce real wages below
what they would otherwise have been. A devaluation raises the cost of
living. If this leads immediately to an increase in money wages sufficient to
offset this cost rise completely, real wages will remain constant and devaluation will have been pointless. The increase in costs would have offset the
balance-of-payments benefits of the devaluation. The attempt to sustain a
certain level of real wages would then have made either unemployment or
a balance-of-payments deficit inevitable.

But evidence suggests the contrary occurs. While devaluations do probably tend to lead to some increases in money wages above the levels prevailing if there had been no devaluations, the net result is still for real
wages to fall below what they would have been. There is clearly a lag;
eventually money wages may catch up, but in the interim, the balance of
payments improves.

Money wages are rigid or nearly rigid downwards while real wages are
not because wage contracts and bargains are struck in money terms for
institutional reasons and because of elements of money illusion. The
smaller the country and the more open its economy, the less money illusion
there is. Hence a very small economy may not be a feasible currency area.
But most of the present and prospective EC members are at present feasible currency areas so that the precise considerations determining the
borderline between a feasible and an infeasible currency area, and the
appropriate policy for an infeasible area, need not be pursued here. The
argument helps to explain, however, why France should be free to have
its own exchange rate, but Nice (or Monaco) should not, and why it is
appropriate for Luxembourg to have formed a monetary union with
Belgium.[2]

2. The concept of the *feasible* currency area is discussed more fully in Corden,
Monetary Integration. It is related to the concept of the *optimum* currency area.
Some of the main ideas come from Ronald I. McKinnon, "Optimum Currency
Areas," *American Economic Review*, Vol. 53 (September 1963), pp. 717–25, and
from my colleague, Peter M. Oppenheimer.

Is the Solution Trade Union Integration?   ·

Europe is becoming more integrated. In response to the spread of the multinational corporation, trade unions are perhaps becoming more international in their outlook, and the general liaisons and attitudes encouraged by European integration are likely to foster greater contact between trade unions, and may eventually lead to some significant formal trade union integration. It is likely that intra-European wage comparisons will be made more often. These can be made much more easily if exchange rates within the EC remain fixed. Crucially, if there is a complete exchange rate union, a single currency unit (the Europa?) could, and probably would, be established; this, of course, would facilitate and even invite wage comparisons.

There is one reason for expecting that this trade union or wage integration will reduce the need for relative exchange rate changes, and so reduce or eliminate the central problem of monetary integration. Bursts of trade union activity and trade union pushfulness in one country but not in another will be less likely to occur. Indeed, wage negotiations might be Community-wide. Rates of increase in money wages might tend to become harmonized.

But that is not the whole story. First, while rates of wage increase might become harmonized, rates of productivity increase might not. Contrary to the views of the cruder advocates of British entry into the EC, there is no general presumption that British entry will raise Britain's growth rate to that of her prospective partners. If money wage rates increase at the same rate in Britain and Germany while productivity continues to grow much faster in Germany, their exchange rate relationship will certainly have to change. What is probably true is that disequilibria resulting from sharp, sudden bursts of wage pressure in one country, as in France in 1968, will be rather less probable. But dynamic disequilibria might not decrease, and in any case would not be eliminated.

Second, with wage comparisons becoming much easier there will be a tendency for the wage rates in particular occupations to become uniform throughout the Community. This could be a very important effect. With labor productivity varying between countries, and hence the real wage appropriate to full employment varying, there would be unemployment in the low-productivity countries. This is the familiar regional unemployment problem, with which individual present and prospective member countries of the Community are familiar.

To put it dramatically, if this type of wage integration really came to pass, Britain might turn into a vast depressed area. That is why, of course, it could not happen. But even such an outcome would not prevent trade unions from pushing for wage integration and exerting tremendous pressure on the system of monetary integration.

The conclusion drawn from the above arguments is that trade union integration may have harmful rather than beneficial effects.

Is the Solution Labor Mobility?

With high labor mobility in an exchange rate union, balance-of-payments adjustments could take place with little more than transitional unemployment. Restrictions on labor movement within the Community are to be removed eventually; there are, even today, fewer restrictions than in many other countries. One might expect, therefore, to find an escape from the central problem of monetary integration through labor mobility.

Consider the simplest case of a pseudo union. Suppose that country A acquires a deficit and country B a surplus. Country A deflates its economy to maintain its foreign exchange reserves and country B inflates its economy. Initially, this creates unemployment in A, so labor migrates from A to B. The expanded labor force in B makes it possible to maintain its increased level of monetary demand while avoiding further inflation. Alternatively, with a complete exchange rate union and a single central bank, the normal interregional adjustment process would create unemployment in some regions and excess demand in others. The central point is that labor mobility makes less necessary the adjustment of real wages upward or downward in response to changing demand and supply conditions. Hence, it is less necessary to use exchange rate alterations as an instrument of real-wage adjustment.

There have been large movements of unskilled temporary labor from southern Europe, mainly from outside the Community, to Germany, France, and Belgium. These labor movements are temporary, they have created social stresses, and have been induced by high real-wage differentials. Can it really be imagined that a U.K. depressed-area problem could be solved by the large-scale migration of British workers to Germany? It is conceivable; but when Britons are reluctant even to move from Scotland or Tyneside to the south, though the language is almost the same, it takes some imagination to conceive of labor mobility solving the central problem of monetary integration. It may marginally reduce problems of internal balance caused by integration, but it would take prolonged unemployment generating a spirit of hopelessness to lead to substantial emigration out of some of the Community countries into others. Furthermore, if monetary integration gets too far ahead of psychological integration—the suppression of existing nationalisms and sense of attachment to "place," in favor of a European nationalism and an American-style geographic rootlessness—then it is not hard to imagine the intensity of nationalistic reaction to any country's "depopulation."

A further more subtle point: If British workers, with their tea breaks and their relaxed habits, migrate to Germany because their "productivity" is too low for the level of real wages demanded for them by their British trade unions (and if the level of real wages in Germany is no lower), can one be sure that British habits will change and productivity increase to German levels?

Hence, if monetary integration leads to the enforcement of Community-wide levels of minimum real wages, it may create inevitable unemployment irrespective of the geographic mobility of the unemployed.

Is the Solution Capital Mobility?

One leg of monetary integration is the exchange rate union and the other leg is private capital market integration. Can the second leg come to the rescue of the first and overcome the central problem it poses? The answer is that in the short run capital integration can indeed help, but in the long run, while having its own advantages, it cannot really solve the problem. The main point, while often obscured, is very simple. No country or region can borrow indefinitely on a private market, however open and efficient the market is, to sustain levels of real wages, and hence real consumption levels which are too high, bearing in mind the productivity of the country or region.

Consider first the pseudo union. The exchange rate of a country is fixed and fiscal policy is used to maintain a level of aggregate demand which achieves domestic full employment. This leads to a current-account deficit. Either the government can borrow directly on the Community capital market, or the rate of interest can be increased, thereby attracting an inflow of capital. Hence, a capital-account surplus would balance a current-account deficit. This is the familiar monetary-fiscal policy mix which, in the short run at least, can achieve simultaneous internal and external balance with a fixed exchange rate.

But this is only a short-run solution. The integration of the Community capital market will make a temporary solution easier to achieve, so that the Community countries can do without short-run exchange rate adjustments on this account. But any country which continues to borrow to an extent that it absorbs an increasing proportion of the Community's capital resources will force up the rate of interest against it. Furthermore, as its debt obligations increase, the country will become less credit-worthy. Obviously, there is no long-term solution here. Of course, a country can borrow on the capital market indefinitely, or for long periods, if new productive investment opportunities are opening up, but that is another matter.

Essentially, the same point applies within a complete exchange rate union. No region in the United States can borrow indefinitely to sustain real-wage and consumption levels that are out of line with the region's productivity and the demand for its products. Banks, governments, or branches of firms cannot borrow indefinitely, other than to finance productive investment.

Is the Solution Fiscal Integration?

There are three aspects of fiscal integration or disintegration relevant to discussion of the adjustment problem.

The first point to note is that it is conceivable for countries to maintain separate fiscal policies even within a complete exchange rate union. Governments could still run budget deficits, but these would no longer be financed by their respective central banks. They would have to borrow on the Community capital market. The rate of interest and availability of funds on this market would be determined by the Community central bank. But this leads to the point made above: governments can run budget deficits to sustain domestic employment, and finance them on the Community market only for limited periods. If they retain the right to do this, however, their short-run national unemployment problems may be less than when they do not have this right.

The alternative would be for the EC Commission itself to have the right to borrow from the central bank if necessary, and to determine its pattern of spending in the light of national employment situations. The Commission is likely to be less responsive to varying national employment issues than the national governments themselves. Hence, if fiscal integration means depriving national governments of the right to run deficits and surpluses as they choose (as is hinted in the Werner Report but is, in fact, rather unlikely) then in the short run the central problem of monetary integration would probably be intensified, though it would not make any difference in the long run.

The second point concerns regional policies. Are they a substitute for exchange rate adjustment? Regional policies usually entail subsidies from the central fiscal authority to poorer regions in a country, or perhaps to regions suffering losses in real income because of lessened demand for their products. If the demand for British exports declines, for instance, and Britain is not allowed to devalue, financial contributions from the Community coffers can sustain incomes and employment. This is equivalent to foreign aid, just as Britain's prospective contributions under the common agricultural policy (CAP) are a form of foreign aid, principally to France. Conceivably, contributions under such regional policies may be used to ease the adjustment problems of a region or a member nation to changed demand conditions. But subsidization and hence financing are involved, as distinct from pure adjustment.

By contrast, devaluation, when it successfully lowers real wages, is solely a form of adjustment. Of course, it is true that permanent financing might be regarded as a form of adjustment, but it is adjustment by the donors, not the recipients, of the subsidies.

The real issue is whether regional policies are likely to be adequate to compensate for the absence of the exchange rate instrument. It seems most unlikely. At present (in 1972) the sums available to the Community regional funds are very small. A very large expansion will be needed if the Commission is to use such regional policies as a solution to possible problems. Member nations will have to be willing to contemplate large transfers over long periods from the Community as a whole to specific members. The countries in need of assistance may not be the poorest members, they may simply be those that are seeking to live beyond their means, owing to demand shifts against them or the excessive expectations of their workers. It is difficult to imagine other members countenancing such situations. Even now central governments in countries such as Britain are rarely prepared to subsidize their depressed regions to the extent necessary to eliminate the considerable regional variations in unemployment rates.

The third point to remember in regard to fiscal integration is that the centralization of social security payments financed by contributions or taxes on a progressive basis would have some stabilizing and compensating effects and so would modify the adverse effects of monetary integration. But such policies have not yet eliminated regional unemployment problems in existing nation-states, though they have made unemployment more tolerable. In the case of the EC, there is great doubt whether the necessary degree of subsidization across countries will be politically acceptable.

Implications for External Exchange Rate Flexibility

The disadvantages outlined above of the effects of monetary integration on the prospectively integrating countries suggest some doubt that monetary integration will in fact take place. However, assuming that it does, what are the likely effects on the Community's external economic policies?

An exchange rate union is free to alter its common exchange rate relative to the outside world. Hence, the integrated Community could alter its rate relative to the dollar. In principle, leaving aside various difficulties, the Community could allow its exchange rate to float, or it could peg the rate and adjust it occasionally. Is the establishment of such a union, whether pseudo or complete, likely to result in greater or less exchange rate flexibility than in the present circumstances?

The Pseudo Union

A pseudo union is likely to lead to less exchange rate flexibility than a complete union. Each country will continue to have its own reserves and be in charge of its own policies. The countries will agree to keep exchange rates fixed in relation to each other or allow them to fluctuate within a narrow band. In principle, they can periodically agree to adjust their common rates relative to the dollar. But there will always be conflicts of interest; one country will want to devalue relative to the dollar and another to appreciate. All these discussions will lead to speculative capital movements. So it would be safest and easiest to keep all exchange rate relationships fixed; it would be the obvious line of least resistance.

An exchange rate union would thus be achieved by a system of completely fixed exchange parities relative to all currencies. This has been the line of thinking of at least some advocates of European monetary integration. They have wanted their countries to avoid altering exchange rates relative to each other but, since the countries have so far not set up adequate machinery for a proper monetary union, they have tried, albeit unsuccessfully, to avoid all changes in exchange rates, even those in which their rates would move together relative to the dollar. More recently, some advocates of integration have favored a joint float relative to the dollar, but this presents difficulties because of the inevitable conflicts of interest generated by the central problem of monetary integration. [In March 1973 Belgium–Luxembourg, Denmark, France, Germany, and the Netherlands agreed to a joint float of their currencies; they were later joined by Norway and Sweden.—Editors' note.]

All this assumes that a pseudo union represents a genuine attempt to maintain fixed exchange rate relationships within the union. It must be distinguished from an essentially make-believe union with no true commitment to maintain relative exchange rates within the union. In such a union, a country could always opt out when its fundamental balance-of-payments position appears adverse (as Britain did in 1972). It may mean less short-term fluctuations, but in the medium and long runs, exchange rates would be just as flexible as in the absence of any so-called union.

Even if the European Community eventually attains a complete exchange rate union, a pseudo union is an inevitable first step, possibly lasting a long time. The EC will probably continue to push for exchange rate rigidity, with all the problems that that implies. This may lead, also, to the continued accumulation of dollars by European surplus countries, and perhaps to the imposition or tightening of controls on capital movements on both sides of the Atlantic.

Arguably, this is the single most important conclusion of this paper. But, having stated this, the point must be qualified. The main concern of the members of the pseudo union will be not to upset the delicate balance of exchange rate relationships between them. The argument above has been that, for this reason, they may be unwilling to alter any of their own exchange rates relative to any country at all. It means that they will be unwilling to take exchange rate initiatives. But this does not necessarily exclude an outside country from altering its rate. No particular difficulty may be presented when Japan, for instance, appreciates relative to gold or the dollar, or some other country devalues.

What about the United States? It is all a question of the numéraire. If the dollar were the de facto numéraire, as it has been in the past, then there may be a problem. But if gold is the numéraire, as de jure it is now, or perhaps SDRs (Special Drawing Rights), then there is no problem provided the United States is willing to alter its exchange rate. Thus, an American devaluation relative to the EC expressed as a rise in the dollar price of gold might be acceptable, while the same relative devaluation brought about by an appreciation of EC currencies relative to gold would not be.

The essential argument, then, is that an American initiative would be acceptable, and indeed would have to be acceptable, to the Europeans. By contrast, because of the difficulty of reaching agreement within the EC, a joint European initiative would not be feasible, or would be avoided for fear of upsetting the delicate intra-European exchange rate relationships.

The implications of this point are significant. From the point of view of adequate international adjustment, one country, or currency unit, can pursue a policy of exchange rate rigidity, or "benign neglect," in terms of the numéraire provided other countries follow policies of flexibility. Until recently, the United States has been that one country (though the failure of other countries to follow adequately flexible policies has been the cause of inadequate adjustment). If the EC becomes an inflexible unit because of its attempt at monetary integration, it becomes desirable for the United States to forgo "benign neglect" and become flexible, as indeed it has since 1971.

The Complete Union

The preceding argument that an exchange rate union induces exchange rate rigidity relative to outside currencies does not apply if the union is complete. There are two reasons for this.

First, once there is a single currency with a single foreign exchange pool, it is technically possible and simple for the union's currency to float, whether the float be "dirty" (closely managed) or "clean." By contrast, floating in unison in a pseudo union is a difficult, if not impossible, operation.

Second, aside from the possibility of floating, it is easier to alter the common exchange rate occasionally because, presumably, economic decision making will have become more centralized. Conflicts of interest will not, of course, disappear. As some sections of a country benefit now from a devaluation while others lose, so the interests of member nations will continue to differ. But with a common central bank, and no doubt a strong political center to supervise it, exchange rate immobilism is less likely.

There remains the further question whether the complete exchange rate union is likely to lead to more or less exchange rate flexibility than the existing, or recent preunion, situation.

One consideration suggests that a complete exchange rate union may have *more* difficulty in adjusting its common exchange rate unilaterally than most of its individual members have now. The enlarged European Community, if converted into an area of monetary integration, will be a major world economic power. It will then have the same lack of freedom as other such powers, namely Britain until the 1950s (though its constraints were to some extent self-imposed) and the United States to date (September 1972). Major economic powers cannot devalue at will, or at least, they have less freedom in choosing the final net rates. Action is necessarily limited by the reactions of other countries. With the noncommunist world economy dominated by the United States, the EC, and Japan, relative exchange rates can be adjusted only by mutual agreement. For the United Kingdom and Germany this was more or less true in 1972, but it hardly applied to the other present and prospective members of the Community.

Another point worth mentioning (although its importance is debatable) concerns the unilateral devaluation by a European country under present circumstances. If such a country wishes to devalue, it will improve its balance of payments not only relative to outside countries such as Japan, which may be desirable, but also relative to fellow EC members in deficit or in balance and which would be adversely affected by the devaluation. The fellow members will then exert pressure against the first country's devaluation. A chain effect is set up. Finally, a new equilibrium is established where several countries will have devalued. This may well be a desirable equilibrium, but the chain process through which it comes about creates frictions and resentments, and probably inhibits exchange rate adjustment. By contrast, in the complete exchange rate union, there would be a single European decision on exchange rates and so less inhibition to adjustment.

The importance of this point is doubtful because the chain analogy really applies only to the situation existing before there was coordination within the Group of Ten. Chain reactions have been avoided in recent years by the Group of Ten haggling about exchange rates, of which the Smithsonian Agreement is the most notable example.

Exchange Controls of the Monetary Union

Would the monetary union make more or less use of controls of various kinds on current- and capital-account items in its balance of payments with the outside world? All exchange controls within the monetary union will have to be removed, but this does not, of course, exclude controls applying to funds flowing into or out of the union as a whole. Lawrence Krause discusses elsewhere the effects of monetary integration on the capital market. Here only two points should be noted.

First, the need for exchange controls for balance-of-payments reasons depends on the extent of exchange rate flexibility. If exchange rates become less flexible relative to the outside world than they are without monetary union, then the imposition and tightening of exchange controls are more likely since controls, or attempted controls, are a substitute for exchange rate flexibility. On the other hand, if the external exchange rate becomes more flexible, controls are less likely. The conclusion follows that the long period of pseudo union expected if the march to monetary integration is to continue may invite *more* exchange controls, rather than less, affecting the dollar and other outside currencies simply because the pseudo union would lead to more exchange rate rigidity. This conclusion does not apply to a complete exchange rate union since such a union might well adopt a policy of exchange rate flexibility relative to outside currencies.

The second point applies to the complete union, where exchange rate flexibility relative to outside countries is much more of an option than in the pseudo union. The choice between exchange controls of various kinds, however ineffective, and exchange rate flexibility is to some extent ideological. Whose ideology will then prevail in the monetary union? If one were to extrapolate from the past and the present, the answer is obvious. Whereas the Germans and the Dutch, and to a lesser extent the Italians, the Belgians, and the British, are market-oriented, the French have a predilection, if not a consistent policy, in favor of controls. Therefore, the union would probably be control-oriented. In light of recent history, this is not entirely a frivolous comment.

It is worth stressing that, just as a customs union involves not only the removal of trade barriers within the union but also the establishment of a common external tariff, so an exchange rate union involves not only the fixing of relative rates within the union but also the pursuit of a common balance-of-payments policy relative to outsiders. Just as the height of the common external tariff reflects the attitudes to tariffs of different members, so the common balance-of-payments policy will reflect the interaction of the varying philosophies of the more influential members of the union.

Some Realities

The Werner Report, which was endorsed by the EC Council of Ministers in February 1971, was quite specific in its proposals. It recommended "the realisation by stages of economic and monetary union in the Community," concluding that "economic and monetary union is an objective realisable in the course of the present decade."[3] How seriously is one to take this proposal? Its disadvantages for internal conditions in the countries concerned have already been pointed out. The proposals for monetary integration represent a pressure for exchange rate rigidity diametrically opposed to the actual tendencies, based on hard experience as well as the preachings of economists for many years, for greater exchange rate flexibility.

3. *Report to the Council and the Commission on the Realisation by Stages of Economic and Monetary Union in the Community.* Supplement to *Bulletin* 11-1970 of the European Communities, the Werner Group, under the chairmanship of Pierre Werner (Luxembourg: Office for Official Publications of the European Communities, October 8, 1970). (Hereinafter referred to as the Werner Report.)

In 1971, and again in 1972, countries endorsing the proposals have acted quite contrary to them. Germany was represented in the Council of Ministers which met in February 1971, but that did not prevent Germany floating the deutsche mark in May 1971. The British government not only accepted the proposals before the 1972 decision to float, and in fact devalue, but Chancellor of the Exchequer Anthony Barber reaffirmed his support for the movement to monetary integration in the same speech in which he defended his decision to float the pound.

How can a sound economic case for monetary integration be made? There are, to begin with, the inconveniences of destabilizing speculation. But flexible exchange rates combined with some recycling can avoid the adverse consequences of this. There are the inconveniences to trade of fluctuating exchange rates. But these are the inconveniences of jerky exchange rate changes. Changes in exchange rates are themselves required because relative cost levels and demand patterns change. Exchange rate rigidity does not eliminate the underlying changes in cost levels, in patterns of demand, and other changes, which do give rise to genuine inconveniences in one form or another.

There is the theory of optimum currency areas. It might suggest that Belgium and the Netherlands are not optimum currency areas (though even that is doubtful) so it might explain the enthusiasm in these countries for integration. But it would be hard to base a case for integrating Britain, France, Germany, and Italy on these grounds. So this body of theory will not be pursued further here.[4]

An Englishman or Frenchman might hope that monetary integration, whether pseudo or complete, would be a way of obtaining credits and extracting real resources from a chronic surplus country, such as Germany, that are not obtainable on the open capital market. But it is unlikely that integration which involves long-term financing rather than adjustment would be acceptable to Germany.

In any case, none of the advantages can possibly outweigh the cost of large-scale unemployment, the likely result of serious efforts at monetary integration. If rates of change in money wages *and* in productivity converge, the need for relative exchange rate changes may be reduced, or

4. See the discussion in Corden, *Monetary Integration*. The classic articles are Robert A. Mundell, "A Theory of Optimum Currency Areas," *American Economic Review*, Vol. 51 (September 1961), pp. 657–65, and McKinnon, "Optimum Currency Areas."

conceivably even be eliminated. Until this happens, however, it is not likely that the countries concerned will actually adhere permanently to agreed exchange rates.

In assessing the direction of monetary integration policy in the future, a number of considerations are relevant.

First, the common agricultural policy—as at present constructed—is greatly inconvenienced by changing exchange rate relationships within the EC. The aim of the CAP has been to fix in each member country the domestic money prices of agricultural goods and, at the same time, to make these uniform throughout the Community. This is brought about by changing tariffs (variable levies) continuously varied to maintain the domestic target prices, as well as by export subsidies. If France devalues and Germany appreciates then it becomes impossible to stabilize the prices of French agricultural products in francs and German products in deutsche marks and yet at the same time avoid any tariffs between the two countries. If a uniform price level throughout the Community is to be preserved for a particular product, then the domestic price must either rise in France or fall in Germany, or both.

It took a long time to negotiate this policy, and France is a heavy beneficiary: a recipient of foreign aid unrecorded by the Development Assistance Committee of the Organisation for Economic Co-operation and Development. Hence France is, understandably, heavily committed to fixed exchange rates within the EC. But it would be perfectly possible to alter the details of the policy: to replace the present arrangements with ordinary fixed tariffs and direct subsidies to poorer farmers or subsidies on production or exports, while eliminating the fixed target prices. France could then on balance be just as well off as before, but the CAP would no longer be dependent on fixed exchange rates. Naturally, countries are reluctant to touch a policy which raises so many delicate issues and took so long to negotiate. But it seems highly likely that eventually the need for the change outlined above will become apparent and a principal reason for the pressure to integrate will melt away.

Second, a complete exchange rate union would require a powerful Community central bank, and this would, in turn, require a strong central political authority. It seems at present hardly conceivable that either France or Britain would accept this degree of centralization. It would be quite out of character with French positions taken on so many issues in the EC. The French preference is for a pseudo union, mainly for the sake of the common agricultural policy. But a pseudo union has built-in weaknesses. It is likely to survive for any length of time as an area of fixed exchange rates only if it is genuinely believed to be a temporary stage toward a complete exchange rate union, and if there is a clear ideological commitment to the latter.

Third, the French are interested in some form of monetary integration so that Europeans will present a common front in negotiations with the United States on international monetary and other questions. This is not the place to investigate the motives of the French, or what their positions will be, but it needs to be stressed that monetary integration as defined in the Werner Report and in this paper is not necessary for such a common front. Indeed, there may be a confusion about the meaning of monetary integration. Perhaps this will be clarified in time once the full implications of monetary integration are understood. It is true, of course, that a pseudo union would make an effective common front more likely while a complete union would make it inevitable.

There are political and institutional motives for sponsoring monetary integration, or at least for talking about it, or appearing to agree to it, even when governments have apparently no intention of adhering to the implications of the agreements. A discussion of such motives goes beyond the adjustment problem per se. There may also be some straightforward failures of economic understanding, possibly of quite elementary kinds. In any case, it seems highly likely that the full economic implications of monetary integration will gradually come to be appreciated. After some delay the Werner Report is finally giving rise to conferences, research papers, and, no doubt, internal government memoranda. The proposal for monetary integration is politically or ideologically motivated and (aside from the agricultural policy aspect) does not spring from economic need or analysis. Yet governments win and lose elections on the consequences of their economic policies. It seems likely, though of course not certain, that a reassessment of the proposals already tabled will in due course take place.

Impact on U.S. Policy

Finally, what is the American interest? A somewhat arbitrary selection of such concerns could include the following:

Policies to Maintain Internal Balance

A primary American interest is that the federal government and the Federal Reserve Board should be able to pursue policies aimed at internal balance—some appropriate combination of near-full employment and modest inflation—without being obliged to consider balance-of-payments effects. The more flexible the dollar exchange rate relationship with other currencies, the more they will be able to do this.

European exchange rate rigidity which is likely to be encouraged by the pseudo union would then have an adverse effect on the United States if the United States pursued inappropriate policies. But there is no reason why it should do so.

If the Europeans are accumulating dollars and fail to appreciate their currencies, the United States has four main options. The first option is to pursue contractive policies which will indeed reduce the dollar outflow but will also create undue domestic unemployment.

A second option is to impose controls or taxes on imports and on capital movements designed to reduce dollar outflow. Both the above options impose obvious costs and hence involve inappropriate policies. It is not suggested here that all controls on imports and capital movements impose net social costs, but if they are imposed for balance-of-payments reasons they are quite likely to do so by comparison with exchange rate adjustment.

A third option is "benign neglect": to let the Europeans accumulate dollars if they want to. It can be argued that if they fail to appreciate their currencies they must prefer accumulation. It does not do the United States any harm when other countries accumulate its currency. This is a familiar option and a widely held, and convincing, view.

A fourth option is for the United States to devalue by raising the dollar price of gold or whatever finally becomes the numéraire, such as SDRs. As pointed out earlier, the case for exchange rate initiatives by the United States is strengthened if the Europeans become reluctant to alter their rates. In any case, the availability of the latter two options suggests that a *rational* United States need not suffer more unemployment just because the Europeans are following policies of exchange rate rigidity, nor need it distort the flow of international trade or capital.

Reduction of Trade Restrictions

A second American interest is that European countries reduce to a minimum restrictions on trade and capital movements in relation to the United States. In the case of a pseudo union, exchange rate rigidity is likely to be encouraged, and this will cause such restrictions on the part of European deficit countries to increase. In the case of a complete union, if the French view dominates (but not necessarily otherwise), more use is likely to be made of restrictions in preference to exchange rate adjustment.

Avoidance of Continuing International Crises

Exchange rate rigidity in the absence of complete monetary integration encourages an atmosphere of international financial crisis. Each crisis is happily resolved by central banks lending each other money, or governments deciding to alter exchange rates, and the looming disasters that financial journalists and editorial writers hint at never seem to eventuate. But an atmosphere of uncertainty is created; there are profits to be made from destabilizing speculation; politicians, and indeed the general public, are confused; and, arguably, confidence in the private enterprise system that the United States favors is likely to be reduced.

These are all consequences that a pseudo union or make-believe union is likely to encourage. A complete union need not have these effects.

A Smoothly Functioning Monetary System

The operations of American international corporations will be facilitated by a smoothly functioning international monetary system. Particular corporations in particular circumstances may well benefit from specific controls and from the judicious movements of their funds across the exchanges. But, in general, international business will surely benefit when it can concentrate on the production and marketing of goods and services. It might appear that business would benefit from exchange rate rigidity, since unstable exchange rates are the bugbear of practical men. But, as stressed earlier, the real problem consists of unstable basic economic conditions, notably in the relationships between money wages and productivity levels in different countries, and it is to these that exchange rates should adjust. If rates fail to adjust, new problems, which may indeed affect workers rather than the international corporations, are created. And if exchange rates adjust jerkily (as they do under the Bretton Woods system and would be encouraged to do by an unsuccessful pseudo union), the problems of instability are increased.

Agreement on International Monetary Arrangements

A fifth American interest is that it should be possible to reach agreements among the major powers about international monetary arrangements: the creation of SDRs, exchange rate policy, and other important items. Failure to agree will have similar effects as continual crises. The question is whether attempts at monetary integration will make international negotiations easier or, rather, more frustrating.

First, if the Europeans aim at exchange rate rigidity and the United States at flexibility, agreement will naturally be difficult, though it might satisfy all parties if the United States became flexible and the Europeans more rigid.

Second, if complete integration were attained, agreement might be easier since there would be fewer negotiating partners. But this is not certain. A community, loosely tied together, may enter negotiations with a split personality (like the United States in international trade negotiations) and have more difficulty commiting itself to anything. Furthermore, if somewhat perverse French attitudes dominate, so that the EC negotiator is a megaphone for France, agreement may be even more difficult.

A third consideration is probably the main one: If the Europeans are preoccupied with trying to attain a monetary union that creates conflicts among them, that presents numerous technical difficulties, and that finally will not be attained, then decisions on international monetary reform will simply be postponed. In the present situation EC members feel obliged to present a common front but, since there is no natural common front, they find themselves engaging in time-consuming and often frustrating preliminary negotiations among themselves, and they are sometimes unable to arrive at any agreed decisions at all. All this inhibits international negotiations. When these negotiations are aimed at establishing some firm set of agreed exchange rates, the failure to reach agreement may not always be so undesirable, but it would certainly make the life of U.S. negotiators more difficult.

The general conclusion is that a pseudo union, or the attempt to estab- X lish it, may have some adverse effects for the United States. But provided the United States reacts intelligently and, above all, does not allow its domestic economy to run below capacity for the sake of its balance of payments, and also provided that it continues to prefer exchange rate adjustment to controls, then the effects should not be serious and, indeed, the United States may be able to ensure against any adverse internal effects.

Given all these considerations, and bearing in mind the earlier analysis, should the United States exercise pressure or persuasion against European integration? This would seem unwise.

One motive for monetary integration is to set up some kind of common front against the monetary power of the United States: against "dollar ↑ imperialism." Another motive of some advocates is to foster the movement toward a United States of Europe. Monetary integration, it is hoped, will lead to political integration, or, at least, will keep the somewhat ↗ clogged-up wheels of "locomotive Europa" moving. The idea of a United States of Europe is partly imitative of the United States—and imitation is said to be the sincerest form of flattery—but there is also the idea of setting up a rival to the United States, and indeed of weakening the power of the United States. Thus one element is anti-Americanism. It follows that any opposition by the United States to the proposals of the integration enthusiasts might be counterproductive.

As a non-American, it seems to me that the wisest policy for the United States to follow would be to "mind its own business." Let the Europeans work it out for themselves. Perhaps what the Europeans need is some alternative approach which allows for exchange rate flexibility but can be made to look like integration. But since the crucial need is psychological, or window-dressing, it would be best to leave the Europeans to resolve this problem themselves.

An alternative might be active support for monetary integration by the United States. This would be in the tradition of American backing for an integrated Europe and might well have the support of some American-controlled multinational companies. But it would disregard the true interests of the people of Europe, would not be justified by a consideration of

the American interest (apart from the goodwill among integrationists that
the United States might gain), and it would tend to identify the United
States with a cause that seems doomed from the start.

Comments by James C. Ingram

W. MAX CORDEN confronts the central issue in the debate about monetary union. I think he has given us a very careful and thorough analysis.
But perhaps it will help to sharpen the discussion if I focus on points of
dispute. I disagree primarily on the basis of his different assumptions
about the initial situation and the sequence of development in the moves
toward unity.

First, however, let me make a few preliminary comments:

A curious reversal of roles is apparent in this discussion of monetary
union. Economists seem to be saying that monetary union will not work
because sufficient political will is lacking and because the politicians never
do what they say they will do. But I wonder whether we, as economists, are
qualified to make such a political judgment. It seems to me that the economists' interest should be focused on how such a system would work if it
once got started. They should specify what are the minimum requirements
for a workable system of monetary union and then let the politicians
decide whether those minimum requirements are tolerable or not. We
seem instead to be usurping the latter role and saying, "Well, the politicians
will never do it."

In my own view, nations in the European Community do not now have
a great deal of monetary autonomy. With monetary union, they would not
be sacrificing very much on that score, and they might even be acquiring
some policy weapons that they do not have at the present time.

As mentioned in previous discussion, monetary union, if it did occur,
would bring great advantages to the European Community for intra-
Community adjustment. Henry Wallich at one point remarked that if the
Europeans really did integrate fully then there would be no internal balance-of-payments problem: no more reserve problems internally, no more
monetary crises or "hot-money" movements from one European country
to another, no problem of coordinating monetary policy because it would
be obvious no one country could pursue a separate course. . . . But then

Wallich simply stopped and said, "Well, this is a dream world and cannot exist."

Perhaps Wallich is correct. But suppose for the sake of argument that full monetary union were established. Then the central question would be whether nations, as decision units, still had the ability to influence real economic variables within their own borders. I think they do, and I think it is extremely useful here to draw attention to the analogy of regional adjustment within the United States.

Another preliminary comment: I have the impression that a great deal of economic integration has already occurred in the European Community and that perhaps the lag is on the side of monetary integration. Indeed, I think the economic integration that has already occurred has pushed the European Community toward monetary union and will push it further. Then, if the Europeans actually take the step toward monetary union, that step in itself would propel Europe toward integration of its economies in a great many ways, particularly through the capital market.

Although we are to assume that the European Community is going ahead with monetary union and to focus on discussion on the transitional problems, I do not think we are doing that. We are instead bogged down on the question of desirability and workability of the system. Corden concludes in his paper that monetary union is undesirable for the European Community because it would force member nations to accept losses resulting from enforced departures from internal balance.

The implication is that there exists an alternative in which such losses could be avoided, an alternative which in practice seems to be flexible exchange rates.

Much of Corden's paper is concerned with what he calls the pseudo union, which seems to me to be monetary union in name only. I would collapse his first two categories—the make-believe union and the pseudo union—into one, and say they are both unreal and not worthy of a great deal of consideration. I agree completely about their infeasibility and have no more to say about them. The remainder of my comments will be devoted to what Corden terms the complete union, which I think is fairly clearly defined in the Werner Report.

First, a word about the transitional phase. A key problem obviously is to convince the market that exchange rates really are permanently fixed, and that the other commitments, such as complete freedom of capital movements, are irrevocable. A number of actions can be taken by member nations to prepare the way for such a commitment, but in the end I think a kind of quantum leap will be necessary. There is no way to approach this stage gradually—by marginal reductions in exchange rate spread and increasing reserves until finally the market is convinced that the rates are fixed. That approach is unrealistic. To use another zoological metaphor, it is like trying to net a tiger by getting a little closer to him every day and gradually slipping a net around him. To catch this tiger, EC member nations will have to make some rather drastic and sudden changes in their economic policies and institutional arrangements when they go all the way to the stage of irrevocable exchange rates.

For example, every currency might be made legal tender in every country, and commercial banks be required to pay checks at par in any currency requested by the holder of the check. This would be a kind of par clearance system for the European Community. Clearly, this also implies that member nations accept a limit on monetary expansion and to that degree there must be a coordinated operation of monetary policy. Any fiscal deficits beyond the agreed limit on monetary expansion by a single nation would have to be financed by issuing bonds in Community capital markets at going rates of interest. I do not see any great loss of monetary autonomy in this kind of restriction because those countries do not now have real autonomy in monetary policy.

Corden writes of two components of monetary union—the exchange rate union and capital market integration—as if they were separable. In the first four sections of the present paper (and the first six of his Princeton essay to which he refers), he assumes zero capital movements. It is not analytically useful or even possible to make such a separation and to assume that capital movements have no influence in a study of the adjustment mechanism in a monetary union. The opportunity for goods and capital to move freely across national boundaries is inextricably involved in the adjustment mechanism, and the preoccupation with current-account balance commonly found in the theory of payments adjustment can lead to erroneous conclusions in the case of an integrated economy.

A central question at issue in this debate about monetary union is whether a separate monetary policy for each member nation is compatible with economic integration as it now exists and as it is contemplated in the European Community. Corden's answer seems to be that it is. He urges the importance of flexible exchange rates as an element of national policy for members. A flexible exchange rate would allow a member nation to have rates of change in money wages and prices that differed from the rest of the Community.

I think the answer to that question is, No. That is, I think the logic of economic integration leads countries toward common price levels and a single money, and that the existing degree of economic integration in the Community has already indicated a strong tendency toward common price levels.

Corden's preference for exchange rate flexibility depends heavily on his assumption that money illusion exists. Thus, if money wages rise more rapidly in France than in Germany, franc depreciation can preserve external balance because French workers are presumed willing to take the cut in real wages accompanying such a depreciation. Corden agrees that if money illusion does not exist, devaluation would be pointless and would not work.

In my opinion, money illusion is a very weak reed to lean upon, especially in an economic union, even one as closely integrated as Europe is already. If money illusion works at all, the effect will be short-lived. As a long-run solution to the problem of excessive wage demands by powerful organized groups, it seems to offer little help. As economic integration proceeds in a group of countries, firms and individuals will become more aware of Community-wide price levels, and the adjustment in local prices to a currency depreciation will be very quick. The speed of adjustment will increase with increasing unification. In a closely integrated group, there will be Community-wide prices for agricultural products, industrial raw materials, and any reasonably homogeneous goods.

This is not, as Richard Cooper points out in his paper, just a matter of the marginal propensity to import. It is a question of all those goods similar to imports and exports—the tradables. I know of no measures of the proportion of tradable to nontradable goods in such a union. I think it would obviously be much higher than the marginal propensity to import, and high enough to make money illusion a very weak and short-run phenomenon.

It is unlikely that militant labor will long be fooled by money illusion. Renewed demands for still higher money incomes will force further exchange rate depreciation, cause further price increases, and so on. If a national government uses monetary policy to check the spiral, then it has to thwart the demand for higher wages and higher incomes, and tolerate some unemployment. Losses caused by departures from internal balance seem unavoidable in such a hard case.

Corden's discussion, both in this paper and in the Princeton essay, is dominated by these hard, essentially insoluble cases: excessive general wage increases in one country, and attempts to support by foreign borrowing a level of real wages unrealistically far above the Community level. If people were to insist on that kind of real-wage pattern, I would have to agree that a monetary union would be in serious trouble and there would be a great deal of unemployment.

On the other hand, I cannot see that those hard cases will be solved by exchange rate adjustment. My impression is that these scenarios—that depict a wage increase in one country across the board for the entire labor force and similar actions—demonstrate that EC member nations are not accepting the discipline and restraint implied in a complete union, and that they are not really operating as part of a closely integrated economy, responding to Community-wide prices and interest rates and market opportunities. Perhaps it is because Corden is so skeptical about EC members' willingness to accept infringements on their sovereignty that he does not analyze the adjustment mechanism for a complete monetary union. I think economists should at least examine the case on the assumption that the necessary political will to unify exists.

If monetary union were in operation and there were a fall in exports caused by excessive wage demands in an industry or in a firm, by a change in taste, or by some other development, then the adjustment problem would appear to be at least manageable inside such a union.

The deficit nation—say, France—would first have adverse clearing balances which would be readily covered through the sale of financial assets in Community capital markets. There would be a little downward pressure on the French money supply and perhaps some downward pressure on income, but the multipliers would tend to be low. With prices and wages rigid downward in money terms, some unemployment will, of course, occur initially, but French industries producing largely for a Community-wide market would not be much affected by the falling output in this one industry.

So there is a balance-of-payments problem that tends to show up as a regional problem, or as pockets of unemployment in particular areas and industries. These are familiar aspects of domestic adjustment within a single nation. For example, if North Carolina tobacco exports fall off, the sales of the furniture industry are not much affected; the furniture industry produces for a national market. There are a number of ways in which to solve such problems. The solutions do not have to include exchange rate depreciation which, indeed, might be a rather blunt instrument in these particular instances.

First, unemployed resources may be drawn into other industries where output is expanding. This may be too optimistic an assumption, but Community-wide economic conditions are what matter for the development of all industries except those in which the recession occurs.

Second, the presence of unemployed labor in the industries whose exports have dropped may attract investment from other parts of the Community. After all, a time process is involved in which every year sizable new investment is taking place and entrepreneurial decisions are made about where to install new capacity. The presence of unemployed labor can be an attraction to such new investment. On the national level, one can cite cases such as New England where, after the textile firms moved out, labor supply acted as something of a pull to new plant locations. There are, of course, a number of instances, such as that of the unemployed miners in West Virginia, where this incentive is absent. Any system has to face this difficulty.

Third, perhaps emigration of labor to other regions, even to other nations, will be necessary though I do not think that international labor movements can be counted on to help the adjustment process in the European Community for some time to come.

Finally, fiscal policy can still be used as an instrument by the deficit countries to compensate for income declines, and to try to cope with local and regional employment problems. Fiscal policy can be used to expand public investment or to stimulate private investment. Such action beyond the limit of permissible monetary expansion could be financed in a Community capital market at market rates of interest. By encouraging promotion of productive investment, the governments concerned not only stimulate aggregate demand and increase employment, but also facilitate a more basic corrective through increasing capital per worker and raising productivity. So, in time, the deficit position may be remedied, but it need not be completely eliminated—at least the current-account deficit need not be. For very long periods of time, a member country can be a net borrower in the Community capital markets. Corden apparently gives short shrift to this possibility but, as I understand him, he seems always to explicitly assume that the borrowed funds are used for purposes other than productive investment. This proviso is made every time he raises the subject in both of his papers. The public borrowing is for consumption purposes; it is to maintain high levels of real wages, not to increase productive capacity. That stipulation certainly prejudices the outcome and it seems to me to be unwarranted.

Capital mobility is not just a short-run matter. There is no question of indefinitely covering a deficit by nonproductive borrowing, no question of sustaining a level of real wages unrealistically high in terms of the Community level. The countries involved must be forming real capital, and then the ratio of their debt to wealth need not be rising as they proceed to borrow more and more in the Community capital markets. I would be much surprised if there are not regions within the U.S. common market area that have been net capital importers for fifty years, with perhaps an exceptional year here and there.

I do not mean to imply that adjustment is easy. Everybody knows the difficulties of fiscal policy, its management and operation. Adjustment places even greater demands on the skills and talents of fiscal policy makers. So a government may well find itself using its fiscal machinery to stimulate private investment rather than trying to seek out productive investment on its own initiative. But a government can do both. Everybody is familiar with the Puerto Rican case, which is an example in which a local government (a regional government, perhaps) has financed an enormous number of public works, electric power installations, road systems, schools, plants, and buildings to attract industry. It has been a net capital importer on government account—a net borrower in the New York capital market—for about twenty to twenty-five years. The last time I looked at the data, the ratio of Puerto Rican debt to total government revenues was declining. Puerto Rico does not seem to be running into the limit of higher rates of interest and lower credit ratings simply because it is creating real wealth in the process of carrying out this adjustment process.

Let me end with one more comment on the depressed-area problem. Perhaps an entire nation may become a depressed area. That idea, of course, is worrisome, and it seems to me that it runs into some conflict with the principle of comparative advantage, especially if one considers how a country, or region, begins to lose its competitive position. In a monetary union, as costs and wages rise in a particular industry or in some specific firms, the managers have to cut output and lay off workers. There is a Community price level and a firm cannot produce if its costs exceed that competitive price. The presence of unemployment would seem to restrain wage demands which should prevent the loss of competitiveness from spreading to other industries. As saving and net investment take place through time, the nation's comparative advantages should expand, assisted when necessary by governmental fiscal action.

If labor unions and other groups with monopoly power force a rise in wages and prices anyway, or if the nation really has no viable resource base, then the solution may indeed be migration and decline. However, in that event no alternative system seems to offer any better solution. Flexible exchange rates in particular would not offer much help. Such a gloomy outcome seems improbable to me. Member nations in the European Community possess a sufficient range of industries and diversity of resources to allow considerable allocative adjustments to take place. Each nation will tend to specialize in goods and services in which it has a comparative advantage. Allocation will be facilitated by intra-Community movements of capital and labor, and wage and price deviations will be checked by this Community-wide market.

By analogy to Corden's concept of a feasible currency area within which money illusion is strong enough to make effective a reduction in real wages through devaluation, perhaps it can be assumed that member nations are "feasible resource areas," possessing a sufficient diversity of economic resources to support a variety of industries. So, when one industry declines, resources can be shifted to other uses. There seems to be no basis for the fear that *all* industries will decline and an entire nation become a depressed area.

Comments by J. Carter Murphy

W. MAX CORDEN's paper is rich with insights. His theme can be paraphrased; it is that European countries who pursue exchange rate union and capital market integration will find the political burdens intolerable. Individual participating countries will find themselves in internal and external equilibrium conflicts to such an extent that the whole experiment will become a rather transitory group encounter. Meanwhile, the trauma of negotiations aimed at alleviating these conflicts will stiffen the European posture toward exchange rate changes vis-à-vis the rest of the world, above all toward the United States. Hence, the experiment has important implications for Americans.

James Ingram has commented on the difficulties of integrating and harmonizing fiscal and monetary policies; and William Fellner has also spoken eloquently on that point. But difficulties on that score do not constitute Corden's central point. His focus, I believe, is that even if monetary and fiscal integration *can* be secured to a substantial degree, the problem of internal versus external balance will still remain and sooner or later it will put pressure on France, Belgium, or the Netherlands, just as it pressed on the United Kingdom in June 1972, only a few weeks after the U.K. had acceded to the exchange rate union.

I shall begin by looking at Corden's culprit. For him, the villain of the piece is the trade union which demands wage increases that, in relation to productivity change, make the region in which this occurs noncompetitive in its trading relations with others. Corden has monetary and fiscal policies play only an accommodating (validating) role in the inflationary process. The behavior of the trade unions leads to wage pressures that are felt to a different extent in the various countries; circumstances soon arise in which no common monetary-fiscal policy can validate all of these wage requirements simultaneously.

Corden may be right in his identification of the villain, but I would have thought otherwise. It would be much more in keeping with popular ideas about Western Europe—and the West Europeans' view of themselves—that the chief problem is one of disparities at any moment of time among the demand-management objectives of the Community member governments and among their choices of policy instruments, and the respective effects of these instruments on the target variables. If these policy disparities are really the prime source of the disequilibria, rather than wage or price demands enforced by monopolistic groups, then European harmonization of monetary and fiscal goals and of the methods used to attain these goals can eliminate an important source of the disequilibria among member countries that Corden worries about, and one can take a much more optimistic and sanguine view of monetary unification.

It has become commonplace to recognize that there are important cost-push elements in inflation wherever it takes place. Trade unions do have power, and they exercise it; others also have monopoly power. Can anything be said, then, about prospective trade union behavior in a well-integrated monetary and exchange rate union in Western Europe? If American experience indicates anything, it is that the trade unions will adapt and exercise their power within the constraints they confront in the market. Furthermore, they will seek to extend their bargaining domain across regional and national boundaries to make the wage bargaining arena correspond to the market within which the locus of production is highly mobile. The American trade unions have a largely unbroken record of pragmatism. The power of unions in the North and Midwest of the United States was certainly limited throughout much of the latter part of the nineteenth and the early part of the twentieth centuries by the availability of less expensive labor in the South, and, in fact, the Northern unions probably rarely imposed real-wage rates at levels, relative to productivity, which necessitated chronic unemployment. What is tolerable unemployment and what is not is, of course, a political matter, but the important point is that it is a matter to be assessed by trade union members along with other elements of the community.

Of course, there are differences in the productivity of labor among European countries and among regions and industries within countries. But I must suppose that this exchange rate union in Europe will be formed with prices and exchange rates reflecting something close to an equilibrium for the wage rate and productivity structure that exists. It would appear that policy makers in the U.K., for example, in the summer of 1972, felt that they were not close enough to such an equilibrium to look forward to the long future as a viable one. Presumably, however, if the British rejoin the Community's monetary arrangements, they will do so at an exchange rate that is reasonably appropriate and that may also avoid at least strong structural disequilibria in the near future.

In short, I would expect labor to be adaptable and that other forces also will contribute to adaptations to change. What are these forces? The answer that I think Ingram and I, and perhaps others, would give would be that, for some time to come, much of the adaptation to shifts in demand, shifts in technology, and shifts in cost throughout Western Europe will take place through capital mobility.

Corden's treatment of the role of capital mobility is a rather strange one, because, as Ingram noted, Corden sees capital movements only as a means of financing current-account deficits. That is to say, the capital which moves is consumption capital. His current-account deficit, when it occurs, goes into the payment of excessive wage demands and is consumed. Surely, it need not be so. The funds provided from an external source can make possible the production of physical capital that increases productivity and that does something, therefore, to remove disparities in productivity as they emerge as a result of shifts in demand and production circumstances.

My guess is that there will be some debate on that, because already Corden has said, "Why will capital move as investment capital into depressed regions?" That is an interesting question, but one, it is worth noting, that assumes a great deal. It not only assumes that deficits are associated with regional depression, which may not be the case, but it certainly emerges from Corden's image of the world as one in which trade unions, within national boundaries, enforce real-wage demands to which other market participants must adjust. If one cannot accept that image, then one can reason that declining relative wages in stagnant areas, in addition to investment subsidy programs in either buoyant or stagnant areas, can help to induce capital formation which will contribute to productivity.

The nature of the adjustment is also a matter of timing. Consider the sequence in a distressed region of, say, the American economy. I am told that there is in Texas a community with the name of Lopeupandhitch. I cannot say that I know the place personally, but let me use it as an illustration. Suppose that Lopeupandhitch suffers stagnation because demand for the product of its local industry has disappeared or declined; what kind of time sequence for capital imports would one look for? Could capital mobility into such a place be a corrective device? I would suppose that the Lopeupandhitch bank would in the first instance cover its losses in the inter-bank clearings by borrowing outside the community. That is to say, the current-account deficit of that region vis-à-vis the rest of the world would be covered by a flow of funds from other regions which would maintain that community's consumption in excess of its productivity for a time. Sooner or later, however, Lopeupandhitch would be a good candidate to get a new industry.

In the short run Corden may be right, both for the kind of disturbance he hypothesizes and for the one (a deflection of external demand) I have imposed on Lopeupandhitch. In such cases the capital flowing into a depressed area in the early stages of its decline will be of a sort that will primarily sustain consumption. Over longer periods of time, nonetheless, I would expect a capital inflow that would increase productivity. The investment capital will come to take advantage of an available labor force, perhaps relatively lower wages, and perhaps in response to special local government inducements. Capital coming as a factor of production will tend to get to the root of Corden's problem. There is, therefore, a dynamic element in this matter. Political assessment of the strength of monetary union may depend on judgment of how much European countries will tolerate market delays in the introduction of new productive capital to regions in a stage of incipient decline.

The spread of technology across regional and national boundaries can also contribute to adjustments. Frédéric Boyer de la Giroday spoke about the difficulty of finding proper currency with which to tip a porter in one of Europe's new international airports. In connection with the international sharing of technology, I want to emphasize that the new airports have materialized. The communications net in Europe must now be of such a character that technology can spread pretty much like good news. Rapid technological changes in France or the Netherlands are soon emulated elsewhere in the Common Market. For this reason, too, one might believe that Corden's dilemma, which led him to pessimistic conclusions about the hope for exchange rate union, may be overstated.

It should also be mentioned in connection with the discussion of wages and productivity levels that changes in labor productivity have complicated effects on a region's balance of payments, effects that Corden unfortunately has tended to gloss over. Changing a region's rate of productivity growth affects aggregate and sectoral *demand* growth as well as aggregate and sectoral *cost* conditions, so that we cannot take for granted how the region's balance of external payments will be affected, or even that any effects will occur.

In spite of these comments, I would not want to draw conclusions contrary to those of Corden: that exchange rate union and fiscal and monetary integration in Europe obviously will succeed and that there are no problems. But it does seem to me that Corden overemphasizes his case, because there are powerful forces supporting unification, if political toleration is high. These may make the institutions endure and evolve into something like the complete union that he hypothesizes.

In very general terms, my criticism of Corden's analysis of the matter is that he fails to be explicit about his model or image of the European setting and about the nature of the disturbances that he imposes upon it. In these complicated matters one must be specific about definitions and behavior responses in order to determine the possible adjustment forces. One also needs to be precise in regard to the disturbances if one wishes to be clear about the responses. Now, in part, specification is of course an empirical matter. Evidence is needed both to formulate the model and to identify those disturbances that are critical. Corden states that the critical source of disturbance is the trade union. My own contention is that disturbance is more likely to stem from a certain sloppiness in monetary and fiscal policies. That is a question on which evidence can be brought to bear.

I am also disturbed about a discussion on the difficulties of exchange rate union that does not specify the alternatives. Exchange rate unification may be an imperfect solution. Western Europe may not be an optimal currency area. But I am also not certain what the alternatives are. If the alternative, for example, is for the Europeans to continue to live with a system of adjustable pegs for their exchange rates, exchange rate union may look pretty good. If, on the other hand, the alternative is a set of gliding parities of some kind, well, that, too, would have substantial significance for Corden's position.

Corden concludes that the trauma the Europeans may face in dealing with their conflicts between internal and external disequilibria may lead them to be quite conservative, perhaps rigid, in their view of exchange rates vis-à-vis the rest of the world. Here, too, one can take an alternative position, for when a number of countries with close economic relations are having simultaneously to alter their exchange rates, there is an oligopoly problem that unavoidably involves gamesmanship. That is to say, no country can unilaterally determine its effective exchange rate if the others are also engaged in the same process. For example, in fall 1971, many countries appeared to be inconsistently arguing that the United States ought to depreciate the dollar while at the same time none of them was eager to appreciate its own currency. Clearly, governments were reluctant to face the political and economic costs of any exchange rate appreciation at all. But the problem was especially that no country wanted to appreciate so fast and far as to get out of line.

I am reminded of the Sweezy case of the kinked demand curve in which the oligopolist who raises his price fears that the other rascals may leave him isolated in his price increase in such a way that he will lose a substantial amount of his market—the *effective* price increase will have been too high—or that if he lowers his price, the other rascals *will* follow and his price cut will have been in vain. The West Europeans have had an oligopoly problem of this sort vis-à-vis the dollar, but if they reach an effective degree of coordination of their internal and external policies to overcome it, I think they may be able to follow a much more flexible policy vis-à-vis the rest of the world. Corden, I take it, agrees with me but feels that a problem arises in the pseudo union. It seems to me, however, that even in the pseudo union stage, a closer coordination of exchange rate policies could develop that might lead to acceptance of more flexible exchange rates between European currencies and the dollar.

Corden's advice to Americans is, I take it, "Stay home!" I like that advice.

Discussion

DISCUSSION was directed to the model of wage determination outlined in W. Max Corden's paper, to the role of labor market disequilibria in the problem of regional stagnation, and to the importance of money illusion in the adjustment process initiated by exchange rate changes.

Harry Johnson took strong exception to the model of wage determination postulated by Corden which is widely accepted in Britain and assumes that wages are autonomously determined through union pressure and not influenced by conditions in the labor market. An implication of such a model is that exchange rates have to be adjusted to whatever the unions decide to do about money wages. Johnson did not believe this model fits the British case. The money wages of any country involved in an international monetary system with fixed exchange rates must conform to the combination of productivity gains and world price movements. In the face of world price inflation, it is not surprising that British trade unions have tried to push up money wages for members to maintain their real wages at levels to which their marginal productivity entitles them. Union push and militancy, Johnson said, are merely institutional devices whereby market pressures communicate themselves.

It is true that a country with fixed exchange rates can change its exchange rate as a last resort, and this ability will influence the entire process of wage and price determination. As long as the fixed exchange rate holds, money wage bargains bring real improvements in welfare, and even if excessive wage increases force an exchange rate adjustment, the bargainers can hope to come out ahead.

Johnson believed that if governments no longer legitimized excessive

money wage increases through protective devices, such as import surcharges and government purchase orders, and if the possibility of exchange rate adjustments were also eliminated, then union behavior would
change accordingly. Price fixing and wage fixing are interrelated
phenomena.

Regional unemployment problems have, in Johnson's view, also been
inappropriately attributed to arbitrary wage determination. The problems
of regions like the Canadian Maritime Provinces have existed for 150
years. It is hard to believe that a condition lasting that long could be due to
arbitrary wages. In order to establish such a rationale, the argument has
to be couched in terms of sudden shifts of demand and what follows from
them. The situation in the Maritime Provinces cannot be explained by
sudden shifts in demand. The last shift in demand was the substitution of
iron ships for wooden ships back in the 1860s, and it is difficult to believe
such a factor could be a cause of disequilibrium for 110 years. Such a
model is merely a primitive extension of Keynes's hypothesis of rigid wages
in a context for which it was not intended.

Labor has a choice in many situations between high wages combined
with relatively low probability of employment and low wages combined
with high probability of employment, Johnson stated. Since leisure, as well
as income, is a valuable good and since people's preferences depend in
part on the pressures on them, people in different parts of the country may
make different choices. It is no accident that there are very high participation rates and low unemployment rates in large metropolitan areas. The
reason presumably is that the level of rents, attraction of consumption,
and similar factors lead people to choose paid labor and high money incomes at the expense of leisure time. In contrast, in the Maritime Provinces, one finds that leisure is an attractive alternative use of time and that
a subsistence level of cash income is accepted.

If one believes that the market influences the process by which money
wages are determined, then monetary integration not only may work, but
it would be an improvement over the situation where one protects unions
by last-resort devices. This is the fundamental issue.

Walter Salant considered that the Corden paper, in emphasizing downward inflexibility of absolute money wages, fails to take into account that
downward relative flexibility can occur in a world of rising money wages
and may be sufficient for adjustment. It is more feasible than absolute
downward flexibility, although even relative flexibility may be undermined
by nonmonetary aspects of integration.

John Williamson analyzed some implications of Corden's wage-standard model without accepting or rejecting the model as such. If countries are on a wage standard and an autonomous rise of wages causes adjustment problems, the resulting capital flows between regions will be pure consumption loans, limited in time and not a viable long-run solution. If, on the other hand, wages do respond to market factors, then capital flows can transfer resources that are conducive to increased efficiency. Furthermore, with a wage standard, an autonomous rise in wages will be widespread and will affect general prosperity in a region and not be confined to particular industries within the region. Regional problems may be intractable in part because there are no exchange rate policies. Unemployment figures in Iceland, for instance, may be less than in the Canadian Maritime Provinces because of the role of exchange rates. The long-run problem of adjustment among regions in Europe may be eased either because a common wage standard develops in response to closer integration of the economies and policy harmonization or because union behavior is affected by market forces, but, in the latter case, a rather long period of unpleasant unemployment may be required.

William Fellner believed that Corden's conclusions may be valid even if some of his assumptions are not. If the money wage rate is merely insufficiently responsive to market forces or responsive only with long lags, then adjustment problems will arise. Moreover, in addition to union behavior, other factors, such as unemployment compensation and minimum wage laws, rigidify money wages and cause adjustment problems. Furthermore, the real problem may be independent of unionization but result from different preferences of countries on the tightness of their labor markets. Inflation may be generated when labor shortages in certain categories of skill force up some wages; institutional factors spread the wage increase to other types of labor; and this process is permitted by the monetary authorities, who gear policy to very low levels of total unemployment. Thus, different preferences of countries will cause adjustment problems, and the differences may be hard to reconcile.

Richard Cooper noted that in thinking about problems of the European Community, the analogy to the United States with its semi-sovereign states can be carried too far. For instance, the adjustment of New England to the movement of some industries to other regions within the United States was neither quick nor smooth. Indeed, New England might have been better off if it had had an exchange rate to change in the early 1950s. The actual adjustment took ten to fifteen years, was very painful, and may have to be repeated because of the cutbacks in government expenditures on electronic and other high-technology products. Within the European context, one can ask the same question about Ireland. Rather than maintaining rigid parity with the British pound, Ireland might have been better off if it had changed its exchange rate after the Second World War, despite the high degree of capital mobility into Ireland and labor mobility out of it. Even if there are inflows of productive capital, there is no assurance that the resulting competitive improvement will be sufficient to attain or maintain full employment. Ireland for years was the depressed area of the British Isles despite this mobility; it might have been better off if it had devalued its currency relative to the British pound.

Charles Kindleberger took issue with the Corden prescription of exchange rate changes to deal with the adjustment problem arising from autonomous wage movements. Currency depreciation is unlikely to succeed in reducing real wages and therefore will not provide a solution to the adjustment problem. For real wages to be reduced, Europeans would have to suffer from money illusion, which they are as unlikely to do as the Chileans or Brazilians. Furthermore, such changes may be resisted by partner countries because of adverse direct employment consequences in their export- and import-competing industries.

Salant believed that even if money wages are fully responsive to the domestic cost of living, a devaluation ordinarily does not raise them enough to offset all its effects on foreign trade, because the cost of living rises less than the price of foreign currencies. A fully offsetting effect would be greater than necessary to restore the domestic purchasing power of money wages.

Fellner said that the whole concept of money illusion suffers from a lack of clarity. The purpose of exchange rate changes is to prevent a country from trying to live at the expense of another country's resources. The exchange rate change will alter the price structure, and the extent of decline in real wages will depend in part on the extent to which consumption is shifted away from the commodities becoming more expensive. If a deficit is to be overcome, less foreign resources must be absorbed, but there is some leeway on how people adjust to the burden.

Cooper also deemed "money illusion" to be an incorrect term, because it conveys the impression that somehow people are being fooled. It implies that they are willing to take a reduction in real wages due to a rise in prices but are not willing to take a reduction in real wages related to a reduction in money wages, and that this reaction depends on their not seeing the basic similarity between the two. To the contrary, the behavior posited by money illusion may occur when there is no illusion about real wages at all. In a world in which contracts fixed in money are used extensively to govern economic relations among people and in which relative wages are frequently as important to a given worker or group of workers as the absolute level of real wages, there are very good reasons why people will be prepared to accept a reduction in real wages via a more or less uniform rise in prices and yet be unwilling to accept a reduction in real wages that comes about through a very jerky process whereby money wages are reduced, either absolutely or relatively. Thus, a devaluation or indeed a general inflation can cause a reduction in real wages that cannot be accomplished through a reduction in money wages, and this can happen without any illusion whatever.

Furthermore, Cooper said, money illusion in that sense is not necessary for devaluation to work, to the extent that assets are denominated in money terms. Recent theoretical studies have focused on the analytical similarity between currency depreciation and a reduction in the money supply. Depreciation reduces the real value of all money balances in proportion to both the devaluation and the importance of tradable goods in the country in question. Insofar as this effect on real cash balances influences people's decisions, it will make devaluation successful in improving the balance of payments, even without money illusion. The frequent devaluations in Brazil since 1967 seem to be working very well, even though Brazilians may not have any illusions about their real wage consequence (a point also noted by Williamson). To argue that a lack of money illusion will obviate the purpose of devaluations, it must be assumed that governments also lack money illusion. In an economy where the government sector frequently purchases as much as 25 percent of goods and services, currency depreciation is also powerful fiscal policy because it reduces the real value of government expenditures. This reduction has an aggregate demand effect, unless the government raises the money value of government purchases correspondingly. Thus, the disappearance of money illusion in the strict sense of people being fooled is not sufficient to prove that devaluation will not work.

Salant noted that Corden's rationale for a deficit region not being able to borrow indefinitely to finance its deficit depends on the assumption that such borrowing absorbs an increasing proportion of financial resources available to the region from outside. This is not necessarily true in a growth situation; if the growth of financial resources available to the region is greater than the rate of growth of its borrowing, then the process could continue indefinitely.

In response to the discussion, Corden recorded his pleasure at having his paper serve as the mechanism for clarifying the fundamental issues. The two main issues revolve around importance of exchange rates as a mechanism of adjustment and capital mobility. In his view, exchange rates still do matter, and this view must be shared by the many economists supporting more flexibility in exchange rates for the international monetary system as a whole. Exchange rate changes may work because of money illusion; however, they may also work if money wages are forced up, since the catching-up process is incomplete. But, even if exchange rate changes become less effective in the future, it would be a mistake to give them up now because the absence of some flexibility will cause unemployment and real distress for people in places like Manchester and Scotland. If in the future it turns out that exchange rates within Europe are not altered very often because the economies have become more integrated, then this fact can be ratified by fixing exchange rates formally. At the present moment, it is too dangerous to commit countries to a process of fixing rates. As to the question of capital mobility, said Corden, one point of clarification needs to be added. A large amount of international capital movement does take place in response to productive opportunities, such as the capital flowing into Australia, but the extra amount of capital that is accommodating to regional disequilibria is not of this character and is the type of capital discussed in the paper. In conclusion, because Corden felt the process of fixing exchange rates would create unemployment which would be economically unfavorable to a number of countries, he did not believe they were going to be fixed.

WALTER S. SALANT

Implications for
International Reserves

MONETARY UNIFICATION, as envisaged by the European Community, is a process of evolution in stages. It is therefore more complex to analyze than monetary union, which is the final state toward which the process of unification is directed. A full analysis would have to include not only the transitional stages but the complications of alternatives in a number of dimensions, including institutional changes about which decisions have not yet been made, economic variables such as divergences of trends in rates of growth of productivity, and—probably most fundamental—the degree to which natural evolution of ideas and willingness to compromise will bring about a convergence of attitudes concerning targets of policy.

The Council of Ministers of the European Community (EC), in February 1971, adopted the recommendation of the Werner Report that monetary union should be achieved in three stages: an "experimental" first stage; a transitional second stage, which is not outlined clearly in either the Werner Report or the Council's plan but is intended to achieve

The views expressed in this paper are those of the author and should not be attributed to other staff members, officers, or trustees of the Brookings Institution. I am grateful to Fritz Machlup for calling attention in his comments to the care needed to use precisely the terms "margins," "bands," and "maximum permissible fluctuations," and the need to specify whether their relationship is to "parities" or "par values." I am grateful to Patrick de Fontenay of the International Monetary Fund for his careful reading and valuable comments, especially with regard to my usage of these tricky terms.

further ability to take Community-wide decisions and action, either through coordination of national institutions or outright transfer of powers from national to Community agencies; and the final stage of achieved economic and monetary union, with a goal of absolutely fixed exchange rates (that is, with no margin of fluctuation) and "if possible, a common currency."[1] This paper considers only the "experimental" first stage. The present rate of progress makes clear that there will be ample time in the future to consider the complexities of the later stages of unification.

Since events may take so many alternative courses, it is possible only to raise questions, not to answer them. At this early stage in the evolution both of the proposed unification and of thought about its implications for the United States, however, that may be useful, for it is important first to develop the right questions and to identify any research needed to find answers.

The most clearly established and most discussed element in the first stage of unification, as decided by the Council, is the narrowing of permitted deviations in exchange rates between pairs of members' currencies to 2¼ percent of their parities. This step, effective July 1, 1972, limits the maximum fluctuation between them to 4½ percent, half the percentage generally permitted under the Smithsonian Agreement of December 18, 1971. It should be remembered, however, that plans for this stage also called for establishment of a coordination group consisting of national rep-

1. *Report to the Council and the Commission on the Realisation by Stages of Economic and Monetary Union in the Community.* Supplement to *Bulletin* 11-1970 of the European Communities, the Werner Group, under the chairmanship of Pierre Werner (Luxembourg: Office for Official Publications of the European Communities, October 8, 1970), pp. 7–29. (Hereinafter referred to as the Werner Report.) This statement of the goal involves alternatives between which the Werner group did not distinguish. A common-currency area differs from one in which exchange rates are absolutely fixed, not only in excluding the possibility that the rates will be changed and having (presumably) only one issuer of currency, but in the fact that the entire money supply owned by residents of one region of a common-currency area constitutes a reserve acceptable for payments to residents of its other regions. On this point, see Tibor Scitovsky's pioneering essay, "The Theory of the Balance of Payments and the Problem of a Common European Currency," in his *Economic Theory and Western European Integration* (London: George Allen and Unwin, 1958), pp. 79–109. See also Harry G. Johnson, "Equilibrium under Fixed Exchanges," in American Economic Association, *Papers and Proceedings of the Seventy-fifth Annual Meeting, 1962* (*American Economic Review*, Vol. 53, May 1963), pp. 112–19, and Richard N. Cooper, *Sterling, European Monetary Unification, and the International Monetary System* (London: British-North American Committee, 1972), p. 22.

resentatives and a Commission member "to ensure reciprocal and constant information on the member states' short-term economic and financial policies and the coordination of these policies within the framework of economic policy guidelines defined by the Council"; development by national monetary authorities of measures to regulate capital inflows and neutralize their negative effects; steps to finance regional development by measures to be agreed on by October 1, 1972; setting up of a European Monetary Cooperation Fund to coordinate central-bank interventions on money markets and to harmonize reserve policies; and movement toward harmonization of fiscal policies and development of a European capital market.[2]

In considering the plan's implications for reserves, I shall begin with some general propositions concerning the Community's demand or felt need for reserves acceptable to nonmembers (which I shall call "external" reserves) before a Community central bank is established.[3] Its need for such reserves is determined by its need for total reserves less the portion of that need that can be satisfied by reserves acceptable to members but not to nonmembers (which I shall call "internal" reserves) and by substitutes for them in the form of intra-Community clearing arrangements and facilities for mutual extension of credit. The need for total reserves is affected by the amount of reserves needed to settle global imbalances and to provide the desired degree of "reserve ease" but is reduced by pooling of external reserves.[4] The portion of that need that can be performed by internal reserves and internal substitutes for them is positively related to the size of reserves needed to settle intra-Community imbalances

2. Summarized from European Community Information Service, "European Community Background Information," No. 9 (Washington, D.C., March 29, 1972; press release, processed).

3. On the differences among "need," "demand," and "desire" for reserves, see Fritz Machlup, "The Need for Monetary Reserves," *Banca Nazionale del Lavoro Quarterly Review*, No. 78 (September 1966), p. 178; Reprints in International Finance 5 (Princeton University, International Finance Section, 1966).

4. "Reserve ease" refers to the attitude of the relevant authorities with respect to their country's reserves and is used in the same sense in which Fleming uses the term "balance-of-payments ease," i.e., the extent to which the minds of officials are at ease with respect to the balance of payments, which presumably influences them in considering "how they will act on those instruments of policy that exercise a significant effect upon the balance of payments...." See J. Marcus Fleming, *Toward Assessing the Need for International Reserves*, Essays in International Finance 58 (Princeton University, International Finance Section, 1967), p. 5.

but is limited by the reserves desired to be held against the consolidated imbalances of the Community with the rest of the world, since internal reserves and substitutes for them cannot be used for that purpose. Thus, the need for external reserves is affected by all these factors.

If there are no internal reserves or substitutes for them, the need for external reserves is equal to the need for total reserves. Insofar as the latter need is determined by official-settlements imbalances, the imbalances that count are the global imbalances of the members; the distribution of these imbalances between members and nonmembers does not matter. With internal reserves, intra-Community clearing, and/or intra-Community borrowing facilities, however, the need for external reserves is reduced below the need for total reserves. Then the distribution of global imbalances between members and nonmembers becomes relevant, because the economy of external reserves is limited by the total need for intra-Community settlement and the proportion of such settlement that may be made by use of internal reserves or intra-Community substitutes for them, that is, by the amount of internal reserves held for such internal settlement. When internal reserves or substitutes for them may be used to settle all internal imbalances, only the consolidated imbalance of the Community with the outside world requires external reserves; the external surpluses of some members are available to finance the external deficits of others. This maximum economy of external reserves can be attained only when settlement between members requires no external reserves.

Thus, the effect of unification on the need for external reserves depends upon (a) its effects on the total imbalances of the members, (b) the extent of pooling of external reserves, (c) the internal imbalances of members, and (d) the degree to which internal reserves and internal substitutes for them are available and are permitted to be used instead of external reserves to settle internal imbalances.

Accordingly, this paper considers first the Community demand or need for total reserves and discusses the degree to which external reserves are likely to be economized by the development of internal reserves. Then, assuming that the world supply of reserves usable for external purposes is given, the paper examines how the effects on the Community's need for external reserves may be expected to affect the United States and the rest of the world's need for reserves and the demand for dollars. Finally, some policy implications for the United States are suggested.

The answers to many of the questions are obscure, even for a given choice among alternative possible developments. To point out their significance for the United States in a form that is operationally useful for policy also presents a problem; it is not always clear what the United States could do about matters that affect it, even when those effects are foreseeable. But I shall note some aspects that appear to have operational implications for United States policy when they arise. They are also summarized in the concluding section.

The Community's Demand for Total Reserves

How is the demand for total reserves by the Community as a whole likely to be affected by the first steps in the process of unification? In the absence of intra-Community fiscal transfers and official financing of deficit members by surplus members, the Community's total need for reserves would be equal to the sum of the needs of the individual members. The strength or weakness of their currencies would be determined by their global balance-of-payments positions, and the division of a member's total net position between its net positions with other members and with non-members would not affect its total reserve needs. This is approximately the position now. The question then becomes whether the global imbalances of individual members would differ much from what they have been in the past as a result of the enlargement of the Community and the changes in bands. That issue plunges me unavoidably into consideration of the effects of the first steps on the state of imbalances and on the adjustment process.

Perhaps most important is the possibility that enlargement of the Community will reduce the size and duration of a member's imbalances. Changes are most probable in two areas. First, change may arise because of shifts in the trade and autonomous capital flows of the applicant countries between present members of the Community on the one hand, and the countries that will remain outside it on the other. These shifts may affect both the balance-of-payments positions of the members and the responsiveness of the flows to factors tending to cause imbalances, thereby influencing both the size and persistence of imbalances. Second, there is the effect of the enlargement of the Community on private capital flows induced by imbalances in other elements of the accounts, that is, on accommodating capital flows.

The first possible influence arises mainly because the applicant countries will move inside the Community's external tariff and participate in its common agricultural policy (CAP). These changes presumably will shift some of their trade in goods and services from nonmembers to members, which may affect their total balance-of-payments positions. At the same time, these changes are likely to make their balances of payments more responsive to slight changes in competitive pressures from other members. There is no reason to suppose that the shifts of payments and receipts will be exactly offsetting, either for the applicant countries or for the original six members. For example, the United Kingdom White Paper of 1969 appears to have foreseen an adverse change in the current-account balance of the United Kingdom (mainly because of net effects on merchandise trade and contributions to the Common Agricultural Fund) and an increase in capital flows from the United Kingdom to other members.[5] It has also been suggested that there may be an increased inflow of direct investment from the United States to the United Kingdom, which might conceivably offset the adverse change expected in the current account.

To the extent that these shifts reduce the imbalances of Community members, they are likely to reduce the members' need for reserves. Whether redirection of existing gross flows of trade and capital, the development of new ones, and the disappearance of old ones will increase or reduce Community imbalances is uncertain. Aside from pointing out that it is relevant to the effects of enlargement of the Community on its reserve needs, I unfortunately cannot contribute anything new to an appraisal of how enlargement will affect the global balance-of-payments positions of any of the present members or applicants initially.

The entry of the applicant countries, however, may increase the responsiveness of the members' payments to imbalances and, therefore, increase the possibilities of adjustment without changes of exchange rates. Enlargement of the Community presumably will increase the sensitivity of intra-Community trade in response to given changes in relative prices and costs and perhaps also will increase the mobility of labor in response to given changes in relative wages. The reduction of tariffs between the applicants and the Community of Six, for example, would increase the effects of a given fall of the pound sterling in attracting demand from other members,

5. See G. D. N. Worswick, "Trade and Payments," in Sir Alec Cairncross (ed.), *Britain's Economic Prospects Reconsidered* (London: George Allen and Unwin, 1971), pp. 61–100, esp. pp. 92–99.

as compared to a situation in which British goods were subject to the Community's external tariff and their prices were not already at their import points.[6]

The second important possible effect on the total official-settlements imbalances of the members is to increase the intra-Community mobility of capital and consequently to increase equilibrating flows of capital between members. The two developments most likely to increase the mobility of capital in this way are a proposal to give priority to "progressive development of a European capital market" (along with "tax harmonization")[7] and the change in the relationship between members' internal exchange rate bands and their bands with nonmembers.

Before discussing these influences on the mobility of capital, let me make two observations about the effect of greater capital mobility on members' imbalances. The first is that increased mobility obviously can increase disequilibrating as well as equilibrating flows of capital. If strains on the Community's exchange rate band develop and the band is too narrow to accommodate to them before they become severe, speculative flows will develop, and large reserves will be needed to deal with them. Then the whole process of unification, with its assumption of fixed parities within the Community, will have broken down. A more fruitful alternative to discuss is the possibility that progress in unification will cause greater integration of capital markets and thereby facilitate equilibrating capital flows. It should be recognized, however, that the extent to which equilibrating flows will increase—indeed, the possibility that they will increase at all—depends greatly on how determined the authorities of the member countries appear to the public about maintaining the internal margins and the parities of their currencies relative to one another. Public perceptions will be affected by the evidence of the willingness of governments to coor-

6. As noted by Harry Johnson, "free trade may have a powerful . . . effect in increasing the natural competitive pressures for preserving the alignment of national price and cost levels. This would prevent the emergence of the condition that calls for exchange rate changes, namely a serious disparity between one nation's price-cost level and those of the rest of the world." Johnson, "The Implications of Free or Freer Trade for the Harmonization of Other Policies," in Harry G. Johnson, Paul Wonnacott, and Hirofumi Shibata, *Harmonization of National Economic Policies Under Free Trade* (University of Toronto Press for the Private Planning Association of Canada, 1968), p. 35.

7. European Community Information Service, "European Community Background Information," No. 9, March 29, 1972, p. 7.

dinate domestic policies and to establish internal credit facilities, clearing arrangements, or a reserve pool.

Second, I should note my belief that mobility of private capital between regions can be a major element in reducing use of official funds—and not merely because liquid capital flows can "finance" deficits temporarily. As Scitovsky and Ingram have taken the lead in pointing out, a large stock of privately held financial assets that have an intra-Community market making them readily transferable between members would be an important factor reducing the need for reserves, whether one wants to call such transfers "adjustment" or "financing."[8] Current-account deficits involve a loss of net wealth of the households and business firms incurring them, and surpluses involve a gain. To the extent that net wealth influences expenditure, changes in net wealth promote adjustment of current accounts. It may be true, as Max Corden points out, that because such changes affect spending on goods produced within the region as well as its imports, they will not resolve the conflict between external and internal balance in what he calls a "pseudo exchange rate union," that is, one in which "there is no explicit integration of economic policy, no common pool of foreign-exchange reserves, and no single central bank," such as the Community will be during the first years of the transition.[9] Whatever the merits of Corden's conclu-

8. See Fritz Machlup, "Adjustment, Compensatory Correction, and Financing of Imbalances in International Payments," in Robert E. Baldwin and others, *Trade, Growth, and the Balance of Payments, Essays in Honor of Gottfried Haberler* (Rand McNally, 1965; Amsterdam: North-Holland, 1965), pp. 185–213; Reprints in International Finance 2 (Princeton University, International Finance Section, 1965). For major statements of the view that adjustment can come through the transfer of financial assets, see Tibor Scitovsky, *Economic Theory and Western European Integration*, pp. 85–91, and Scitovsky, *Money and the Balance of Payments* (Rand McNally, 1969), esp. Chaps. 5 and 8, and three studies by James C. Ingram: "State and Regional Payments Mechanisms," *Quarterly Journal of Economics*, Vol. 73 (November 1959), pp. 619–32; *Regional Payments Mechanisms: The Case of Puerto Rico* (University of North Carolina Press, 1962); and "A Proposal for Financial Integration in the Atlantic Community," in *Factors Affecting the United States Balance of Payments*, Compilation of Studies Prepared for the Subcommittee on International Exchange and Payments of the Joint Economic Committee, 87 Cong. 2 sess. (1962), pp. 175–207. See also Leland B. Yeager, *International Monetary Relations: Theory, History, and Policy* (Harper and Row, 1966), pp. 78–80, for an excellent short but comprehensive statement of methods of interregional adjustment in an area with a common currency, including adjustment through transfers of financial assets. See also Peter Kenen's comments on this paper.

9. If the governments of deficit countries offset the adverse effects on employment, they will interfere with correction of the deficit, and if they permit correction

sion on that score, such capital movements can be equilibrating in the short run, and reserves are presumed to be needed only to deal with short-run problems. Whether there will be an economy of reserves for internal settlement, therefore, depends upon whether equilibrating flows of private capital within the Community are likely to increase.

I turn now to the two developments most likely to influence the mobility of capital within the Community.

The first, the proposed "progressive development of a European capital market," presumably means progressive reduction of controls over intra-Community flows of capital, more nearly similar rules regarding flotation of new issues, development of similar financial instruments, and other contributions to larger and more efficient financial markets.

Although the Treaty of Rome stipulates, and the Werner Report and the plan of the EC Council of Ministers repeat, that the Community proposes to remove controls over flows of capital between the members, there has been no movement in that direction since the relaxations in December 1971. On the contrary, most of the changes made since then have been to strengthen controls over capital flows, either directly or by making capital movements more costly. Moreover, the proposals for regulation of short-term capital flows adopted by the Community's Council of Ministers on March 21, 1972, apparently did not contemplate requiring members to make any distinction between residents of other Community members and residents of nonmembers, and (so far as I know) few, if any, of the

---

of the deficit, they will fail to offset the adverse employment effects. As Corden argues, even changes in a member country's monetary-fiscal policy mix, which have been proposed to resolve conflicts between internal and external balance, will not do so in the medium and long run in a pseudo union. See W. M. Corden, *Monetary Integration*, Essays in International Finance 93 (Princeton University, International Finance Section, 1972), pp. 30–34. The logic of Corden's theoretical argument about the possibilities of medium- and long-term use of changes in the fiscal-monetary mix in a pseudo union does not imply a conclusion as pessimistic as the one he draws. He states the conditions that would limit the success of that strategy to the short run but neglects the implication that if those conditions do not prevail, neither do the time limits that their prevalence would impose. This objection applies with equal or perhaps even greater force to his equally pessimistic conclusion, based on the same reasoning, that Ingram's view is incorrect. "The argument that capital mobility within a complete exchange-rate union eases the process of adjustment is therefore as much a short-term argument as the argument that appropriate manipulation of the monetary-fiscal policy mix will solve the fixed-exchange-rate problem in ... a pseudo-exchange-rate union" (pp. 33–34).

European Monetary Unification

existing capital controls make that distinction.[10] No relaxation of controls
sufficient to permit capital to move more freely in response to market
forces than it did before August 1971 appears likely for at least a few
years.

In view of this prospect, it may be asked whether market incentives to
shift the direction of capital flows in favor of intra-Community flows will
permit such actual flows to increase. If the exchange rate parities between
the Community members are perceived as sufficiently near equilibrium to
be maintained and the will of officials to maintain them is perceived as
strong, an increase in equilibrating capital flows probably will not be inhibited by existing controls. In the main, these flows would tend to be in a
direction opposite to those that most of the Community members' present
controls seek to prevent.[11] If equilibrating flows between the members do
not increase, it will probably be because the Community arrangements for
maintaining narrow margins around unchanged parities are breaking

10. Germany introduced new controls on corporate borrowing abroad in March
1972. Britain relaxed controls in March but tightened them again in June, when the
pound was floated. France, which had instituted separate exchange rates for financial
and commercial transactions after August 15, 1971, relaxed controls, but Belgium
and the Netherlands, which had earlier instituted such dual exchange markets,
intensified restrictions in March. See International Monetary Fund, *Twenty-third
Annual Report on Exchange Restrictions, 1972*, pp. 5–6 and 7–9; *The Economist*,
Vol. 244 (London, July 15, 1972), pp. 56–57; *OECD Economic Outlook*, No. 11
(July 1972), pp. 32–33, 37; and Morgan Guaranty Trust Company of New York,
World Financial Markets (July 25, 1972), pp. 2–4. The last-mentioned publication
observes, "It is interesting to note that apparently no attempt was made to coordinate
these controls so as to avoid their application to other EEC countries and preserve
greater freedom of movement for capital within the Community than between members and third countries" (p. 3).

11. The German, Belgian, and Dutch controls seek to restrain speculative inflows,
whereas equilibrating movements appear likely, in the next few years at least, to be
outward and unlikely to be discouraged if they occur. The Italian and British controls
seek to limit outflows, and so long as their currencies are weak, the direction of
equilibrating flows affecting them will be inward. In their cases it may be argued that
the parities are not credible because the market will expect the lira to be devalued,
and that any new parity chosen for the pound sterling in the coming year will be
regarded as short-lived in the light of Britain's postwar performance. Although there
is ground for such pessimism, it should be noted that widespread pessimism about
Italy's ability to eliminate its deficit in 1963 without devaluaton of the lira proved to
be unfounded and that the present weakness of the lira is accompanied by a much
stronger current account than Italy had in 1963. On the 1963 episode, see Marcello
de Cecco, "Appendix: The Italian Payments Crisis of 1963–64," in Robert A.
Mundell and Alexander K. Swoboda (eds.), *Monetary Problems of the International
Economy* (University of Chicago Press, 1969), pp. 383–89.

down. In that case, equilibrating capital flows will be inhibited for reasons far more fundamental than the continued existence of present controls, or indeed of any prospective capital controls, since they are likely to be directed against speculative disequilibrating flows. Such speculation itself will reflect a failure of effective policy coordination too great to permit the system to operate.

The second development affecting the intra-Community flow of capital is the change in the relationship between the intra-Community exchange rate band and the band with nonmembers. Although the decision to maintain exchange rates between the members' currencies within 2¼ percent of their parities is generally referred to as the "narrowing of the band," it represents a substantial narrowing only in relation to the 4½ percent band around par values (or central rates) agreed to at the Smithsonian meeting on December 18, 1971. For most members, the actual band before August 15, 1971, was in practice 1½ percent in relation to the dollar, so that the maximum permitted fluctuation of the Community members' currencies against each other was 3 percent. Now that deviations above and below their parities with each other have been limited to 2¼ percent, this maximum has become 4½ percent.[12] That is substantially narrower than the 9 percent maximum that would have been possible under the Smithsonian Agreement's 4½ percent band in relation to par values, but that fact is relevant only if one is comparing the consequences of the present Community band with what would be permissible under the Smithsonian Agreement, and since the latter band was only six months old when the intra-Community arrangement went into effect, such a comparison would be too hypothetical to be useful. It is more useful to compare the present (September 1972) Community arrangement with the one that prevailed before the Smithsonian Agreement. The new maximum possible percentage fluctuations in exchange rates within and between various categories of countries and the changes in them are summarized (subject to qualifications for some countries) in tabular form below. The maxima prevailing before the Smithsonian Agreement are indicated as "old maximum fluctuation"; those prevailing in September 1972 (that is, based on the

12. A 2¼ percent band limits the difference among national interest rates on three-month money to 9 percent if funds are free to move and the parities are not expected to change, whereas the 1½ percent band limited it to 6 percent. Even the smaller of these two spreads has rarely occurred, however, so this increase of the theoretically possible spread is not likely to have much practical effect.

Smithsonian Agreement as modified by the EC's own agreement) are indicated as "new maximum fluctuation."[13]

	Old maximum fluctuation (percent)	New maximum fluctuation (percent)	Change (percentage points)
Between members of EC	3	4½	1½
Between members of EC and nonmembers of EC, other than the United States	3½	9	5½
Between the United States and members of EC	1½	4½	3
Between the United States and nonmembers of EC	2	4½	2½
Between nonmembers of EC, other than the United States	4	9	5

13. Qualifications are necessary because the table does not take into account all combinations of arrangements that affect bands of fluctuation. It assumes, for example, that before August 15, 1971, all Community members maintained margins of ± ¾ of 1 percent vis-à-vis the dollar and that all nonmembers maintained margins of ± 1 percent vis-à-vis it. It also assumes that all the present and prospective members maintain the 2¼ percent band, although Denmark, Ireland, and the United Kingdom stopped maintaining the narrow margins when the British pound began to float. Moreover, the table implies that after the Smithsonian Agreement all countries other than the United States that will not be members of the Community established central rates or maintained parities with respect to the dollar, whereas this is true for only some forty-five nonmember countries. Twenty-one nonmembers, in fact, maintained unchanged par values in terms of gold, and ten nonmembers that changed their par values continued to define them in terms of gold. For most of these thirty-one countries the maximum permissible fluctuation of their exchange rates with respect to the dollar, to currencies of Community members, and to each other is 9 percent. Furthermore, countries that use a currency other than the dollar as an intervention currency are allowed a 1 percent margin of fluctuation on either side of that currency. If that currency can fluctuate by 9 percent in relation to a third currency, then the currency using it as an intervention currency can fluctuate by 11 percent in relation to the third currency. Neglect of these complications, however, does not greatly impair the usefulness of the table as an indicator of changes in the bands that affect the main potential flows of mobile capital. It should also be noted that the applicant countries are in the "EC" sector in the situation labeled "new maximum fluctuation" but are in the "non-EC" sector in the situation labeled "old maximum fluctuation."

These changes create the possibility of a substantial inducement for owners of capital, especially short-term capital, to shift the directions in which they are inclined to move it. While the new band arrangement augments the maximum possible loss on transfers between member currencies, it reduces that loss relative to the maximum possible loss on transfers between one of them and dollars from twice the latter ($3:1\frac{1}{2}$) to equality with it ($4\frac{1}{2}:4\frac{1}{2}$).

This widening of the permissible fluctuations with nonmembers by a greater amount than those with members is likely to divert capital that, under past exchange rate arrangements, might have moved between member currencies and the dollar. If it does, these flows are likely to do more than in the past to maintain exchange rates between member currencies within the limits of the band. The change will therefore probably reduce the need for official intervention and the need for reserves.

This change also may be expected to induce some shift from the private use and holding of dollars to the use and holding of member currencies. In particular, the relative reduction in the maximum fluctuation between member currencies is likely to increase the willingness of banks in the Community to hold currencies of other members, and otherwise to increase equilibrating flows of private funds in response to movements in the intra-Community exchange rates themselves. Although this would dampen any increase that might otherwise occur in official demand for Community currencies, it does not appear likely to dampen the decrease in demand for dollars to use and to hold. While this shift is going on, the central banks of the member countries presumably would have to take over some of the dollars that the private sector wanted to unload.

To summarize the conclusions about the Community's need for total reserves, one cannot know how the balances of member countries' current accounts and autonomous capital flows with all areas are likely to be altered by enlargement of the Community and by the change in the difference between the permissible intra-Community and extra-Community exchange rate fluctuations. But one can reasonably expect that the responsiveness of trade in goods and services and the prospect for equilibrating private capital flows within the Community will be greater than before. If other conditions provide incentive for use of this expanded scope, these effects may be expected to reduce the variance of the total imbalances of the members around any trend and thus to reduce the members' need for total reserves. The probability of this outcome is strengthened insofar as the widening of the band with nonmembers facilitates the adjustment process and thereby reinforces these effects.

Community Substitutes for External Reserves

The next point to consider is how fully internal reserves and other official arrangements within the Community are likely to satisfy the Community's need for total reserves and therefore to reduce its need for external reserves. Intervention to maintain intra-EC margins is to be carried out in Community currencies when the spread between the strongest and weakest Community currencies reaches the limits permitted by the Community band (the "snake") and this band is not at the limits of the 4½ percent band (the "tunnel"). The use of strong currencies to support those at their floors is a form of official borrowing. According to the rules, the countries whose currencies are supported must settle with the supporting countries in external reserves at the end of the month following the one in which the intervention occurred.

This interval, while short, does afford deficit countries some economy in their required average holdings of external reserves. Under some circumstances, this economy could be a substantial fraction of the average holdings that they would require for this purpose if they had to intervene with external reserves daily. It will reinforce the effect of any reduction in the official-settlements imbalances of members that may result from the widening of exchange rate margins with nonmembers and enlargement of the Community.

The present requirement for monthly settlement within the Community implies that the members are clearly not yet ready to finance each other's deficits over any protracted period of time. This has implications for the prospect that members' external reserves will, in fact, be pooled, a step that has been suggested by academic experts, that is contemplated by Community officials, and that would produce further economies in total and external reserves. Such pooling implies extension of credit for indefinite periods. If the members now are not even willing to extend credit to each other for more than two months at most (and, on the average, one and one-half months), it seems reasonable to infer that pooling is not likely to occur for several years.

The members' willingness to finance each other's global imbalances greatly affects the aggregate need of the Community for reserves. It especially affects whether the sum of the members' total imbalances or the consolidated imbalance of the Community with the outside world is more relevant to its felt need for reserves. This question raises the issue between nationalism and "Europeanism." How important that issue is depends in great part on how a member's net balance is distributed between other members on the one hand and nonmembers on the other. To see how a nationalistic view of balance and of policy in general can create difficulties, it is necessary to consider some issues that may be generated by the structure of net balances, and to identify the problems of adjustment and need for reserves that some structures of net balances may create.

Imbalances of Members versus the Consolidated Imbalance of the Community

One can easily imagine situations in which the Community as a whole and a single member have persistent and opposite imbalances; for example, when the Community has a consolidated surplus with the rest of the world and a member has a global deficit. Adjustment of the Community's surplus through appreciation of its band in relation to nonmembers' currencies would then worsen the position of the member already in deficit, since its currency would presumably already be low in the Community band and would therefore rise with the band.

If global balance for each member is not demanded, there is no payments problem for the Community as a whole. Even then, however, balance in the Community as a whole implies that members in global surplus make available to other members not only the portion of their own global surpluses required to settle any deficits with them, but the rest of their surpluses as well. All surpluses are required to finance other members' deficits with the outside world. If a member in global deficit is not in surplus with members in surplus, it must obtain access to the needed portion of those surpluses by some other means. If those means are unilateral fiscal transfers, official long-term loans, or private long- or short-term loans—all of which are above-the-line transactions in balance-of-payments accounting—then net official-settlements balances, which would have been global surpluses and deficits in the absence of these transfers, are zero net balances, and no settlements requiring use of official liquidity (that is, either reserves or extension of official credits) need be made. Without above-the-line transfers, global balance for the Community as a whole is sufficient only if surplus members make official credits available to deficit members without limit. In that case, although the need for official liquidity is greater than it would be if global balance for all members were insisted upon, the need for official reserves is smaller. In either case, abandonment of the idea that all members must be in global balance requires that interregional, nonreserve transfers must be available.

If, in contrast to this situation, global balance for each member apart from such compensatory arrangements is insisted upon, the external reserves needed are greater, since the deficits of some are not financed by the surpluses of others and a member's need for reserves to finance deficits is not reduced by the reserves of others.

Thus, how much the Community's need for external reserves will fall will depend greatly on the extent to which the Community acts to develop fiscal or other means of making intra-Community transfers, thereby enabling balance in the Community's payments, rather than in that of its member nations, to be the criterion of payments equilibrium. In the absence of such transfers, insistence on global balance for each member nation is likely to make the felt demand for external reserves substantially larger than it would be if balance for the Community as a whole is regarded as sufficient.

This conclusion must be qualified in two respects. One is that a global imbalance that would have required a member to take unacceptably drastic domestic fiscal or monetary measures before enlargement of the Community might be corrected by less drastic measures after its enlargement. The reason is that when two countries have opposite global imbalances, the changes in their aggregate domestic demands required to achieve a given reduction in the imbalances of both at a given exchange rate are smaller, the larger are the proportions of changes in their total trade that affect directly their trade with each other.[14] If this effect is

14. See Ragnar Frisch, "On the Need for Forecasting a Multilateral Balance of Payments," *American Economic Review*, Vol. 37 (September 1947), pp. 535–51, for an analysis of how the direction of trade affects the total change of trade required to remove a given imbalance when a country's trade with all partner countries is changed in the same proportion. Frisch uses this result as an argument for making nonproportional changes to minimize the total change needed to correct imbalances, whereas the argument here is that the total amount of proportional changes can be smaller, the more the countries with opposite imbalances trade with each other.

strong enough, the constraint that the Community band imposes on adjustment through exchange rate changes may be less serious than is often supposed, and the persistence of imbalances and the need for reserves correspondingly less.

The other qualification is that, although limits have already been placed on deviations of spot exchange rates between member currencies from their parities, changes in the parities are not ruled out until the last stage of unification; parities may be changed during the experimental stage and apparently even in the transitional stage, although in that stage the restraints on them are clearly intended to be greater.[15] If needed parity changes are made before large-scale financial transfers become available and are ruled out or eschewed only after that, the demand for external reserves will be less than if such transfers become available only after parities have become rigid.

Taking both of these points into account, my conclusion is that, given the constraints of the Community band, the effect on the need for reserves of the difference between the nationalistic and the Community-wide views of balance depends in great part on whether large-scale financial transfers do or do not become available when domestic macroeconomic changes remain infeasible and parity changes have also become impracticable. If such transfers do become available before then, the need for reserves will be little affected by a failure to give up a nationalistic view of balance; if they do not, it will be much affected.

The requirement of the Community-wide view of balance, that is, that members in global surplus must be willing to finance the global deficits of other members, is no different, in principle, than the corresponding requirement within the United States (or any other country), where it is presumably satisfied. But in the United States, nobody—not even a president of a Federal Reserve Bank—knows or even asks whether an-

15. According to the Werner Report, in the first stage "it is desirable that the solidarity of the member countries in the determination of their exchange parities should be supported by a reinforcement of the consultation procedures in the matter" (p. 22). In the second or transitional stage "progress ... should be such ... that the Member States no longer have to resort on an autonomous basis to the instrument of parity adjustment. In any case, it will be necessary further to reinforce the consultation procedures laid down for the first stage. Only at the moment of transition to the final stage will autonomous parity adjustments be totally excluded" (p. 25). In the final stages of union the Community currencies will have "immutable parity rates, or preferably they will be replaced by a sole Community currency" (p. 12).

other Federal Reserve district is in global deficit and, if so, whether that deficit is being financed by his own district's global surplus, let alone objecting to the latter possibility. It appears likely, however, that a long time will elapse before all members of the European Community, deeply concerned as they long have been about national payments imbalances, will be equally indifferent either to their own deficits or to the use of their surpluses to finance the global deficits of their fellow members. Greater flexibility or a float between the Community's band and the currencies of the outside world obviously will not solve this problem, since any change in the position of the Community's band that would reduce the global imbalance of some members would increase the opposite imbalance of others. If concern with the global imbalances of individual member countries persists, the likelihood that a serious problem will arise depends in great part on whether members are likely to have global imbalances that are not only opposite but persistent.[16] Because discussion of adjustment seems to be based on an implicit assumption about this question, it is worth brief comment.

If the global imbalances of members merely reverse the direction of preexisting imbalances and therefore reverse the positions of the currencies concerned, so that one moves from the ceiling to the floor of the Community band and the other from the floor to the ceiling, the resulting change in the rates between them might suffice to adjust their payments positions. This possibility would be decreasingly useful as the permissible change, now 4½ percent, is progressively narrowed. Indeed, if their

16. This problem, which concerns the relevance of individual members' *global* imbalances, is different from the problem that would arise if the restoration of global balance for members forced increases in bilateral imbalances with other members, and members in bilateral imbalance with a partner country objected to the *bilateral* imbalance, even though the partner country were in global balance. If such objections do arise, they might also present a problem, because in some situations exchange rate or domestic macromeasures that restore global balance necessarily increase bilateral imbalances. These imbalances reflect the structure or direction of demand and supply, and a simultaneous decrease in both global and bilateral imbalances requires measures that affect this structure. Insofar as the structure of demand and supply giving rise to bilateral imbalances results from intra-Community barriers, these imbalances would be reduced by legally required removal of the barriers, but insofar as they result from unrestricted market forces, their reduction by erection of intra-Community controls is supposed to be ruled out. I shall not deal with the problem of bilateral imbalances here, however, as the objection to intra-Community imbalances of countries in global balance seems less likely to arise and therefore less deserving of discussion than other problems.

present imbalances are perceived as likely to be reversed in the future, accommodating flows of capital are likely to be induced. In either of these cases, financing by official reserves would not be needed.

During the 1960s, however, the imbalances of the individual countries tended to be persistently in one direction. This is true even if one omits the last years of the decade on the assumption that world monetary reform will eliminate recurrence of the acute financial crises that marked them. Before 1968, the original EC members had persistent surpluses. In the period 1961–67, which contains thirty-five country-years for the five original balance-of-payment entities of the Community, there were twenty-nine official-settlement surpluses and only six deficits. The United Kingdom, however, was in deficit for six of those seven years. As a result, the original members had total surpluses over the period 1961–67 of $9.9 billion and the United Kingdom a total deficit of $5.5 billion, as shown in Table 5.[17] (The figures for 1968–70 are also given to emphasize their extraordinary difference from those of the preceding years.)

The implicit assumption of most discussions of the Community band is that this divergence between the original members of the Community and

17. The balances of Denmark and Ireland have been omitted because comparable data on their total official-settlements balances were not available at the time of writing. The data shown are net changes in the external assets and liabilities of monetary authorities, as given in the 1971 Yearbook of the Statistical Office of the European Communities, *Balance of Payments 1960–1970*, Tables 11.1–11.6. They differ slightly for a few years for some countries from the balance-of-payments data shown for 1966–70 in Tables 4.1–4.6 of the source. The differences are not large enough to affect the conclusion drawn from the table.

The annual sum of imbalances without regard to sign, which has been used as a measure of annual payments imbalances, was as follows for the original six members and the United Kingdom (in millions of dollars):

	Sum of annual average imbalances	Annual average consolidated imbalance
1961–67	2,798	745
1961–69	3,893	1,565
1961–70	4,812	2,717

For use of figures that disregard signs to show imbalances and to measure trends in imbalances over time, see Rudolf R. Rhomberg, "Trends in Payments Imbalances, 1952–64," International Monetary Fund, *Staff Papers*, Vol. 13 (November 1966), pp. 371–95, and other documents by the IMF staff in *International Reserves: Needs and Availability*, Papers and Proceedings, Seminar at the International Monetary Fund, 1970 (IMF, 1970).

Table 5. *Official-Settlements Balances, European Community, Six Original Members, and the United Kingdom, 1961–70*

Millions of dollars

Year	BLEU[a]	France	Germany	Italy	Nether-lands	Total, European Community	United Kingdom	Total, European Community and United Kingdom
1961	244	1,066	26	613	82	2,031	-987	1,044
1962	-34	715	-223	481	-19	920	843	1,763
1963	224	845	687	-602	165	1,319	-477	842
1964	252	781	108	332	248	1,721	-1,882	-161
1965	160	666	-326	960	72	1,532	-343	1,189
1966	34	374	477	288	42	1,215	-1,294	-79
1967	248	305	-41	518	169	1,199	-1,335	-136
1961–67	1,128	4,752	708	2,590	759	9,937	-5,475	4,462
1968	-284	-3,279	1,702	-61	-165	-2,087	-3,207	-5,294
1969	112	-1,547	-2,912	-704	62	-4,989	1,412	-3,577
1961–69	956	-74	-502	1,825	656	2,861	-7,270	-4,409
1970	296	2,087	6,167	480	702	9,732	3,348	13,080
1961–70	1,252	2,013	5,665	2,305	1,358	12,593	-3,922	8,671

Sources: Statistical Office of the European Communities, *Balance of Payments, 1960–1970* (Luxembourg: The Statistical Office, 1971), Tables 11.1 to 11.6 for the original Community members and total, and Table 4.6 for United Kingdom, 1966–70; International Monetary Fund, *Balance-of-Payments Yearbook*, Vols. 16–20, Table 3, for United Kingdom, 1961–65.

a. Belgo-Luxembourg Economic Union.

the United Kingdom will continue. That assumption, however, should not be accepted uncritically. In Germany, unit labor costs in manufacturing appear to have risen substantially relative to the average of those of its competitors, when both are adjusted for exchange rate changes to express their relative movement in a common currency, and even when they are expressed in national currencies.[18] The rise after adjustment for exchange rate changes has been so great as to suggest that the deutsche mark is overvalued compared to almost any base in the early or mid-1960s, despite the market's contrary valuation. Unless the data for manufacturing costs are wrong or these costs are unrepresentative of costs for all tradable goods, one can only conclude either that Germany's surplus, persistent except for 1969, will be reversed in the next few years, which implies that the market is a poor indicator of the exchange rates consistent with fundamental equilibrium, or that changes in relative costs have been and will continue to be outweighed by other factors, which implies that persistent surpluses and deficits are not determined mainly by relative rates of inflation. Both alternatives challenge conventional wisdom and should be given more serious attention.

That does not mean, of course, that the position of Germany will be reversed. If such a reversal does not occur, however—and perhaps even if it does but the United Kingdom relapses into chronic deficit—the divergence of trends within the enlarged Community will create a major problem of intra-Community transfers.

A divergence of trends among the members has frequently been recognized as a major problem for the Community, but the source of the problem has been identified as potential divergence in national price and cost trends, and it is generally believed that the only way in which the narrow band can be made viable is to prevent the potential divergences from being realized. The rise of Germany's unit labor costs in manufacturing suggests that the coexistence of persistent surpluses of one member with persistent deficits of another cannot be identified only with divergence of national price and cost trends; it might persist without that divergence or not exist despite it. This fact and others mentioned earlier also indicate that the coexistence of virtual imbalances is not necessarily incompatible with maintenance of the EC band. However, if virtual im-

18. See International Monetary Fund, *Annual Report for the Fiscal Year Ended April 30, 1971*, pp. 65 and 67, and Arthur Neef, "Unit Labor Costs in the U.S. and 10 Other Nations, 1960–71," in *Monthly Labor Review*, Vol. 95 (July 1972), pp. 3–8.

balances in the private sector become actual imbalances despite increased responsiveness of intra-Community flows of goods, labor, and capital to given intra-Community changes in relative prices, income, and wealth, then maintenance of the band will require a great expansion in the means and willingness to make equilibrating intra-Community financial transfers. In the absence of sufficient official lending, this means fiscal transfers. Given a sufficient expansion of such transfers, national surpluses and deficits on account of other transactions can coexist and, indeed, persist, as they almost surely have among the regions within countries, even if no exchange rate movements at all are possible. If such fiscal transfers do develop, great economy in the need for external reserves may be expected.

The degree to which reserve needs will be affected, therefore, probably turns largely on whether, and how rapidly, the Community will act to develop a Community fisc or some other means of providing intra-Community transfers. Each person may make his own appraisal of that prospect. While mine would be that the prospect does not appear very promising, my personal judgment is less important than the conclusion that a big push to promote such transfers may well be necessary, both to make the consolidated imbalance of the Community rather than the aggregate of members' imbalances the determinant of the Community's need for reserves and, what is more important, to permit the whole process of monetary unification to proceed.[19]

19. The importance of fiscal harmonization or transfers may be the aspect of monetary integration about which economists disagree most. It is discussed by Corden in *Monetary Integration* (cited in note 9), as well as in his paper in this volume. Lutz noted that both the Werner Report and the report of the Council of Ministers seem to regard harmonization of members' budgetary policies as a condition for a monetary union but said, "In my view, this is not a necessary condition. The cantons of Switzerland, for example, each have a separate budget policy without this meaning that Switzerland ceases to be a unified monetary area." (See Friedrich A. Lutz, "Foreign Exchange Rate Policy and European Economic Integration," in Fritz Machlup, Armin Gutowski, Friedrich A. Lutz, and others, *International Monetary Problems* [American Enterprise Institute for Public Policy Research, 1972], pp. 107–23.)

Robert Triffin agreed with Lutz, saying, "The experience of Switzerland—and, I would add, of the Latin Union before World War I and of the Belgium-Luxembourg Union today—amply demonstrates the fact that full budgetary and fiscal unification is *not* a prerequisite for monetary union." ("Discussants on Professor Lutz's paper" in *ibid.*, p. 125.) But Erik Lundberg disagreed: "I think that the parallels he [Lutz] draws with Swiss cantons or the Federal Reserve System do not hold up very well when referring to national autonomous states having their independent political

Demand for Dollars in the Community and the Rest of the World

Even at the present early stage of unification, some reduction in the Community's demand for dollars for internal settlements is likely to result from the use of Community currencies to maintain the Community band and from the use of reserves other than dollars to settle part of the debts incurred by members when their currencies receive Community support. The question arises whether this reduction, which will probably be moderate for some time, will be reinforced by reductions in the Community's demand for dollar reserves for external settlement and in the demand of the rest of the world for dollar reserves.

This question cannot really be answered without knowing how the reduced foreign exchange value of the dollar, the widening of bands, and other recent developments will affect the regard in which the dollar is held and what provisions the reform of the world monetary system will make for adjustment of parities, which presumably also affects the need for total reserves. Two relevant considerations may be noted, however. In the first place, intervention by members of the Community to maintain the 4½ percent band, as well as to finance part of the settlements arising from maintenance of the Community band, will continue to be conducted in dollars. Second, there is the more important and more complex question of what is likely to happen to the private demand for dollars as a transactions currency and a store of wealth. This is relevant because the use of the dollar as a reserve currency derives in large part from the private demand for it. If and when unification has progressed, one of the Community currencies (or *the* Community currency) will undoubtedly become more attractive for the conduct of transactions and the investment of liquid funds. It is then likely to become a closer rival of the dollar. If that

---

entities and institutions. ... If 'unharmonized' fiscal policies are carried out ambitiously, the balance-of-payments consequences will imply the need of big transfers of funds from 'strong' to 'weak' economies. ... Efforts to coordinate monetary policies with regard to some conformity as to rates of inflation ... would probably be quite insufficient." (*Ibid.*, pp. 129–30.) Tibor Scitovsky agreed with Lundberg's stress on the harmonization of fiscal policy and said, "The intra-state balance-of-payments problem of the United States was only resolved when it became psychologically possible to have federal policies that favored one part of the country with their cost partly borne by other parts." ("Statements by participants" in *ibid.*, p. 133.)

currency is used to finance its own country's deficits or the deficits of the Community as a whole by increasing its country's liabilities, such financing will cut the felt need for the present types of external reserve assets on the part of both the Community and nonmember countries. The United States will then need more (nondollar) reserve assets at a given fixity of exchange rates, because it will be less able to finance deficits with dollars. But that course of development is dependent on a Community currency's becoming a more important vehicle currency.

It appears to be widely believed that a diminution in the dollar's role as a vehicle currency is not imminent. One reason given is that the commercial habit of denominating and settling transactions in dollars is hard to change. I doubt that this inertia alone would prevent a shift to denominating and settling in another currency if there were clear disadvantages in continuing to use dollars for these purposes. Rather, the question is whether the dollar's recently acquired disadvantages or loss of advantages are believed to be past, or whether new ones will be expected to develop. The belief that the dollar's old advantages will continue to diminish may persist for a while, even if the facts should cease to justify it; this is another inertia but one that works to diminish the role of the dollar. It is difficult, therefore, to know even the direction in which inertia will operate, let alone the weight to be given to it.

Another consideration, however, is probably more important. The use of the dollar to make payments and to hold wealth, like the use of sterling in earlier decades, has depended heavily on the wide variety of financial instruments denominated in dollars, the ease of disposing of dollar assets at minimum transactions costs and capital loss, and other benefits arising from the size, efficiency, and competitiveness of American financial markets. It would take time for European financial markets to develop these characteristics. I would concede, as a valid counterargument, that European financial markets have improved in recent years, and that the effect of British entry could speed their further growth greatly. While margins between borrowing and lending rates, which are a good indication of competitiveness, are much higher in the national financial markets of continental Europe than in the United States, they are less in the Eurodollar market. If the London banks that dominate that market should develop markets in Europounds or Euromarks, a substantial shift to greater use of these currencies at the expense of the dollar could occur in a few years, if not sooner. But there is strong resistance to price competition in banking on the continent, and this resistance is likely to impede such a development. My guess is that the continent's financial industry will seek to limit such activities on the part of the banks of the new partner, which in general will be eager to behave acceptably to the rest of the club for at least the first few years. Therefore, while I can readily see the potentiality for more advanced Community financial markets, I doubt that the potential will be sufficiently realized to reduce the transactions and portfolio roles of the dollar greatly in the next few years, so far as countries outside the Community are concerned.

An offsetting consideration, however, applies to capital owned by residents of member countries. As was pointed out earlier, the threefold increase in the maximum possible fluctuation between a member currency and the dollar, when the corresponding maximum possible change in relations between member currencies has risen by only 50 percent, reduces the risk of holding assets denominated in a Community currency relative to the risk of holding assets denominated in dollars. This reduction of relative risk may weaken the demand for dollars. The demand of member central banks for dollars would also be likely to decline, because their intervention to maintain the Community band is carried out in members' currencies when this band is not at the limits of the 4½ percent band.

These two influences, one affecting the private demand for dollars and the other the official demand, make for a decline in the *stock* demand for dollars. This decline would have only a transitory effect if the world economy were not growing in nominal terms. In a world of nominal growth, however, stock demand rises, and these influences reduce the dollar amount of that rise, that is, they reduce the private and official demand to *acquire* dollars. Such influences may be powerful enough to outweigh any factors tending to strengthen the dollar as a vehicle currency.

The net result of these opposing considerations is difficult to assess, but my "inconclusive conclusion" is that no change in the vehicle role of the dollar is to be expected so long as there is great uncertainty about whether European monetary unification is likely to succeed. If it appears that it will, the vehicle role of the dollar is likely to diminish, and that is likely to diminish its reserve role, too. But if conflict among members makes it appear that monetary unification is headed for the rocks, the dollar will remain a strong vehicle currency, perhaps a strengthened one. In that case, the movement to diminish its reserve role will be weakened.

World Reserves: Their Distribution and Growth

To the extent that European monetary unification reduces the Community's felt need for external reserves, the present difference between the "reserve ease" of the Community and the United States will be increased, although it is hard to say whether by little or much. Insofar as reserve ease depends on the relation between actual reserves and variables such as total money supply, gross national product, or others that, for the Community as a whole, are equal to the sum of those variables of individual members, the increase in reserve ease would come entirely from whatever economy of external reserves is made possible by substitution of other means of settling imbalances. That economy might not be very large. But to the extent that the felt need for external reserves is reduced because changes in the structure or responsiveness of private transactions or official transfers reduce intra-Community official-settlements imbalances or because these imbalances are settled primarily through internal reserves or substitutes for them, the Community's felt need for external reserves will be related mainly to the imbalances in the transactions of its members with nonmembers. Even now, these transactions are only about half the sum of its members' total international transactions, judging from available data on transactions in goods and services. If, when world payments get closer to equilibrium, the ratio of future to present felt needs for reserves even approximates this fraction, the increase in European reserve ease will be very great.

Reserve Levels

A crude indicator of comparative reserve positions and of the change in the position of the Community that would result from consolidation is a comparison of the European and American ratios of external reserves to merchandise imports. This frequently used measure has often been charged with having no rational basis, but it can be given one if certain necessary assumptions are charitably accepted.[20]

20. For a rational justification, see Walter S. Salant, "Practical Techniques for Assessing the Need for World Reserves," in *International Reserves: Needs and Availability*, pp. 287–88. (See note 17 for full citation.) As noted therein, the ratio of imports to reserves may be a useful criterion for comparing adequacy of reserves, even if money supply is regarded as the variable to which needed reserves are related. Although the money supply of a union of countries is the same as the sum of those of its members, consolidation of the members into a union reduces the ratio of needed reserves to money supply.

As may be seen from Table 6, the ratio of reserves at the end of April 1972 to merchandise imports in 1971 for the United States was slightly less than 28 percent, which is about the same as for BLEU (Belgo-Luxembourg Economic Union) and the Netherlands, slightly below

Table 6. *Monetary Reserves, April 30, 1972, and Merchandise Imports, 1971, Selected Countries and Regions*

Amounts in billions of U.S. dollars

	Reserves			
		Percentage of world	*Merchandise*	*Reserves as percentage*
Country or area	*Amount*	*total*	*imports*[a]	*of imports*
European Community				
BLEU[b]	3.6	2.6	12.9	27.9
France	8.5	6.0	21.3	38.9
Germany	20.1	14.3	34.3	58.6
Italy	6.6	4.7	16.0	41.3
Netherlands	4.3	3.1	15.4	27.9
Denmark	0.8	0.6	4.6	17.4
Ireland	1.1	0.8	1.8	61.1
United Kingdom	7.9	5.6	23.9	33.1
Total, European Community				
Including intratrade	52.9	37.6	130.2	40.6
Excluding intratrade	52.9	37.6	64.3	82.3
Other countries or areas				
United States	13.3	9.5	48.3	27.5
Japan	16.5	11.7	19.7	83.8
Canada	5.9	4.2	16.8	35.1
Rest of world	52.1	37.0	114.9	45.3
World total				
Including EC intratrade	140.7	100.0	329.9	42.6
Excluding EC intratrade	140.7	100.0	263.3	53.4

Sources: International Monetary Fund, *International Financial Statistics*, Vol. 26 (August 1973), pp. 18, 37. Reserve figures, expressed in Special Drawing Rights, were converted into U.S. dollars by multiplying by 1.0857. Imports of Community countries from their partners were derived by applying to total imports of members the percentage obtained from other members of the enlarged Community, as given in International Monetary Fund and International Bank for Reconstruction and Development, *Direction of Trade* (June 1972), pp. 78, 80–85. Component figures are rounded and may not add to totals. Reserves as percentage of imports are calculated from the rounded figures in the table.

a. The figures for 1971 imports, as given in the source, are based on monthly figures in national-currency values translated into dollars at the corresponding monthly averages of daily exchange rates in 1971. If, in an effort to make them comparable with figures for the April 1972 dollar values of reserves, they were converted into dollars at the exchange rates prevailing in April 1972, the import figures for countries whose currencies had appreciated relative to the dollar would be raised in proportion to the change in the dollar prices of their currencies, and their ratios of reserves to imports would be lowered. Such an adjustment, however, would imply that the dollar values of imports would have changed in proportion to the change in the foreign-currency prices of the dollar. Since this assumption has no more basis than the one implied by the table, the conversion has not been made.

b. Belgo-Luxembourg Economic Union.

the United Kingdom's 33 percent, and far below the ratios of France (40 percent), Italy (41 percent), and Germany (58 percent). For the enlarged Community, the ratio of reserves to its members' total imports was approximately 40 percent. For Japan it was 84 percent, for Canada 35 percent, and for the rest of the world it averaged 45 percent. If the Community's imports are treated on a consolidated basis by eliminating intra-Community trade, however, its ratio of reserves to imports doubles, rising to nearly 82 percent, and the existing disparity, on this criterion of reserve ease, between the United States and the Community is greatly increased.

Whether an increase in the abundance of reserves necessarily has much or any effect on the price level or balance of payments of the country or area experiencing it is a point about which there appears to be no clear consensus, although it is generally agreed that the direction of any effect that does occur is expansionary and toward reducing any surplus in the balance of payments. In the case of the Community, any such effect would tend to reduce the United States deficit or replace it with a surplus and make for reconstitution of U.S. reserve assets. (It would also tend to increase Japan's surplus.) At the same time, it would also give impetus to world inflation. But these results would occur only if the increase in "excess supply"—I use the expression loosely—had some significant economic effect in the Community. Whatever the normal effect of an increase in the supply of reserves relative to felt need that results from absolute growth of reserves, in the case of the Community the increase would result from a reduction of felt need. It would therefore have none of the monetary or possible income effects of an actual inflow of reserves. Moreover, it would occur in a situation in which the members are already concerned about excessive internal liquidity and inflation. It is unlikely, therefore, that it would either have expansionary effects on markets or stimulate the authorities to embark on significantly more expansionary policies. Perhaps some easing of the United States balance-of-payments and reserve-asset positions would result, but I should not expect that effect to be great.

The increase in the disparity between the reserve positions of the United States and the Community (and also Japan) has been great on any criterion. One need not believe, therefore, that their ratios of reserves to imports should be equal to conclude that some reduction in the present disparity is desirable. It is true that the present distribution of reserves partly reflects the large capital outflows from the United States to Community countries and Japan occurring during the crises of the past few years and that it may be partly reversed in the next few, but it appears unlikely that such a reversal would eliminate the disparity.

If the United States needs an increase in its reserve assets for reasons of monetary independence, negotiating position, prestige, or any other reason, it has an interest both in the continued creation of SDRs (Special Drawing Rights) and in having the Community's proportion of new allocations reduced below the proportion based on the sum of its members' present quotas, which is now the basis of allocations. Such a reduction could be carried out gradually and would be logically consistent with the principle of distribution in proportion to IMF quotas, for if the Community gradually becomes a single monetary entity, it and not its members should have a quota, and that quota should be less than the sum of the present quotas of its members.

Reserve Growth

So far, I have discussed only levels of reserves. Something needs to be said about reserve growth. Over time, countries or groups of countries undergoing economic growth normally want an accompanying growth of reserves for both internal money and external settlements. If external reserves are used for both purposes and grow too slowly, the development of substitutes for their internal use releases external reserves for external use. The history of the monetary use of gold is largely one of such substitution, other domestic moneys having replaced it and released increasing proportions of it for external purposes.

This generalization suggests that the Community must have a policy for growth of its internal reserves, just as the world community through the IMF must plan for growth in world reserves and the Federal Reserve System must have a policy for increasing member bank reserves in the long run rather than depending on increases in the monetary gold stock to expand the monetary base. However, as Marcus Fleming has pointed out, a high stock and a high rate of growth of reserves are substitutes for each other from the standpoint of balance-of-payments ease.[21] The Community now has an enormous volume of external reserves. Although a reversal of the United States' balance-of-payments position could extinguish a large part of the original members' $30 billion or more official dollar hold-

21. See *Toward Assessing the Need for International Reserves* (cited in note 4), pp. 5–11, 21, which includes analysis of the factors affecting the rate of substitution between the stock and the growth of reserves.

ings, and although its $16 billion of gold reserves are widely regarded as immobilized for practical purposes, neither fact nor the combination of them means that its reserve position would be less easy than it is now. The use of gold might be reactivated by the extinction of a substantial amount of dollar reserves, and it would be reactivated by adherence to the provision that a member must repay debts arising from support of its currency in assets proportional to the composition of its reserves. Therefore, I see no reason to suppose that the need for reserves to grow with transactions and wealth presents any problem in a unifying Community—either for it, for the United States, or for the rest of the world.

There is another aspect of reserve growth, however, in addition to the need to maintain an adequate stock of reserves. Some economists, including myself, have stressed that there are countries that want surpluses in their balance of payments even when they regard the levels of their reserves as more than adequate. Attainment of that objective implies a world aggregate of surpluses, which in turn implies that the global amount of *net* reserves must grow, either because the alternative of currency appreciation has employment effects that are more objectionable to them or for other reasons. Insofar as that is the case, high levels of reserves are not a substitute for growth of reserves. If enough countries want surpluses, "The stock of international reserves in the world could conceivably be adequate and even excessive by many of the various criteria that have been proposed, but the increments could still be too small in relation to the net balances of payments that monetary authorities desire, for the authorities may well refrain from reducing surpluses even when they are satisfied with the levels of their reserves. For example, exporters and import-competitors may resist measures to reduce a trade surplus or private borrowers may resist any reduction in their access to foreign capital, while the authorities themselves, fearing inflation, do not wish to make domestic capital more readily available."[22] In addition to these reasons, the alternative to a sur-

---

22. See Walter S. Salant, "International Reserves and Payments Adjustment," in *Banca Nazionale del Lavoro Quarterly Review*, No. 90 (September 1969), pp. 281–308. This article contains a full statement of the view that growth of net reserves is needed to reconcile national targets for surpluses. For other statements of that view, see Fritz Machlup, *Remaking the International Monetary System: The Rio Agreement and Beyond*, Committee for Economic Development, Supplementary Paper 24 (Johns Hopkins University Press for CED, 1968), pp. 45–49, and Milton Gilbert, *The Gold-Dollar System: Conditions of Equilibrium and the Price of Gold*, Essays in International Finance 70 (Princeton University, International Finance Section, 1968).

plus and the consequent reserve growth under the fixed-rate system was to tolerate or engineer an expansion of money demand, which the Community countries regard as undesirable.

While the argument that some countries (and the aggregate of countries) want surpluses retains some general validity in the absence of a joint float of the Community currencies against those of nonmembers, it may have little force with respect to the growth of external reserves when the Community is at an advanced stage of its monetary unification, and perhaps also less with respect to most of its members after the very early stages of unification. For one thing, the desire of some members for surpluses can be satisfied partly by growth of internal reserves. Second, the alternative to accepting reserves is not now likely, for the Community, to be wholly an expansion of domestic money demand but at least partly an appreciation of its currency band in relation to the dollar and other currencies, which is counterinflationary. It is possible, of course, that currency appreciation, now a more respectable alternative to reserve inflows than it was a few years ago, will be even less accepted than monetary expansion was, when the presumption was that parities would be maintained. In that case, there would still be pressure to maintain surpluses. But the possible currency appreciation for a single member of the Community is now presumed to be limited and is supposed to become increasingly so, and appreciation of the Community band does less damage to Community exporters and import-competitors than the earlier alternative of appreciation by a single country, since it leaves exports to and import-competition from other members relatively unaffected.

Moreover, so far as SDRs are concerned, the argument that pressure for surpluses implies pressure to acquire reserves even when reserve levels are high was always weaker with respect to SDR allocations to Community countries than it was with respect to reserves they earned. The reason is that in those countries the counter-entry to such allocations is not generally regarded as a true credit and does not have the same economic effects as growth in earned reserves, on which effects the argument relies. This weakness or even lack of connection between pressure for surpluses and pressure to acquire SDRs by allocation implies that even if the Community is reluctant to see its surpluses reduced, its appetite for SDR allocations may decline. For countries outside the Community, however, the pressure for reserve growth may be as great as it was before. This situation may contain the seeds of increased future conflict over the creation of SDRs, with implications for the United States that are pointed out below.

Some Policy Conclusions

A few conclusions relevant to policy may be brought together from the foregoing discussion.

1. Even if there is no reduction in the Community's need for total reserves, there will be some economy in its need for external reserves, owing to the substitution of internal reserves for external reserves.

2. There is likely also to be some economy in the Community's need for total reserves, owing to the expansion of intra-Community official borrowing facilities and improved adjustment through the operation of market forces on trade and private capital flows, including accommodating short-term flows. Any success in policy coordination and progress in development of a Community-wide public expenditure and tax policy would further reduce the Community's need for external reserves. (So would greater flexibility in the relation between the Community's band and the dollar, of course, but that would depend more on the changes made in the world system than on monetary unification in the Community.)

3. As European monetary unification progresses, one of the major member currencies will probably become more attractive as a vehicle currency and a medium for investment of short-term funds. As a result, it will become more competitive with the dollar as a reserve asset for other countries, including nonmembers. This development will tend to reduce the need of other countries for gold, SDRs, IMF positions, and dollars as official reserves. The corresponding reduction in the ability of the United States to finance deficits by increases in its dollar liabilities may be offset by a decrease in the need to do so resulting from the greater flexibility of the exchange rate between the dollar and other currencies, but if no such reduction occurs, the United States' need for reserve assets will increase. Even if increased flexibility of exchange rates dampens an increase of this need, the need is already great.

4. Because of the three preceding influences, the present aggregate reserves of the Community members, already abundant, will become superabundant, and even more disproportionate to United States reserves than

they are now. The Community's interest in the further creation of SDRs may be expected to wane, except insofar as SDRs are created to replace its dollar holdings. This raises the question whether the present voice of Community members in determining how many SDRs are to be created will not become disproportionate to their legitimate interest in SDR creation, compared with that of the United States and other nonmembers. If they aspire to become a monetary union and claim to be making progress in the process of unification, logical consistency calls for treating them increasingly on a consolidated basis. Consolidated Community imports are less than half of the sum of the members' national imports, so that their present voice in the creation of SDRs—and, indeed, their quotas and voting rights on all matters, insofar as these are influenced by imports and other variables that are reduced by consolidation—will become progressively more excessive as consolidated figures become increasingly relevant. A reduction in their quotas is therefore a logical implication of their unification.

5. Since the United States has an interest in increasing its reserve assets, there is a potential conflict between it and the Community with respect to decisions about both the aggregate amount of SDRs to create and the proportions of the total that the Community should receive. This consideration suggests that the United States, taking the Community's intention to unify at face value, has an interest in pressing the logical implication of unification by seeking reduction of the Community's quota, which would reduce both its voice in decisions about SDR creation and its proportionate share in their allocation, as well as its voting rights on other matters.

6. Unification also affects the question of who should receive the Community's allocation of SDRs. If and when the Community achieves the goal of monetary union, it will make no sense to have SDRs allocated to its individual members. If the United States wishes to stimulate the process of monetary unification, it can move to have *part* of the members' share of SDRs held in escrow, so to speak, for distribution to the Community central bank or to its common reserve pool before either is established, so as to stimulate their establishment, with the amounts so held being distributed to the first of the two to function. After they are in operation, the United States should insist that the entire Community share be so distributed.

7. In the later stages of unification, when there is a Community central bank, it will become easier to make changes in the parities between the

dollar and the European currencies, since any required negotiations to that end will presumably be conducted with the Community's central bank, instead of with the national authorities. Even before that bank is set up, such changes should be easier to make as soon as the Community band is firmly established. One reason is that since the parity of each member's currency with the others will be firmly set, none will have to worry about what the other members will do if the United States changes or proposes to change the par value of the dollar. Another reason, which applies when the United States must depreciate in relation to the Community, is that appreciation of Community currencies may be expected to evoke less resistance on the part of European exporters and import-competitors than now, because only exports to and imports from nonmembers would be affected, which may be expected to cut such resistance approximately in half.[23] This is a problem of adjustment that perhaps need not be discussed in a paper on reserves, but negotiations with Europe involving both reserves and adjustment should presumably be discussed with the same European authorities. The United States, therefore, should insist on discussing both the problems of reserves and exchange rate changes with the same single Community authority. In theory, that authority should be the responsible member of the Commission or the chairman of the Community's "Coordination Group," if it is established. Should the appropriate Community authority lack sufficient power and the United States wish to give impetus to unification, the United States should refuse to deal with the members individually and insist that the appropriate Community official or body be given the necessary power.

Comments by Peter B. Kenen

WALTER SALANT has presented a comprehensive, thoughtful treatment of the subject. There is little I can add and little to subtract. I am led, therefore, to comment broadly on the subject of his paper, not to examine

---

23. This figure is based on the ratio of intra-Community to total members' 1971 merchandise imports only. A more appropriate basis is the corresponding ratio for the sum of exports and competitive imports, defined to include both merchandise trade and services, including receipts and payments of investment income that would be adversely affected by appreciation but excluding other investment income.

minutely his arguments, and will stress the later, less certain stages of monetary integration rather than the first.

Salant's paper is a survey of three distinct topics bearing upon the felt need for reserves, each one connected to the others. It deals with the implications of financial integration, with the somewhat simpler outcome of new arrangements for settling internal imbalances, and with the effects of consolidating completely national accounts and national reserves. I shall review them one by one, ignoring for the moment their several connections.

Suppose that the process of monetary integration could take place without creating new machinery or instruments for settling imbalances within the European Community and without consolidating national accounts or reserves. Imbalances within the Community would have still to be settled by transfers of "external" assets; each country would retain responsibility for its own balance of payments, including its balance with the rest of the Community, and each would retain its own stock of reserves with which to finance its global deficits. Financial integration would still have a number of dimensions, and progress in each would probably occur at its own rate. The stages described by the Werner Report are, in fact, distinguished by the emphasis attached to the progress required in each of several directions.

Three such dimensions are important for the present purpose. They are the unification of exchange rates, the unification of financial markets, and the harmonization and eventual unification of monetary policies and, to an uncertain extent, fiscal policies.

The unification of exchange rates, taken by itself, is apt to increase the felt need for reserves. The chief reasons are furnished by Salant. If a single member of the Community has a large surplus in its global payments and a change in its exchange rate is required or desired, some other member may be thrust into deficit. An appreciation of the first country's rate by more than the girth of the "snake in the tunnel" will cause all other rates to appreciate vis-à-vis nonmembers. This simple fact has two implications.

First, it may have an inhibiting effect on a member country's willingness to change its exchange rate or, through the Community's decision-making processes, on its ability to do so. Members may have then to finance larger or more enduring imbalances and may want to hold more reserves in order to do so. (It may also mean that the United States has more interest than ever in preempting the right to alter the exchange rate for the dollar.)

Second, rate changes, when they occur, will expose member countries to new imbalances. Joint changes in rates will serve in part to shift one country's imbalance to the other members of the Community, changing its sign in the process. This, too, can cause the members to desire more reserves.

These two effects are not additive. The second arises only if the first does not materialize (or, more precisely, is not perceived to do so), and I would be inclined to stress the first for the time being. The second, however, may emerge as the more important long-term consequence of exchange rate unification (especially if coupled to new flexibility on the part of the United States).

The next effect of integration, increased capital mobility, may offset this long-term tendency. There is bound to be more internal mobility if exchange rates inside the Community can be contained within the band, if the band itself is narrowed during the next few years, and if the Community removes all controls on internal capital movements. Internal mobility can be delayed only if the joint or separate use of capital controls vis-à-vis outsiders limits members' access to the Eurocurrency market—the most important meeting place for the banks of member countries.

Salant is right to warn that mobility has both negative and positive features. It can serve to magnify disturbances even as it fosters a species of adjustment. But he is also right to stress its stabilizing role. The scope for disruptive disparities in credit conditions is apt to diminish as the members harmonize monetary policies.

Mobility, however, has two aspects, corresponding roughly to the first and later stages of policy harmonization. For as long as member countries retain for themselves the technical initiative in monetary policy—the right to conduct open-market operations and to set separate discount rates —the financing or correction of imbalances by capital movements has to be induced by monetary policy. Differences in credit conditions and short-term interest rates produced deliberately by central banks are probably required to induce corrective flows of funds. And these flows are the more likely to take place when the members' banks and other investors have cause to believe that exchange rates will be stable inside the Community. (The need to foster such confidence is itself sufficient cause for welcoming a narrowing of the snake in the tunnel, whatever other reservations one may have concerning that objective.)

What happens, however, when the central banks are merged or surrender their autonomy in the determination of money-market conditions and commercial bank reserves? At this point, Salant invokes the processes described by James C. Ingram and Tibor Scitovsky. If a country runs a current-account deficit (whose locus, one must add, is in the private sector), that country's citizens must liquidate assets. Liquidation may have the direct equilibrating effect stressed by Scitovsky: people with less wealth are apt to spend less, setting in train a contraction of income and imports. But it is apt to have the additional effect stressed by Ingram. Liquidation will depress the prices of the assets sold, driving up their yields. The size of the price decline and the nature of the resulting payments adjustment will depend on the degree of capital mobility. If capital does not respond to changes in yields, the decline in asset prices is limited only by the willingness of residents to substitute the cheaper assets for money (the same money that must be transferred to foreigners to finance the deficit). In this instance, the decline in asset prices can aid the balance of payments only by curtailing domestic investment and setting in train a further contraction of income and imports. If, instead, capital is mobile, foreign investors will step in to acquire domestic assets, accepting them in lieu of money and arresting the decline in asset prices. In this instance, the decline in asset prices serves to correct the payments deficit by improving the capital account, not mainly by deflating domestic expenditure and reducing imports.

General, endogenous interest arbitrage may be the most important method of financing-*cum*-adjustment between the separate regions of the United States and of other countries with integrated capital markets, though it is hidden from view and has escaped systematic analysis (save by Ingram, in the case of Puerto Rico). The assets traded between regions are, in the main, supraregional (for example, government and high-grade corporate securities), and the chief participants, commercial banks and other financial institutions, conduct this form of arbitrage in the normal course of adjusting their portfolios to daily changes in their cash reserves.

Salant has suggested that interregional adjustment differs importantly from international adjustment because, in the former, the means of payment available for settling imbalances are coextensive with the total money supply. The process I stress suggests a different formulation. Interregional adjustment is distinguished by generalized arbitrage conducted in large stocks of assets acceptable in other regions; the means of interregional payment are conserved by continuous portfolio adjustments. If processes like these can be developed within the European Community, they will help to reduce or settle imbalances between the members and substantially to reduce the felt need for reserves arising from fixed internal exchange rates.

Returning to the illustration furnished earlier, suppose that one member of the Community has a surplus and opts for appreciation, dragging with it the currencies of other members. Those which now experience global deficits can seek, even at this stage, to correct their positions by restricting credit, inducing a capital inflow from the outside world and from their partners. (Remember in this connection that I still assume the use of "external" assets for internal and external settlements, so that a country's surplus with its partners furnishes the assets needed to finance an external deficit.) With further financial integration, however, the partners need not take deliberate action nor need they experience a sudden, serious deflation in consequence of a joint appreciation. The current-account deficits attending that appreciation, even if quite small, will set in motion portfolio adjustment and endogenous arbitrage. The deficit countries will earn "external" assets from the country that began in global surplus. (Note that these same processes will dictate a smaller appreciation by the surplus country than would be required without them. The surplus country should not appreciate sufficiently to eliminate its global surplus. It should, instead, remain in surplus with the outside world in order to earn the "external" assets required to finance its partners' global deficits.)

These same processes, however, require something more than the absence of barriers to capital mobility. Banks and other private financial institutions must have available to them sufficient stocks of assets—public or corporate debt—acceptable throughout the Community. The advent of sufficient financial integration may therefore await the consolidation of fiscal policies or, at least, of national debts and the development of Community-wide markets for financing large enterprises. One would be too optimistic to assign it much importance until the last stages of integration.

The third aspect of financial integration is perhaps the most important for present purposes. Much that has been written on payments adjustment and the need for reserves, including Salant's paper, would seem to assume that payments problems arise exogenously (or quasi-exogenously) out of differences in cost-price trends reflecting differences in institutional arrangements or national policy preferences. Recent work on this subject, however, suggests the opposite, and while I do not place great confidence in these new results, for reasons I plan to articulate elsewhere, they cannot be dismissed out of hand. Research by Michael Michaely and others suggests that most major imbalances are "non-dilemma" cases, reflecting errors in demand management rather than autonomous shifts in the determinants of trade and capital flows. One has, therefore, to ask how the process of financial integration, including policy harmonization, will affect the magnitude and frequency of errors in management.

I am far from sure of the answer but will venture a guess. In the early stages of financial unification when harmonization is incomplete in the several domains of national policy, such errors may be smaller in aggregate than they have been in the past, reducing imbalances. Later on, however, when harmonization gives way to the unified direction of demand management, these errors may be enlarged (relative, at least, to the early stage). My reasons for this guesstimate are simple, perhaps naïve. In the early stages, the Community as a whole may succeed in restraining national policies. Later, however, the Community itself will have the power to make large errors of its own. One may hope that it will not do so, but recent experience in the United States suggests that large countries with powerful policy instruments may not have more wisdom than their smaller neighbors.

The chief effects of financial integration itself can perhaps be summarized as follows. The limitation of national autonomy in exchange rate policy is apt to *enlarge* the felt need for reserves by individual member countries. This will be so whether it results in more rigid exchange rates and, therefore, longer imbalances or whether it results in more frequent joint changes in rates and, therefore, the migration of imbalance from the countries from which they originated to the partners whose exchange rates were made to change too. Unification of capital markets is apt to *reduce* the felt need for reserves because it will lead to larger internal flows of private capital in lieu of official reserves. This offsetting effect may be delayed, however, as the principal market now available for shuttling private funds across the Community may be walled off by capital controls aimed primarily at outsiders, and the Community itself has yet to develop internal markets and debt instruments suitable for general endogenous arbitrage. Finally, the coordination of national policies could lead to smaller national imbalances in the short run, *reducing* the felt need for reserves, but the margin (and cost) of errors may grow larger again at subsequent stages.

Each of these suggestions is predicated on one other pair of suppositions—that internal settlements have still to be made in "external" assets and that each member country retains responsibility for its own balance of payments. Put differently, I have been assuming heretofore that the Community's felt need for reserves is the sum of separate national needs and that each need is based on the member's expectations concerning its global balance of payments. Salant has dealt extensively with the effects of relaxing these assumptions but perhaps has elided some of those effects.

Consider first the implications of financing internal imbalances with internal assets, and suppose, for the sake of simplicity, that there is no limit upon the supply of these assets.[24] There is at once a major saving of reserves; no member has to hold "external" assets in anticipation of internal deficits. But there are important offsets to this saving. Recall the illustration mentioned earlier. If one member country opts for appreciation, dragging the others with it, its partners may experience global deficits. Under the arrangements posited earlier, these could be financed by capital flows from the member with the surplus. Under the arrangements now posited, these financial flows could no longer help, for they would not bring with them the "external" assets needed to finance the partners' deficits with the outside world. The partners would have to attract capital from outside the Community or deflate sufficiently to eliminate their deficits. To put this same point differently, the larger felt need for reserves that may arise in consequence of joint exchange rate changes may be exacerbated, not relieved, by the perfection of a separate system of internal settlements. To put the point in more general terms, the introduction of such a system could work to the disadvantage of countries used to covering external deficits by internal surpluses (on average or at the margin in times of overall deficit).

My conclusion here is similar to one drawn by Salant. Internal financing is an uninhabitable halfway house. Countries cannot dwell in it together unless they are also prepared to consolidate their "external" accounts and assets without quarreling among themselves concerning each member's potential claim upon the household's total assets.

To abandon the metaphor and to come to the point, new machinery for settling internal balances can function effectively only when members of

24. This supposition is twice removed from current reality. At present, monthly settlements within the Community, resulting from intervention to contain the girth of the snake, are made in packages of external assets. The next step in unification may be the substitution of a new bookkeeping system, but no one has yet suggested that members should have the right to unlimited debit balances.

the Community are prepared to take one more step. They have also to pool their reserves and, more importantly, to forgo individual proprietary claims on the new pool of "external" assets. They must act as though they had a single balance of payments with the outside world. (To suppose, as I have, that countries would grant each other limitless drawing rights on an internal bookkeeping system is, of course, to make much the same assumption. If countries are prepared to disregard internal debts, which are, after all, mortgages on real resources, it should not be too much more difficult for them to disregard their individual claims on debts to a pool of "external" assets. Salant says the same thing negatively when he observes in a different context that "a long time will elapse before all members of the European Community . . . will be equally indifferent either to their own deficits or to the use of their surpluses to finance the global deficits of their fellow members.")

Total consolidation of this variety must await the unification of policy instruments. One cannot have a single balance of payments without having ways to manage it collectively. Consolidation is the last step logically in monetary unification and would seem to be the last step chronologically in the timetable contemplated by the Community. It should be pointed out, however, that this final step could work to enlarge the felt need for reserves compared to what it was at the previous step, not to reduce it. I shall use algebra to illustrate this point.

Pretend that the balance of payments of a single country can be described by a simple stochastic process and that a country's felt need for reserves depends in a direct linear fashion on the expected variance of the stochastic series:

$$(1) \qquad\qquad R_i = a_i \sigma_i^2$$

where R_i is the desired level of reserves for the ith country, a_i is a constant, and σ_i is the expected standard deviation of the balance of payments (whose mean is zero).

Now divide the balance of payments into two components, an external balance w_i and an internal balance u_i, and assume that each component has a zero mean. In this case:

$$(1a) \qquad\qquad R_i = a_i(\sigma_{w_i}^2 + \sigma_{u_i}^2 + 2r_i\sigma_{w_i}\sigma_{u_i})$$

where r_i is the simple correlation between w_i and u_i. Notice that this formulation isolates one of the effects described early in these comments. An increase of endogenous capital mobility can be said to decrease algebraically the value of r_i, reducing the felt need for reserves.

Turning to a union of two such countries, one can now define the joint need for reserves, R_T, on each of the three suppositions considered thus far. Suppose, first, that each country retains responsibility for its own balance of payments and has to finance all imbalances with "external" assets. In this case, the joint need for reserves is a simple sum:

$$(2) \qquad R_T = R_1 + R_2 = a_1(\sigma_{w_1}^2 + \sigma_{u_1}^2 + 2r_1\sigma_{w_1}\sigma_{u_1})$$
$$+ a_2(\sigma_{w_2}^2 + \sigma_{u_2}^2 + 2r_2\sigma_{w_2}\sigma_{u_2})$$

or

$$(2a) \qquad R_T = a_1\sigma_{w_1}^2 + a_2\sigma_{w_2}^2 + \sigma_u[\sigma_u(a_1 + a_2) + 2a_1r_1\sigma_{w_1} + 2a_2r_2\sigma_{w_2}]$$

because $u_1 = -u_2$, so that $\sigma_{u_1} = \sigma_{u_2} = \sigma_u$. When, further, $a_1 = a_2 = a$ (the two countries have identical "demand" functions):

$$(2b) \qquad R_T = a[(\sigma_{w_1}^2 + \sigma_{w_2}^2) + 2\sigma_u(\sigma_u + r_1\sigma_{w_1} + r_2\sigma_{w_2})].$$

The only effects on the need for reserves resulting from financial integration are those that may change σ_{w_1}, σ_{w_2}, and σ_u and those that can affect the correlations r_1 and r_2. I have already listed some of these.

Next, consider the halfway house—the financing of internal imbalances with "internal" assets. In this case, all terms involving σ_u vanish from the argument, leaving as the joint need for "external" assets:

$$(3) \qquad R_T = a(\sigma_{w_1}^2 + \sigma_{w_2}^2).$$

I have already suggested that the argument of equation (3) will be smaller than that of (2b) but that the net reduction in R_T may not be large if financial integration has had a substantial impact on the two correlations in equation (2b).

Consider finally the complete consolidation of national accounts and reserves. The Community's need for reserves has now to depend upon the expected variance of the consolidated balance of payments:

$$(4) \qquad \sigma_T^2 = E[(w_1 + u_1) + (w_2 + u_2)]^2 = E(w_1 + w_2)^2;$$

and the need for reserves can be written as:

$$(5) \qquad R_T = a(\sigma_T^2) = a(\sigma_{w_1}^2 + \sigma_{w_2}^2 + 2r\sigma_{w_1}\sigma_{w_2}),$$

where r is the simple correlation between w_1 and w_2. It is not possible to compare this last equation directly with equation (2b) or (3). It relates to different institutional arrangements, including at the very least the joint determination of monetary policies to manage the Community's joint balance of payments. In other words, the terms σ_{w_1} and σ_{w_2} may not be the same as they were before. Notice, however, that one new term appears (the correlation between the members' imbalances with the outside world) and that, as indicated earlier, the process of policy unification may enlarge this term.

I cannot, then, second Salant's assertion that this final logical step in monetary unification will by itself reduce the need for reserves relative to the need perceived at any earlier stage. The shift to a collective view of the Community's needs focuses attention on interactions that were present all along but do not appear explicitly until reserves are pooled.

Combining these last observations with those made earlier, I find it hard to forecast the net effect of unification, in all of its dimensions, on the Community's felt need for reserves. I hope, however, that this reformulation has helped to identify some of the questions deserving more study as the process of unification proceeds.

Much of Salant's paper deals with the effects of unification on the status of the dollar as a reserve asset and offers additional comments on the private transactions-*cum*-investment demand for dollar balances. I will offer a few brief amendments or reservations on these issues rather than a systematic survey.

Salant anticipates a reduction in the private demand for dollars, now that the bands for exchange rates have been aligned, increasing the potential for exchange rate changes vis-à-vis the dollar by more than the potential for changes between Community currencies. I would attach more importance to the overall *increase* in variability than to the relative change. Banks and other institutions holding transactions balances in foreign currencies may be inclined to reduce all such balances, not to change their composition. If there is cause to anticipate a substantial substitution of Community currencies for dollars, it derives from an effect Salant has mentioned in a different context. Further growth in the Community's internal transactions, resulting from the accession of new members and from the liberalization of internal financial transactions, may increase the transaction demand for Community currencies and diminish the demand for dollars.

Next, I would stress additional reasons for expecting a decline in the use of the dollar as an official reserve currency. Salant suggests that the arrangements for internal intervention to contain the girth of the snake will entail more frequent official use of Community currencies. Since the snake and the tunnel have both grown fatter in the last twelve months (and the Community will not intervene in dollars unless the snake bumps the tunnel), intervention using the Community's currencies is apt to substitute for intervention using dollars. By implication, there will be an increase in the official transactions demand for Community currencies and a corresponding decline in the demand for dollars.

To this must be added another possibility. If the United States should seize the initiative in exchange rate policy, as I have urged earlier, it may also want to intervene more frequently in the spot markets. It can, in fact, be argued that the United States should assume exclusive responsibility for intervention in dollars vis-à-vis the currencies of the Community. Such an arrangement would be much more symmetrical than any we have seen thus far. The Community would keep the snake thin. The United States would keep the snake inside the tunnel. If the task were divided this way, however, the United States would have to hold or borrow other countries' currencies. More important, intervention by the United States may substitute for intervention by members of the Community, further reducing the transactions demand for the dollar.

Finally, one must make allowance for the possibility that outsiders may wish to participate in any new arrangement for settling imbalances within the Community. The Community has developed an extensive network of preferential arrangements embracing most of the Mediterranean countries, as well as the former colonies of its six original members. It is, in addition, the most important single trading partner for many countries outside its preferential network. Some of these countries may seek and obtain access to whatever future bookkeeping system is established to settle some or all of their future imbalances with the Community. The participation of outsiders would be limited; they could not enjoy unlimited drawing rights. Any significant participation, however, would no doubt reduce their demand for other reserve assets, including the dollar. Arrangements of this type, moreover, would not contravene the Community's vow to avoid use of its currencies and of any new Community currency as reserve media. Bookkeeping credits in a new settlement system would not be freely convertible into other reserve assets, nor could they be invested at will in the money markets of the Community. Such credits would not be reserve currencies in any of the important disadvantageous meanings of that term.

Upon rereading Salant's paper, after writing these comments, I was impressed by the very large measure of agreement between us but also by the enormous concurrent uncertainty. There is much more work to be done on all aspects of this subject.

Comments by Fritz Machlup

IN READING Walter Salant's paper I agonized over his use of the words "parity," "par," "margin," and "band." Aside from the helpful distinction between par value and parity made in the Fund's 1971 report[25] and mentioned by Salant, I want to point out the need to specify clearly what one means by the word "band." The band of permissible fluctuations around parity is, of course, the sum of the margins above and below parity. In addition, if only one numéraire is used to define par values, the band around the parity between any two currencies other than one used as the numéraire is as wide as the sum of their bands around the numéraire. This makes clear that one must specify, when using the word "band," the band of fluctuation around what.[26] The EC countries have agreed to avoid having a band between their currencies that is double the band of each around the dollar and have narrowed their bands to the width of that between each of them and the dollar, that is, to 4½ percent.

One of the chief aims of Salant's analysis is to find out how the countries' needs for external reserves are likely to be affected by the enlargement of the Community and by the narrowing of the band around the parities for the Community currencies. In this connection, I want to call attention to a useful terminological innovation in Peter Kenen's discussion; instead of "need," he refers to "felt need" for reserves. There is a great difference between a need that is objectively determined and a "felt" need. Speaking of such a felt need for reserves, Salant assumes that it will be determined by the countries' payment deficits. I find this formulation misleading. Just as we distinguish the demand for "money to hold" and for

25. International Monetary Fund, *Reform of the International Monetary System,* A Report by the Executive Directors to the Board of Governors (IMF, 1972), p. 17.

26. See Walter S. Salant, "A Partial Glossary of International Finance," at the end of this volume.

"money to spend," we should distinguish between a felt need for reserves to hold and for reserves to spend. A potential deficit may increase the felt need for reserves to hold, but an actual deficit financed out of the existing reserves reduces the reserve holdings of the deficit country. Reserves are needed for expected future deficits, and these expectations are often based on experienced past deficits. Current deficits affect felt needs for reserves through the expectations they create regarding the future.

Salant speaks a great deal of equilibrating capital flows and leaves it open whether they should be regarded as adjustment or as the financing of an imbalance. In some contexts, I had the impression that he may have a third supposition in mind. He seems to use the word "equilibrating" also for autonomous capital movements that happen to offset an imbalance on current account. The last type is very different from accommodating capital movements that finance a given current-account deficit and also from other induced capital movements that are somehow generated by a process of equilibration. A distinction must be made between a capital movement that happens to offset an imbalance in other parts of the balance of payments and a capital movement that is induced either in a process of adjustment or as an effect of a given institution designed to accommodate payments of the imbalance.

Salant also refers to "equilibrating movements" out of Germany, Belgium, and the Netherlands as "likely, in the next few years at least, to be outward," whereas equilibrating movements in the case of Britain and Italy "will be inward." This need not be understood as a prediction but rather as an implication of Salant's expectation that the Dutch, German, and Belgian currencies are now undervalued, so that it would be normal for these countries to run surpluses on current account. Capital movements would then deserve to be called offsetting or "equilibrating" if they happen to be "outward"—the opposite, of course, for the pound and for the lira, where Salant says that the capital movements will be inward. He does not really predict that they will be inward, but I presume he would call them "equilibrating," or rather offsetting, if they were inward and were, therefore, compensating the expected deficit on current account.

Private foreign reserves may be good substitutes for official reserves, as Salant points out. He fails to state, however, that the existence of large private external reserves may sometimes, because of fluctuations in asset preferences, give rise to changes in supply and demand conditions in the foreign exchange market; to offset these changes authorities may need larger, not smaller, reserves. One might also want to add that, just as official reserves are sometimes held in medium-term securities, private reserves may also be held in the form of foreign medium-term securities and that sales and purchases of the latter securities may take on the appearance of either accommodating or disturbing capital movements.

Salant speaks of "speculative disequilibrating flows." One thinks of the massive flows that force the monetary authorities to give up supporting an unrealistic exchange rate. What is disequilibrating in such a situation? Is it not the fixed exchange rate or perhaps the monetary policy which made a rate that may have once been right into a disaligned rate? The speculative capital flow that forces the authorities to adjust the rate is, in my view, more equilibrating than disequilibrating.

Salant is most ingenious in working out the possibilities and probabilities that the official demand for dollar reserves will be reduced in the process of European monetary unification. Assume that, with many opposing forces at work, the demand, or the felt need, for additional dollar reserves is actually reduced. Just what consequences do we derive from this knowledge? Will the monetary authorities, finding that they want to hold fewer dollars than they possess, show greater inclination to appreciate their currencies, to let them float upward, or will they decide to reduce their import barriers or to increase their aid to developing countries, or will they buy American securities, or will they arrange for domestic monetary expansion with income and price inflation? Many options are available to the countries with surplus dollars, and no one knows which of these options they will take. With present attitudes, the most likely outcome might be that they will take none of the enumerated options but, instead, decide to live with the surplus dollars for a few more years, perhaps until they are no longer regarded as surplus, possibly because the countries will have become used to having them.

Note. The controversy raised by aspects of the Corden paper left no time at the September 1972 conference for general discussion of the Salant paper.

RICHARD N. COOPER

Implications for Integration of the World Economy

THE IMPACT of European monetary unification, or moves in that direction, on the integration of the world economy is the subject of this paper. It is an especially difficult topic to consider. Moves toward European monetary unification can take many different forms. So far, only the first tentative steps have been specified by the European Community (EC), leaving ground for conjecture about what comes next. Furthermore, "integration" of the world economy is not a well-defined concept. It has taken on almost as many shades of meaning as there are writers using the term. Some use the term "integration" to refer to institutional development at the international level (for example, the United Nations and its specialized agencies); others like to apply it to the degree of cross-national feeling or empathy. Even within the more circumscribed economic realm, integration can take on several meanings, ranging from the absence of economic policies, such as import tariffs, that discriminate on a national basis through the evolution of single worldwide markets to the full development of common economic policies, especially with regard to money.[1] The most meaningful *economic* definition of full integration presumes the existence of a

1. For a further discussion of the alternative uses of "integration" and references thereto, see Richard N. Cooper, *The Economics of Interdependence: Economic Policy in the Atlantic Community* (McGraw-Hill for the Council on Foreign Relations, 1968), pp. 8–11.

single market with a single price (after allowance for transportation costs) for comparable goods. This definition automatically entails the absence of tariffs or other government policies that insert a barrier, or wedge, between prices in two geographic areas, but it also requires actual market linkages between the areas.

The picture is further complicated in two respects. Integration can be regarded either as a process or as a state of affairs. If it is to be regarded as a continuum along a certain dimension, rather than the extreme point of that dimension (for example, the attainment of a fully unified market), then there is an important ambiguity in the context of three or more countries, or market areas: Is the "world" economy more or less integrated if there is a high degree of integration between two of the countries but a low degree between them and the rest of the world than if there is just a moderate degree of integration among all countries? Such ambiguity continues to provide grounds for dispute between the advocates of a regional approach to integration of the world economy, regarded as a process, and the advocates of the universal or global approach. There are, of course, proponents of regionalism as an end in itself, but others instead regard it as the most efficacious route toward an integrated world economy; regionalism becomes instrumental rather than an objective in its own right. Like-minded countries, this school of thought argues, can push ahead toward integration rapidly, setting an example for the more laggard and skeptical countries, rather than being held back by them. This difference in tactical approach has underlain a number of the institutional tensions of the postwar era, such as the disharmony between the International Monetary Fund and the European Payments Union in the early fifties, and between the General Agreement on Tariffs and Trade and the European Community and other common markets in the sixties. Thus, verbal similarities can conceal real differences of view regarding process or end result.

Rather than speculate further on the appropriate meaning of integration or how best to achieve it in the world economy, I will try instead to outline some of the probable effects of European monetary unification on the world economy, viewed from the vantagepoint of the United States, and leave it to the reader to decide whether they have advanced or retarded world economic integration. In doing so, it is useful to divide the discussion into three parts: (1) the effects of European monetary unification on the world economy after unification has been achieved, and all the dust has settled; (2) the effects on the world economy during the period of transition to the aforementioned state of affairs; and (3) some of the political consequences of the relative shifts in economic importance between the United States and Europe, making allowance, among other things, for the fact that the European Community has not really decided on the path toward monetary unification.

Long-run Effects

Unification of existing currencies into a single European currency— call it the Europa—would in itself probably have *no* substantial long-run effect on the world economy. Trade flows and capital movements would not be appreciably different from those obtaining without European union. The world economy would not look very different, except of course within Europe.

This somewhat startling proposition requires qualification, for it is only a first approximation. It does not suggest that the world economy will look the same, say, two decades hence as it looks now in 1972, only that the presence or absence of a single European currency, in and of itself and taking no account of transitional difficulties, will not much influence the many changes that are probably going to take place in any event. The adjustment process will certainly look very different then. There will be either greater or less exchange rate flexibility than at present; but European currency unification will not determine the outcome except within the European Community, where by assumption the countries will have adopted permanently fixed exchange rates.

Europe by then will probably be a far larger net exporter of long-term capital than at present; but the forces in that direction are already observable (high saving rates and declining rates of return on the continent, low rates of return within Britain) and are not likely to be influenced much by the presence or absence of a unified currency.

The international monetary standard may well be different by then, having shifted to a modified Special Drawing Right (SDR), an International Monetary Unit (IMU), possibly even with a growing volume of *private* assets denominated in IMUs. But if this eventuality does not come about, the foreign assets held in both private and official hands are still most likely to be the U.S. dollar. A unified European currency, in contrast to a united position by European countries on international monetary reform, is unlikely to influence the outcome.

The historical headstart of the dollar combined with the large size and relative efficiency of American money and capital markets, reinforced by dollar markets in Europe, are likely to permit the dollar to outcompete an incipient Europa for short-term asset-holding. The dollar could of course be weakened by unsound monetary policy in the United States in competition with sound monetary policy in Europe, but that is an improbable conjunction. It could also be eroded if Europe as a trader with the rest of the world were to become very much larger than the United States, so that a much larger value of foreign trade would be denominated in Europas than in dollars. This, too, although possible if the United States becomes heavily protectionist, is unlikely to occur.

The assertion that there will be no effect does, however, have to be qualified in a number of respects. There will of course be identifiable effects, and it is partly a matter of taste whether they are emphasized or deemphasized, since every situation has some similarities and some differences from every other (real or hypothetical) situation. I choose to deemphasize the differences because I believe, with one possible exception, they are of secondary importance when compared with the similarities to what the world will look like without European monetary unification.

Several economic effects arising from monetary unification per se can be identified. First, by internalizing the payments between European countries within a single monetary area and, in effect, pooling reserves, the European demand for foreign exchange reserves will be reduced below what it would be without unification.[2] Thus, unified Europe will find itself with an even greater excess of reserves than it now has, and this will either stimulate spending abroad (a once-for-all, although possibly prolonged, effect) until the excess is exhausted, or it will leave Europe chronically restive about excess reserves, less willing to vote SDR creation, earning more in interest payments, and similar effects.

The introduction of a single currency for an area as large and economically important as Europe will also undoubtedly lead some other countries, whose economies are closely connected to the European Community, to hold their private and official working balances in Europas rather than in dollars (or sterling), and to that extent also the demand for non-Europa reserves will be below what it would be without the Europa.

2. Circumstances can be imagined in which the internalization of some portion of international payments would lead to an increase in demand for reserves, but these are not likely to obtain in the case of Europe. For a more complete discussion, see the paper by Walter S. Salant.

Again, economies with close trading ties with the European Community can reduce their risks and transactions costs if they use Europas. For this reason, a higher proportion of international trade (even excluding intra-European trade) will be denominated in Europas than is now denominated in continental European currencies, thus reinforcing the tendency to hold working balances in Europas. Shifting the currency of denomination to that of the area in which the bulk of trade takes place may somewhat reduce risk by avoiding some short-run variation in the terms of trade arising from using the currency of a third country. By the same token, transactions costs will also be modestly reduced, since the direct buy-sell spread between countries' currencies and the Europa will presumably be lower than the buy-sell spread between them and existing European currencies with the dollar as an intermediary. Hence, total trade may receive some stimulus from this reduction in risk and transactions costs.

If the Europa were to spread beyond the small area of "satellite" economies and if it became a global reserve currency, then the pattern of world trade and capital movements would be affected substantially. In that event most, or perhaps all, countries would hold at least some of their reserves and most of their private foreign currency balances in Europas, and, in the long run, countries would convert their present private and official dollar balances into Europas. To accomplish this, the United States would need adequate payments surpluses and Europe would need equivalent deficits in the transition period. Moreover, in the long run, the United States would still have to run payments surpluses in order to provide for a secular increase in American balances of Europas; the roles of Europe and the United States during the past two decades would be reversed. The two additional implications mentioned in the preceding paragraph—the alteration of patterns of risk and the reduction in buy-sell spreads for the Europa—would apply on a global rather than just on a regional scale, and there would be a corresponding increase in the buy-sell spread between the dollar and any currency other than the Europa, for the Europa would mediate exchange between the dollar and other currencies. But, as indicated above, this evolution of the Europa to a global reserve currency, while possible, is unlikely.

Finally, the most important qualification to the basic, "no effect" proposition (aside from the possibility of the Europa displacing the dollar as the principal international currency) concerns monetary policy. With a single currency, Europe will perforce have a single monetary policy, and its monetary policy will strongly influence world monetary conditions, just as U.S. monetary policy does today. The detailed effects on the world economy of greater monetary autonomy in Europe depend on the character of the international monetary regime with respect to reserve holdings and with respect to exchange rate adjustment. Europe's influence will be greater by virtue of size even if the Europa were not a reserve currency, that is, even if the world were on an SDR or a dollar standard. Its influence would be reinforced if the Europa became a reserve currency, because the feedback to domestic monetary conditions from movements in Europe's payments position induced by its monetary actions would be correspondingly less negative in Europe, just as it is for the United States under the present dollar standard, and it would thereby increase Europe's monetary autonomy.

The greater impact of Europe as a union on world monetary conditions would diminish the relative importance of the United States, but the latter's influence would remain strong. Even more than at present when Europe's influence is more diffuse, this would give rise to conflicts in monetary policy on both sides of the Atlantic with occasional tugs-of-war between the two areas, one trying to tighten world monetary conditions, the other trying to ease them. Some kind of coordination of policy would be necessary. Coordination is of course needed even today, but the preponderance of the United States as an organized entity, reinforced by the reserve currency role of the dollar (and after August 1971 by the inconvertibility of the dollar under a regime of fixed exchange rates) means that in a showdown the United States always wins, or else forces other countries to change their regime. This happened in March 1971 when Germany floated the mark, essentially for domestic monetary reasons. [Note. It happened again in March 1973 when several countries engaged in a joint float against the dollar to prevent massive net inflows of funds.—R.N.C.]

A further complication will develop if both the Europa and the dollar have reserve currency status; then differences in monetary policy between Europe and the United States will induce some holders of foreign exchange, official as well as private, to shift to the assets with the higher yield. The exact implications of such shifts depend on the nature of convertibility obligations at the time. Presumably some such obligations will exist. If so, differences in monetary policy could evoke large movements in reserves. It will be necessary either to coordinate monetary policies closely, relying more on fiscal policy for domestic economic stabilization, or to make provision for vast recycling operations from one area to the other, in a way that will not affect the disparity in monetary conditions that gave rise to the capital movements in the first place.

In short, the use of monetary policy by the Community and the United States will be complicated by the emergence of a unified European currency, since the United States will have less control than it now does and Europe will have more, but still not have decisive control. This development will encourage efforts to coordinate monetary policy at the trans-Atlantic level, or it will induce a search for mechanisms to insulate one area from monetary influences in the other, for example, through the institution of tight controls over yield-sensitive capital movements.

A unified Europe will greatly influence world monetary conditions under any exchange rate regime, ranging from one that is completely fixed to one that is fully floating. This may seem surprising in view of the frequently expressed contention that a regime of freely floating rates fully insulates an economy from external monetary influences. But, for open economies, tradable goods and services comprise a consequential part of the total purchases within the economy. Therefore, changes in their prices have an important effect on the real value of cash balances, thereby affecting the degree of monetary ease or tightness. Thus, tight money in a united Europe will lead under floating rates to an appreciation of the Europa relative to other currencies, reducing the real value of cash balances in countries that trade extensively with Europe, thereby transmitting tight monetary conditions to the latter countries as their residents attempt to reconstitute the real value of their holdings of money. If variations in real balances arising from currency fluctuations were to become sufficiently severe, residents of such countries would increasingly hold their balances in Europas rather than in local currency. An open economy is an open economy, under fixed or flexible exchange rates. It is undoubtedly true, however, that the international transmission of European monetary actions would be more direct and more immediate in their monetary impact under a regime of fixed exchange rates, including gliding parity variants, than under freely floating rates, and that even under floating rates the real-balance effect noted above would be of consequential magnitude only for countries with strong economic ties to Europe.

It is highly unlikely, moreover, that the world will have a regime of freely floating exchange rates. More likely, it will have moved toward a regime of absolutely fixed exchange rates with a high degree of policy coordination and other linkages such as labor union activity between major industrial economies. Or there will be a regime of controlled flexibility. Under either of these regimes the need to coordinate monetary policies between the United States and Europe will, in the absence of comprehensive and effective controls on capital movements, be serious.

A regime of controlled flexibility in which there are two reserve currencies will, in addition, be subject to shifts in private and official holdings between the two currencies in response to changing expectations about movements in the exchange rate between them. Because of these shifts, which could only be partially inhibited through monetary policy within the political constraints of modern economies, such a dual reserve currency system would be unstable in the long run.

Effects during the Transition

The transition to the state of affairs described above may be so long that the "long run" is beyond the horizon. The sterling exchange standard, which reached its heyday just before the First World War, has been disintegrating for a long time, but a residuum still exists over forty years after it began its marked decline in 1931. It perhaps had its symbolic end in 1972, when the pound was floated under market pressure. Of internationally important countries, only India maintained its currency link to the pound. Others pegged their currencies to the dollar; most had been shifting their international reserves from sterling for a number of years.

What then might be involved in the transition to the long-run situation following European currency unification? The transition can be divided into two phases: (1) the period between the present and successful unification of European currencies, and (2) the period from unification to the "long run" after rivalry with the dollar has subsided. Only the economic aspects of these two phases are considered in this section; political aspects, especially of the first phase, are reviewed in the following section. The distinction is artificial but useful.

Under the conditions of managed money prevailing for the past quarter century, the task of unifying national currencies is extraordinarily difficult. Historically, with only one exception, all currency unions have either *followed* political unification, rather than preceded it as proposed in the case of the European Community, or they have been markedly one-sided, with a clearly dominant partner, as in the case of the Belgo-Luxembourg and Switzerland-Liechtenstein unions. The one exception is the Scandinavian monetary union (1873–1915), where the banknotes of each country circulated freely in the other countries. But this union antedated the era of deliberately managed national monetary conditions; all members maintained their currencies fully redeemable in gold, and the union collapsed under the differential monetary pressures of the First World War. Thus, in pledging itself to monetary unification, the European Community has embarked on an enormous undertaking, which among other things will require:

1. The development of a supranational monetary institution to manage monetary policy for the Community as a whole.

2. The establishment of a central political authority to which the monetary managers are responsible.

3. The introduction of more flexible fiscal policies at the national level to compensate for the loss of national monetary autonomy in dealing with excess or deficient aggregate demand at the national level (a requirement that will disappear over time as the various national economies become fully integrated into one European market).

4. The development of a Community-wide fiscal policy that will, in effect, transfer purchasing power from "regions" within the European economy suffering from excess demand to regions with deficient demand: the generation of so-called regional policies, which, to be successful, will almost inevitably involve fiscal transfers from some regions to others.

The mere listing of these requirements indicates how difficult the task will be, and how preoccupying of European official thought and energy. This preoccupation will necessarily draw European attention away from global concerns and will make it hard to induce Europe to respond constructively to non-European concerns and initiatives. This European immobilism will be reinforced by rather sharp disagreements within the Community on underlying objectives.

European immobilism will affect not only broad international questions, such as improvement of the balance-of-payments adjustment mechanism and creation of SDRs, but also the adjustment mechanism within Europe. To many observers, the commitment to eventual monetary unification implies a commitment to fixed exchange rates during the intervening transition.[3] Yet such a commitment, without the coordination

3. This implication is far from logical, and indeed it could be argued that the most effective way to achieve monetary unification would be to start with a regime of *freely floating* rates among European currencies and then gradually to align monetary and other policies to the point at which exchange rates do not alter, even though they are free to do so. De facto monetary unification will then have been achieved, and can readily be made formal.

of policies and other essential ingredients for unification, is bound to result in acute balance-of-payments strains, leading to large and disruptive movements of speculative capital during the transition, necessarily involving outsiders as well as residents of the European Community. These movements in turn will prompt the imposition of controls to preserve the fixed exchange rates. And, even further, the flexibility of European currencies within the allowable band of flexibility will be affected. Disputes will arise—indeed, they have already arisen—over whether the "snake" of European currencies should be allowed or encouraged to move up or down relative to the dollar.

In discussions leading to Britain's entry into the Community, the need for an eventual devaluation of the pound was widely recognized, even if not officially proclaimed. But there was a nearly universal underestimation of the probable effect, at then prevailing exchange rates, on Britain's balance of payments of freeing movements of capital from Britain to the continent. The floating of the pound in June 1972 and its subsequent depreciation relative to most European currencies neutralized this issue for awhile. But uncertainties about the appropriate valuation of the pound when Britain is undergoing vast economic readjustments to its new membership and is at the same time under strong pressure to maintain a fixed exchange rate with its European partners are bound to unsettle the international financial scene generally, and will have repercussions on the dollar and other non-European currencies. These disturbances are not likely to be different in kind, however, from those that have plagued international transactions almost annually after 1966.

If the move toward European monetary unification survives the turbulent first phase, then the second phase of the transition to the "long run" will give rise to rivalry between the new European currency and the U.S. dollar for the position of primacy in international finance.[4] As noted above, the coexistence of two reserve currencies is not likely to be stable in the long run, partly because of the economies of scale inherent in the use of money, including international money, and partly because greater flex-

---

4. This assumes that the rivalry will not have been obviated by the introduction of a new, nationally neutral international medium such as a modified SDR, or International Monetary Unit (IMU), available for private as well as official transactions. For a discussion of the relationship between the use of the dollar as a reserve currency, and its use in private international transactions, and the difficulty of untangling the two roles, see Richard N. Cooper, "Eurodollars, Reserve Dollars and Asymmetries in the International Monetary System," *Journal of International Economics*, Vol. 3 (September 1972), pp. 325–44.

ibility of exchange rates in any form is likely to make one currency more attractive than the other. Unless the U.S. economy is extraordinarily badly managed, or unless the European economy is extraordinarily well managed, the headstart of the dollar probably gives it a commanding lead in this rivalry.

If, however, for one reason or another (including a concerted political effort by Europe), the dollar should begin to yield to the Europa, then the world will be involved in the difficult and possibly turbulent process of changing a large volume of international assets, private and official, denominated in one currency for assets denominated in another. Even before the decisive tipping point has been reached, however, countries will find themselves in the politically awkward position of having to decide whether to maintain their financial ties to the dollar, by holding reserves in dollars, linking exchange rates to it, and using it for market intervention—or whether to switch to the Europa. If at that stage the United States is inadvisedly trying to preserve the international role of the dollar, while Europe is attempting to diminish it and enhance the role of the Europa, then this could become a source of latent if not open tension between them and a leading foreign policy issue between each region and third countries.

The value of dollars in private and official hands outside the United States exceeded $150 billion in 1972. It is not entirely clear how much the claims in the Eurodollar market represent double counting, for existing figures do not net out all interbank deposits. But the claims will undoubtedly grow larger in the next two decades, in the absence of some international agreement to fund them. Conversion of these balances into Europas, even if spread over ten to twenty years, will call for very substantial alteration in the pattern of world payments. The United States will have to run a substantial payments surplus, and Europe will have to run a correspondingly large deficit, both measured on a net liquidity basis. (The need for a U.S. surplus to permit foreigners to liquidate short-term dollar claims could, of course, be avoided if U.S. banks and firms issued short-term claims denominated in Europas to satisfy the hypothesized demand for them. Creditors and debtors would thus remain unchanged, and only the currency of denomination—hence allocation of exchange risk—would change.) Give prevalent neomercantilist attitudes, the rest of the industrial world will be reluctant to accept the required U.S. surplus. But when the time to adjust comes, attitudes might well be different.

Once a tipping point in composition of private and official balances is reached, the shift can accelerate, unless counteracting pressures are exerted. Britain was preoccupied for two decades with maintaining sterling balances. To that end it engaged in high interest rate policies, allowed preferred access to capital markets, directed foreign aid and preferential procurement (for example, in sugar and bananas) toward sterling area countries, and in addition called upon the great store of good will and political pragmatism that characterized the British Commonwealth.

If a tipping point for the dollar is reached, or anticipated, the United States may be tempted into a similar course of action, piecemeal. Indeed, such a course has already been adopted on a modest scale. Canada and Japan, like the less developed countries, both received partial exemptions from the interest equalization tax, thus being accorded some preferential access to the U.S. capital market. The voluntary credit restraint program covering American banks and the mandatory control of American corporate investment overseas also have preferential categories, mostly but not exclusively for less developed countries. The U.S. government is known to have had conversations with a number of aid-receiving countries about the composition of their reserves. These actions have not yet gone so far, or become sufficiently focused geographically, to be designated meaningfully as a dollar area, analogous to the sterling area. But the signs are already there, and the tendencies may be much stronger if the U.S. dollar has a serious rival in another currency, as sterling did. Moreover, the pressures would be very hard to resist if, at the time the tipping point were reached, the United States had an obligation to convert dollars into some form of reserve asset and only imperfect control over its exchange rate; as indicated above, the potential conversions would be massive.

The United States should strongly resist being drawn further down this path. Fortunately, such a course is not necessary or even tempting so long as the U.S. dollar is inconvertible into other reserve assets, and the United States should resist making the dollar convertible without adequate safeguards. Instead of trying to create a subglobal community of financially loyal countries, a dollar area which in the long run will only lead to unnecessary friction and strain with both members and nonmembers, the United States should exert its influence to achieve an adequate adjustment mechanism (which would mitigate but not fully solve the problem outlined here). It should seek consolidation of dollar holdings in the IMF or some other international body; this would also lessen but not solve the problem so long as large private balances remain outstanding. The United

States should also see that a contingency plan is prepared involving either foreign acceptance of a free exchange rate (such as Britain adopted in June 1972) or of massive recycling from Europe if a tipping point is reached.

European Commitment: Political Dimensions

The above discussion has been predicated on the assumption that monetary unification is desired in Europe and that it will take place. But there is reason to suspect that the objective is not fully accepted, even for the distant future, let alone for the end of the present decade. The British government is known to have serious reservations, and with good reason. The question is less widely debated on the continent, outside of Germany, but it is worth recalling the immediate antecedents to the Hague commitment to monetary unification in December 1969. That year had been one of considerable turmoil in European financial and commodity markets. The surprise devaluation of the French franc took place in August, and the German mark floated temporarily for some weeks in the autumn.

Early in the year intra-Community trade had been disrupted by French restrictions on imports, by special German border taxes to slow exports and stimulate imports, and by wide discrepancies between spot and forward exchange rates, all of which interfered with the functioning of the Common Market and particularly with the common market in agricultural products. Then came the unexpected resignation of de Gaulle in April, an event that simultaneously made French devaluation possible and removed the major obstacle to further progress of the European Community.

By late 1969, the new French government wished to make a gesture of cooperation toward the European Community to restore its credibility as a full partner in that enterprise. It also perceived currency difficulties as a threat to the Community's hard-won common agricultural policy (CAP) and desired therefore a common commitment to an exchange rate regime that would insure minimum interference with French agricultural exports. Finally, the French government was still smarting from the rebuffs received from its European partners in 1968 and 1969, when it was decided over French opposition first to establish the machinery for SDRs and then to activate that machinery for the first creation of SDRs in January 1970. European agreement to these actions was largely in response to U.S. leadership and was not, in the French view, sufficiently European in identity.

For a variety of reasons, therefore, the French government found it convenient to espouse closer monetary cooperation in Europe, which it interpreted as closer coordination of the European position on international monetary questions, that is, coordination of EC members' external monetary policies. One important strand in French thinking also favors the coordination of domestic monetary policies within the Community similar to that achieved by the theoretical gold standard of the nineteenth century; but that view, although present, is by no means ascendant.

French interest in greater monetary harmony among European countries coincided with the need of both the EC Commission and the proponents of European unity throughout Europe for a new goal, a dramatic symbol around which further progress toward unity could be rallied. By 1969, the Common Market was formally and officially complete. The transition provided for in the Rome Treaty, except for the provisions on majority rule, was over. Further progress was stalled and morale was low from the buffeting the Community had taken from de Gaulle. To prevent Europe from becoming solely a commercial union, the "Europeans" of Europe sought a new target, and monetary unification met the immediate requirements more plausibly than possible alternatives, such as revival of the idea of a European Defence Community. Thus, the Commission and the European-ists in other European countries welcomed the French initiative at The Hague. It served a temporary convergence of interests that concealed fundamental disagreements on principles. Some parties saw European monetary unification as the mobilizing force of the seventies toward European unity, just as formation of the Common Market had been the mobilizing force of the sixties. Others saw it as a vehicle for projecting a European policy onto the global scene and, in particular, successfully confronting the United States on international monetary questions.

If this assessment is accurate, it puts a very different complexion on the first transition phase already discussed in economic terms. To the preoccupation with internal affairs and the immobilism involved in having undertaken an intrinsically difficult task would be added sharp disagreement on the ultimate, or at least the proximate, objectives of "monetary unification." The European Community is going to find it difficult both to take constructive initiatives with respect to external affairs and to follow the initiatives of others, notably the United States. Thus, there may be a vacuum in effective world leadership at a time when the basic ground rules governing international trading and financial relationships during the past quarter century are in need of substantial modification, if not complete overhaul.

There are sharply different conceptions of "world economic order," both within Europe and between France, in particular, and the United States. France will attempt to harness the European objective of monetary unification, which requires the member countries to collaborate on and coordinate external monetary policies, to the French conception of world order.

This conception has never been published officially, and indeed may well not even be formulated internally within the French government, but French statements over the years have a consistent theme which can be summarized in the following propositions, in which the monetary precepts of Jacques Rueff are strongly evident:

1. There should be an impartial international monetary standard, preferably gold (necessarily at a much higher price).

2. The international role for national currencies should be eliminated, except in regions of special metropolitan influence, such as Francophone Africa, remnants of the sterling area, and those countries (as in Central America) that are, or seem in Europe to be, exceptionally closely tied to the United States.

3. There should be fixed exchange rates.

4. There should be controls on capital movements of all types, but especially direct investment and short-term banking movements.

5. World commodity markets should be "organized" so as to reduce price fluctuations and establish fair prices for primary products.

6. Trade preferences should be a legitimate instrument of foreign security and cultural policy.

7. International organizations should be given a minimum authority.

The first four of these propositions of course harken back to the original Bretton Woods Agreement, of which France has become a vigorous proponent recently. All seven planks are evident in French foreign economic policy during the past decade, although with fluctuating emphasis. There is undoubtedly no unanimity of view on them, even within the Pompidou government. Moreover, it should not be assumed, as is done occasionally in the press, that these views are put forward because they are narrowly self-serving. French concern about an international monetary system based on national currencies is widely shared. French devotion to fixed exchange rates also has considerable support outside France; it is not motivated merely by a desire to preserve French advantages under the common agricultural policy. Liberal French observers argue that flexible exchange rates of any kind will lead to a proliferation of trade controls; only under fixed rates will trade be increasingly liberalized and monetary policies sufficiently harmonized to encourage progress toward an integrated world economy.[5]

In the French position, there is a common thread, more philosophical than ideological in nature, that favors government interference in economic activity, not merely for macroeconomic management, which is more or less accepted in the United States, but for detailed market influence, or *dirigisme* as it has come to be known. A predisposition to *dirigisme* is probably general in Europe, outside of Germany and Switzerland, and marks an important philosophical difference between Europe and the United States, as it bears on the pursuit of world economic order. Britain has a strong liberal, that is, *nondirigiste*, intellectual tradition. But its practices in recent years have veered so markedly away from that stand that it is still unclear how Britain's presence will affect the outcome of what so far has been mainly a Franco-German dispute within Europe.

If the *dirigiste* view prevails within the European Community, as it is likely to do at least in some important dimensions (possibly as a condition for continuing French cooperation with the Community), there are two important corollaries for international monetary arrangements. First, the European Community will attempt to maintain direct controls over the international movement of capital. These controls will not be entirely successful, but efforts to prevent evasions may well lead on to a more comprehensive set of controls. Second, the commitment to fixed exchange rates will be strong and bolstered by a willingness to resort, if necessary, to direct government intervention in international transactions, mainly in regard to capital movements but if necessary in other transactions as well. Examples would be import quotas and special surcharges on imports, such as those used by France in 1968 and Britain in 1964, in both cases to avoid changing the exchange rate and in violation of solemn undertakings to preferential trading partners as well as less solemn global agreements. It will become more difficult to apply such restrictions *within* the Com-

5. See, for example, Paul Fabra, "Should a European Currency Become a Reserve Currency?" *The World Today* (London), Vol. 27 (June 1971), pp. 249–55.

munity as time goes on, but pressure will correspondingly mount to apply restrictions on a uniform basis to all external transactions. Continuing disagreement among member governments, notably between France and Germany, over the desirability and effectiveness of such controls will represent one of the most important difficulties in the transition toward monetary unification.

What does at present command common agreement in Europe is the desirability of diminishing, if not entirely eradicating, the reserve currency role of the U.S. dollar. For the reasons given above, there is no corresponding and complementary agreement on improvement in the international adjustment process, but rather a dominant view that fixed exchange rates remain viable, bolstered if necessary by controls on international capital movements. This conjunction of views, if carried into practice, will unquestionably be *dis*integrative of the world economy, however that term may be defined.

Comments by Bela Balassa

FOLLOWING time-honored custom, I will emphasize my points of disagreement with Richard N. Cooper rather than points of agreement. Cooper makes the provocative statement that the unification of existing currencies into a single European currency will in itself have *no* substantial long-run effect on the world economy. It seems to me that the key words are "in itself." They may be interpreted to mean that monetary policies, in Europe and elsewhere, are not going to be affected by currency unification. Yet one can hardly assume that this will be the case and, if I add some more qualifications to those made by Cooper, his statement will prove to be empty of content. I hasten to add that this conclusion does not imply any basic disagreement between Cooper and myself; it reflects, rather, differences in emphasis and in the evaluation of probabilities as regards possible actions.

Let me begin by putting forward the proposition that the final outcome will depend on the steps taken during the transitional period toward monetary integration. Cooper notes that to many observers the commitment to eventual monetary unification implies a commitment to fixed exchange rates during the intervening transition. While he points out that this implication is far from logical, he assumes that such a route would be followed.

As I argued elsewhere, this alternative is both undesirable and unworkable.[6] In view of intercountry differences in tradeoffs between inflation, unemployment, and economic growth, as well as in the relative valuation of these objectives, the maintenance of unchanged parities among EC currencies would entail compromising national policy objectives. In order to establish fixed exchange rates among these currencies, it would be necessary to modify such national policy objectives relating to price stability, employment, and economic growth, and to coordinate monetary, fiscal, and wage policies; neither step is expected to occur in the near future.

Correspondingly, efforts made to maintain fixed exchange rates within the EC are bound to fail and to lead to recurrent crises, as they have in recent years. Any such attempts not only involve a misdirection of energies but tend to jeopardize the possibilities for coordination in other areas, including regional policy and industrial policy in the Common Market.

Cooper has emphasized the danger of "immobilism" in the integration process that might result from attempts to achieve monetary integration via the fixed-exchange-rate route. But one needs to go further and explore alternative possibilities. It might then be possible to escape the "Alice-in-Wonderland" feeling that I, for one, have experienced during discussions on the impact of monetary integration in Western Europe on the United States. Union may not occur at all and, if it does, it may be a long way off and take a different route from the one at present envisaged. In the intervening period, the world economy and the international monetary system will have undergone changes, so that current assumptions and presumptions on which today's discussions are based will no longer be realistic.

It seems to me that either European countries will persist in taking the fixed-exchange-rate route, leading to recurrent monetary crises, or they will opt for a different course. In the first eventuality, we should discuss the implications of failure and the resulting crises for the United States rather than those of an imaginary situation. In the second, we should consider the possible outcomes under alternative assumptions. I now turn to the second possibility.

6. Bela Balassa, "Monetary Integration in the European Common Market," Proceedings of the Conference on Europe and the Evolution of the International Monetary System (Geneva: Graduate Institute of International Studies, Jan. 13–15, 1972; processed).

In my Geneva paper, I suggested creating a common unit of account for the European Community around which the currencies of the EC countries would fluctuate during a transitional period. Similar proposals have been made in other quarters, most recently by Magnifico and Williamson,[7] and it seems to me that, with the enlargement of the Common Market, the ensuing changes in the composition of the Commission, and the increased understanding of the disadvantages of the fixed-exchange-rate route, such an alternative will eventually come into focus. Its implications are considered below.

Establishing a common unit will not by itself alter the position of the U.S. dollar on the international monetary scene. But it can hardly be assumed that the EC countries would limit themselves to creating a new unit without taking steps to assure its use in official and private transactions and to make it a "pivot" for European currencies. These steps are bound to affect the role of the dollar in international financial markets and they are likely to be accompanied by a conscious effort on the part of the Common Market to reduce the dollar's present preeminence.

There are various actions that may be taken. They include employing the new unit in all EC operations in place of the great variety of units now used, among other purposes, for setting agricultural prices, for calculating the budget of the Community, and in the transactions of the European Investment Bank. The new unit also offers a medium for the operations of the European Reserve Fund and, eventually, for interventions on foreign exchange markets.

The last-mentioned purpose presupposes the wide acceptability of the new currency unit. This can be promoted by permitting commercial banks to establish accounts denominated in this unit; by permitting and eventually requiring commercial banks, pension funds, insurance companies, and other financial intermediaries to hold obligations denominated in it; and by national governments using it for some of their national debt issues.

It can be expected that traders, investors, and tourists would increasingly resort to the new currency unit in their transactions as it becomes widely acceptable among the member countries and its employment entails reducing the exchange risk associated with the use of national currencies and the dollar. If the new unit proves to be of more stable value than the U.S. dollar—a possibility Cooper does not seem to consider realistic—the

7. Giovanni Magnifico and John Williamson, *European Monetary Integration,* Federal Trust Report (London: Federal Trust for Education and Research, 1972).

replacement of the dollar in European transactions would be accelerated. Some movement in this direction is already apparent in issuance of bonds and travelers' checks denominated in multiple currencies. The role of the dollar would further be reduced if the new unit were used as an intervention currency.

The proposed solution would probably release energies for policy coordination in other areas, such as regional and industrial policies, a prerequisite for eventual integration in the monetary sphere. Monetary integration in Western Europe would thus be furthered by the meshing of such policies as well as by the avoidance of monetary crises. At the same time, pressures would be created to alter national policies and thereby reduce fluctuations around the common currency unit. And, if the political will were there, eventually further moves would be taken toward monetary *and* economic integration.

Parallel to these changes, Europeans will increasingly make their presence felt in international monetary negotiations. Such developments are likely to take place during the transitional period in negotiating the value of the new common currency unit vis-à-vis the dollar, in dealing with problems of speculative capital flows, and in reacting to U.S. initiatives on such matters as the convertibility of the dollar into other reserve assets. Although Cooper opposes the reestablishment of convertibility, it is considered to be in the interest of the European countries.

The picture that emerges is that of a duopoly between two leading currencies. Cooper has ably discussed the potential disadvantages of this outcome. But the question is not only what disadvantages this alternative would have and how it would affect the position of the United States but also what it holds for European countries whose governments are critical of the present supremacy of the dollar. At the same time, the potential disadvantages of a duopolistic structure can be mitigated by flexibility in the exchange rate between the new European unit and the U.S. dollar.

Comments by William Diebold, Jr.

IN READING Richard N. Cooper's paper, I faced the problem I have faced so often before when reading his studies. It is full of neat analyses and interesting original twists that make me think about a number of related but disconnected issues. Much of the content of his paper I agreed with, not least the outcroppings, in the midst of an analysis, of sound policy advice on, for instance, the inadvisability of trying to foist the dollar on other countries and a warning that the kind of policies implicit in some of the French approaches are serious because they are views shared by many more people than the French.

However, when I asked myself what the real thrust of the whole paper was in terms of direction, I found myself a little confused. So, on reviewing his arguments, I attempted to sum up the most pertinent issues and I came out with a series of statements that seem to point in different directions. The procedure is not really fair to Cooper because my statements overlook some of the qualifications, time dimensions, and other explanations that he considers necessary. But perhaps my propositions are close enough to his main line of reasoning to permit me to say that the result, while not a portrait, is a caricature—and a caricature, after all, should reveal something about the original.

The initial proposition is the one to which Bela Balassa objected: the existence of a European currency is not, in the future, going to be of great importance to the world economy. The next statement I came up with is that such monetary unity would make Europe of much greater importance in the world than a Europe which is now divided.

At that point, Cooper's argument is ambiguous as to whether it is monetary unity or unity of position on international monetary issues that will give Europe greater importance. However, the third proposition—that the increased weight of Europe in the world and its impact on monetary issues does not depend on whether there are fixed or flexible exchange rates in the system generally—suggests that true unification is the key.

Fourth, quite rightly pointing out that the Europeans have embarked on an extremely difficult course, Cooper notes that this may well lead to immobilism and unwillingness or inability to deal with international monetary reform. To the extent that the Europeans do achieve unity, some degree of rivalry with the United States will result and Cooper sees trouble ahead unless a new system is developed in which some currency, other than the one for the European Monetary Union (EMU) or the dollar, serves not only as the general reserve unit but also as the substitute for the EMU currency and the dollar in private use; problems due to great shifts in private balances would thereby be avoided. Failing those circumstances, Cooper sees that rivalry may push the United States into a policy of trying to create a dollar area or retain a degree of dollar supremacy.

The fifth and sixth propositions concern the ways in which the concept of monetary unity can be used in Europe. The fifth states that EMU is treated as a symbol of unity, but a very weak one since many Europeans either do not really want a united Europe or are not truly committed to the idea—which will become apparent when they are asked to pay the price. Nevertheless, the sixth proposition is that the French could use this symbol of unity as leverage to produce all the bad results of the kind of policy the Americans do not want. This suggests considerable diplomatic skill on the part of the French.

When I put these six propositions together, I find that I am enlightened as to the possibilities of the situation but not so much as to the probabilities. However, Cooper goes further in his analysis by emphasizing those outcomes that he considers more rather than less probable. But even without this guidance, I have found his paper quite helpful in the way it takes account of a whole series of contradictory forces at work in this difficult situation. Each of the themes he develops, it seems to me, may very well be correct, with the exception of the implication of the first proposition that if EMU were achieved it would not be really important. Nonetheless, I would like to raise some additional questions that seem relevant to the weighing of alternatives.

Cooper's paper—and the others in this volume—have this one omission in common: failure to consider alternative forms of monetary integration in Europe. Almost all analysis has hinged on the tacit assumption that only one type of European monetary integration is possible, namely, one emphasizing fixed exchange rates within the group. At the same time, analysis has shown that that particular form of monetary integration is open to many very cogent objections, and it is very difficult to achieve. Does this not mean that sooner or later the Europeans will try to get what they want from monetary integration by another route? Would other methods work better? Would they have the same international impact? Would they be objectionable to the United States?

There seems to me to be a distinction, hitherto undiscussed, between the taking of common positions on monetary reform and the actual process of integration inside Europe; this tie-in may turn out to be a crucial factor. It would certainly seem to have great bearing on the matter of French leverage (which is more powerful, I should imagine, when countries consider taking a common position than it is when they are considering ways of achieving true internal integration). On the one hand, the kind of resistance each effort generates in Europe is different and, on the other hand, a solid front against the Americans appeals to both France and Germany and could be achieved more quickly if they took a common position than if they had to wait until there was true internal consolidation. Taking a common position on an issue in international monetary reform should be regarded as an act reflecting common interests, not just as a matter of attitudes, philosophies, and sentiment. Who, within Europe, would actually gain or lose by alternative forms of international monetary integration?

My other main question in this connection is whether the taking of a common position creates significant pressures for true integration. That integration generates (or requires) common external positions is obvious, but how strong is the influence in the other direction?

This leads to questions about the transition and the dynamics of integration. That process is very familiar in trade. The first essential both for prosperity and economies of scale was to eliminate internal barriers in Europe. The existence of a big American market with no internal barriers has played a part in the thinking of those who established the Common Market. However, with its creation, new problems arose for the United States to which the latter's response was the Trade Expansion Act that later led to the reduction of other barriers. Clearly, by almost anybody's standards, there was a gain in integration from this whole process.

Does that sort of situation pertain when it comes to monetary matters? The internal inducement, in terms of European problems, has not been dealt with in depth; although significant references have been made in discussion suggesting that the positive forces for monetary integration may be strong, this line of argument has not been pursued.

There is no doubt at all, however, that there is an international inducement to develop a common policy since, otherwise, Europe's influence on international monetary reform would be weak compared with the American influence. But then comes the question: If European nations join forces, what kind of response will this stimulate in the United States? It seems to me that Cooper's paper is right on that score both in regard to the alternatives he names and their respective lack of wisdom.

Basically, the United States has three possible courses open to it: One, to react against European monetary union, is clearly disintegrative; another is to attempt either to coordinate policies or at least to help smooth any transition; and the third is what I would call a true globalizing solution.

Americans should accept the idea that a new kind of international monetary regime is being established which has to be handled by the two parties —Europe and the United States—working together.

To go further into the dynamics of integration means dealing with such matters as short-term capital movements and direct investment. In the latter case, once again there is a pattern of European-American interaction that can be compared to the trade experience and the potential experience in money already referred to. So far, the European Community has failed to agree on a common investment policy. But I suspect that over the next ten years, even if the label "common investment policy" is not used, the Europeans will, through a series of actions concerning industrial policy, competition, nontariff barriers, government procurement, and the like, take a number of steps that affect direct American investment.

It is no longer adequate to treat direct investment primarily as the movement of capital. It is more a matter of entrepreneurship and industrial organization. There is, of course, still a close link with capital movements and a good deal of what has been said about the danger that different types of controls will be imposed bears on what is done about direct investment. There is also an interaction. Lawrence Krause makes a good point when he says that the liberalization of capital movements and the unification of capital markets inside the Community would, as a practical matter, have to apply to all enterprises within the Community, whatever their ownership. That would represent a big change because in spite of pledges about national treatment and legal equality, there are several kinds of discrimination against American companies. One is in access to national capital markets, accorded to truly European companies on a preferential basis, in part to compensate them for not having the freedom of their American-based competitors. As long as the European governments feel the need for such preferential treatment (and it seems to me they are likely to feel it at least as much in the future as in the past), it will be an obstacle to the true unification of the capital markets.

Then, there is another line of questioning that might be labeled, "How to think about the problem." Is there some way of eliding the process of regional integration in monetary affairs? In other words, could the Europeans get what they really want out of monetary integration from an improved global system?

To explore that issue means understanding European needs. How these are interpreted and how one views the possibility of eliding the regional factor both have a bearing on the kind of proposals for monetary reform that the United States could most usefully make. They are also important in judging whether the Europeans can avoid the difficulties inherent in any attempt to maintain fixed rates among themselves. They may be able to do this either because a different road to union is made possible by the reformed global system or because union no longer seems necessary.

A distinction must be made between the long-run substantive advantage for the Europeans of any such global system and the rather different kind of advantage they might see in taking a common position vis-à-vis the United States in negotiations for monetary reform.

The Europeans certainly cannot get what they want if the world system is dominated by the United States. As systems need managers, there is then the question of how the global system will be administered if not by the United States alone. If it is to be managed internationally (and there is a considerable consensus among experts that it should be), who are the other parties? Just Europe? Also Japan? Still others? If there is a European component, can it be anything other than a spokesman for a complete European monetary union?

Another branch of this line of inquiry would be to ask how, if there is a European monetary union of some sort, serious friction can be avoided between the United States and the new entity; the dangerous possibilities are outlined in Cooper's paper. If there are two large entities of this sort, there is bound to be a certain amount of dissension. That does not mean that agreement is impossible, nor does it mean that antagonism should dominate thought and that a combative position is justified. The question is whether the friction can be contained and the conflicting views and interests reconciled sufficiently to prevent a breakdown in communication so that it seems reasonable for one or the other to insist on a disintegrative course of action. Cooper quite rightly warns that there are forms of international management of the economy that are not really compatible with American thinking, so it is possible that a point could be reached at which a disintegrative step was preferable to the only terms on which broader agreement could be attained.

Finally, as to U.S. policy, I am only going to say it is clear to me that in the foreseeable future the United States has to be able to contend with two entirely different kinds of Europe so far as monetary affairs are concerned. This means that Americans have to be capable of finding ways of moving toward international monetary reform that can accommodate either a divided Europe that is or is not taking seriously the effort of getting together or one that is so concerned with getting together that it does not wish to pay attention to the problems of the world monetary system.

This is an extraordinarily difficult task, particularly if one also imposes the condition that it would be better in the long run for the United States not to try to run the show or even have the degree of influence it has had in the past. And yet, sometimes action will depend on American insistence and pressure. When later discussion explores this dilemma more fully, Cooper's paper will prove extremely helpful.

PHILIP H. TREZISE

Implications for U.S. Policy toward Europe

"Our support for the strengthening and broadening of the European Community has not diminished. . . . We consider that the possible economic price of a truly unified Europe is outweighed by the gain in the political vitality of the West as a whole."   —*Richard M. Nixon, 1970*[1]

"The United States has always supported the strengthening and enlargement of the European Community. We still do. We welcome cohesion in Europe because it makes Europe a sturdier pillar of the structure of peace."
—*Richard M. Nixon, 1971*[2]

"In 1971, several of the fundamental goals of United States policy in Europe came measurably closer.
    "The unification of Western Europe made a major advance."
—*Richard M. Nixon, 1972*[3]

EUROPEAN UNITY has been an objective from which American foreign policy has not deviated since it was first articulated in the Marshall Plan. Underlying the objective, in the first instance, was the premise that Western Europe's intermittent civil war could be ended only by bringing France and Germany into association and cooperation as members of a larger

1. *United States Foreign Policy for the 1970's,* Message from the President of the United States, February 18, 1970.
2. *U.S. Foreign Policy for the 1970's,* A Report to the Congress by Richard Nixon, February 25, 1971.
3. *U.S. Foreign Policy for the 1970's,* A Report to the Congress by Richard Nixon, President of the United States, February 9, 1972.

276

community. This was followed by the hope or the expectation that a unified Europe would both provide for its own defense against the military power of the Soviet Union and also with the United States as a partner work for stability and peace elsewhere in the world.

The first premise, arguably, has been satisfied. Franco-German rivalry no doubt has some latent force in European political life, but a renewal of internal military conflict in Western Europe is simply not conceivable. Peace within Western Europe is strong and secure. But the concept of an identifiable "Europe" with an independent military capability and a single foreign policy is most unlikely to become a reality, at least for this decade, except, possibly, if the United States were to end its commitment to European defense and the Soviet Union were to show unmistakably hostile intentions.[4] Although there is a sizable faction in Western Europe which, for various reasons (including the wish to be more independent of the United States), strongly favors union, the European political process does not seem to be working decisively in that direction.

Now, however, comes European monetary unification heralded as a route to political unification. The group headed by Pierre Werner (and which included B. Clappier of France) did not dissemble about what unification in the monetary realm is intended to accomplish. The Werner Report states: "Economic and monetary union thus appears as a leaven for the development of political union."[5] Or, again, "The centre of decision of economic policy will be politically responsible to a European Parliament. The latter will have to be furnished with a status corresponding to the extension of the Community missions, not only *from the point of view of the extent of its powers, but also having regard to the method of election of its members.*"[6] The process of monetary unification inescapably would lead the participant countries into matters of critical political importance and would require new or expanded supranational institutions. An eventual Community with its central bank, its "centre of decision" for economic

4. It is by no means clear that a "European" defense structure, presumably with a nuclear component, would be desirable if it could be achieved but, perhaps fortunately, we will not need to face that eventuality soon.

5. *Report to the Council and the Commission on the Realisation by Stages of Economic and Monetary Union in the Community.* Supplement to *Bulletin* 11-1970 of the European Communities, the Werner Group, under the chairmanship of Pierre Werner (Luxembourg: Office for Official Publications of the European Communities, October 8, 1970), p. 12. (Hereinafter referred to as the Werner Report.)

6. *Ibid.*, p. 13; emphasis added.

policy, and a genuine Parliament would surely have a close resemblance to a European federation.

It is not inherently impossible that the Werner group's approach might bring about such a federal Europe. If it does so, however, it will probably not be because of the logical progression by stages foreseen so persuasively in the Werner Report. Instead, there could be a series of disputes with the United States: about monetary reform, about American investment in Europe, about agricultural trade, about commercial policies. These conflicts would draw European political leaders together around a common external objective which would be to contend as "Europeans" with American economic power. European preoccupation with internal difficulties, particularly those associated with monetary integration, could gradually give way to resentment and bitterness against American policies and American demands that seem to run counter to Europe's aims. In these circumstances, sovereignty might be relegated to Community agencies as the essential feeling of "European-ness" overtook and supplanted nation-state loyalties.[7]

I am not suggesting that this is what will happen. For one thing, it supposes a substantial diminution of the proximate external threat arising from the imbalance of military power between Western and Eastern Europe. Failing such an abatement, the security ties between the United States and Western Europe no doubt will continue to dissuade each side from outright confrontations with the other. Beyond that, economic conflict between Europe and the United States would be costly to both sides, and this will be a substantial deterrent. But if union is to be effected within a short period, say, a decade, it is likely to require the kind of direct political impetus that is perhaps most readily provided by common hostility toward an outsider.

The most suitable American attitude toward the objective of European monetary unification is probably a passive one. We can go on saying, and meaning, that European union is desirable and that it has our support, without favoring a particular set of procedures intended to hasten its attainment. But to quarrel with the monetary union objective is to quarrel

7. As Raymond Aron says, "the community power, animated by a community desire . . . conscious of its uniqueness and determined to assert and affirm it in the face of all other collectivities." Raymond Aron, *Peace and War: A Theory of International Relations* (Doubleday, 1966), p. 747.

with the whole European idea, for surely political union must encompass monetary union, whichever is the leader in the integration process. At the practical level, moreover, U.S. opposition can only strengthen those proponents of monetary unification who see in it the creation of a countervailing power to the United States. And in the end, the specific features of an eventual monetary union, and thus its meaning for the United States and the world, will depend in largest part on the series of decisions and actions leading to it. If the process of unification requires extensive controls against outsiders, then the final stage will find Europe an inward-oriented unity; and if the interim is one of progressive liberalization, the result will be to foster an open world economy. But once implemented, the European monetary union most probably will be beyond the control or influence of the United States.

If it is a correct judgment that the United States had best take an agnostic view of monetary union, and it is difficult to imagine Washington having any other official position, then the policy problems revert as usual to more immediate matters. In this case, they center on prospects for revision of the international monetary arrangements. European aspirations to form a monetary union obviously need not conflict with a reform of the Bretton Woods system. At the moment, in fact, such overt indicators as are available suggest that the European Community and the United States are in broad agreement on the principles of reform. But it is prudent to suppose that difficult negotiations are still to come.

Past experience and an objective view of the situation argue that the single most serious obstacle to international agreement will be the inability of the European states to reach a consensus. Europeans would have had difficulty agreeing among themselves even if the common commitment to begin working toward monetary union had never been accepted. The differences between France and Germany relate to fundamental principles; they have not been bridged in more than a dozen years of association in the Community. On each new occasion of Community decision making an effort has to be made to resolve disagreements. And the hope in Europe that the accession of the United Kingdom will expedite the Community's processes may not, in fact, be realized when it comes to deciding upon monetary questions.

At any rate, the agreement to seek monetary unification can scarcely fail to complicate the already unwieldy and slow-moving machinery in Brussels. The normal requirement to search for a Community position is almost a political absolute. Another meeting like the one in Stockholm in 1968, with France as odd-man-out, is but barely imaginable. Yet if the Community members are themselves deeply absorbed in the monetary problems of the Nine, they may take a long time to reach agreement on common responses for the issues to be raised in the Committee of Twenty.[8]

Should negotiations on monetary reform drag on inconclusively, one must suppose that the Community reply to the dollar's inconvertibility will be an extension of controls on capital movements and, in some circumstances, on trade flows as well. Furthermore, the probability is that the industrial countries will deem it necessary to halt consideration of other economic questions until the outcome of the monetary talks is more clearly discernible. In the present economic climate (of September 1972), that can only mean a continuing retreat from multilateralism and a further erosion of the General Agreement on Tariffs and Trade; the Community's preferential trading system, which soon probably will extend over all of Western Europe and most of Africa, will assume an air of permanence; and the political understandings required if anything is to be done about agricultural trade will probably not be attainable.

But if European immobilism does not stall the negotiations, does the Community's pledge to unification make international agreement on monetary reform much more difficult or impossible?

At the heart of the matter must be the adjustment process and the role played by exchange rate flexibility. The agenda outlined in the Smithsonian communiqué of December 1971 indicates no other point on which the commitment to unification in Europe intensifies the difficulties of reaching an international accord (except, of course, as the political necessity for intra-Community agreement has been enhanced and the French position thereby strengthened).

Of course, one may ask: Is not convertibility of the dollar made much more difficult? Aside from the relationship of a better adjustment process to making dollar convertibility workable, the other problems—which concern the disposition to be made of outstanding dollar balances—may be hard to resolve but they are not aggravated because the Community has decided on monetary union.

8. For a description of the origin and purpose of the Committee of Twenty, see International Monetary Fund, *IMF Survey*, Annual Meetings Issue, Vol. 1 (October 8, 1972).

Also, what will be the place of gold, reserve currencies, and Special Drawing Rights (SDRs) in the system? More than a lingering European attachment to gold and an active desire to phase out the reserve currencies may be expected, but these attitudes do not stem from adherence to the concept of monetary unification.

Similarly, with the "appropriate volume of liquidity" and with measures to deal with short-term capital movements, there may be a European position contrary to that of the United States or Japan, but it is not evident that it will be swayed much by the doctrines of the Werner Report.

When it comes to the "means of establishing a suitable degree of flexibility" and "the division of responsibilities for defending stable exchange rates," one cannot be so sure.[9] There is the London statement of understandings among the finance ministers of the then Ten, which included "easily adjustable" parities and "equal rights and obligations" between deficit and surplus countries.[10] In principle, furthermore, the embryo European monetary union could operate within a system having a "suitable degree" of flexibility: by joint adjustment of Community rates relative to outside currencies, or by abandoning the Werner Report prescription for (more or less) fixed rates among the members.

At that stage, the Nine probably would fight shy of any commitment to adjust their rates jointly against the dollar. The experience thus far affords no basis for confidence that separate payments positions within the Community will move in reasonable harmony over the next few years. Yet if there are significant divergences, one or another participant is bound to veto changes that would worsen its national problem, and rightly so. A Community of Six could not agree on a joint float during the crises of May and August 1971, and it seems most doubtful that an enlarged Community will be prepared to take a pledge that will be extremely difficult to honor.

Why not depart from the idea of fixed rates within the Nine? The argument that the common agricultural policy (CAP) relies on unchanging rates can hardly be sustained in the face of the large parity adjustments made since 1969. Occasional small changes in parities would certainly be less disruptive of the CAP than the sizable revaluations and devaluations of 1969. And there is an increasingly persuasive case anyway for moving

9. International Monetary Fund, *International Financial News Survey*, Vol. 23 (December 22–30, 1972), p. 418.

10. Reported in *New York Times*, July 18, 1972.

the CAP from price supports to income supports.[11] The stronger argument may issue, paradoxically, from the devoted integrationists and from France. The integrationists, just like the Werner Report, can see relative fixity of intra-Community rates as a central factor in forcing the pace of monetary-political unification. With the exchange rate excluded as a means of adjustment, the Community will need arrangements and institutions to harmonize national policies and to deal with regional imbalances. As time goes on and experience is gained, "the principal decisions of economic policy will be taken at Community level and therefore . . . the necessary powers . . . transferred . . . to the Community plane."[12] France, still unfriendly to this kind of supranationalism, can nevertheless see fixed rates as a key element in a managed Community economic system, with exchange controls, a wide preferential trading system, and "organized" commodity markets.

If the fixed rate view prevails and the Community negotiators prove unwilling either to consider joint or separate parity adjustments subject to presumptive rules of some kind, might not the United States, Japan, and Canada agree on procedures for greater flexibility for their currencies, leaving the Community members free to make discrete changes in those extreme cases that will still arise? Japan will surely resist any such idea, and Canada, with its aspirations to diversify its markets beyond the United States, will be dubious. In any case, a differential rule of this sort is bound to lead to a regime of European exchange controls unless the principal nations of the Community consistently inflate faster than the United States. It is hard to see how a desirable and reasonably durable reform can be achieved without the active and full participation of the Community states in the adjustment negotiations.

Pessimism may be unjustified, for the London communiqué of the Ten (issued when Norway was still expected to join) may mean literally what it said. In that event, the task of finding agreement on a scheme for quasi-

---

11. The "Mansholt Report" in 1968 observed that "it is a fact that [farm incomes] still lag badly behind the incomes of other social and occupational groups. . . . Unless the common agricultural policy can show substantial progress in this matter in the course of the next few years, there will assuredly be a crisis of confidence and one of the main foundations of our Community will thereby be endangered." Commission of the European Communities, "Memorandum on the Reform of Agriculture in the European Economic Community," COM(68) 1000, Part A (Brussels: 1968; processed), p. 2.

12. Werner Report, p. 26.

automatic, or anyway frequent, small parity changes still looks formidable enough, but less difficult than the alternative: that the Community insist on a path to monetary union via rigid exchange rates.

In sum, the Community's choice of monetary unification as an ultimate objective leaves American policy pretty much where it would be or ought to have been without that decision. The interest of the United States, which may or may not be pursued with requisite vigor, is in a more open world economy. As events have developed so far, the next and necessary step to be taken in that direction is the restructuring of the Bretton Woods system. In nominal negotiating terms, the United States can offer to Western Europe, Japan, and Canada a willingness to forswear the reserve currency "privilege" for the dollar in return for agreement on an orderly mutual process of adjustment of future imbalances. In fact, the object of the exercise is to rebuild a system in which the industrial countries can cooperate to mutual advantage. It will be ironic if this bargain should become more difficult to strike because the Community has elected—in part as a reaction to the special position held by the dollar—to seek a unified European monetary system.

Comments by Edward R. Fried

THE BREVITY of Philip Trezise's paper on policy implications may seem surprising. Policy, however, deals with what governments can influence at tolerable costs with instruments at their disposal. Hence, the broad terrain of the workability of the European Monetary Union (EMU), the possibilities of achieving it and even its consequences for U.S. interests do not, for the most part, involve issues for U.S. policy. Nonetheless, these questions may provide some guide as to the costs the United States may be willing to incur to avoid losses or to achieve gains.

To start with first principles, I take it that U.S. interest in the political unification of Europe remains undiminished, or nearly so. Trezise cites statements to that effect in each of President Nixon's foreign policy reports. I would note two caveats. Where the President's 1970 foreign policy report dutifully reports that part of the catechism which says that the political gains of European political unification would outweigh the possible economic costs to the United States, his reports in 1971 and 1972 include no mention of possible costs. Second, the U.S. rhetoric of confrontation with

Europe over agriculture, sharing of defense burdens, and exchange rates over the past year or so has sounded more appropriate to an adversary than an alliance relationship. Nevertheless, the President makes these foreign policy statements each year, and whether everyone in the administration hears them or not, they are unambiguous statements that the U.S. policy is to support the political unification of Europe for overriding political and security reasons.

That being the case, should not European monetary union have the active support of the United States? If it succeeded, it could bring impetus to political unification. Furthermore, the current discussion at this conference suggests that, if EMU worked and if it were achieved in an expanding international economic environment, it would, on balance, have economic benefits for the United States—second-order benefits, to be sure, but benefits accompanied by potentially large political and security gains.

Nevertheless, active U.S. support of EMU would not be in order. Even before the United States assumed a less active role and before it was widely recognized that economic power had become diffused in the world, the United States learned that active support of policies that Europeans considered to be their internal matters had its disadvantages. Furthermore, the economic costs to the United States of active support could turn out to be large. A relatively sanguine view of these costs assumes that EMU can be achieved and can work well. Transitional problems, however, could create difficulties for the United States; so would an attempt to achieve EMU that failed.

Would this be reason for the United States to quarrel with Europe over its commitment to EMU? Surely not. To do so might indeed be one way that European monetary union could be achieved but only in circumstances and in a form unfavorable for all countries. Lawrence Krause has made the distinction between movements toward European monetary union that are externally and internally motivated. In the former instance, which could result from active U.S. opposition to EMU, economic confrontation between the United States and Europe would be more frequent and more strident, creating the danger that restrictions and controls on international activity would spread. In this environment, security and political relations with Europe would also suffer, perhaps critically.

That leaves us with a passive policy regarding European efforts to achieve monetary union, not benign neglect but, in Trezise's terms, "agnosticism," in W. Max Corden's terms, "minding our own business," and in J. Carter Murphy's terms, "to stay at home." Richard Cooper and Charles Kindleberger suggest this may not be possible, but I suspect they have in mind not the issue of EMU in general but how EMU may concern other matters under active negotiation with Europe.

Assuming a passive U.S. policy, how will Europe's effort to achieve monetary union affect Atlantic relations? Here Trezise focuses on its possible consequences for the negotiations on monetary reform. In principle, they need not be serious; in practice, they might be.

First, agreement to seek European monetary union could greatly complicate the problem within Europe's Nine of reaching a common position in discussions of the Committee of Twenty. Cooper and others pointed to the external complications that could arise if Europe were preoccupied with internal matters. Joseph Nye's emphasis on the differences within the Community over objectives as well as means paints this problem more vividly. All this could mean that the negotiations for international monetary reform might degenerate into an exercise in tedium and frustration—another Kennedy Round, even longer drawn out. The Kennedy Round had to be completed within five years or else U.S. legislative authority would have expired. In the case of the monetary negotiations, the only pressure against European immobilism would be the onset of crisis. Financial crises have their uses, but in today's environment, there is less assurance they will have a benign outcome.

Second, aside from the question of European immobilism in the negotiations, will the Werner Report prescription of more or less fixed exchange rates cause the Europeans, in Trezise's words, to fight shy of any commitment to adjust their rates jointly against the dollar? It seems reasonable to believe that likely divergences among the separate payment positions of countries within the European Community over the next few years will increase the difficulties of reaching a common Community position on changes in rates against the dollar.

What, then, is to be done? Corden suggests that the United States be prepared to take the initiative and devalue as a means of dealing with this aspect of immobilism in European exchange rates and, presumably, on the assumption that the Europeans would permit this to happen. Perhaps this would work but only on the assumption that Japan will be prepared to take up the adjustment slack by revaluing (assuming, for this discussion, the continuation of the present pattern of imbalances in payments). This may turn out to be too optimistic an assumption, particularly after taking into account Japan's excessive concern over its competitive position in third countries vis-à-vis European surplus countries. I am left with the conclusion that it is difficult to envisage a satisfactory adjustment mechanism in which Europe does not play an active role.

The danger is that the effect of the commitment to EMU on European negotiating flexibility and on Europe's willingness to adjust its rate against the dollar on the basis of presumptive criteria could delay the negotiations on monetary reform and could even place them in jeopardy. If so, there are likely to be increasing arguments over convertibility and no progress in negotiations on industrial tariffs, nontariff barriers, and agriculture. Irritation in the United States over Community preferences and the common agricultural policy, together with European irritation over the United States' failure to return to convertibility and the continued "privileged" role of the dollar, might then move everyone further toward a world of restrictionism.

This may be far too gloomy a prospect, however. As Trezise points out, the London communiqué of the finance ministers outlines a negotiating position that would be compatible with an effective system of exchange rate adjustment, and in principle, the move toward EMU could provide for small and frequent changes in European rates against the dollar.

In any event, the implications for U.S. foreign economic policy would seem to be the same, with or without the Community objective of monetary integration. To build a workable international system, the United States, Europe, and Japan must share responsibility in the adjustment process regardless of how European internal affairs are organized.

Comments by C. Fred Bergsten

BOTH THE PROCESS of European monetary unification and the eventual achievement of European Monetary Union (EMU) can have a major impact on U.S. foreign policy through their effects on domestic politics in the United States. In turn, U.S. policy can significantly affect the evolution of EMU by affecting policy attitudes within Europe. My comments will focus on the close relationships between these two sets of "domestic" politics.

EMU is the third major functional phase of European integration—the first was the creation of the customs union (CXT, for the common external tariff which best symbolizes it); the second was the creation of the common agricultural policy (CAP). The discrimination of the CXT could have seriously upset U.S.-European relations, by making American industry and labor more protectionist. But the U.S. responded positively by passing the Trade Expansion Act and proposing the Kennedy Round, and by investing heavily behind the new tariff wall, and Europe replied in kind by negotiating the Round to a successful conclusion and avoiding restriction of American investment. The CAP has seriously upset U.S.-European relations, however, by undermining the crucial support of the U.S. farm community for a liberal U.S. trade policy and (along with the European Community's preferential arrangements) by cooling U.S. enthusiasm for European unification itself by signaling Europe's disregard for the interests of outsiders. This has happened because the United States rejected the Community's offer to limit increases in its agricultural supports (the *montant de soutien* or MDS proposal) in the Kennedy Round, and because the Community has obstinately continued to expand the CAP and the preferential arrangements despite increasingly shrill American and other protests. The basic question in assessing the broad foreign policy effect of EMU is whether it will follow the CXT or CAP precedents.

It is virtually certain that major economic conflict between Europe and America would decisively undercut the ability of any U.S. administration to maintain any significant (let alone the present) level of U.S. troops in Europe.[13] Senator Mike Mansfield bizarrely saw the monetary crisis of May 1971 as an "attack on the dollar," and used it in the Senate to mobilize support for legislation requiring an immediate 50 percent cut in those troops. He lost by only eight votes, and only after the most intensive lobbying carried out by the Nixon administration on any single issue. Pressures for cuts in the defense budget, especially abroad, are already very severe. U.S. economic interests that would be hurt by U.S.-European economic conflict would surely seek to retaliate on issues of security, even if the administration were wise enough not to try to use its leverage on those issues to extract economic concessions, as Nye suggests it might. Such a result would obviously have a major impact on overall

13. I focus on the troop level because it is the most obvious manifestation of the U.S.-European political relationship. However, the analysis applies to the entirety of that relationship.

U.S. foreign policy.[14] The broad foreign policy costs of economic conflict were, of course, also demonstrated vividly in late 1971, when British Prime Minister Edward Heath refused to meet President Nixon to discuss the President's forthcoming trips to Peking and Moscow until the United States called a meeting of the Group of Ten (which took place in Rome) to negotiate a solution to the deepening international economic crisis.

The flash point is trade (and perhaps investment), not money. Wilbur Mills told *Der Spiegel* in fall 1972 that he could move the Burke-Hartke bill through Congress "tomorrow," if he wished. Allowing for political hyperbole on the part of Chairman Mills, it remains true that protectionist pressures now run exceedingly deep in U.S. politics, and that the process of trade deliberalization which has been accelerating since at least 1967 will accelerate even further and faster if new liberalizing trade negotiations do not begin soon.[15]

Here enters the link to EMU. A major trade negotiation is unlikely to be launched unless negotiations toward fundamental monetary reform are already under way, both because Europe quite properly wants America to play by some (presumably new) monetary rules if Europe is going to play by the trade rules, and because America also wants to be assured of an effective adjustment process before increasing still further the scope for international economic interpenetration. Indeed, the avoidance of renewed disequilibrium in the exchange rate of the dollar is a sine qua non of the avoidance of serious protectionism in the United States.

EMU could thus play a decisive role in avoiding major problems for U.S.-European relations if it expedited reform of the international monetary system—or it could play a decisive role in generating such problems if it impeded such reform. (The United States itself must of course play a constructive role in achieving monetary reform; European cooperation is a necessary but by no means sufficient condition. Here I wish to treat EMU as *the* independent variable, however, so I assume a constructive U.S. role.) It will thus have a major effect on U.S. foreign policy over the next few years.

14. I do not argue that the present (or any particular) level of U.S. troops in Europe is optimum. I do argue that their precipitate withdrawal would be highly destabilizing to world politics, and that *any* withdrawal in reaction to economic conflict—which could imply that, on security grounds, they were still needed—would have a similar effect.

15. For a detailed analysis, which holds with at least as much strength now as when it was written, see C. Fred Bergsten, "Crisis in U.S. Trade Policy," *Foreign Affairs*, Vol. 49 (July 1971).

Unfortunately, there is at least a strong possibility that the process of reaching monetary union in Europe will impede progress toward global monetary reform. Many Europeans want to move first on EMU, deferring global reform talks for at least several years, because they feel that its success will greatly enhance their bargaining position on global reform and that they will be able to take a stronger position on global monetary reform if they know its shape much more precisely.[16] This could provide decisive support for the views of the majority of European trade officials, who have little understanding of the political need to heed the U.S. call for early and meaningful trade negotiations (see the Rey Report),[17] and the majority of European, especially Community, bureaucrats, who boggle at the thought of simultaneous negotiations on EMU and global reform.

Indeed, EMU *without* global reform would not merely inhibit progress; it would almost certainly make the global monetary problem much worse. EMU promotes the international use of national currencies within the Community, as the members intervene in each other's currencies, for *both* intervention and reserve purposes.[18] But history demonstrates quite clearly the dynamic spread of key currencies once they are in circulation, and how, after that, they develop their own momentum. It can confidently be predicted that these currencies will be widely used—for both vehicle and reserve purposes—*outside* the Community as well, in the absence of negotiated reform that provides for *international* regulation of world liquidity.[19] Indeed, the data suggest that such developments are already widespread. Most EC countries say that they oppose extra-Community use of their currencies, but they are powerless to stop it in view of the Euro-currency markets. Moreover, some do not really oppose it, viewing the

16. I argue below that EMU is *least* likely to succeed under this scenario, despite the opposite views (or hopes) of many Europeans, because it would then lack the external pressures which are probably needed to push its members to the crucial decisions which they must make.

17. Organisation for Economic Co-operation and Development, *Policy Perspectives for International Trade and Economic Relations*, A Report of the High Level Group on Trade and Related Problems, Jean Rey, chairman (OECD, 1972).

18. For example, Governor Guido Carli stated in the 1972 Annual Report of the Bank of Italy that he aimed to hold 20 percent of his reserves—$1.0 billion to $1.5 billion at that time—in other EC currencies.

19. I disagree with Richard Cooper's paper in this volume on two related points. A unified European currency *would* play a larger world role than the sum of the individual European currencies, and thus might well "influence the outcome" of whether an SDR standard eventuates. And *either* a common European currency or the sum of the individual European currencies will play a much larger role relative to the dollar than the latter do now.

expansion as one route to greater "equality with the dollar" and hence an improvement of their own bargaining position. The result would be a multiple reserve currency standard, which was seriously studied a decade ago and rejected by virtually all observers as highly unstable and the worst possible approach to monetary reform.[20] In addition, as Richard Cooper points out in his paper, U.S.-European rivalry for key currency supremacy could replicate the U.S.-British rivalry of the interwar period and exacerbate both the economic and foreign policy difficulties which would already be extremely serious.

The adjustment results could be even worse. If EMU prevented global reform, it would probably assure the further proliferation of controls over international transactions and unregulated exchange rate changes. Both would provide juicy temptations to mercantilist approaches in both Europe and America, as indeed they already have. This, in turn, would promote the highly undesirable foreign policy trends described above, as indeed it already has. Corden argues persuasively in his Princeton essay that EMU would lead to EC immobilism on global exchange rate issues, because the conflicting needs of its members will be impossible to reconcile.[21] Hence, Europe would probably not contribute to constructive exchange rate changes in the absence of new presumptive rules and an international institutional framework through which they were implemented.[22] Yet EMU would itself increase the need for adjustment reform by enabling Europe better to withstand monetary pressures from the United States, as Cooper points out in his paper in this volume.

In view of the major political and economic interests of the United States in avoiding such developments, and the serious risk that they may in fact develop, the United States has two major concerns about EMU: that its development not impede early movement toward global monetary reform, and that its eventual shape be compatible with a more viable global system. Both steps call for a major U.S. initiative toward constructive global reform at the earliest possible date.

20. For a much more detailed analysis, see C. Fred Bergsten, *Reforming the Dollar: An International Monetary Policy for the United States,* Council Papers on International Affairs: 2 (Council on Foreign Relations, 1972), esp. pp. 5–13.

21. W. M. Corden, *Monetary Integration,* Essays in International Finance 93 (Princeton University, International Finance Section, 1972).

22. This probability also strengthens the case for an active U.S. parity policy to make the new regime work. The basic case for such a policy, involving the "triple comparative advantage" of the United States in initiating parity changes, is developed in my *Reforming the Dollar,* pp. 39–41.

U.S. pressure for global reform will *help* Europe achieve EMU by forcing decisions on its external manifestations which will in turn force decisions on its internal aspects. U.S. pressure for the Kennedy Round helped Europe achieve its CXT and CAP, and the absence of early U.S. pressure, or even response to the MDS proposal, let European agriculture develop in a manner which carries exceedingly high costs for most Europeans. There are no internal pressures sufficiently strong to force reconciliation within the EC of the sharp conflicts among its members on EMU issues. Indeed, external pressure for global monetary reform is the *only* force likely to do so.

But this external force must be applied in the proper way, and toward the proper ends. Much of the development of EMU so far is in *defensive* response to uncooperative pressures from the United States: massive dollar flows into Europe, efforts to preserve the key currency role of the dollar far beyond what is possible or needed in the 1970s and beyond, gyrations between "benign neglect" and Connally-style confrontation. To be sure, the United States could probably push EMU further by more such uncooperative pressures: by elimination of its present capital controls, more "benign neglect" coupled with obvious efforts to keep the world on an inconvertible dollar standard by evading global reform, and the like.[23] But recent history strongly suggests that this kind of U.S. approach could tilt the intra-EC debate in favor of the French model, based on controls and rigid parities, instead of the German model, whose focus on liberal trade and payments and greater flexibility of exchange rates is far more compatible with U.S. national interests.[24] The history of the negotiations on Special Drawing Rights is an instructive parallel, where active U.S. pursuit of an objective shared by most of the Six tilted the balance against France and achieved a result which served both global and American interests.

There is thus a strong foreign-policy, as well as economic, case for an urgent U.S. initiative on constructive international monetary reform. It

23. Some European economists, for example, Rinaldo Ossola, have argued that such a U.S. approach would destroy rather than promote EMU. I am dubious, in view of the political commitment of all EC countries to the idea; however, it might reduce EMU simply to negative immobilism which would block all constructive global reform. In any event, the effects on U.S. foreign policy of either destroying EMU or rendering it impotent are highly undesirable—unless we were to place achievement of a dollar standard very high on our list of international priorities.

24. Overt U.S. opposition to EMU would be even more certain to do so, as Trezise points out in his paper.

is clear that the United States should not be dissuaded from seizing the initiative—as it was in 1970—by pleas from some Europeans to "wait until EMU is on the track." Fortunately, the kind of reform which would maximize U.S. interests—greater flexibility of parities in response to pre-sumptive rules with international sanctions to back them up, much wider margins, annual injections of sufficient amounts of SDRs, a special issue of SDRs to consolidate any present reserves held in undesired forms (in-cluding the "dollar overhang"), dramatic expansion of the quantity and quality of the swap network to recycle liquid capital flows—is compatible with the existence of either EMU or separate European participants.[25] It is incompatible only with further delay. Instead of resisting U.S. pressure for monetary reform, Europe should thus welcome it as promoting both its own internal and external policy objectives.

Comments by Robert R. Bowie

WHEN I taught in law school, I remember calling on a student to state the facts of a case. His response was, "Well, I don't exactly understand the facts, but I think I could explain their significance." My task here is to comment on the political significance of monetary relationships about which I feel, at least, uncertain.

Moreover, at this stage of our discussion, it is hard to say anything new. So my role is largely to indicate how I see the political aspects within this ambiguous context. I will limit myself to a few points:

First, the monetary issues cannot be isolated from the whole matrix of relations between Europe and the United States. As others have said, the various elements interact. The handling of monetary reform and the European Monetary Union (EMU) will affect trade and commercial rela-tions. The economic relations are bound to influence cooperation on security and foreign policy generally.

Effective collaboration among the United States, Western Europe, and Japan across a wide spectrum is essential for their own interests and for the long-term effort to create a viable international order. These regions cannot do what is necessary separately. They must work intimately to-

25. For details, see my paper, *Reforming the Dollar*, pp. 48–95.

gether. Thus, partnership with Europe and Japan still seems to me a valid and necessary objective for the United States.

Second, the European Community (EC) will offer the best basis for such cooperation with Europe if it becomes a more effective entity for common action by its members. Key Europeans see it as the means to put Atlantic relations on a footing more acceptable to them. In shaping the American course, it is essential to be clear about the European motives in seeking unity.

These motives have evolved since the start of the integration movement in 1950. At that time, the Europeans had consensus about where they wanted to go, and about priorities and the price they would have to pay. They were seeking a United States of Europe and they seemed prepared to make the requisite sacrifices.

Even then, they understood, as Jean Monnet stressed, that unity could not be achieved by a sudden movement, but only by stages. Each step could make it easier to take the next. It would so change the situation that possibilities for further progress would open up. That is still the operative concept, although there have been changes in the motives and the clarity of purpose.

In the beginning, the key purposes were: (1) to bring about a reconciliation of France and Germany, (2) to benefit from a larger market, as well as (3) to exert more influence. Today, everybody assumes that the first of these has been achieved. Europeans also enjoy the second in the form of greater prosperity, although they still have problems in managing intra-Community relationships.

The third purpose has become much more important. It is expressed in various ways: the desire to play a greater role, to have more control over their own affairs, to be able to stand up to the United States. This motivation has both its positive and negative aspects. In some quarters the negative, the anti-American, is the stronger. Others, in more positive vein, are eager to become more effective partners.

How far do these feelings produce a genuine consensus on what should be done? Here, one should be realistic. How far does any society know precisely what it wants? The political process is messier than academic model-building.

The Europeans, at least, have a considerable amount of what I call shared imagery. They want to see Europe enough of an entity to be able to manage its own affairs domestically and also to deal effectively with the outside world, particularly with the United States, but also with the Soviet Union, developing nations, and the rest of the world. That is no blueprint; certainly, it is not as precise as the original concept of federal Europe.

Yet, European leaders seem well aware that this goal requires the transfer of much authority from national governments to some form of European entity. Even Georges Pompidou, for example, in one of his press conferences, said as much explicitly; indeed, he volunteered the comment.

But, although this is understood, the Europeans are ambivalent in practice. They are not eager to give up authority, certainly not more than they have to. They are uncertain how much they will have to transfer, in what form, or through what institutional structures, in order to achieve their image of what Europe's role should be.

Third, monetary union will ultimately pose these issues in stark form. What is at stake is the authority and responsibility for managing the economies of Europe. For effective monetary union, the member states will have to transfer this function to central control of some kind. They may be able to creep up on the decision piecemeal, but they will finally have to take the major leap. No one can be sure they will cross that threshold.

Some of the discussants have suggested that the route of the Werner Report, and especially fixed exchange rates, may not be the best route to achieve monetary union, that it might make more sense to let the exchange rates remain more flexible until other policies had been more closely harmonized.

But the present course is not immutable. The Europeans have shown over a period of twenty years that they are quite capable of changing their techniques and approaches. Later on, after a succession of failures with fixed exchange rates, they might adopt another course. In any event, I do not think the present approach should be treated as if it were written in granite. To me, it is significant that the Europeans revert over and over to this goal which the Werner Report itself describes as a major route toward political unity.

Fourth, even if the Community succeeds, it is not likely to provide panaceas for U.S.-European relations. There will be, as Richard Cooper says, a long period of transition, even if the Europeans proceed toward unity in an expeditious way and more skillfully than they have done so far. During that period, inside Europe, there will be all sorts of pulling and hauling and backing and filling and compromising and the like.

The Community will almost surely be excessively rigid in its dealings with the United States because it will be able to reach common positions among members only by compromises, which it will hesitate to modify. That phenomenon is not unknown within the U.S. government, and if it is true within a single government, it is much worse for a group of nine countries more or less sovereign and not under similar compulsions. We must therefore accept that we are going to have rough sledding in practical negotiations.

Finally, what does all this suggest about U.S. policy and action? I agree with C. Fred Bergsten's view for both economic and political reasons.

The United States cannot intervene directly even if it would like to see the Community proceed more expeditiously toward monetary union. But that does not mean that Americans cannot exercise considerable influence by affecting the context within which the EC members make their decisions. U.S. initiative for constructive monetary reform seems the best route to achieve this.

Like Bergsten, I believe that the United States should present constructive proposals which manifestly attempt to take account of some of the wider needs and concerns. That is the most effective way to force the Europeans to come to some conclusions about what they want and what they are prepared to do. Such an approach would have the advantage of strengthening the leverage of the more constructive forces.

In any event, I do not see anything else useful for the United States to do. To stand around and wait, on the theory that everyone can live with a dollar standard, will mean missing the chance to shape the environment in which the Community will have to act. In narrow monetary terms, such a stance might be defensible. But in terms of the larger purpose of U.S. relations with Europe, in building a cooperative basis for a large number of other activities, that is not good enough. The result could be resentment and noncooperation that will spill over into many other fields where it will be very costly.

Discussion of the Cooper and Trezise Papers

DISCUSSION focused on the concern that Europe's attempt to create monetary union would immobilize it with respect to the larger issues of international monetary reform, on policy prescriptions for the United States government, and briefly, on the philosophy behind alternative economic policies.

Edward Morse raised some questions concerning the supposed contrast between U.S. goals of international economic policy—a presumed liberal world order—and the French views, which presumably support a world order based on *dirigiste* patterns. This contrast is of some importance for the next stage of development of the international system, particularly the relations of the United States and Europe; it also has implications for possible changes in American foreign policy.

First, is "liberal" a proper description of American foreign policy and is it appropriate as a normative approach for the future? Other countries do not regard the United States as liberal in matters of economic policy. Furthermore, these liberal rules have created a mechanism which has particularly benefited the United States because of the asymmetry in economic relations between the United States and other powers. What are the advantages of those rules if the asymmetry no longer exists?

Second, are liberal rules desirable given the many noneconomic goals of societies which may point in directions other than toward the most economically efficient solution?

Third, is it appropriate to pose the policy options only as those between liberal and *dirigiste* rules? In a world in which the tremendous imbalance between the United States and other power centers is ended and the United States cannot have its own way in international policy matters, is a fully integrated world economy desirable? Can American foreign policy adjust to a nonliberal world with alternative visions of order and with plans for other kinds of mechanisms that can allow for a high level of economic integration but that are not based on liberal rules? These questions need to be examined for future policy consideration.

Benjamin Cohen raised the possibility that the concern expressed by many discussants over European immobilism on global monetary reform might be exaggerated. As Europeans ponder the future two or three years hence and consider the consequences of not reaching a global monetary reform because of their own preoccupation with EMU, they might not like what they see. The Europeans might view their alternatives to global reform as appreciating their currencies, inflating their economies, or imposing self-destructive controls. In the face of these alternatives, they might shift attention to global reform. It is important that the United States actively pursue global reform so that the European position on reform will not arise from frustration that would make them hostile to the dollar.

Henry Wallich stated that a modification of the traditional American support for European unification may be desirable. This tradition was attributed to a belief that European unification is a "good thing" and that the United States benefits from good things and from traditional U.S. activism in support of new proposals, which may result from the U.S. government being heavily overstaffed. Taking into account the diminished relative importance of the United States in the world, the inability of previous forms of economic unification to bring about political unification as they were supposed to do, and the disagreeable features that have been produced, like the common agricultural policy, a different approach might be expedient. Furthermore, one motive for active U.S. support in the 1950s—the cementing of friendship between France and Germany—has disappeared. Under these new circumstances, the United States might avoid economic costs by adopting a low-profile policy. With respect to international monetary matters, the United States can live with or without EMU as long as minimum requirements such as freedom for U.S. monetary policy, some control of the dollar exchange rate, and less-than-full-scale convertibility are present. If the Europeans achieve EMU, that will be fine, said Wallich. But little would be gained for the United States by becoming involved in shaping the process. In the short run, many difficulties stand in the way of EMU, even though it may be achievable in the long run. The United States can have little influence on EMU and it would be much better to let events take their own course.

Richard Cooper believed that it is neither possible nor desirable for the United States to stay out of the process of EMU, however pleasant that course may seem. If there were a really solid international monetary system in which the Europeans could shape their own system without disturbing the larger system, then it would seem feasible and sensible for the United States to remain a bystander. But this condition does not exist; instead, the whole global structure has to be rebuilt. The United States cannot remain indifferent to the process of creating EMU because that process is bound up with the issue of what the world economic order is going to look like. Will it be a system that relies very heavily on controls, on exchange flexibility, on world capital mobility and fixed exchange rates, or on something else entirely? The United States has a deep interest in this question. Furthermore, if as some believe, there is an intimate political, if not economic, connection between the North American assessment of what is going on in Europe and U.S. policy responses, then American policy and stance toward the world economy is affected directly by the process of creating EMU.

William Fellner noted the possibility that a European attempt to create EMU might be desirable even if not successful, because it could develop a cooperative attitude concerning exchange rate adjustments. Exchange rate adjustments will take place in the future, and a more cooperative attitude about the proper criteria for adjustment and who should interpret these criteria could develop in the attempt to establish EMU. While the reverse could happen, it is less likely.

Edward Fried, responding to the discussion, in the absence of Philip Trezise, noted that the United States needs to take the initiative in monetary reform whether EMU is a going concern or not. EMU does not add appreciably to the dangers of the current situation. The United States cannot remain passive about global monetary reform, although it might with respect to EMU alone. The basic issue concerns the adjustment process and it is with respect to the adjustment process that the United States might find difficulties in the creation of EMU.

HARRY G. JOHNSON

Summary of the Conference

CONFERENCE CHAIRMAN Leonard Weiss explained on behalf of the Department of State that the Conference on Implications of European Monetary Unification for the United States had been called on September 21–22, 1972, because the European decision to establish a common currency was the first instance of a group of national states deciding to achieve full economic integration, and it was important for the American government to understand the implications and probable effects. There was also the question of how far the world could proceed with the reform of the international monetary system when there was so much disagreement within Europe itself over monetary policies and objectives.

The first session was devoted to the reading and discussion of Arthur Bloomfield's background paper. Summarizing succinctly the movement toward monetary union, he said that the history of the Common Market could be divided into two periods: from the Treaty of Rome to 1968, when the main effort went into administrative organization, and from 1968 on, when the European Community (EC) encountered a series of monetary crises and, as a result, turned to the aim of monetary integration. The effort had had no real success so far (September 1972) in achieving a common external monetary policy, liberalizing internal capital movements, and integrating the European capital market. The reason was not lack of administrative procedures—these proliferated after every crisis—but unwillingness of member nations to sacrifice their national interests to the common objectives when crises occurred. Until there was an actual transfer of power to the Community from the member nation-states, there

299

was a need for some transitional arrangements in the foreign exchange markets. But these arrangements could take a great variety of forms and might even be replaced by an effort to harmonize domestic economic policies.

The first commentator, Benjamin Cohen, contributed a classification of possible meanings of monetary integration into fixed exchange rates (currency integration), integration of capital markets (financial integration), and policy harmonization (pure monetary integration), and asserted that feasibility decreased and importance to the United States increased as one went down the list. Cohen also raised the question whether the monetary integration objective was motivated by internal or by external forces (that is, the Community's own interests or reaction against the policies of the United States). The second commentator, Gottfried Haberler, raised the question whether monetary integration was possible without more basic economic unification and gave his views briefly on the subjects to be discussed in the subsequent more technical sessions.

Discussion thereafter was somewhat diverted by Haberler's use of the "cart before the horse" analogy, which lent itself to rich analogical elaboration. (If one puts the bridle on the horse's tail, is this a mistake or is it because the horse bites? If one puts the bridle in his mouth, is this because he kicks? Do you have first to feel out the shape of the horse?) It ended with Peter Kenen's suggestion that not only was the horse really a camel, but that it had two humps, one representing quantitative monetary policy and the other representing credit policy. The main question, which seemed the point of division between the "pro-Europeans" and the cooler American participants—a division that persisted throughout the conference— was whether the Europeans were making progress in their own way and, if they were, why the process was one of "two steps forward, one step backward." In this connection, it was argued that the political process of contending with enormous economic policy problems is bound to be messy and apparently irrational, that it will necessarily focus on apparently neutral technical issues, and that by so doing it will be able to survive one failure after another. Lawrence Krause made the important point that the United States will probably benefit from any development in the Community that is motivated by internal considerations but lose from developments motivated by reactions to the behavior of the United States itself. Frédéric Boyer de la Giroday, an official of the Community who was invited to respond to the discussion, stated that monetary integration was being forced on Europe by technological developments within a particular geographical setting.

In the second session participants discussed Joseph Nye's paper on the political context of monetary integration. The main impressions that emerged from the application of Nye's integration theory was that European monetary integration is unlikely to succeed because it lacks sufficient self-reinforcing mechanisms. The presentation also showed that "the Monnet method" (which consists of promoting apparently technocratic issues that actually have far-reaching implications for the rest of the social system) could lead to disintegration as well as to further integration. The two discussants, Theodore Geiger and Edward Morse, both of whose comments were scholarly, succeeded mainly in conveying the message that Europe was currently in a state of malaise (what Harold van B. Cleveland later described as "waiting for Godot"); and this idea, together with a certain amount of economists' horseplay about positive-sum and zero-sum games, formed the focus of the subsequent discussion. In this connection, Robert Bowie stood out from the rest in maintaining that Europe had been making bigger and more rapid political decisions than the United States, and that there had been a general forward motion. W. Max Corden contributed a useful taxonomy of European motives, including the helpful neology of "megaphonism," that is, the desire of the former imperial powers, Britain and France, to amplify their present (reduced) international political power by using "Europe" as their mouthpiece.

The first afternoon session was concerned with Harry Johnson's paper on narrowing the bands among European currencies. The main points were that narrowing the European bands while retaining the full band against the dollar involved two constraints on national exchange rate policies, that some decision had to be reached on the average European rate against the dollar, and that there were two simple and two difficult methods of solving the problem, depending on whether Europe could establish its own numéraire currency and whether it was prepared to use the dollar as intervention currency.

Edward Bernstein, as commentator, pointed to two problems. First, if Europe settled intra-European imbalances in a European asset and settled extra-European imbalances in dollars, there would be a tendency to strive for balancing both sets of accounts separately, which would be against the U.S. interest. Second, it would be wrong to let either deficit or surplus countries use their exchange rate policies in a way that limited the freedom of others to avail themselves of the permissible range of exchange rate variation against the dollar. Hence "the snake within the tunnel" was against U.S. interests.

William Fellner pointed out that European policies were sufficiently different to make the maintenance of fixed exchange rates difficult. There was the possibility of using controls, but these would have to be capital controls coordinated against the rest of the world. The snake in the tunnel would prevent most currencies in the snake from utilizing the full leeway of the tunnel. Among currencies restricted by the snake, one that was at the floor of both the snake and the tunnel could not rise to the ceiling without changing its position relative to others in the snake, and if it did change that position the other currencies could not utilize the full leeway of the tunnel. Although alternations in the direction of harmonization could enable first one snake currency, then another, then a third, to make full use of the tunnel, there is no presumption that the system would operate in this peculiar way; in reality, the snake would limit movements of currencies in the tunnel.

John Williamson defended the Magnifico-Williamson proposal to establish the Europa against Johnson's criticisms. The problem was to establish a weighted average of the contrary pulls on the different currencies; the Europa was an interim medium for this purpose. Johnson's criticism that forcing the use of the Europa would sacrifice microeconomic efficiency (for example, by imposing reserve requirements in Europas on commercial banks) ignored the proposal's infant-industry justification. There were economies of scale in the use of money, and once the Europa became established, people would find it useful.

Richard Cooper maintained that the problem set in Johnson's paper was a well-defined one—to narrow the bands among European currencies while maintaining the same band against the dollar—which the European countries had faced and resolved. There were three alternatives:

1. To abandon the market and have the central banks decide the rates and make the market, thereby eliminating any special role for the dollar. This alternative would involve sacrificing the efficiency of the present market mechanism.

2. To use a single European currency as the intervention currency for all of Europe except possibly one country. One variant was the Europa; however, it would be very difficult to make the Europa a market currency,

and much easier to choose an existing European currency. The pound sterling was the obvious choice, with Europe becoming the sterling area; but this was politically unacceptable.

3. By coordinated intervention. The Werner Report envisaged the dollar being used as intervention currency, which would have meant Europe's taking a position on the dollar. The actual decision was to intervene with any other European currency when a currency hit the limit of the European band and to intervene with dollars only at the limit of the band against the dollar. This avoided the need to take a position on the dollar but involved a nonmarket exchange of assets among central banks. Cooper thought that the implicit surrender of freedom to intervene within the European band meant that the arrangement probably will not last, because central banks sooner or later will want to intervene within the band.

Subsequent discussion ranged over the questions of whether the European arrangements would facilitate or retard international adjustment, and how they might affect U.S. interests.

The second afternoon session was devoted to Krause's paper on the effects of European monetary integration on private capital markets. Krause took as his text the Werner Report's flat declaration for total liberty of capital movements within the Community. He argued that capital movements were necessary for adjustment within the Community; adjustment by labor migration was politically unacceptable, while intergovernmental transfers could not provide the whole solution. He further argued that, while capital market integration would have little if any effect on total saving and investment, there would be a significant qualitative microeconomic effect through the narrowing of interest rate spreads. However, there would be associated concerns about the possible abuse of market power by large financial institutions, and the loss of domestic monetary autonomy. So long as there was no discrimination against U.S. financial institutions operating in Europe, the effects for the United States would be of second-order importance only. Krause argued also that the Eurodollar market existed partly because of European restrictions on the mobility of capital, and partly because of American restrictions on access to American capital markets. He said that European capital market integration would therefore remove part of the reason for the market's existence; if the American restrictions were also removed the Eurodollar market might well disappear.

All of this analysis was based on the assumption that the final objective had been achieved. But there was a problem of transition. With capital market liberalization, existing exchange rates would become disequilibrium rates. Current national interest rate levels reflected differences in expectations about inflation. Harmonization of interest rates would require a new set of exchange rates. To arrive at these rates there was a need to provide for small changes in parities; there was a danger of premature rigidification of rates. Europe might attempt to postpone exchange rate adjustment by capital market controls, but this would merely postpone, not solve, the problem.

The discussion of the paper was generally mystical about the benefits and the likelihood of the capital market integration Krause foresaw. Cleveland foresaw instead a proliferation of capital controls against the outside; he also argued that with integrated capital markets small changes in national monetary policies might be very effective in maintaining balance-of-payments equilibrium whereas exchange rate changes might take a long time to exert their effect. Charles Kindleberger argued that no one really knows whether exchange rates should be fixed at the start or at the end of the integration process and that history speaks both ways on the issue. He also argued that there is private as well as government discrimination against international capital movements and that capital may well move in the (economically) wrong direction. And he suggested that for economic reasons a capital market has to have a geographical center (the costs of long-distance communication) and asked where that center was likely to be.

Henry Wallich found Krause's picture of the future too rosy to believe because it would entail no freedom for national monetary policy; he argued that policy coordination would have to come before capital market integration. Frederick Strauss emphasized the need for a common industrial policy, stressing the importance of reducing restrictions on mergers across national borders. Others discussed the need for barriers against capital movements to and from outside countries as a precondition of internal freedom of capital movements; Corden argued that capital was likely to flow out of, not into, a depressed region. Cooper pointed out that modern theory suggests that the more open an economy is, the more effective monetary policy and exchange rate policy will be in correcting external disequilibria because of the real-balance effect, up to the point where people stop using the national money and use foreign money instead. In reply to the discussion, Krause defended his assumption of capital market liberalization by asserting that controls on international capital movements were too difficult to be feasible in the contemporary world. Given the existence of multinational corporations (European as well as American), such controls would have to reach down into every detail of the daily operations of firms.

The conference resumed early the next morning with discussion of Corden's paper on monetary integration and the adjustment problem. The comments by James Ingram and J. Carter Murphy covered the issues in such detail that the conference was really confronted with three very meaty papers. The chairman, however, was well advised to let this session run overtime, and to transfer one of the sessions scheduled for the morning to the afternoon, because many found the discussion so provocative.

Adequate summary of such detailed argumentation is impossible. Corden set out to be deliberately provocative. He distinguished make-believe monetary integration, pseudo integration, and real integration. His central theme was that countries are on a wage standard; money wages influence demand, but real wages can be altered by exchange rate changes. The autonomy of national wages has implications for the debate about whether narrowing of exchange margins should follow or precede harmonization of policies (the "economist"–"monetarist" debate in the European sense). The former position is incompatible with the wage standard. Also, complete capital market integration would not provide a long-term solution, since autonomous wage changes would create areas of depression within the Community that would not be corrected by capital inflows (which would be unprofitable). Corden was pessimistic about the likelihood that monetary union would be more flexible in the matter of exchange rates and felt that the United States would have to take the initiative. As regards exchange controls, he expected a pseudo union to utilize them more; in a complete union it would depend on whose philosophy prevailed. He concluded with some remarks on the U.S. interest. So long as the United States maintained full employment without inflation it had little to worry about; it should mind its own business and leave Europe to itself because monetary integration in Europe was a loser; the United States would be badly advised to support it.

Ingram began by remarking that economists who say that monetary union will not work because the political will is lacking are making political judgments, and he questioned whether they have any special qualifications for doing so. Europe has litle monetary autonomy now; it might acquire some, but monetary integration would require a quantum leap. He felt that Corden's presentation was dominated by the hard cases, that is, an excessive *general* wage rise in one part of the Community; that countries would not support real wages above the competitive Community level; and that if they were able to do so exchange rate adjustment would not work either. He examined cases he thought more probable and the potentialities of market-induced movements of capital and labor and of fiscal policy for dealing with them. Murphy conceded to Corden's view that trade unions have the power to raise costs and that they exercise it, but thought that in a well-integrated monetary union they would be constrained by the market. They would also try to extend their bargaining domain to the whole Community, reducing the strains of divergent cost movements within the Community that Corden feared. Murphy thought as Ingram had, that increased capital mobility would also help bring about adjustment by helping to remove disparities in productivity. He ended with the general observation that Corden's model had not been explicit enough about the European setting and the nature of the disturbances.

Opening the general discussion, Johnson said that Corden, like most British economists, was distorting the Keynesian assumption that wage rates were autonomously determined in the short run by applying it to the long run. It is true that wage determination has in fact taken place against a background of governmental ability to impose trade and payments controls to defend an existing rate and to devalue that rate if necessary. This does encourage union militancy, but there is no reason to think that if governments were deprived of these safety valves by full economic and monetary integration, the process of determining wage levels would not become more disciplined. Disparities in regional unemployment rates within countries were often adduced in support of predictions of national depressed regions in a monetary union. But such disparities had lasted in some cases over a century, and it was difficult to believe that they represented disequilibrium pricing of labor; instead, there was a choice for labor between full-time employment at lower wages per time-unit and high-paid employment for part of the time, the latter alternative permitting the enjoyment of more leisure. It was no accident that low unemployment rates prevail in large cities, where most enjoyment of leisure has to be bought with work, and high unemployment rates in remote regions, where much leisure can be enjoyed with low cash income.

Kindleberger discussed money illusion and its limitations. Cohen pointed out that coordination of policy is not the same as equality of policy. Walter Salant took issue with Corden on capital movements by moving the model from a static to a long-run growth context. Many people took issue with Corden on the capital movements question. Williamson sided with Corden in asserting his belief that wage rigidity would lead to regional problems but declared himself agnostic on whether such rigidity really exists. Cooper pointed out that money illusion is neither necessary nor illusion in a world of contracts and of real-balance effects. Corden replied to his critics in his usual modest and graceful fashion.

The second morning session dealt with Salant's paper on European monetary integration and international reserves. Salant's main conclusions were that there will be no change in the vehicle role of the dollar so long as there is uncertainty about European monetary unification, and that Europe may want a smaller rise in international reserves than suits the United States and others. In this connection he observed that if a European monetary union, once achieved, were to be concerned with its consolidated payments position and monetary reserve, it would logically be entitled to less weight in international decisions about reserve-creation than the aggregate of its membership now has, a potentially explosive suggestion that no conferee showed any sign of having noticed. Kenen, in a comprehensive discussion, agreed in large measure with Salant's conclusions but also noted that there was great uncertainty about the outcome of the issues raised and that much more work was needed on all aspects of them. Fritz Machlup's comment, after noting that differences in the use of the terms "band," "par value," and "parity" had caused confusion about technical but substantive matters, said that even if monetary unification reduces Europe's felt need for reserves, the reduction may have no significant consequences; the members of the Community, instead of appreciating their currencies, reducing import barriers, or increasing investment on foreign aid, are more likely to live with the surplus dollars. C. Fred Bergsten made the point that Salant's conclusion that European monetary unification would make the European currencies more attractive relative to the dollar rested on present ceteris paribus assumptions that could change.

Leading off the first afternoon session by presenting his paper on European monetary unification and integration of the world economy, Cooper argued that the present preponderant influence of the United States would change, and the international monetary system become more symmetric.

There might even be a reversal of roles between Europe and the United States—the danger here was that the United States might be forced into *dirigisme*. Bela Balassa maintained that the effort to establish fixed exchange rates in Europe was a misdirection of European energy. William Diebold's comments, which ranged widely over the issues, included the suggestion that alternative forms of monetary integration should be considered and that this consideration should be approached by studying the dynamic process involved in integration. This session was limited to the paper and discussants, owing to shortage of time.

Philip Trezise's paper on foreign policy implications of European monetary union was presented by Edward Fried, who unfortunately was bound by the need for brevity. He confined himself to raising a few of the main questions posed in the paper. Bergsten took a much more positive line; European Monetary Union (EMU) was the third phase of the Community's development. The first was the customs union, which the United States had managed to live with via the Kennedy Round. The second was the common agricultural policy, which the United States had found adverse to its interests. A major trade negotiation was unlikely unless global monetary reform had first been brought under way, but European monetary unification would block international monetary reform for some years ahead. European unification without global monetary reform would be bad for global reform. The United States had two major interests: that EMU should not impede global monetary reform, and that its final shape should be consistent with global monetary reform. The United States should press for global reform, though external pressure should be applied in the proper way. Bowie, as second commentator, argued generally that the United States should help Europe to solve its problems.

In general discussion, Cohen pointed out that there was virtual unanimity on the immobilism of Europe with respect to international monetary reform. Morse raised the question of the validity of the liberal view of the world on which U.S. foreign economic policy and most of the discussion had been based.

Wallich expressed the opinion that the United States need not assume that it has to take an interest in developments or nothing will happen. As regards European monetary unification, other forms of integration in Europe have not done what they were supposed to do. The United States should pursue a low-profile policy; it can, after all, live with a wide range of European arrangements.

The final session was devoted to Johnson's summary of the conference (necessarily briefer than that presented above). Johnson began by saying that he thought it had been a worthwhile conference, though more as a background to policy formation than as a guide to what policy should be. He concluded his summary by remarking that there were two types of Americans present at the conference: those who had labored over European integration in the immediate postwar period of the cold war and had as their aim the strengthening of Europe as an ally, and those of a younger and maybe less involved generation that looked at Europe with a colder concern in light of current U.S. economic and political interests. It might be considered a weakness of the U.S. policy position and policy formation that so many people now senior had an emotional and career attachment to making European economic integration work, especially as the Europeans now tend to be resentful of U.S. power and U.S. pressure. Johnson tended to side with Krause, Corden, Wallich, and others, who thought that the United States should leave the Europeans to their own devices and their own mistakes in the area of European monetary integration. In the brief discussion that followed, Cooper argued that if the United States wants global monetary reform it must come to grips with the movement for European monetary integration. Johnson admitted this but responded that the United States should not get actively involved in the details.

WALTER S. SALANT

A Partial Glossary of
International Finance

To INCLUDE a glossary of international finance in a book likely to be read
mainly by experts may appear unnecessary and even useless. The appearance,
however, is deceptive. At the conference on which this book is based, it
became evident that even the assembled experts were using some terms familiar
to all of them in different senses. Indeed, at one point what appeared to be a
difference of opinion turned out to be a difference of understanding about the
meaning of the widely used word "band." This discovery, in turn, led to a
realization that some other terms were being differently used or were ambiguous, and that some words often thought to be synonymous might better be
distinguished.

The resulting confusion persuaded the editors that it was desirable to include
the glossary that follows and, in addition, to change the terms used by authors
and discussants—with their consent, of course—to conform to the definitions
given below when the editors noticed that they used the same term differently.

The glossary itself is not intended to be complete. It is confined to terms
used in the papers and discussion, and even among them, to those that caused
misunderstanding among the conferees or appear likely to do so among
readers.[1]

The glossary is followed by a discussion designed to illuminate the definitions
of some of the terms.

1. Some other terms are defined and explained in glossaries published in International Monetary Fund, *IMF Survey*, August 14, 1972, p. 7, and August 28, 1972,
p. 32. Other terms commonly used in analytic discussion of balance-of-payments
problems are explained in "Notes on Terminology," in William Fellner, Fritz
Machlup, Robert Triffin, and others, *Maintaining and Restoring Balance in International Payments* (Princeton University Press, 1966), pp. 243–54.

310

Glossary

Band: The distance between the two limits within which the price of a currency is permitted to vary in the foreign exchange markets in a spot exchange transaction involving another currency. This distance is expressed as a percentage of one currency's parity with the other currency. The band is equal to the sum of the permitted margins above and below parity, and therefore is twice the margin when the margins above and below parity are equal. To avoid ambiguity, however, one must specify around what the variation is permitted. The main reason is that if the exchange rate for spot transactions of a currency is permitted to vary within a band of x percent around its parity with its intervention currency while another currency is permitted to vary within a band of y percent around its parity with the same intervention currency, the band of permitted variation in spot exchange transactions between them is $x + y$ percent of their parity with each other. Moreover, since countries may not be using the same intervention currency, it is necessary to specify not only whether the band referred to is the band around a currency's parity with its intervention currency or with nonintervention currencies, and also to identify the other currency (or class of currencies). The band of a currency around its parity with another currency whose par value is defined in terms of the same numéraire is the sum of the bands around their par values. (See Discussion, item 3, below.)

Central rate: A de facto substitute for a par value intended to be a temporary basis for the maintenance of a stable rate of exchange, but differing from a par value in not having been established in accordance with the rules of the International Monetary Fund (IMF) relating to par values. Whereas par values, under the IMF Articles of Agreement, had to be expressed in gold or a U.S. dollar having the gold value of July 1, 1944, central rates, as an extralegal concept, could be declared in gold, in SDRs, or in a currency.

Cross rate: The exchange rate between two currencies, calculated as the ratio of the exchange rates between each of them and a third currency. For example, if £1 = $2.40 and 1 DM = $0.30, the cross rate between pounds and deutsche marks is £1 = $\frac{2.40}{0.30}$ DM = 8 DM.

Exchange rate: The price of a specified unit of one currency measured in a specified unit of another. For example, $1.00 (U.S.) = 4 DM, or 1 DM = $0.25 (U.S.), which is an alternative expression of the same exchange rate. The definition and the alternative expressions in the example make clear that it is meaningless—and should be forbidden—to say that an *exchange rate* rose or fell, because that leaves uncertain which currency's price rose or fell. If the price of one currency measured in units of the other rose, the price of the other currency measured in units of the one must have fallen, the two being reciprocals of each other. An unambiguous statement requires specifying which currency's price rose or fell.

Intervention currency: A currency which the monetary authority of a country stands ready to buy and sell to prevent the market price of its currency from deviating beyond its permitted range.

Margin: The permitted deviation of the price of a currency, in an exchange transaction involving another currency, on one side of its parity with that other currency. The term should not be used without explicit or clearly implied reference to the *direction* of the deviation and, as in use of the word "band," without clear indication of the point of reference from which the deviation is measured. Thus, one should say "the margin *above*" or "the margin *below*" parity *with Currency Y* (or "the margin *on either side* of" parity *with Currency Y*, if the margins are equal). For the purposes of exchange transactions, margins must be calculated on the basis of parities because such transactions involve two currencies. For the purposes of gold transactions, which involve only one currency, margins are calculated on the basis of the par value of the currency involved.

Numéraire: A unit of measure or common denominator in terms of which the par values of currencies are defined. More generally than in the field of international finance, any good that is used as a unit of account and (as the term was originally defined by Léon Walras) for which the demand, if any, was associated only with its nonmonetary attributes. The latter quality, however, does not apply to the recent use of the term in international finance; there is a monetary as well as a nonmonetary demand for gold, but gold may nevertheless be called a numéraire in international finance. (See Discussion, item 2, below.)

Par, par value: The value of a currency defined as a specified number of units of a numéraire. To be distinguished from "parity." (See Discussion, item 1, below.)

Parity: The ratio between the par values of two currencies. The parity must be based on some common denominator in which the par values of the two currencies are expressed. Since the term involves two currencies, one should not speak of the "parity of a currency" but of its parity with another currency, and specify what other currency. (See Discussion, item 1, below.)

Spot exchange transactions: Purchases or sales of foreign currency for "ready" delivery, which in practice normally means within two working days. For purposes of the Fund's Articles of Agreement, the term excludes transactions in banknotes and in coins.

Discussion

1. There is a widespread tendency, even among experts, to use the terms "par value" and "parity" interchangeably. Par values, as defined above, are of interest chiefly because they provide the basis for determining the parities between currencies. It may be noted that, from this point of view, the numéraire in terms of which the par values of two currencies are defined need not have a value observable in the marketplace in order to permit their parity to be determined and observable. To establish the parity between them, it is

necessary and sufficient that their par values be defined in terms of the same numéraire or of numéraires whose values are commensurable, since the ratio of their par values can then be related to each other. Thus, if the par value of the mark were five ounces of a specified quality of moon dust and that of the franc were four ounces of moon dust of the same quality, their parity would be established as 1 franc = 0.80 marks or 1 mark = 1.25 francs, even though there is no observable price for moon dust. Their parity would also be determinate if the franc were defined as a specified number of units of Mars dust, so long as a relation between moon dust and Mars dust were specified. Since the parity between two currencies can be defined if their par values are the same or can be related and since their actual exchange rate is observable in the marketplace, the deviations of their actual exchange rate from their parity is also observable.

The distinction between "par value" and "parity" is made in the IMF Articles of Agreement, but it is not widely recognized, or at least honored, outside IMF circles.

2. While the possibility of using a numéraire whose value is not observable may have been of merely theoretical intellectual interest in the past, it has become of more practical interest now that proposals have been made to define par values in terms of Special Drawing Rights, for which a market value is not observable. If the numéraire does not have an observable value, the deviations of a currency's market value from its par value, in contrast to its deviations from its parities with other currencies, are also not observable.

3. The conference on which this volume is based revealed a difference in use of the word "band" that most of the conferees had apparently not recognized before. At the conference Walter Salant referred to the "band" under the Smithsonian Agreement as 4½ percent, meaning the band around par values or central rates but not so specifying because he thought that was the accepted meaning, and referred to the "maximum permissible fluctuation" between two nondollar currencies as 9 percent, that is, as the sum of their bands. Fritz Machlup thought Salant's reference to the band as being 4½ percent for nondollar currencies was an error of fact and said that the correct figure was 9 percent. He used the word "band" to mean maximum permissible fluctuation in an exchange rate around the parity between any pair of currencies.

A cursory review of the literature shows that the word "band" has not always been used in the same way, even by the same writers. It appears to have come into wide use after George Halm used it in the title of a paper.[2] In that paper and others, the word is generally used in a way that raises no question as to whether the variation being discussed is around the defined par value (which at that time was equivalent to the parity with the U.S. dollar) or around the parity with another currency. Even when a writer specified "around parity," that did not necessarily remove ambiguity, because so many writers

2. George N. Halm, *The "Band" Proposal: The Limits of Permissible Exchange Rate Variations*, Special Papers in International Economics 6 (Princeton University, International Finance Section, 1965).

used and still use "parity" to mean the same thing as "par value" rather than the ratio of par values.

In *The "Band" Proposal*, Halm refers to "the presently permitted span of 2 percent" (p. 20). "Span" as used here clearly means "band" or the sum of the margins. This use of "span" by Halm could not have referred to the maximum possible variation in the exchange rate between two currencies because it was widely known that the Fund, under an Executive Board decision of July 24, 1959, permitted the spot exchange rate between two currencies to be 2 percent on either side of their parity (under conditions that, in effect, came to mean primarily between two currencies other than the dollar), thereby permitting the rate between two nondollar currencies to vary not by 2 but by 4 percent.[3]

Machlup refers to "the band between the maximum selling price and the minimum buying price" of the dollar as "2 percent, as stipulated in the Fund Agreement." Although this is the same as the maximum permissible fluctuation against the dollar, his use of the term does not favor either view of its meaning because, in the case of the exchange rate between another currency and the dollar prior to the devaluation of the dollar, the par value and the parity were the same. No references to the band were found that clearly use the word to refer to the maximum permissible swing of an exchange rate between two nondollar currencies.

Obviously, the term "band" is ambiguous unless the user makes explicit reference to what the band is around. The same can be said of "margin."

3. How this substantive change was accomplished is itself an interesting story. The actual case which brought the question to the attention of the International Monetary Fund was the decline in sterling to more than 1 percent below its parity with the lira in the Milan and Rome exchange markets in 1958. The British view was that the IMF Articles of Agreement obligated Italy to prevent a decline in sterling in its markets below the 1 percent limit from parity, even if that meant acquiring and holding inconvertible sterling. Under Article IV, section 3(i), of the IMF Articles of Agreement, the margins of 1 percent governed spot exchange transactions between a member's currency and the currencies of all other members. The Executive Board's authorization of 2 percent margins therefore appears, at least to the layman or the nonlegal expert, as flatly inconsistent with this provision of the Articles. It was legally reconciled with the Articles by treating the wider margin as a "multiple currency practice," which the Articles give the Fund authority to approve. This 1959 decision, which in effect doubled the permitted margins around the parities between nondollar currencies, was briefly reported in International Monetary Fund, *Annual Report for 1960* (IMF, 1960), p. 31. Fuller accounts may be found in the Fund's official history, J. Horsefield (ed.), *The International Monetary Fund, 1945–1965: Twenty Years of International Monetary Cooperation*, Vol. 1: *Chronicle*, pp. 469–70, and Vol. 2: *Analysis*, pp. 80–82 (IMF, 1969), and in an article by the Fund's general counsel, Joseph Gold, "The Legal Structure of the Par Value System," in *Law and Policy in International Business*, Vol. 5 (Washington, D.C.: Georgetown University Law Center, 1973), pp. 185–88.

Conference Participants

Leonard Weiss *U.S. Department of State (Conference Chairman)*
Bela Balassa *Johns Hopkins University*
C. Fred Bergsten *Brookings Institution*
Edward M. Bernstein *EMB (Ltd.), Research Economists*
Arthur I. Bloomfield *University of Pennsylvania*
Robert R. Bowie *Harvard University*
Frédéric Boyer de la Giroday *Commission of the European Communities*
Harold van Buren Cleveland *First National City Bank of New York*
William C. Cates *U.S. Department of the Treasury*
Benjamin J. Cohen *Fletcher School of Law and Diplomacy*
Richard N. Cooper *Yale University*
W. Max Corden *Oxford University*
William B. Dale *International Monetary Fund*
Kenneth W. Dam *U.S. Office of Management and Budget*
William Diebold, Jr. *Council on Foreign Relations*
William J. Fellner *Yale University (Emeritus) and American Enterprise Institute for Public Policy Research*
J. Marcus Fleming *International Monetary Fund*
Edward R. Fried *Brookings Institution*
Theodore Geiger *National Planning Association*
Kermit Gordon *Brookings Institution*
Gottfried Haberler *Harvard University (Emeritus) and American Enterprise Institute for Public Policy Research*
Deane R. Hinton *Council on International Economic Policy*
James C. Ingram *University of North Carolina*
Harry G. Johnson *University of Chicago and London School of Economics and Political Science*

315

Peter B. Kenen *Princeton University*
Charles P. Kindleberger *Massachusetts Institute of Technology*
Lawrence B. Krause *Brookings Institution*
Fritz Machlup *Princeton University (Emeritus) and New York University*
Edward L. Morse *Princeton University*
J. Carter Murphy *Southern Methodist University*
Joseph S. Nye, Jr. *Harvard University*
Henry D. Owen *Brookings Institution*
Joseph A. Pechman *Brookings Institution*
Jacques J. Polak *International Monetary Fund*
Walter S. Salant *Brookings Institution*
Frederick Strauss *U.S. Department of Commerce*
Philip H. Trezise *Brookings Institution*
Henry C. Wallich *Yale University*
John H. Williamson *International Monetary Fund*

Index

Abs, Hermann J., 135, 135n
Ansiaux, Baron H., 138
Aron, Raymond, 278n

Balance of payments: capital flows to adjust, 207–08, 239, 248; effect of devaluation on, 174; exchange rate changes and, 25, 25n, 78, 96–97, 100, 175–76; under exchange rate union, 160–61; labor productivity and, 195; mutual support for, 2, 2n, 7, 11–12, 32; "openness" and, 143–45, 156–57; reserve requirements and, 217–24, 242–45; use of reserve assets to settle, 104
Balance-of-payments ease, 205n, 231
Balassa, Bela, 27n, 137, 137n, 266–69, 308
Baldwin, Robert E., 210n
Band of exchange rate fluctuations, 311. *See also* Exchange rate margins; Intra-Community exchange rate margins
Banking, under monetary integration, 124–27
Barber, Anthony, 177
Barre Report, 9, 9n, 10, 11
Belgium, 1n, 15, 17n, 29, 172, 192, 212n, 248
Belgo-Luxembourg Economic Union (BLEU), 16, 229
Bergsten, C. Fred, 110, 111, 286–92, 288n, 290n, 295, 307
Bernstein, Edward M., 71, 97–105, 109, 112, 301
BLEU. *See* Belgo-Luxembourg Economic Union

Bloomfield, Arthur I., 1–36, 70–77, 299
Bonds, international, 120–23. *See also* Eurobonds
Bowie, Robert R., 75, 292–95
Boyer de la Giroday, Frédéric, 73, 74, 195, 300
Brandt, Willy, 57, 58
Brazil, 201
Bretton Woods Agreement, 102–03, 115, 139, 182, 264, 279

Cairncross, Alec, 134, 134n
Canada, 17n, 145–46, 156, 198, 199, 230, 261, 282, 283
CAP. *See* Common agricultural policy
Capital flow. *See* Capital movements
Capital market, European, 6–7, 7n, 14, 23, 273; effect on capital flow, 211–13; geographic location of, 152–53
Capital market integration, 32, 142, 154, 159–60, 168–69, 209, 239, 303, 304
Capital markets, private: borrowing in, 118–23, 151; competition in, 127–28; impact on U.S. of development of, 139–40; investments through, 123–24, 151, 152; monetary integration and, 118–32, 139
Capital mobility: effect on asset prices, 239; effect on credit conditions, 238; exchange rate fluctuations and, 168–69; factors influencing, 209–15; to finance current-account deficit, 169, 190, 193–94; importance of, to monetary integration, 116–18; obstacles to, 150, 157
Capital movements: controls over, 8,

317